S0-AEU-160

DATE DUE

Unless Recalled Earlier

DEMCO, INC. 38-2931

THE ECONOMY OF ESTEEM

The Economy of Esteem

An Essay on Civil and Political Society

GEOFFREY BRENNAN AND PHILIP PETTIT

RECEIVED

SEP 1 2 2005

MINNESOTA STATE UNIVERSITY LIBRARY
MANKATO, MN 56002-8149

OXFORD
UNIVERSITY PRESS

HM
1041
.B74
2004

OXFORD
UNIVERSITY PRESS

Great Clarendon Street, Oxford OX2 6DA

Oxford University Press is a department of the Univers
It furthers the University's objective of excellence in resea
and education by publishing worldwide in

Oxford New York

Auckland Cape Town Dar es Salaam Hong Kong Karachi Kuala Lumpur
Madrid Melbourne Mexico City Nairobi New Delhi Shanghai Taipei Toronto

With offices in

Argentina Austria Brazil Chile Czech Republic France Greece
Guatemala Hungary Italy Japan South Korea Poland Portugal
Singapore Switzerland Thailand Turkey Ukraine Vietnam

Oxford is a registered trade mark of Oxford University Press
in the UK and in certain other countries

Published in the United States
by Oxford University Press Inc., New York

© G. Brennan & P. Pettit 2004

The moral rights of the authors have been asserted

Database right Oxford University Press (maker)

First published 2004

All rights reserved. No part of this publication may be reproduced,
stored in a retrieval system, or transmitted, in any form or by any means,
without the prior permission in writing of Oxford University Press,
or as expressly permitted by law, or under terms agreed with the appropriate
reprographics rights organization. Enquiries concerning reproduction
outside the scope of the above should be sent to the Rights Department,
Oxford University Press, at the address above

You must not circulate this book in any other binding or cover
and you must impose this same condition on any acquirer

British Library Cataloguing in Publication Data

Data available

Library of Congress Cataloging in Publication Data

Data available

ISBN 0-19-924648-3

3 5 7 9 10 8 6 4 2

Typeset by Kolam Information Services Pvt. Ltd, Pondicherry, India
Printed in Great Britain
on acid-free paper by
Biddles Ltd., King's Lynn, Norfolk

3705412

5049458

For John Braithwaite

Preface

One of the authors of this book is an economist, the other a philosopher, but we are each ill-disciplined enough to have interests in the large set of theoretical and normative questions that connects our subjects. As colleagues for fifteen years at the Research School of Social Sciences, Australian National University, we got into the habit of meeting for a weekly lunch to discuss questions of common interest. And somewhere around 1990, we stumbled across the topic of esteem. The upshot, many lunches later, is this book.

We were pressed into thinking about the role of esteem in social life by a number of prompts. First, a sense of dismay at the strengthening political assumption that there were only two disciplines on which government could rely in seeking to spend the tax dollar wisely: tough management or resort to the market. Second, a feeling, nurtured by rereading Adam Smith, that even if economics and game theory did well to focus on self-interested motivation, they had lost sight of the rich resources of self-interest associated with the desire for esteem. And third, disappointment at finding that, despite the long history of emphasis on the importance of this desire, the other social sciences did not offer anything approaching a systematic theory of esteem or an agreed set of findings on the topic.

Prompted by these motives, we stuck with our lunchtime conversations about esteem and later, as our commitment stiffened, spent many sessions poring over blackboard jottings together. We drew shamelessly for advice and references on our colleagues in disciplines other than our own, ranging from history to criminology to psychology. And gradually, bit by bit, we found that we had something we thought was worth saying. We hope that readers will share our sense that however well or badly we ourselves handle the topic, there are enormous riches to be mined in and around this area.

One colleague whose advice, direction, and encouragement played a crucial role in keeping us at this book is our friend, John Braithwaite. He himself gave enormous importance to what he described as 'reintegrative shaming' in his influential work on *Crime, Shame and Reintegration* (Braithwaite 1989), and the theory developed there was itself an important factor in leading us to give attention to social esteem. Conscious of the extent of our debt—and of the pleasure of many conversations—we are delighted to be able to dedicate this book to him.

The themes and theses of the book are common property that we are each happy to own and for which we each expect to be held to account. But the actual writing of the book posed something of a problem, given natural differences of disciplinary and individual style. Our solution was to give the penning of the long middle part of the book to Brennan—this goes into some detail in looking at the economics of esteem—while leaving the rest of the material, which has a more philosophical, scouting character, to Pettit. We hope that any differences of style in the presentation are reasonably justified by differences in the sort of material covered.

We are conscious of the length and relative complexity of the book. With a view to making things easier for readers, we provide a short concluding section at the end of each chapter. We have a preamble at the beginning of each of the three parts of the book to give overall guidance on how the argument goes. And we use the Introduction to set the scene and to orient readers to the issues we cover.

Apart from John Braithwaite, three people read much or all of an earlier version of the manuscript for us: Dharmika Dharmapala, Richard McAdams, and Michael Wenzel, and we are most grateful to them for their advice. More generally, we are indebted to a large number of colleagues at the Research School of Social Sciences and elsewhere, and to an even larger number of Australian and international visitors to the School. At the risk of overlooking someone, we would like to mention in particular Michael Baurmann, Valerie Braithwaite, Arudra Burra, Conal Condren, Bob Cooter, Steve Dowrick, Jon Elster, John Ferejohn, Frank Foreman, Bruno Frey, Bob Goodin, Knud Haakonssen, Alan Hamlin, Russell Hardin, Richard Holton, Susan James, Harmut Klient, Martin Krygier, Niki Lacey, Melissa Lane, Rae Langton, Julian Le Grand, Margaret Levi, Christian List, Iain McCalman, Victoria McGeer, Tim O'Hagan, Mark Philp, Quentin Skinner, Michael Smith, David Soskice, Kim Sterelny, Steve Stich, Bob Sugden, Wojciech Sadurski, Jean-Fabien Spitz, Tom Tyler, Bruno Verbeek, and David Vines. We are also grateful to Nic Southwood for preparing an excellent index. And, finally, we must mention Andrew Schuller, who was the model of an enthusiastic, insightful, and patient editor. Wittingly or unwittingly, all of these people did something to shape this book. We hope they won't be embarrassed to discover the fact.

Contents

List of Figures   xi

Introduction: Rediscovering the Economy of Esteem   1

PART I: TOWARDS THE ECONOMICS OF ESTEEM   11

Introduction   13

1. The Nature and Attraction of Esteem   15
2. The Demand for Esteem   34
3. The Supply of Esteem   50
4. The Economy of Esteem   65

PART II: WITHIN THE ECONOMICS OF ESTEEM   79

Introduction   81

5. A Simple Equilibrium in Performance   83
6. A More Complex Equilibrium in Performance   106
7. Multiple Equilibria and Bootstrapping Performance   125
8. Publicity and Individual Responses   141
9. Publicity and Accepted Standards   161
10. Seeking and Shunning Publicity   178
11. Voluntary Associations   195
12. Involuntary Associations   222

PART III: EXPLOITING THE ECONOMICS OF ESTEEM   241

Introduction   243

13. The Intangible Hand in Profile   245
14. The Intangible Hand in Practice   267
15. Mobilising the Intangible Hand   289

References   322
Index   331

List of Figures

5.1. Individual esteem incentive. (a) Relation between esteem
and performance level—total and marginal.   86
    (b) Marginal value of esteem for X-performance.   87
5.2. Individual reaction curve.   88
5.3. The reaction curve derived from the underlying indifference
map. (a) Indifference map between esteem and other 'goods'.
(b) Corresponding reaction curve.   91
5.4. Equilibrium in the performance domain.   95
5.5. Comparative statics in the performance domain.   97
6.1. Comparative statics when standards are influenced by ideals.   107
6.2. Individual esteem incentive in the 'three-range' case. (a) Relation
between performance level and total esteem. (b) Marginal
esteem and marginal value of esteem.   112
6.3. The distribution of performances. (a) Distribution of
performances without esteem effects. (b) Distribution with
esteem effects.   114
6.4. Esteem and risk-in-performance.   119
7.1. Frequency and the supply of esteem.   128
7.2. Esteem required at various levels of compliance.   130
7.3. Equilibrium compliance levels.   131
7.4. Equilibrium vulnerability. (a) Low-compliance equilibrium
vulnerability. (b) High-compliance equilibrium vulnerability.   134
7.5. The effect of increased publicity.   136
7.6. Effects of changed perception of proportion complying.   137
8.1. Marginal esteem incentives as publicity increases.
(a) Relation between performance and esteem in the low
publicity case. (b) Marginal esteem curves for varying
publicity contexts.   144
9.1. Misperception of failing practice corrected.   165
10.1. Trade-off between effort expended in performance
improvement and in publicity-seeking.   183
10.2. The enfant-terrible case.   191

11.1. Relation between marginal esteem benefit and
expanding group size. 202
11.2. Esteem-maximising group size. 216
12.1. Free-riding in promoting one's association. 232

Introduction: Rediscovering the Economy of Esteem

The third desire

The three ruling passions in human life are often said to be the desire for property, the desire for power, and the desire for prestige or status or esteem (Ricoeur 1965: 168 ff.). The effects of the first desire are charted in standard economics, the effects of the second in political science—and of course in the annals of history. But the effects of the desire for esteem have escaped the sustained attention of social scientists. It is almost as if there were a conspiracy not to register or document the fact that we are, and always have been, an honour-hungry species.

The drives for property, power, and prestige have all figured in the books of the moralists. It has been standard, and standard within a variety of traditions, to observe that each of these passions is hard to moderate in the soul of the individual and that each, therefore, can lead a person into a pattern of behaviour that is destructive of the personality and of good interpersonal relations. On this front there is no discrimination against the third desire. But whereas the disciplines of economics and politics have grown up around the study of the competition for property and power, nothing of that systematic kind has occurred with esteem.

What economics and politics reveal in the domain of property and power is that the unintended consequences of people's desires congeal into aggregate patterns that affect in turn what individuals can and choose to do. The competition for property dictates the prices at which individual goods can be obtained, for example, while the competition for power dictates the opportunities for individuals to find a place among others and to exercise influence. Both disciplines, however, have a normative as well as a positive or empirical side. They not only seek to reveal how things actually turn out as a result of people's interactions, but also try to identify ways in which they might be made to turn out better. Thus economics specialises in identifying more efficient systems of production and distribution, politics in charting more stable ways of organising the dispensation whereby power is allocated among individuals and groups. And specialists in each discipline equally argue for improvements that would have beneficial consequences, not just for endogenous ideals like efficiency and stability, but also for ideals—perhaps more controversial ideals—like freedom, community, and equality.

We see no reason why there shouldn't be a study that serves these same positive and normative ends in regard to the system generated by people's desire for esteem. Were it distinct enough to earn a Greek name on a par with 'economics' and 'politics', we might call it 'kudonomics': the study of the laws governing the system of *kudos* or renown. We tend to think of it ourselves as an extension of economics, however, since the discipline of economics has been extended in recent times beyond the realm of things that can strictly be bought or owned—commodities and services—to include other goods, including indeed the goods associated with power. There is an economy in property, an economy in power, and there is also, so we believe, an economy in esteem.

The economy of esteem

Economies are systems whereby scarce resources are allocated among competing parties. In particular, they are systems of allocation that have an interactive or aggregative dimension. What individual agents do gives rise to aggregate patterns that feed back in turn into the things that determine what individual agents do; they feed back, for example, into the determination of people's opportunities and expectations.

This more or less standard account of an economy is completely general, abstracting from the sorts of resources that are allocated. But the generality is often moderated in the practice of identifying and analysing economies. The resources within the remit of economic studies have been extended greatly in recent decades to include even resources of power, as already mentioned. But they are still usually restricted to goods of an action-centred kind: goods that materialise via the things people do and are disposed to do. They do not include goods, like esteem, that come into being by virtue of what people think and feel about the person esteemed: that is, by virtue of their attitudes rather than their actions.[1]

---

[1] For some notable exceptions, see Akerlof 1984; Frank 1985; Levy 1988; Hollander 1990; McAdams 1992, 1995, 1997; Bernheim 1994; Klein 1997; Kuran 1995; Akerlof and Kranton 2000; Le Grand 2000; Ellickson 2001; O'Neill 2001; Cowen 2002.

Our aim in this book is to look at the scope for studying, in the manner of an economics, the system whereby perhaps the most important resource of this attitudinal kind—esteem—is allocated among individuals. Esteem in the sense intended includes the positive asset of approbation and the negative liability of disapprobation. We describe the negative liability as 'disesteem' but we often use the term 'esteem' to describe the positive asset as well as the generic entity; the context will make our intentions clear in such cases.

Esteem cannot be given away or traded in the ordinary manner, for there is no way that I can buy the good opinion of another or sell to others my good opinion of them. We shall be seeing later why this is so. But though it is non-tradable in that sense, esteem is still a good that is allocated in society according to more or less systematic determinants; and it is a good whose allocation has an interactive, aggregative aspect. Thus there is room, at least on the face of it, for studying both the positive results of that emerging pattern and the normative prospects for changing that pattern in a way that is generally beneficial.

The fact that there is an interactive, improvable system for the allocation of esteem, despite esteem not being a fully tradeable resource, suggests that the economy of esteem ought to be an intriguing area of investigation. And so indeed we think it is. We hope that our book will show that the economy of esteem is a system that economists and other social scientists ought to be actively investigating. It has received a little attention in the sociological study of social exchange (Blau 1964; Heath 1976; Coleman 1990: 129 ff.). But it is deserving of a lot more analysis, in particular analysis of an economically oriented variety.

Some economists will say that esteem is taken into account in standard theory to the extent that reputation—say, the reputation for delivering on time or for delivering at a certain level of quality—is seen as an important resource for someone in the market. But reputation is distinct from esteem in our sense. Esteem may accrue to someone who is not reidentifiable—someone who lacks a recognisable name or face—whereas reputation presupposes reidentifiability. And the two notions come apart even where reidentifiability is assumed. Esteem does not entail market reputation, since it may often be given for properties that are irrelevant to market behaviour. And market reputation does not entail esteem. It is often equivalent to brand or name recognition, for example, and can be purchased by a new producer, and provided by consumers, without any connection with esteem. Consumers may reason that the new producer will try to maintain the quality of the old brand or name, without in any way esteeming that company or person. And the new producer can reckon that that fact gives market value to the reputation involved.

The tendency among economists who discuss the value of reputation is to see it as deriving entirely from the value of the commodities it enables an agent to secure. Like money, esteem is taken to give an agent a certain purchasing power in the domain of consumption goods—an expectation of being able to use it to obtain such goods—and that is assumed to be the reason it is attractive. We do not think that this reductionist view of market reputation carries over to esteem more generally. We seek esteem or shrink from disesteem among people we are very unlikely to meet again; we even seek esteem or shrink from disesteem among those who will live after our time and whom we will never meet. It is hard to see how this could make sense if esteem had no value for us other than as a means of securing consumption goods. We will return to this point—and indeed to other observations registered here—later in the text.

Two reasons for investigating the economy of esteem

There are two main reasons for investigating the economy of esteem. The first consideration, which is purely theoretical or intellectual in character, is that there is something truly strange and wonderful about the way the economy of esteem works as a matter of positive or empirical fact. We try to make this vivid in the first and second parts of our book, where we look at the nature of esteem, the way it is supplied, the basis on which it is demanded, and some of the interactive, aggregative effects of the strategies whereby individuals try to pursue it.

The second reason for investigating the economy of esteem, however, goes deeper in our own way of thinking. The economics of any system of allocation tries not just to understand the system, as mentioned, but also to see how far it can be made to work better and to work for the better promotion of what is regarded as the common good. It constitutes a normative as well as a positive economics. And there is enormous scope, it turns out, for exploring the normative potential of the economy of esteem.

It is common nowadays to think that there are only two reliable controls available for ensuring that people will act in a manner that conduces to the common good: the one is the invisible hand of the market, the other the iron hand of law and administration—the iron hand of the state. The assumption that there are just two forms of social discipline shows up in the directions of government over the past decade or so. Governments have tried to market more and more of the services that used to be provided in the non-marketed sector of the economy—services in education, research, health, counselling, and the like. And, where marketing is impossible or problematic, they have sought to impose a tougher regime of monitoring and management: they have tried to subject those providing the services to ever more intrusive forms of surveillance and accounting.

We think that this dichotomous picture of regulatory possibilities is misconceived. In particular, we think that it overlooks the possibility of subjecting people to a quite different sort of discipline: that involved in being required to act so as to secure esteem and escape disesteem. We think of this discipline as an intangible hand that complements the invisible and iron hands that have monopolised the attention of regulators (Brennan and Pettit 1993; Pettit 1993, 1997). The forces of esteem are distinctively associated, not with the market, and not with the state, but with what is nowadays often described as civil society. One of the most interesting projects in institutional design is to investigate the conditions under which the intangible hand can be expected to work well and, in particular, to work for the production of what is generally seen as the common good.

The distinction between the iron hand, the invisible hand, and the intangible hand is analytically well grounded. The iron hand involves actions that intentionally sanction agents—reward or punish them—so that they behave in a certain way; it is represented, for example, in the legal and regulatory initiatives of the state. The invisible hand also involves actions that serve to sanction agents—for example, the actions of consumers in seeking out the cheapest provider of a certain good—but those actions are not designed intentionally to elicit a certain pattern of behaviour, such as competitive pricing; they serve as rewards and penalties that elicit that pattern but they are not necessarily intended by their agents in that role. The intangible hand is like the invisible hand, and unlike the iron hand, in deploying non-intentional sanctions of this kind. But it is unlike the invisible hand, in that the sanctions deployed involve the formation of attitudes—rewards of esteem, penalties of disesteem—not, or at least not necessarily, the performance of actions.

The third and final part of the book is explicitly focused on the normative as distinct from the positive study of the economy of esteem though much relevant material already surfaces in the second part. This normative study amounts, in effect, to an examination of the ways in which we might expect the intangible hand to be made to work for good in our societies. We look at how far the economy of esteem might work efficiently: that is, how it might work well by standards inherent in the system. And, more importantly, we look at how it might work effectively in the production of other socially endorsed values: how it might work to promote conformity with certain ideals, and in particular how it might encourage politicians and professionals and those who serve on various public bodies to stick faithfully to their assigned briefs.

We mentioned that governments often try nowadays to market services like education and, where marketing is impossible, to monitor and manage the service providers in a tougher measure. If we are right about the opening for the intangible hand, then it might make more sense for governments to look at how far educational services can be disciplined—and at how far, therefore, taxpayers can be assured of getting value for their money—by setting things up so that esteem goes with high performance, disesteem with low performance.

We are particularly sensitive to this possibility, as we wrote this book while working together in a public institution: the Australian National University. Like many other countries, Australia has begun to submit teachers and academics to a pattern of relentless scrutiny and continuous accounting that consumes an extraordinary amount of time, demoralises and destabilises those in the business of education, and makes the education profession less and less attractive to young talent. We would argue that such external scrutiny and accounting has gone further than is needed, given the availability of the discipline of esteem; and that it may even have gone so far that that discipline has been seriously weakened.

How the economy of esteem escaped attention

As we worked on the themes in this book over the last decade or so, we became ever more perplexed at the failure of economics to address the topic more centrally. A book on the economy of esteem ought not to have been necessary. Economics and social science is two hundred years old, after all, and the importance of esteem has been recognised for at least two thousand (Lovejoy 1961; Adair 1974). So why has the economy of esteem escaped much attention or analysis?

Adam Smith, the founder of economics, was himself a great believer in the attraction that people feel for esteem, and the repulsion that they feel for disesteem. 'Nature, when she formed man for society', he wrote, 'endowed him with an original desire to please, and an original aversion to offend his brethren. She taught him to feel pleasure in their favourable, and pain in their unfavourable regard' (Smith 1982: 116). In adopting this view, Smith was following a tradition of emphasis on the importance of the esteem motive that had been present in Western thought in the time of the Greeks and the Romans, had resurfaced with emphasis in the Renaissance, and had become a major theme in the moral and social treatises of the seventeenth and eighteenth centuries. We say something more on that tradition in later chapters of the book.

The belief in the power of esteem led Smith even to argue that the reason why we seek out wealth, the reason why we want to have more and more to spend on what he called baubles and trinkets, is that by achieving conspicuousness in such possessions, we win distinction and esteem. 'It is the vanity, not the ease or the pleasure, which interests us' (Ibid. 50). Writing in 1790, John Adams (1973: 33) gave nice expression to the same idea. 'Riches force the opinion on a man that he is the object of the congratulations of others; and he feels that they attract the complaisance of the public.'

But this view that it is an interest in esteem that fuels the desire for material goods and services largely disappeared with the development of mainstream economics. Most economists came to assume that people naturally sought accumulation and wealth and only the odd renegade like Thorstein Veblen stood against the trend. He argued that in the pursuit of accumulation 'the struggle is substantially a race for reputability on the basis of invidious comparison' (Veblen 1905: 32).

We can think of three main reasons why esteem may have slipped out of focus among economists and social scientists in the two centuries since Smith wrote his path-breaking books. One is that with the advent of economics, in particular with the discovery of invisible-hand possibilities of social ordering, it became unfashionable to give attention to any mode of social discipline that invoked virtue in some way (Hirschman 1977). Bernard Mandeville, in his *Fable of the Bees*, was very influential in preaching that private vice was public virtue (see Mandeville 1924) and, albeit Smith wanted to distance himself from Mandevillean irony, the invisible hand gave a certain substance to that rather paradoxical lesson. The centrepiece example of the invisible hand was the open and free market in which, so it was claimed, the individual pursuit of advantage—shameless self-seeking, as it appeared to many—would guarantee that goods were made available, to the benefit of all, at competitive prices.

The scepticism about virtue, and an enthusiasm about the invisible hand model of social ordering, may well have provided reason not to pay any serious attention to the economy of esteem. For esteem will rule people's lives only so far as they can continue to believe in the possibility of estimable or virtuous behaviour and only so far, therefore, as there are at least some individuals who offer persuasive examples of virtue (Pettit 1995). It is because of being taken to issue from virtue, after all, that many forms of behaviour will win esteem for an agent. Esteem and virtue go closely together (see Lovejoy 1961: 185). Thus in letting go of individual virtue as a source of collective order, economists and social scientists may have let go at the same time of the desire for being thought to be virtuous as a source of such order.

But there may also have been a second force at work in leading such thinkers to neglect the economy of esteem. As Enlightenment figures looked for a secure basis on which to predict and plan for social ordering, they looked beyond the motives of traditional aristocrats to the things that were likely to move the ordinary run of men and women. It was natural for them in this enterprise to pay no attention, therefore, to the forces that seemed to be distinctively associated only with aristocratic circles. And among those forces the love of esteem and the hatred of disesteem must have seemed like characteristically aristocratic traits; indeed such a view can already by found in Aristotle (Elster 1999: 70). The language of honour and dishonour was aristocratic in provenance and seemed to be powerful only in sustaining aristocratic patterns of behaviour, many of them patterns of behaviour, like dueling, that were anathema to Enlightenment tastes (Holmes 1990; Stewart 1994).

While David Hume (1994: 24) was prepared to concede that 'honour is a great check upon mankind', for example, he himself had come to think that it was often a debased currency, associated with aristocratic 'debauchees' and 'spendthrifts' (Hume 1994: 294). This critique was deepened and developed, later in the eighteenth century, by the extremely influential figure of William Paley. 'The Law of Honour is a system of rules constructed by people of fashion, and calculated to facilitate their intercourse with one another; and for no other purpose' (Paley 1825: 2). Enlightenment figures like Hume and Paley, and in particular the new profession of economists, put the economy of esteem beyond the bounds of serious attention as they explored the prospect of building social order on the hard-nosed common sense and the honest self-interest of the bourgeoisie (Gunn 1993: 29). In scorning the pretensions of old-style aristocrats, it may have seemed natural to banish the system of honour and esteem from the ambit of their concerns.

We think that the assumption, clearly implicit in Paley's work, that ordinary folk have no interest in honour and esteem and that it belongs only to the aristocracy is a grievous error.[2] He would have done well to hearken in this regard to the little-known eighteenth-century author, Abraham Tucker, whom he singles out for praise in the dedication to his book. For Tucker (1834: 191) directly confronted and rejected that assumption. 'We currently pronounce the vulgar void of honour because they want those notions of it instilled into us by education and good company: but if they had not a sensibility of their own,

---

[2] It is ironic that the traditionally aristocratic culture of honour may now survive in its most florid form among those on the other end of the socioeconomic spectrum. See Nisbett and Cohen (1996).

they would never be moved unless by blows or something affecting them in point of interest, whereas we find the meanest of mankind as apt to take fire upon opprobrious language or defamation, when they understand it, as the most refined.'

Tucker's comment still holds true today, as a number of authors remind us. We ordinary folk may not pontificate about honour in the manner of seventeenth- and eighteenth-century aristocrats but we are surely still sensitive to its demands. This is more obviously true in some circles than in others (Nisbett and Cohen 1996). But we think that it is true to some extent in all. 'Honor is not dead with us. It has hidden its face, moved to the back regions of consciousness, been kicked out of most public discourse regarding individuals (though it remains available for use by nation-states to justify hostility); it can no longer be offered as a justification for action in many settings where once it would have constituted the only legitimate motive. But in spite of its back-alley existence, honor still looms large in many areas of our social life, especially in those, I would bet, that occupy most of our psychic energy' (Miller 1993: x; see too Baurmann 1996: 81, and Ogien 2002: 21–3).

A third reason why social thinkers like Paley and those who followed him may have turned away from the role played by the desire for esteem, concentrating on the possibilities held out by invisible-hand modes of ordering, is that putting any faith in people's desire to be thought virtuous must have seemed close to putting faith in the power of hypocrisy. Throughout the long period from Cicero to Hume in which the desire for esteem is recognised and presented as a potential force for good, the very people who hail esteem often show themselves to have a bad conscience about doing so. If a person seeks esteem for virtue only when they are truly virtuous—only when their virtue is sufficient to ensure that they behave well—still that suggests a focus on the views of others, and an eagerness to please others, that does not sit easily with Stoic or Christian values (Leeman 1949). And if a person seeks esteem for virtue when their virtue alone would not be sufficient to ensure proper behaviour—when the reward of being thought virtuous plays a non-redundant role—then that is surely a sort of deception, perhaps even a sort of self-deception.

The longer tradition had ways of living with this unease. It was common, for example, to distinguish between hypocrisy proper, often described as dissimulation, and the much more moderate sort of hypocrisy associated with acting out of a desire to be thought virtuous. Whereas dissimulation involves pretending to have acted virtuously when one has acted badly, this latter sort of hypocrisy only involves acting virtuously when one is not fully virtuous; it involves simulating—that is, simulating virtue—rather than dissimulating

(*Oxford English Dictionary* 1971: 765). Notwithstanding this sort of distinction, however, there is evidence of a continuing unease about socially relying on the power of a desire that does not speak well for the people who are moved by it— the basis of the unease was most forcefully expressed in Montaigne's Stoic reflections—and this may well have prompted social thinkers like Paley to look elsewhere. Given that the invisible hand was now available as the model for an alternative form of social ordering, there was somewhere else for them to look. That hand might operate in the market on the basis of shameless self-seeking, but at least that basis involved no hypocrisy.

The retreat from esteem meant that in sharp contrast to the eighteenth and seventeenth centuries, those who wrote about government in the nineteenth only very rarely suggested that the governors might be disciplined by the desire for esteem. In the eighteenth century American Republicans like James Madison and English Whigs like Joseph Priestley were agreed that government was to be curtailed, in good part, by the forces of esteem, arguing that honour in Montesquieu's (1977: 30) words 'reigns like a monarch over the prince and the people' (Madison, Hamilton, et al. 1987: 406; Priestley 1993: 33). But their radical counterparts of the following century, the utilitarians, dispensed almost completely with the idea. It is ironic that perhaps the most powerful invocation of the esteem motive in nineteenth-century discussions of government came in Lord Macaulay's 1829 attack on James Mill's 'Essay on Government'. 'The fear of resistance and the sense of shame operate, in a certain degree, on the most absolute kings and the most illiberal oligarchies. And nothing but the fear of resistance and the sense of shame preserves the freedom of the most democratic communities from the encroachments of their annual and biennial delegates' (Lively and Rees 1978: 116).

We have mentioned three considerations that may have been influential in leading to the loss of interest in people's desire for esteem and in the influence of that desire in social life. We think that none of these considerations ought to have been important. We believe, as Adam Smith believed, that it is nature that endows people with an attraction for esteem, not just the corrupt culture of an old-style aristocracy. We believe that even if the invisible hand is a potent force of social order, still there is a lot of force attaching also to the intangible hand. And we hold that the fact that the intangible hand operates on the basis of what many will see as a moral weakness does not mean that we can afford to ignore this force in thinking about how social order is or can be achieved. We hope that our discussions in this book will bear out those beliefs and that they will alert economists and social scientists to a dimension of social life that has lain too long below the threshold of theoretical attention.

PART I

TOWARDS THE ECONOMICS OF ESTEEM

Introduction

The chapters in this part of the book set out the basic building blocks with which we work. The first chapter sketches the conception of esteem that we are using here, distinguishing it from a variety of other attitudes. And it goes on to argue that esteem in that sense is something that we human beings find attractive, perhaps inherently—perhaps as a result of biological priming—but certainly for its instrumental benefits: it clearly helps us attain other goods and makes it easier to think well of ourselves, to have self-esteem. Esteem emerges as a domain of desire that is relatively autonomous in relation to the domain of consumption goods and that holds out the prospect of an autonomous economy.

The second and third chapters look at what is required if there is to be an economy of esteem and argue that the requirements are actually fulfilled, though in a distinctive manner that gives that economy a character of its own. Esteem must be something that it makes sense for people to demand and seek out by their own efforts, thereby giving rise to unintended, aggregative consequences; it must be more than something that they welcome but can do nothing about attaining. And for a fully developed economy esteem must be something that people are able to supply in response to the demands of others; there must be a possibility of exchanging esteem, whether for reciprocal esteem or for other benefits.

While it seems at first that neither of these requirements can be met, we argue that this appearance is misleading. We maintain that people can demand esteem, and can supply esteem—or, more strictly, the services that confer esteem—so far as, in particular, the demand and the supply is virtual in character. People may act for esteem-independent motives in these areas but their action will be virtually controlled by an interest in esteem, if its failure to deliver esteem would lead to reconsideration and revision. The last chapter of this first part of the book illustrates the sort of economy that comes into view in the light of these arguments and prepares the way for the more detailed investigations of Part II.

1

The Nature and Attraction of Esteem

The word 'esteem', like the Latin root 'estimare', can mean either to estimate or to estimate positively, whereas its opposite 'disesteem', like the Latin 'dis-estimare', can only mean to estimate negatively. Our general topic in this book is esteem in the neutral sense of estimation: the sense in which it may come in a negative or positive form. In this opening chapter we want to set out the basic elements of esteem, and to look at why people desire the positive esteem of others—we touch upon self-esteem only in passing—and the absence of their disesteem. The chapter is in two main parts, the first given to the basic character of esteem, the second to its status as something attractive to people.

The arguments of this chapter set up the questions pursued in the two chapters following. First, how far is esteem a matter of effective pursuit, and disesteem a matter of effective avoidance, in social life: how far does the desire for esteem translate into a demand, in the standard, economic sense? And second, how far are esteem and disesteem matters of effective supply in social life, with people conferring the one as a reward, the other as a penalty? We argue in the second and third chapters that esteem is effectively demanded and supplied in social life, notwithstanding the difficulties that stand in the way of such processes. On this basis there emerges the possibility of a genuine economy of esteem operating in people's dealings with one another. We sketch the possibility of that economy in the fourth and final chapter of this first part of the book and then go on in the second part to present some exercises in the analysis of that economy.

1   THE ATTITUDE OF ESTEEM

The first thing to say about esteem, in the sense in which we shall be concerned with it here, is that it essentially involves an attitude, not an action, and that it may or may not be expressed in praise or criticism. Sometimes the word 'approval' is used in place of 'esteem', both in its neutral and positive senses, but one unfortunate aspect of that usage is that the word 'approval' signifies the act—usually the linguistic act—of approving as often as it does the attitude of approving. We think that that ambiguity has led to serious misunderstandings, as in the argument that approval always involves effort and cost, and should only be expected of agents who are willing to pay that cost (for a critique see Pettit 1990). We discuss that argument in Chapter 14.

A corollary of this observation is that if the esteem given to a person by others is a good, the disesteem a bad, then they are attitude-dependent goods and bads. I can enjoy the esteem of another, or suffer their disesteem, only so far as they actually have the attitudes required. There is nothing they can do to confer their esteem or disesteem upon me, short of having the required attitudes. This marks off esteem and disesteem from the action-dependent goods that figure in most economic discussions. Action-dependent goods are all services or products or resources that are obtained by virtue of what agents or providers do. Whether or not the goods are successfully obtained does not depend on the attitudes held by the people involved (Pettit 1993: 266).

The attitudes of esteem and disesteem, when we describe them without qualification, should always be taken as attitudes that one person has towards another. But they are also, of course, attitudes that people can hold towards themselves. We say a little about self-esteem later in the chapter, believing that there is an intimate connection between the esteem in which others hold a person and the esteem in which that person may hold himself or herself. But our core topic in this book is social esteem, not self-esteem.

An evaluative attitude

There are three features by which the attitude of esteem is distinguished. It is an evaluative attitude, because it involves rating a person in one or another respect. It is a comparative attitude, because in most cases the intensity of the esteem depends, not just on the absolute rating, but on how the person compares with relevant others in the ratings given. And it is a directive attitude, because the ratings are given in areas where the assumption is that agents can do something about their performance; they can generally invest more effort, for example, and improve the rating they receive.

The fact that esteem is an evaluative attitude marks it off, most saliently, from an attitude like love or attachment. When I come to love someone, there is almost always an explanation to be given of why that attitude appears: the person attracts my love in virtue of this or that feature or set of features. But I may have no special access to that explanation; I may only be able to speculate about it. And there may be no other sense in which I am in a position to say what I love the person for. I will love the person, period, not love them for this or that accomplishment.

Things are very different, however, with esteem. This is always based on a rating of the person for how they perform in respect of some characteristic, negative or positive. If I esteem someone positively I will do so for their being kind or fair, brave or bold, a good parent, a conscientious colleague; or, in a more egocentrically focused way, for their being kind or fair, a good parent or a conscientious colleague, in their dealings with me. And if I disesteem someone I will do so for their being cruel or unjust, cowardly or snide, an uncaring parent or a sloppy colleague; or again, more egocentrically, for their displaying dispositions of those kinds towards me. There will always be a dimension in respect of which I grade the person and the esteem or disesteem will always be given in a proportion that answers in part to that grading. Even when I grade the person for how he or she behaves towards me, the implied base of evaluation—for example, the base implied in saying 'that is an unkind way for you to treat me'—is always a general consideration that anyone in my position might invoke; it applies to me in virtue of my being in that position, not because of who I am. So at any rate we shall assume.

The dimensions in respect of which esteem is given to a person come in many varieties. I may esteem or disesteem someone for their possession of standard properties of the kind illustrated above, whether these are considered egocentrically or from a more neutral point of view: properties like kindness, fairness, cowardice, or snideness. But I may also esteem or disesteem someone for a positional property, such as being the most or least honest person in the company, the one who wins the race or the one who comes last. Or I may esteem or disesteem someone for a sortal property, such as being a kind nurse, an honest politician, a corrupt accountant, or whatever. And of course I may esteem or disesteem someone for the higher-level property of being a person who scores very well or very badly in respect of a range of other, lower-level properties. The possibilities are legion.[1]

Some of the words whereby we pick out dimensions of esteem do not indicate dimensions of disesteem, and vice versa. Take the terms in which we may esteem someone highly: say 'benevolent' or 'brave'. We do not necessarily disesteem someone on grounds of lacking benevolence or bravery, even when we fail to esteem them positively in such terms; the lack of positive esteem does

---

[1] Although esteem is an evaluative, dimension-based attitude, someone may be held in esteem in a general sense that does not point us to any particular dimension. When a person is esteemed in a range of audiences, and across a variety of characteristics, it will make perfect sense to say that he or she is widely esteemed, without enumerating the various dimensions relevant. All that the evaluative character of esteem implies is that, if the esteem is well placed, then there are such dimensions to be identified.

not necessarily constitute disesteem. In such cases, however, there are almost always other words or phrases that can be thought of as representing the same dimension, now in the range of disesteem rather than positive esteem. Corresponding to 'benevolent' there is 'malevolent', corresponding to 'brave' there is 'cowardly', and so on. Our usage in this book will be to think of the dimensions on which behaviour is estimated as being picked out, with different ranges in view, by both sorts of word. Thus there is a single benevolence–malevolence dimension, so we suppose, and a single bravery–cowardice dimension, and it is possible in each case to win esteem or disesteem or, at least for most such examples, to score in an entirely neutral way. We may think of the dimension being scaled with positive numbers for degrees of esteem, negative numbers for degrees of disesteem, and with 0 representing the neutral score.

The fact that esteem is an evaluative attitude in the sense explained means that when we invoke the desire for esteem in rational explanation of what people do, as of course we shall be invoking it here, we are not 'going radical' in the fashion of some rational choice theories. We are not providing the sort of explanation that begins from an austere picture of human beings as centres of self-interest that operate out of society, without any normative expectations or evaluations of themselves or one another. Our explanatory enterprise is more circumscribed and modest, presupposing the existence of habits of normative assessment among the people to whom it applies. We do not think that this limitation is particularly severe, however, since it is hardly questionable that we are an evaluative species and we see no special mystery attaching to how this comes to be so (Pettit 2001*b*).

A comparative attitude

That I rate someone at the high or low end of a dimension of assessment will not inevitably determine, on its own, that I give them this or that level of esteem. The reason is that esteem is normally sensitive, not just to the basic rating I award, but also to the level at which I think that people generally rate in the person's reference group: that is, in the constituency of comparison that is taken to be relevant.

Comparison affects esteem directly when the esteem is given for a positional property like that of being the most or least honest in the company. But in other cases, so we urge, it also affects esteem. It has an indirect effect, with the comparator group made explicit, when esteem or disesteem is given for a sortal property like that of being a kind nurse or a corrupt accountant. And it has an indirect effect, with the reference group left to be determined by context, when it is given for an absolute property like honesty or kindness or corruption.

This claim about the sortal and absolute cases is not as self-evident as the claim in the positional case but it is intuitive and plausible. Suppose I think that someone is honest 95 per cent of the time. That may lead me to form a high estimate of them, if the person is a politician and I have a poor view of the performance of politicians on this front. But equally it may lead me to form a low estimate of them, if the person is a priest and my assumption is that priests are generally punctilious about honesty. The sensitivity to comparison may only be partial, of course, so that a poor comparison has less and less effect on the esteem I give the person, the higher the absolute rating achieved. But there can be little doubt that some sensitivity is present in all cases. 'We judge more of objects by comparison', as Hume (1967: 593) said, 'than by their intrinsic worth and value; and regard every thing as mean, when set in opposition to what is superior of the same kind.'

When we give esteem and disesteem to someone, then, we usually take them as a member of some explicitly mentioned or contextually salient constituency: as a member of this or that profession or organisation, as a person of a certain religion or ethnicity, as a citizen of the local country or perhaps just as a human being. And whether we find them estimable or disestimable for the presence of a certain disposition, or the performance of a certain action, is in some part a function of how others in that constituency behave. The point goes through as a matter of definition with positional dimensions of assessment. And it goes through as a plausible observation with non-positional properties of the absolute or sortal kind. Having assessed someone on such dimensions, we give them esteem in a way that is sensitive to their departure from what we take to be the normal performance—the mean, the median, the mode, or whatever—in their reference group. Thus the degree of esteem that people earn for being honest, or the degree of disesteem they suffer for being dishonest, is affected by the baseline of normal practice. Honesty is an ideal of performance in such a case but, to invoke terminology used later, the standard that determines the degree of esteem forthcoming is almost invariably a function both of that ideal and of the prevailing practice, not of the ideal alone.

Consider a community where it is the statistical norm for dog-owners to clean up any mess that their dogs make in public, such cleanliness being an ideal for the people involved. The fact that that is prevailing practice will mean that those who are careless about letting their dogs soil public areas will attract considerable disesteem: certainly more disesteem than they would suffer if their carelessness was fairly typical. Or consider a community where it is the statistical norm for householders not to bother cleaning up rubbish on the pavement or nature strip outside their garden fences, though cleanliness of that kind remains an ideal. In such a community the person who makes an effort to keep the nearby public space as unlittered as their own garden—assuming this does not look like unproductive folly—will almost certainly win a high opinion among those who know of their behaviour; that person will tend to do better in the opinion stakes than they would do if every householder behaved in the same way.

The fact that it is an evaluative attitude means, as we saw, that esteem is distinct from the attitude of love or affection. The fact that it is a comparative attitude means that it is distinct from the equally important attitude that we might describe as giving the person recognition or countenance or standing (Darwall 1977; Taylor 1992; Taylor 1995: ch. 12; Honneth 1996).[2] Being comparative, esteem involves the grading of people against one another on a more or less continuous scale. And it contrasts in this way with recognition.

Suppose that I give someone esteem or disesteem in a given dimension. I will recognise that person—I will give them respect or countenance—just so far as I treat them as falling within the domain of those who are subject to estimation, positive or negative; I will let the person count. The esteem I give in this sort of case will come in degrees and the degree given will be sensitive to the comparative performance of relevant others. But the recognition I give will not come in degrees and will not be sensitive in the same way. Recognition can come in degrees only so far as it is given in respect of a smaller or larger set of estimative dimensions, or by a smaller or larger number of people.

We shall return to the discussion of recognition in Chapter 10, since it turns out that the economy of esteem—the order resulting from people's pursuit of esteem—can be affected in relevant cases by the desire for recognition. People may find attention and recognition so attractive in itself that they are prepared to work for it, even when the cost is being disesteemed rather than esteemed. Bad publicity may be thought to be better than no publicity at all. But we shall not explore that theme at this stage. For now the important thing to notice is just that the attitude of esteem is distinct from the related attitude of recognition.

The comparative nature of the attitude of esteem has a consequence that is, as we shall see, of considerable significance for the operation of the economy of esteem. It implies that esteem is scarce, not just in the familiar, economic sense that it is costly to earn—it doesn't fall like manna from heaven—but also in the

---

[2] Fukuyama (1992) may confuse recognition and esteem in taking 'isothymia'—the desire for recognition as the equal of others—as being continuous with 'megalothymia', the desire for recognition as superior to others.

more specific sense that there is an element of interpersonal competition in people's attempts to acquire it. This competitive scarcity has an important impact on the nature of the economy of esteem. People are not only going to have to work at earning esteem, as the wider sense of scarcity implies. They are also going to have to work at earning esteem—and at avoiding disesteem—in a context where the efforts of others make it harder for any individual to attain it. They are going to have to compete in the pursuit of esteem.

Not everybody can be first in an ordinal ranking, so it is clear that the positional rating of a person, and the esteem that goes with it, is going to be scarce of supply in this competitive sense. But not everyone can be above average either—above the mean, the median, or the mode of performance— and so the same lesson goes through with esteem that is based on non-positional ratings. Even the dog-owners who avoid disesteem by not letting their dogs soil public areas are in competition for a scarce good in this sense. Let fewer and fewer dog-owners allow their dogs to soil the pavement and it will be harder and harder for a given owner to avoid disesteem; the occasional or partial lapse will become less and less forgiveable. Let more and more dog-owners allow their dogs to soil the pavement and it will be easier and easier to avoid disesteem; any effort to control a dog, however desultory, will earn the owner a degree of positive esteem.

A directive attitude

Many evaluative and comparative attitudes are non-directive, in the sense that there is no suggestion that the person could have done anything to earn or not earn those attitudes. Such attitudes will amount to positive or negative re-sponses towards the agent, for the possession of properties that do not redound to the person's credit or discredit, not being within intentional control. The admiration or awe that I may feel for someone who is naturally beautiful or intelligent—beautiful or intelligent in a way that is not due, in however small a part, to their own efforts—will be non-directive in the sense explained. And so will any negative attitudes like disgust that are occasioned by recognising the presence of complementary properties of ugliness or stupidity.

Esteem in the sense in which we are concerned with it here is different from admiration—or indeed disgust—as it is different from affection and recogni-tion. Like admiration, and unlike affection, it is evaluative. Like admiration, and unlike recognition, it grades people against each other on a more or less continuous scale. But unlike admiration, or disgust, esteem represents a directive form of evaluation. It doesn't just communicate the message: this is good or this is bad. It communicates the message that the sort of performance esteemed or disesteemed is one to be emulated or avoided in the agent's circumstances.

But though esteem is directive in the sense explained, and admiration non-directive, there is one misunderstanding that it is important to guard against. This is that while there may be no possibility of my improving myself in respect of certain properties for which I am admired, or for which I am the object of disgust, there will often be a possibility of my avoiding publicity, or of my taking steps to have the properties in question cast in a more important or less important light. In that sense the attitudes from which we are distinguishing esteem may remain directive and may give rise to adjustments on the part of those who enjoy being subject to them, or wish to avoid being subject to them (Miller 1997). Much of the material on publicity in Part II, for example, is relevant to issues that go beyond questions of esteem to issues of admiration as well.

The fact that esteem is directive in the sense explained means that its domain is restricted to those actions and dispositions that we think people can be held responsible for. The dispositions esteemed will be various, ranging from long-standing traits and habits to more or less transient policies and desires; so far as they are generally esteemed these will be treated as virtues in the agent; so far as they are disesteemed they will be seen as defects or vices. The actions esteemed will include the exercises of such dispositions but can also extend to performances that may be brought off with more or less aplomb, depending on the virtuosity of the performer. Like the elegant dance or the display of mathematical acumen or the sporting achievement these performances may be matters of esteem—or disesteem—even when the talents involved are not something for which the agent is responsible, and even when they are exercised out of a disposition that does not earn esteem: say, vanity, or a desire to impress. Virtuous dispositions, virtuous actions, and virtuoso performances—and corresponding failures—are objects of what we describe as esteem, not just objects of admiration or disgust, so far as they are susceptible to a degree of self-regulation and self-control on the part of the subject and can count as matters of credit or discredit (Pettit and Smith 1996; McGeer and Pettit 2002; Pettit 2001a).

The directive aspect of esteem suggests that people will try to adjust their performances so as to increase the esteem they enjoy and diminish the disesteem they suffer. In other words, although esteem as such is attitudinal, the economy of esteem involves a crucial behavioural dimension. We may expect to be able to affect people's behaviour, then, by reshaping the system of rewards and penalties on offer: by making it more probable, for example, that the quality of people's performances, high or low, will not generally escape notice. We may expect the economy that emerges from the demand for esteem to be open to initiatives of institutional design. We may expect the behaviour that emerges from that economy to be open to policy modification.

This lesson, already emphasised in the Introduction, is that so far as esteem is a directive attitude, the economics of esteem can have a normative as well as a positive aspect. There will be a contrast in this respect with the economics of admiration or disgust. It will certainly be possible to chart the ways in which people position themselves so as to be more prominent objects of admiration, or less prominent objects of disgust; it will be possible to have a positive economics in this domain. And it may also be possible to have a normative economics that identifies ways in which people can all be better off, obtaining at lesser cost the results they seek in the domain of admiration and disgust. But there is no prospect of having the full sort of normative economics that is possible, as we shall see, with esteem. Many of the points we make in this book will be applicable in the domain of admiration and disgust, as well as in the domain of esteem proper; that is particularly true of the points about publicity developed in Part II. But our focus will generally be on the economy of esteem in the narrower sense.

2 THE ATTRACTION OF ESTEEM

As we noted in the Introduction to the book, there is a very long tradition of holding that positive esteem is one of the most important values that people recognise in their day-to-day behaviour, negative esteem—disesteem—one of the most important disvalues. The idea is that among the things that may be expected to move people most reliably and forcibly is the desire to be thought well of by their fellows and the aversion to being regarded badly. People, so it was generally held, live under the regime or law of opinion and that regime moulds all that they are and do. It provides a gravitational field that silently shapes their dispositions and their doings, exerting a long, insistent influence that can only be resisted at the cost of considerable effort and self-sacrifice. It is hard to believe that a tradition of this kind can fail to reflect something deep about our human nature. The tradition provides evidence, in itself, that people are deeply attached to the esteem of others.

People who contributed to this tradition wrote at many different times and with many different concerns and, even in the same period, wrote in different idioms. Commenting on authors in the seventeenth and eighteenth centuries, for example, Arthur O. Lovejoy (1961: 129–30) wrote, 'Their terminology, when they discoursed on these subjects, was exceedingly variable and confused. Different names were given, by different writers, to the same passion (as shown by the contexts), and the same names to different passions.' (For further background see James 1997.) This variation of interest and idiom makes the business of exact interpretation hazardous but it does not cast doubt on the general claim that up to the nineteenth century the virtually unanimous view of writers in the area was that the love of esteem is a powerful human motive. The unity on this topic sounds through all the discordance of terminology and all the difference in context, emphasis, and intent.

A particularly striking example of someone within this tradition is Adam Smith. He enjoys almost iconic status in the history of economics, and he is often identified with the idea that society can be bound together solely by market-like disciplines of self-interest. But he was himself insistent on the power of the desire for esteem, writing as follows in 1759:

Nature, when she formed man for society, endowed him with an original desire to please, and an original aversion to offend his brethren. She taught him to feel pleasure in their favourable, and pain in their unfavourable regard. She rendered their approbation most flattering and most agreeable to him for its own sake; and their disapprobation most mortifying and most offensive. (Smith 1982: 116).

But here Smith is merely reflecting and endorsing a view that prevailed in his time, and that has a long and venerable pedigree.[3] We make the point by quoting, without further comment, from some of the major writers involved.

Cicero (first century BC*):* The sages, taking nature as their guide, make virtue their aim; on the other hand, men who are not perfect and yet are endowed with superior minds are often incited by glory, which has the appearance and likeness of *honestas*. (Lovejoy 1961: 156. On Cicero, and his Greek forebears, see Leeman 1949)

Aquinas (mid-thirteenth century): Honour is the greatest good among external goods. (Aquinas 1958: Index 156)

Thomas Hobbes (1642): Few except those who love praise do anything to deserve it. (Hobbes 1998: 23)

John Locke (1678) The principal spring from which the actions of men take their rise, the rule they conduct them by, and the end to which they direct them, seems to be credit

---

[3] Whereas Smith took the view that our very concepts of right and wrong are forged within an esteem context, however—roughly, what is right is what the impartial spectator or interlocutor would find estimable—earlier writers thought of the force of esteem as having only a motivational impact on moral performance.

and reputation, and that which at any rate they avoid, is in the greatest part shame and disgrace. (Locke 1993: 236)

Pierre Nicole (1676): The goals pursued by interest, ambition and pleasure often hinder the effectiveness of *amour-propre*, but they never completely extinguish it. It is always alive in the depths of our hearts, and as soon as it finds itself free of constraint, it is always active, carrying us towards whatever can procure for us other people's love, and making us avoid whatever we imagine might attract their dislike. (Nicole 1999: 4)

Edward Young (1726–8):

> The Love of Praise, howe'er conceal'd by art,
> Reigns, more or less, and glows in every heart:
> The proud, to gain it, toils on toils endure;
> The modest shun it, but to make it sure.

> (Young 1968: 348–9)

Christian Wolff (1732): Nothing pre-eminently great has ever been done in the world which did not flow from glory as its source. (Lovejoy 1961: 167)

Voltaire (1734): God has wisely endowed us with a pride which can never suffer that other men should hate or despise use. To be an object of contempt to those with whom one lives is a thing that none ever has been, or ever will be, able to endure. (Lovejoy 1961: 181)

David Hume (1751): Another spring of our constitution, that brings a great addition of force to moral sentiment, is, the love of fame; which rules, with such uncontrolled authority, in all generous minds, and is often the grand object of all their designs and undertakings. (Hume 1983: 77)

Edmund Burke (1757): God has planted in man a sense of ambition, and a satisfaction arising from the contemplation of excelling his fellows in something deemed valuable amongst them. It is this passion that drives men to all the ways we see in use of signalising themselves, and that tends to make whatever excites in a man the idea of this distinction so very pleasant. (Burke 1987: 50)

Abraham Tucker (1760s): There is no man utterly destitute of honour, because no man but finds the expedience of it in some degree or other: nor is there a possibility of living in any comfort or tranquillity under universal contempt. (Tucker 1834: 190)

Kant (1786): A craving to inspire in others esteem for ourselves, through good behaviour (repression of that which could arouse in them a poor opinion of us) is the real basis of all true sociality. (Lovejoy 1961: 193)

John Adams (1790): no appetite in human nature is more universal than that for honor. (Adams 1973: 51)

Instrumental reasons for desiring esteem

This long tradition of emphasising the role played by the desire for esteem testifies irresistibly to its importance. But tradition apart, there is every reason to think that esteem is something that we all naturally care about. At the very least, there are reasons of prudence why creatures of our kind should always display a concern to be esteemed.

A first reason of prudence for being responsive to the esteem of others is pragmatic in character. To the extent that I am positively esteemed by others, my interactions with them are likely to run smoothly and to the extent that I am disesteemed, my interactions are likely to hit rough patches. I can expect those who hold me in esteem to put their trust in me, and those who hold me in disesteem to withold their trust. I can expect those who hold me in esteem to testify to my good standing and recommend me to the trust of others. I can expect those who hold me in disesteem to testify to my poor standing and to recommend against my being given such trust. And so on (see Posner 2000). The eighteenth-century writer Abraham Tucker (1834: 188) put the point with wonderful candour: 'we find it so extremely and continually useful to have the good opinion and esteem of others, which makes them friendly and obsequious to our desire, that this is enough to give us a liking to esteem, and consequently to those actions or qualities tending to promote it.'

This pragmatic reason is supported by an evidentiary reason of prudence why I should cherish the esteem of others, and flee their disesteem. Enjoying the esteem of others provides me with evidence, though of course only defeasible evidence, that I am living up to the ideals assumed in the background evaluations; if I share those ideals, as I normally will, then it should be welcome news that others think that I live up to them. And enjoying the esteem of others provides me with corresponding grounds for thinking well of myself and for developing a degree of self-esteem. These considerations work in the negative case as well, since the disesteem of others will suggest that I am falling short of ideals I very likely espouse and, short of self-deception, will thereby reduce the self-esteem I can feel. The idea that social esteem has this evidentiary value is intuitively plausible, fitting with received wisdom (Lovejoy 1961: 161). But it is also supported by a wide range of psychological research and theory (Miller and Prentice 1996: 802; Fletcher and Clark 2001; Leary 2001).

The pragmatic reason for desiring esteem suggests that people will be concerned to increase the size of the audience that thinks well of them, and to reduce the size of the audience that thinks badly. Other things being equal, such an effect on audience size would make it more likely that their economic and other interactions will be with people who hold them in esteem. (The pragmatic reason suggests also, of course, that people will want especially to be esteemed by those with whom they are likely to have significant relations—say, as trading partners, employers, or clients—and by those who have authority over them: say, their teachers, the police, or those in public office.)

The evidentiary reason for desiring esteem points in a different direction. While it may be pragmatically better, other things equal, to have the esteem of more people rather than of fewer—even of those whom one does not esteem oneself (Elster 1999: 89)—evidentiary considerations suggest that it will be more attractive in any area to have the esteem of those with greater competence to evaluate one's performance than the esteem of those with less (Williams 1993: ch. 4). And while it may be better, other things equal, to have the disesteem of fewer people rather than of more, these considerations mean that it will be more attractive in any area to suffer the disesteem of those with lesser competence to evaluate than the disesteem of those with greater. The judgement of ourselves that we are led to have in any area of performance is going to be more responsive to the opinion of those we treat as more expert than to the opinion of those we treat as less.

As on so many matters in this area, David Hume (1967: 321) puts the point with particular force and clarity:

tho' fame in general be agreeable, yet we receive a much greater satisfaction from the approbation of those, whom we ourselves esteem and approve of, than of those, whom we hate and despise. In like manner we are principally mortify'd with the contempt of persons, upon whose judgment we set some value, and are, in a great measure, indifferent about the opinions of the rest of mankind.

This implication of the evidentiary value of esteem is not inconsistent with the implication of its pragmatic value, though it does mean that it may often be difficult in practice to predict how people will reconcile pragmatic and evidentiary considerations. One point worth noting, however, is that the preference for being esteemed by those with greater competence to judge one's performance may have a pragmatic as well as an evidentiary rationale. Those with greater competence in any area are also likely to be more influential in spreading amongst others the opinion they happen to form of one's competence and performance. And so they may serve people better in pragmatic as well as in evidentiary ways.

Given that people desire esteem for a mix of pragmatic and evidentiary reasons, what does this say about the preferences they are likely to have in regard to defective esteem, as we might call it? The esteem provided by others may be defective in either of two ways. Not being informed by ideals that are valid and relevant by the lights of the esteemed person, it may be ideal-defective. Or not being based on the facts about how the person esteemed actually behaves or is disposed to behave, it may be fact-defective. How are people likely to feel, then, about ideal-defective and fact-defective esteem (Hume 1967: 324)?

The fact that disesteem is defective in these two ways—by the lights of the disesteemed person, as we assume—does not mean that it will necessarily cease to be repugnant. Ideal-defective or fact-defective disesteem may not have evidentiary disvalue—I may not be worried by the evidence it gives of my own lack of performance or character—but it is still going to make interaction with others more difficult.

It is doubtful if defective esteem—positive esteem—will remain motivating to the same extent. The fact that someone esteems me in a ideal-defective or fact-defective way is not going to have much evidentiary payoff, since I can't use it to support my self-assessment and self-esteem. As Hume (1967: 322) argues in connection with the evidentiary value of esteem: 'Whatever esteem a man may have for any quality, abstractedly considered; when he is conscious he is not possesst of it; the opinions of the whole world will give him little pleasure in that particular, and that because they never will be able to draw his own opinion after them.'

What, however, of the pragmatic payoff associated with defective esteem? Is it likely to make interaction with others smoother? We think that it will reliably do so only in the case where there is a misperception of a more or less trivial fact: a fact, not about my general dispositions and ability, but only about a particular performance. In cases where the esteem is ideal-defective and in cases where it is seriously fact-defective, there will often be no real prospect of my being able to live up to the associated expectations. And so there will be little pragmatic reason for me to want it.

There are a couple of queries that may arise about the evidentiary value of esteem. It is obvious why the unsolicited esteem of others—their positive esteem, or the absence of disesteem—might help me to think better of myself. But won't there be a problem if the esteem of others is secured only by dint of my personal effort to make sure, say, that they are aware of me and see me in a good light? Not necessarily. There would be a problem if the esteem that I manage to secure were obtained on the basis of deception. I would have to be self-deceived to think well of myself on the basis of esteem that I obtain from others by deceiving them about myself. But we see no problem when such deception is not involved. The fact that I had to work to get people to notice me, or to see me in the best light, does not take from the evidentiary value of their being led to think well of me under such prompts.

Another query arises, not with attempts to win esteem, but with attempts to avoid disesteem. Suppose that I have done something disestimable and am fully aware of this. How can I be enabled not to think badly of myself through lacking the evidence that the disesteem of others would provide, when that evidence is lacking only because I have taken steps to ensure that others do not know of what I did? The answer, we think, goes back to some familiar facts of human psychology. It is easy to explain to oneself the fact of having done something disestimable, and to salvage one's self-image thereby, when all of this occurs in an internal, private forum. But it is much harder to restore a positive self-image when others clearly know of what one did and, equally clearly, form an unflattering image. It may be easy to convince oneself in wholly private reflection that, for example, the foul deed was out of character. But this will prove much more difficult if there are others who, knowing about that action, continue to give one the cold or critical eye.

Is esteem intrinsically attractive?

These considerations, pragmatic and evidentiary, suggest that esteem will remain attractive so long as it serves the purposes mentioned. They even suggest that esteem is a primary good in Rawls's (1971) sense. Given the ubiquity of the pragmatic and evidentiary concerns mentioned, it is plausible that no matter what else a person desires, at least among the desires that human beings reliably have, those desires will tend to be well served by the enjoyment of esteem.

But there is evidence that to some extent esteem also has an intrinsic or unconditional hold on us, being something that nature has primed human beings to find attractive, perhaps for reasons of biological fitness. We often care about esteem where there is little or nothing to be gained in pragmatic or evidentiary terms. We care about our standing among people we are unlikely to meet—say, those who come after us—and among people who know so little about us that their opinions can hardly give evidentiary support to our view of ourselves.

Contemporary authors like Richard A. Posner and Eric Rasmussen (2000: 21) acknowledge that esteem seems to bother us with strangers, even when there is no further interaction in prospect. 'It is remarkable how sensitive people are to manifestations of disapproval even by strangers and even when unaccompanied by any implicit or explicit threat.' But for a really forthright statement of that point of view, the best source is the nineteenth-century historian, Lord Macaulay:

men feel extremely solicitous about the opinions of those by whom it is most improbable, nay, absolutely impossible, that they should ever be in the slightest degree injured or benefited. The desire of posthumous fame, and the fear of posthumous reproach and execration, are feelings, from the influence of which scarcely any man is perfectly free, and which in many men are powerful and constant motives of action. (Lively and Rees 1978: 105–6)

The idea that the desire for esteem is to some extent biologically hardwired is not outlandish, since a person's inclusive fitness would seem to be increased by the presence of that desire. It might be hardwired in this way, so far as it exists as a modular, motivational force that operates independently of information about the effects of its satisfaction (Fodor 1983). Just as modularisation ensures that we see the stick in water as bent, so that it looks bent even when we know it is straight, so modularisation might ensure that we desire the esteem of others, so that such esteem will look attractive even in circumstances where it serves no other desires and where we know that that is so.

We do not need to argue here for the biological credentials of the desire for esteem, however, nor for its modular status within our psychology, in order to establish the claims we make for the economy of esteem. The importance that we give to the economy of esteem requires that esteem have an attraction that does not reduce to the attraction of material commodities and services—consumption goods. And such irreducibility or autonomy is plausible, even if esteem is attractive only for the pragmatic and evidentiary reasons given. Since the evidentiary reason invoked does not involve consumption goods, the attraction of esteem may be independent of the attraction of the consumption goods it helps an agent to secure.

What would it mean to say that esteem goods were reducible to consumption goods, so that esteem was not really an autonomous domain? Basically, that a given kind and level of esteem is like money in having no attraction for human beings that is not fully explained by the consumption goods it is capable of securing for them. Were the attraction of esteem to be fully explicable in that way, then it would go to zero in the case of strangers, and those in future generations, from whom we can hope to gain little or nothing. And were it explicable in this way, then the indifference curves representing the degree to which an agent is willing to trade-off esteem bundles for consumption bundles would be straight lines. People would not be more inclined to trade-off esteem goods, the more such goods they had; nor would they be less inclined to do so, the fewer esteem goods they had. Esteem would attract them—as money attracts ordinary, non-fetishistic folk—only for what it could buy them (see Posner 2000; Ellickson 2001: 22). We suspect that economists who speak of the value of market reputation do think that esteem is attractive on this basis, as a way of securing business and, ultimately, consumption goods. Not only do they focus on just one specific kind of esteem; they also fail to recognise that the esteem is a genuinely autonomous domain of attraction.

We think that esteem goods are irreducible to consumption goods, for ordinary people clearly do care about the esteem and disesteem of strangers and, equally clearly, are unlikely to be willing to trade esteem goods for consumption goods at a constant rate. But the belief in such irreducibility does not mean that the desire for esteem is biologically hardwired into people. Irreducibility may obtain, even under the assumption that the attraction of esteem goods derives wholly from their evidentiary as well as their pragmatic significance. After all, no quantity of consumption goods will serve the evidentiary purpose of enabling people to think better of themselves. Were people to want esteem for an evidentiary reason, then that in itself would explain why they might treat it as desirable independently of its value in the space of consumption.

The fact that esteem goods do not reduce to consumption goods does not establish in itself, of course, that there is good reason to separate out the economy of esteem as a distinct area of study. We might just as well have thought of separating out the economy of apples or the economy of one or another particular variety of esteem, since irreducibility also obtains among such sub-species of goods. The claim that the economy of esteem is worth isolating in this way must turn on how far the evaluative, comparative, and directive aspects of esteem combine to ensure that the system is subject to some distinctive laws of its own.

The desire for esteem in today's world

Despite psychological evidence on people's concern with esteem (Baumeister and Leary 1995), and despite sociological evidence on how this concern can mutate into a cultural obsession (Nisbett and Cohen 1996), some people maintain that the desire for esteem has little significance in modern or postmodern society. Not everyone takes this line, as emphasised in the Introduction (see e.g. Miller 1993: x; Baurmann 1996: 81; Ogien 2002: 21–3). But many argue that forces of approval and disapproval work effectively only in small-scale societies and have little or no power in the modern, anonymous world (Toennies 1887).

It is easy to see what motivates this thought. You are generally going to be known to others in a small-scale society and so it is certainly true that the benefit associated with someone's noticing you do something good, or the loss associated with their seeing you do something bad, is multiplied by their capacity to remember that it was you, someone recognisable by face or name, who did it and by their related capacity to report on your action to others. If you lose the esteem of a friend, you may also lose their friendship. If you lose the esteem of a stranger, that may be the sum total of what you lose.

Jon Elster (1999: 75) gives a vivid image of what life in such a premodern society must have been like in a description of the world of Aristotle:

> It is intensely confrontational, intensely competitive, and intensely public; in fact, much of it involves confrontations and competitions before a public. It is a world in which everybody knows that they are constantly being judged, nobody hides that they are acting as judges, and nobody hides that they seek to be judged positively.

But this is not to say that the forces of approval and disapproval have no place in modern, more or less anonymous society (Braithwaite 1993). We appear to cherish approval, and worry about disapproval, even when we are not known to others or, if we are known, even when we are not going to have further dealings with the others in question. Consider how we flinch at being seen doing something embarrassing, even when total strangers are involved: think of being seen picking your nose by another driver, for example, as you sit in a traffic jam. Or consider how we shrink from looking silly in a context like that of the jury room, where we may never again see the people who witness our embarrassment. Or consider the result of a study of New York public washrooms which revealed that whereas only about 35 per cent of women washed their hands after using the toilet when there was no one else present in the washroom, nearly 80 per cent did so when there was someone else there (Munger and Harris 1989).

But in any case the anonymity of modern society is easily exaggerated. While we may each lack a name on the street of a big city, that namelessness is quite consistent with being well known in a range of the interlocking circles that fill the space of the modern world. Some of these circles will be small of radius, like the circles of friendship and workplace and sports associations; others will be of much larger compass, like the circles of the extended family, the professional association, even the email network. There may not be the same concentration of recognition and identity in the modern world that there was in small-scale, premodern society. But your having a name in many different, partial communities may facilitate the forces of approval and disapproval just as powerfully as it would have done, had you been a member of a single community in every aspect and period of your life. And in any case we inhabit a world in which large numbers can hear our voice on talk radio, if we care to speak, or see us on television if we manage to appear. Not everyone in the large metropolis is anonymous. Many have a degree of exposure that goes far beyond anything that was feasible in the heyday of esteem theorists.

CONCLUSION

We have looked at two questions in this chapter, bearing on the nature and the attraction of social esteem. On the nature of esteem, we argued that it is an attitude towards others that is marked off by three characteristics. It is an evaluative attitude, unlike love or hate, that involves a ranking of others on certain dimensions. It is a comparative attitude whose intensity depends, not just on the estimated person's absolute ranking, but on their performance relative to others in their reference group; in this regard it contrasts with recognition or respect. And it is a directive attitude that presupposes that the agent esteemed or disesteemed could have been different, or could have done something different; unlike admiration or disgust, esteem proper is given for something within the agent's control.

On the attraction of esteem—the second topic we investigated—we pointed to a long tradition that testifies to people's desire to be thought well of by others and we investigated the sources of this attraction. Whether or not social esteem attracts people on a hardwired, biological basis, it is certainly attractive for its pragmatic and evidentiary payoff. Positive esteem, or just the absence of disesteem, smooths the paths of interaction with others and provides a ground for the agent's self-estimate and self-esteem.

The pragmatic and evidentiary payoff of esteem explains why people prefer to be esteemed by more rather than fewer, and nevertheless why the esteem of the better informed is preferable to that of the less well informed. And it also explains why people don't have the same degree of interest in esteem that is informed by ideals they do not share or that is based on deep misperceptions of fact. Even if that instrumental payoff were the only reason why people found esteem attractive, so we saw—even if social esteem did not attract people on a hardwired, biological basis—esteem goods would still not be reducible to consumption goods; they would not serve, like money, as a way merely of securing such goods.

Some have argued that the desire for esteem plays a less important part in the modern world than it did in earlier times. We argued that there is little evidence for this claim and that, notwithstanding the decline of theoretical interest in esteem, there is reason to think that it remains a powerful force in social life.

2

The Demand for Esteem

When economists speak of some scarce commodity or service or resource being in demand, they do not mean that, like good weather, it is welcomed and appreciated by those who get it. They mean that not only is it savoured in that passive way, it is also in effective demand. People adjust their behaviour so as to increase their chance of getting more of the good in question, given that any scarce good requires effort to attain: it is not like manna from heaven. And, if the good is scarce in the more specific, competitive sense—if one person's efforts at attaining the good can drive up the cost to others of doing so—then they will compete and perhaps bargain with one another about it.

We saw in the last chapter that esteem is a good desired by all and scarce in both the competitive as well as the generic sense; we saw too that how far individuals achieve that good depends on factors within their individual control. But for all that this shows, esteem may still only be a benefit that is much appreciated, like a stretch of good weather, not a benefit that induces any interactive adjustments among people. We turn in this chapter to the issue of whether there is reason to think that it amounts to something more than this: whether it is a good that can be in effective demand.

The chapter is in two sections. First, we look at a reason, associated with the so-called teleological paradox, why esteem may apparently fail to be in effective demand. And then, in the second section, we argue that this reason is not compelling. We show that the paradox does not arise in every case, and that where it arises it can be avoided by recourse to concealment or, more typically, by the sort of effective demand that we describe as virtual rather than active. The paradox may show that there are limits on how far certain forms of esteem can be in active, transparent demand but it is quite consistent with esteem being in effective, though virtual demand.

1 THE PROBLEM

The teleological paradox

We have seen that social esteem is something that everyone desires and that how much esteem people receive depends on how they perform in this or that domain. This observation may seem to entail, all on its own, that esteem will be effectively demanded among rational agents and that we can look with confidence to identifying patterns of esteem-pursuit in the way that rational agents behave and compete. But this would be a mistake, at least on the assumption that effective demand means active demand. Esteem may be a good that people desire and attain in a measure that depends on factors within their control. But that does not mean that it must, therefore, be rational for people to try to control those factors with a view to increasing the esteem they enjoy: that is, to demand or pursue esteem actively. For it may be that though the esteem enjoyed depends on those controlled factors, the attempt to exercise the control with an eye to esteem—the attempt to target esteem, as we may say—would be self-defeating or counterproductive.

Consider the so-called paradox of hedonism (Sidgwick 1907: 48). This holds that while the pleasure that people enjoy will depend in good part on the things that they choose to do, still the attempt to do things that will bring them pleasure may be self-defeating or counterproductive. While the pleasure people attain will depend in good part on factors within their control, still the attempt to exercise control with a view to maximising such pleasure may be irrational. It may mean that less pleasure will be attained than would have been the case had the agents kept their eyes on some other goal instead, and had they let the pleasure emerge as an unintended or at least not directly intended byproduct (Elster 1979, 1983).

The hedonistic paradox is familiar from a range of traditional discussions but it exemplifies a possibility that is even more striking in the case of other objects of desire. Take the good, as we may presume it to be, of psychological spontaneity and now consider the steps that it would be rational for an agent to adopt with a view to increasing his or her spontaneity (Smart 1987: essay 22). Whatever the agent is to do, it should be clear that taking direct account in every choice as to what is best for the promotion of spontaneity will not be a rational procedure. Exercising control with a view in each instance to maximising spontaneity—that is, targeting spontaneity—will be directly self-defeating.

While the spontaneity achieved will depend on factors within the agent's control, spontaneity will not rationally lend itself to being targeted in that way.

The more general paradox that looms in the area has recently been described as the paradox of teleology (Scanlon 1998: 383). The paradox affects any of a range of goods or goals. It implies in each case that though the *telos* in question may depend on factors within an agent's control, that does not mean that it is rational for the agent to target it and make it in that sense a matter of active demand. It does not mean that the agent should shape the exercise of control in every instance with a view—even among other things—to the promotion of the *telos* involved.

The reason why the argument of the last section does not establish that esteem is in effective demand among people is that, for all we have said, the good of esteem may be subject to the teleological paradox. It may be that though the esteem that people enjoy depends on factors within their control, still it would be irrational for people to try to exercise control with a view to increasing the esteem they enjoy. The targeting of esteem might be self-defeating or at least counterproductive. Assuming that demand is effective only when it is the active form that involves the targeting of the good in question, the possibility that the teleological paradox affects esteem means that we cannot leap from the observations of the last chapter to the conclusion that esteem is in active demand among people.

Esteem and the teleological paradox

As it happens, Jon Elster (1983) argues that esteem does indeed fall foul of the paradox of teleology. Making the achievement of esteem an active, targeted goal is counterproductive, he maintains, in much the way that the parallel pursuit of pleasure or spontaneity is counterproductive. If one makes the achievement of esteem one's explicit goal, then that very fact will tend to undermine the provision of esteem by others. 'The general axiom in this domain is that nothing is so unimpressive as behaviour designed to impress' (Elster 1983: 66).

It is incoherent to think of making spontaneity a targeted goal: spontaneity consists precisely in not having such a self-focused aim. It is psychologically implausible to contemplate making pleasure a primary goal: pleasure tends to come, as a matter of human experience, from absorption in the pursuit of something distinct. It is going to be interpersonally self-defeating, so Elster suggests, to envisage making esteem a targeted goal. For esteem-seeking is not itself an esteemed form of behaviour, so the argument goes, and any attempt to win esteem that wears its character openly is not going to do well in the esteem stakes. Esteem comes from others and it is a general rule that esteem is given only to those who do not explicitly seek it.

The Elster axiom says that behaviour designed entirely to impress is entirely unimpressive, and makes no comment on behaviour that is designed partially to impress. But in that sense it would not have much bearing on real life; there is rarely going to be reason to think that someone is motivated exclusively by the desire to impress. We prefer to take the axiom in a more challenging way as a claim that behaviour will be unimpressive to the extent—usually, the partial extent—to which it is designed to impress.

Understood in this way, the axiom is plausible with behaviour that is designed to elicit in the observer the belief that the agent is virtuous in some way: say, that he or she has a disposition to be honest, for example, or forthright, or kind. To the extent that I believe that someone is acting in an honest or forthright or kind way in order to win my approval I will lack evidence that he or she really is of an honest or forthright or kind disposition. The belief will inhibit the inference to the conclusion that in any suitable situation—and regardless of the absence of an audience—the agent would behave in a similar way and manifest that disposition. Thus it is unsurprising in such cases that I will not be impressed—I will not come to think that the agent has the virtuous disposition paraded—if I think that the behaviour that is presented as an instance of the disposition is actually produced by the desire to impress me. On the contrary, I will take the agent to be intentionally deceptive in pretending to act out of a virtuous disposition and so I will have a reason in this respect to disesteem that behaviour. And that will be so, moreover, even if I think that the agent is self-deceived as well: even if I think that he or she is unaware of being moved by the desire to be thought virtuous.

This line of thought is not an original way of explaining why people disapprove of actions designed to impress the observer with the agent's virtue. It is to be found, quite explicitly, in the work of the seventeenth-century French moralist, Jean de la Bruyère (see Lovejoy 1961: 144).

At heart men wish to be esteemed, and they carefully conceal this wish because they wish to pass for virtuous, and because to desire to gain from virtue any advantage beyond itself would not be to be virtuous but to love esteem and praise—in other words, to be vain. Men are very vain, and they hate nothing so much as being regarded as vain. (See too Nicole 1999: 4–5.)

We concede, in view of this sort of argument, that esteem is subject in considerable measure to the teleological paradox. Or at least that it is subject to that paradox, so far as people find it difficult to conceal any targeting of esteem: that is, so far as the targeting of esteem, conscious or unconscious, is often going to be salient to others. That salience may be a matter of degree, with people holding by certain judgements as to the likelihood that agents in general, or this or that agent in particular, is moved by the desire for esteem in certain behaviour.

This concession about the relevance of the teleological paradox generates the challenge that we address in the next section. But before coming to that challenge, it is important to note that the paradox does not cut so deeply, nor apply so widely, as Elster's formulation suggests. It does not apply as widely as he suggests, because it arises only with an agent's attempt to impress on us that he or she has a certain virtuous disposition, as we mentioned earlier, not with every attempt to impress. Typically, we will prefer that someone act virtuously out of non-virtuous motives than act viciously and so we may give a certain esteem to such a person, not for being virtuous, but at least for behaving in a virtuous way. And with other forms of action—virtuoso rather than virtuous performances—we will ignore the motive involved. The fact that someone is clearly trying to impress us with their ability at mathematics, or their elegance in ballet, or their virtuosity at the piano, or their effectiveness in providing a speedy and high-quality service does not undermine the impression that they achieve. It may lead us to think that they are not very modest but it will not undermine the evidence that they give of their ability, or elegance, or proficiency, or effectiveness.

As the paradox does not apply so widely as Elster suggests, so it does not cut so deeply. This appears in the fact that while many thinkers have castigated the hypocrisy involved in the pretence of virtue, it has not been universally or unconditionally condemned. We saw earlier that hypocrisy may take the form of simulating virtue or dissimulating vice, in terms that were common in the seventeenth and eighteenth centuries. It may involve acting as if one were virtuous of disposition, when in fact one is not; or it may involve hiding the fact that one's actions, not just one's dispositions, are non-virtuous. Simulation never seemed as bad as dissimulation to those who deplored hypocrisy; it was taken, in Pope's expression, to be a happy frailty—if you like, a saving vice (Lovejoy 1961: 169).

That the paradox does not cut so deeply as Elster suggests appears also in the fact that where we do fault people for seeking esteem in a certain way, and allow this to detract from the esteem we give them for being virtuous, we do not assign a particularly heavy weight to this negative aspect of their performance (Kamtekar 1998). In many cases, for example, we will prefer someone to behave more virtuously, if with a greater desire for esteem, than to have them behave less virtuously but with a lesser concern to be admired. Oskar Schindler found it hard to live with the disesteem of his Jewish workers and it was partly for this reason, we may suppose, that he worked so hard to save them from the Nazi death camps. But we would surely rank his behaviour much higher than that of a less vain counterpart who did nothing for those exposed to Nazi threats.

2 TOWARDS A RESOLUTION

Some concealment strategies of resolution

The limitation on how widely the teleological paradox applies means that esteem can be actively demanded, without any counterproductivity, when agents are seeking to impress an audience about the quality of their behaviour, not their virtuous dispositions. But what about the virtue case, which is a central part of our own concerns? Even if we acknowledge that the paradox does not cut as deeply as Elster and la Bruyère suggest that it does, still it represents an important challenge. And so the question is whether there are any other grounds for thinking that people can exercise an effective demand for such esteem. Are there any other grounds for holding that it may yet be rational for people to pursue virtue-based esteem?

It may be rational for people to pursue such esteem so far as they can make that demand non-transparent. They might hope to achieve non-transparency, for example, by actively hiding their desire to be esteemed, resorting to the various artifices of duplicity. But the duplicity option is unpromising. Where someone is being duplicitous about the pursuit of esteem, then it is all too likely that that aspect of their psychology will quickly become obvious to those who know them. Even if they are poker-faced enough to be able to hide the various ways in which a targeting of esteem is naturally expressed, the pattern of their duplicitous behaviour over the long haul is likely to give them away.

Where this strategy involves personally concealing the fact that one is actively seeking to promote the reputation for being virtuous, two other concealing strategies involve a social sort of concealment. In the first, the person hires or contracts in some way with another agent for that other agent to promote the esteem enjoyed by the principal. In the second, the person becomes an agent for promoting the esteem of a principal with whom they are associated and in whose growing esteem they can share.

The strategy of hiring an agent is well illustrated in the way literary agents, political lobbyists, media liaison personnel, and public relations officers operate in the contemporary world. There is no disesteem attached to targeting the esteem of another person for promotion and so agents of these kinds can operate under contract and avoid the counterproductivity that would bedevil the principal's own attempts at self-promotion.

What of the strategy of pursuing esteem for an associated agent, on the grounds that one's own stocks will go up as the stock of that principal goes up? The most straightforward example is the case where people spend a lot of their energy singing the praises of an aggregate body to which they belong. Here the associated agent is a nation, a neighbourhood, an organisation, a network of friends, or whatever. The fact of openly working to increase the esteem of such a body is likely to look selfless and admirable and to earn esteem within the group; this, indeed, may be why people find it rational to sing the praises of the group and not wait, in the style of the free rider, on others to do so. And the effort is likely to serve at the same time to increase their own esteem as a member of the very body that they present as estimable.

The strategies of social concealment are likely to be more important, we believe, than the strategy of personal concealment, and we shall be supporting that claim in later analyses in Chapters 11 and 12. These strategies require a degree of social specialisation and organisation but they are not susceptible to discovery and disruption in the manner of personal duplicity.

Demand, active and virtual

The strategies of social concealment cannot be deployed generally, only in special circumstances; they offer only a side-entrance to the economy of esteem, not an open portal. But we are not excessively concerned by this limitation, as we think that there are non-active ways in which people demand and pursue virtue-based esteem—and esteem more generally—and that these quite straightforwardly circumvent the problem raised by the teleological paradox. People can effectively demand a certain good through virtually but not actively demanding it.

When people actively demand a certain good—when the desire for that good motivates their behaviour, wholly or in part—then they consciously or unconsciously see their behaviour as a means to achieving that good. The presence of the desire ensures that people see the behaviour as attractive and motivating. But there is another possible way in which people might have their behaviour shaped by a desire and in this case the desire does not motivate them or play any such causal role.

Let the desire in question be D1, and the behaviour B1. The scenario we have in mind will obtain under the following conditions (Pettit 1993: ch. 5, 1995, 2000).

- People perform B1 without being motivated by D1; they are led to perform B1 by habit or inertia or some other desire, D2.
- But B1, as it happens, does satisfy the desire, D1.
- Moreover, were the motivating factors to lead the agent to B2, not B1, and were B2 to frustrate the desire, D1, then D1 would motivate people to return to behaviour B1.
- After returning people to B1, D1 would quickly cease to play such a role in sustaining the behaviour; that role would again be taken over by habit or inertia or some other desire like D2.

In conditions like these the desire, D1, certainly shapes the behaviour that people display. But it does not motivate that behaviour, at least in the ordinary run of things. It constitutes a standby cause which is ready to kick in if things go amiss and the agent is led away from the behaviour, B1, but it does not play any active causal role, short of being activated in the event of B1 failing. Without driving or even steering the behaviour of the agent, it rides herd on what he or she does; it is there to ensure that the behaviour sticks to a certain path. It is not an active moulder of what the agent does but it is ready to activate at the moment that the behaviour departs from the original mould. The desire, D1, is in virtual control of the behaviour, though it does not figure actively in its causal genesis.

In stating the teleological paradox, we observed that a person's desire for a certain good, even a good that depends on factors within their control, may lead them to welcome its attainment without their demanding the good actively: that is, without their targeting the good by trying to exercise control with a view to its maximisation. What we now see is that there is a third alternative, over and beyond the passive welcoming of what their behaviour achieves and the active targeting, conscious or unconscious, of that result. There is also the possibility that while the desire for the good does not lead to active targeting—does not constitute active demand—it still plays a much more important role than ensuring that the good will be welcome. It may be there as a standby or virtual controller that will activate and shape the behaviour to its own satisfaction, but only in the event of that being necessary: only in the event that other forces do not already ensure the appearance of the behaviour required.[1]

---

[1] For the record, there is also a salient fourth alternative, involving a weakening of the virtual strategy. It would consist in people's moving out of any behaviour that ceases to provide the good, and then going on a

To say that a desire, D1, virtually controls for the appearance of behaviour, B1, is to say that B1 normally materialises and that should any other behaviour appear in its place, then D1 will tend to restore B1. Habit or inertia of some other desire, D2, puts B1 in position under normal conditions but D1 ensures that B1 is the only behaviour available to be given a tenured position; it is there to cull any alternatives that might present themselves. We can describe this role in familiar psychological terminology as one of inhibiting alternatives. And we can also say that D1 thereby reinforces the behaviour, B1, ensuring the absence of challenges and strengthening the habit or inertia or alternative desire that is at work. It may even be that D1 reinforces the behaviour B1 more positively, by giving the agent *ex post* pleasure and reducing the likelihood of regret or reconsideration. The control exercised by D1 will remain virtual in our sense just so far as it plays no part in the *ex ante* planning—conscious or unconscious—of the behaviour.

If a desire operates in this virtual manner to support a given pattern of behaviour—say, a kind or forthright pattern—then an incidental effect may be that that sort of behaviour becomes second nature for the agent; it assumes a powerful hold on their mind and heart, coming to constitute a natural mode of response. We might call this the Aristotelian observation, for Aristotle (1976) is famous for emphasising how patterns of virtuous behaviour, even patterns supported crucially by non-virtuous considerations, can become second nature in the agent; they can come to be the expression of a virtuous disposition. We shall return to this observation at various points, though nothing crucial in our argument depends on its accuracy.

The virtual demand for esteem

However limited people's active demand for esteem may be, we believe that they do routinely demand or pursue it in the virtual mode. We will try to make this claim plausible and thereby show why we need not despair of the possibility of finding an economy of esteem in which the populace are generally implicated.

Let us suppose, plausibly, that people grow to adopt certain patterns of behaviour under the influence of training and imitation and moralising and other such cultural factors, even if they diverge from these in spasmodic displays of innovation (see Hurley and Chater, 2004). In other words,

---

random walk, as it were—a random walk, rather than an active search—until stumbling across a form of behaviour that delivers the desired good.

let us think of their patterns of behaviour as being initially generated in a spontaneous manner over which they may have only a very partial degree of control. Under this assumption people will routinely be led by cultural cues to perform this or that action, as their situation requires. They will spontaneously do what the cultural logic suggests they should do. They will act as etiquette or fair play or friendship requires, for example, and they will act in those ways without a second thought as to whether this is for the best in some ulterior set of terms. Their motivation will be exhausted by a sense of what is expected of them under the cultural framing of their situation.

Let us postulate, in addition, that while people care greatly about the esteem in which they are held by others, as we argued in the last chapter, this is not a motive that receives endorsement within standard cultural framing; as the teleological paradox underlines, it is in many cases a disestimable motive to act on. Under this additional assumption, we may expect that while people will be concerned about the extent to which their behaviour wins them positive esteem or enables them to avoid disesteem, this concern will not register with them in the fashion of more standard cultural cues. My culture may attune me to recognising that since someone has asked me for directions, I should help out as far as I can; or that since it would be unfair to a friend to do such and such, I should avoid it; or that since I am a member of this or that group, I should play my part in some collective endeavour; and so on. But my culture will not attune me in the same way to recognising that since I could make a better impression on someone by varying what I do—since, in particular, I could give them a better impression of my virtue—that is indeed the course of action I should adopt.

What to expect, then, in such a scenario? We think it is plausible that the concern for esteem, in particular the concern for being thought virtuous in some way, will come to play a virtually but not an actively controlling role. It cannot be expected to assume an active role in general, given that it is not culturally endorsed. And yet it cannot be expected to play no role at all, given its importance in people's psychology. The likely prediction is that it will play a virtual role, remaining normally in the background but being primed to assume an active profile as soon as evidence suggests that an otherwise attractive pattern of behaviour carries serious esteem costs.

The idea is that people will each have a background aspiration level so far as esteem is concerned—a level that may vary, of course, from individual to individual—and that any signal that a course of behaviour will take them below that level is likely to activate the desire for esteem, raising the question of whether the behaviour really should be adopted or sustained. They may decide that it should indeed be maintained, despite the esteem costs; but, assuming that the desire for esteem is relatively powerful, they will routinely be led to revise what they do.

Conceived in this way, the virtual demand for esteem may play a silent but enormously powerful part in shaping our lives. It may have no phenomeno-logical or motivational presence across vast tracts of behaviour and yet it may quietly ensure that behaviour in those areas serves us well in esteem terms. We may seek out colleagues or associates because we share common interests and values, for example, and we may prize those with whom we bond for their merits as contributors in that area. But it may still be that were those colleagues not to serve us well in esteem terms—were they to reflect an image of ourselves that we found unflattering—then we would move on and find associates elsewhere. The bonds would not be reinforced in the manner described above.

There is nothing cynical about this picture. It puts in centre place the fact that our motives in doing what we normally do—our motives, for example, in sustaining various associations—are entirely as the cultural framing of those actions suggest they ought to be. It merely goes on to register that if the actions offend in a certain measure against the desire for esteem then that desire is likely to be powerful enough to prompt a drift away from the commitments in question. There is no cynicism involved in that admission, only realism and common sense. The Aristotelian observation made above gives us reason, no matter how idealistic we may be, to rejoice in the dispensation of esteem that we have been describing. For it enables us to think that as culturally framed patterns become reinforced by the returns they bring in esteem, they will become products of spontaneous habit and, assuming that the patterns are desirable, products of spontaneous virtue.

When economists speak of people demanding a certain good, they normally assume that they will look for levels of that good which are optimal from the point of view of their overall utility function. Is there reason to expect that under a regime of virtual demand, what is demanded—in this case esteem—will be achieved in such optimal quantities? Or should we think rather of people looking only for an adequate level of esteem: seeking only to satisfice in the space of esteem, not to optimise (Slote 1989)? We need not judge on the question for purposes of this inquiry. But it is worth remarking that if people only begin to worry actively about esteem when a certain aspiration level is breached—if in that sense they only seem to be concerned about getting enough, not as much as possible—still the procedure they follow may guaran-tee them the optimal amount. An alternative, active procedure might raise the expectation of the esteem to be attained but do so only at a risk—say, a risk of exposure—that they are unwilling to bear; thus it might not maximise their expected utility. The regime of virtual demand may exemplify the cunning of reason, and not any willingness to settle for less than the best.

The virtual strategy of resolution

We hope that these remarks may prove sufficient to establish the plausibility of the picture under which people virtually demand esteem. If we are happy to endorse that picture, then the spectre raised by the teleological paradox fades almost entirely out of view. It may be disestimable to act on the desire to be thought virtuous, for the reasons given earlier: this is to pretend to act on an estimable motive, when actually one acts out of quite a different one. But it will not necessarily be disestimable to give the desire the role of a virtual but not active controller of what one is and does.

The reason we disapprove of people's acting out of the concern for esteem, as presented earlier, is that doing so involves duplicity and deception. But that critique does not apply to just having the desire for esteem, when it is not actually operating as a concealed motive: when it is present only as a standby control, to be activated in the event of the esteem failing to appear. And so there is no reason why the possession of a concern for esteem, where this has a virtual but not any active role, should make a person disestimable.

As it happens, there is positive evidence that even where we disapprove of a person's acting out of the concern for esteem, pretending to be virtuous, we do not disapprove of the presence in the person of a desire for esteem. If we thought that the very presence of the desire was bad, then presumably we would hold in the highest regard those virtuous agents who are wholly indifferent to whether and what others think of them. But that is not so. Most of us think that a person who is wholly indifferent to *whether* others have the opportunity to form an opinion of them is excessively self-confident. How could anyone be so sure of the value of what they are or do as not to care whether others can ever scrutinise and assess it? And most of us think that someone who is wholly indifferent to *what* opinion others form of them, when others have the chance to exercise scrutiny, is little short of a moral monster: we must see them as totally shameless. Writing in 1676, Pierre Nicole (1999: 42) gave forceful expression to a view that will command general assent: 'there is almost nothing more dangerous than people whose minds can sustain irrational, bizarre conduct in the fact of public opinion, and can, against all reason, place themselves above the judgment of those who know them.'

It is not surprising, then, that many of those in the tradition of emphasising the role of esteem were willing to praise people for having such a desire, if not for acting duplicitously and deceptively on the basis of that desire. They thought that while it is bad to want to be thought virtuous when one is not, it is the sign of a noble mind that one cherishes the esteem won for being virtuous and for behaving in a virtuous manner. Cicero often gives expression to such a view, though he is not without ambivalence on the point (Leeman 1949). Perhaps its most forceful exponent is David Hume (1983: 71): 'A desire of fame, reputation, or a character with others is so far from being blameable, that it seems inseparable from virtue, genius, capacity, and a generous or noble disposition.'

What does the virtual desire for esteem explain?

With the model of virtual demand in place, we need have no hesitation in thinking that not only is esteem something that people desire, as argued in the previous chapter, it is also something that is in effective demand among people generally. Thus we can see our way towards how an economy of esteem might emerge. But it is one thing to say that the virtual demand for esteem shapes a person's behaviour. It is quite another to show exactly how it serves to explain that behaviour, as it must presumably be able to do. We turn, in conclusion, to this question.

Under the picture of people's virtually demanding esteem, there are two scenarios to distinguish. In one a person acts in a certain fashion and derives a good deal of esteem from so acting but the desire for esteem is never activated as a control on his or her behaviour; the behaviour is driven by other habits and motives and, since they happen to serve esteem well, the desire for esteem remains a purely virtual presence. In the other the person generally acts in that same fashion, and is generally moved only by those other habits and motives, but on one or two occasions in the past the desire for esteem has had to come into play in shaping up those habits and motives.

How does the virtual demand for esteem serve to explain what the person does under the first scenario? It does not explain why the person actually does what he or she does on a given occasion, nor why he or she actually continues with that behaviour. Such questions are answered quite satsfactorily by reference to the actual habits and motives that are causally responsible for the behaviour. So what can the virtual desire for esteem—an unactivated, standby cause in this first scenario—explain?

Our answer is that it can explain why the pattern of behaviour in question is relatively resilient: why it has the modal property—independently discerned or made visible by the esteem story itself—of being such as to withstand contingencies under which the actual motivation is disturbed or generates a new pattern of behaviour. So far as it serves esteem well, the behaviour in question is more robust than otherwise might have been expected; if the agent moves away from it, then the desire for esteem will tend to reinstate the behaviour. And this robustness or resilience can only be made intelligible by reference to the regime of virtual control (Pettit 1993: ch. 5, 1995).

The explanation of resilience envisaged here is an instance of equilibrium explanation or, more strictly, stable-equilibrium explanation. This is the explanation of a fact or pattern which does not show how it emerged or why it is present, but which demonstrates that the pattern is more or less inevitable, at least in a certain context, by pointing out that any ways in which it is liable to be disturbed would lead to correction. As an example Elliott Sober (1983) offers us R. A. Fisher's explanation of the 1:1 sex ratio in many species. The idea is that if a population ever departs from equal numbers of males and females, then there will be a reproductive advantage favouring parents who overproduce the minority sex and the 1:1 ratio will tend to be restored. Such an equilibrium explanation can be seen, in our terms, not as a distinctive way of explaining things—not as a distinctive *explanans*—but rather as a way of explaining a distinctive *explanandum*. That the sex ratio is in equilibrium, or that any pattern represents an equilibrium—strictly, a stable equilibrium—is a way of saying that it enjoys a particularly high degree of resilience. Being in stable equilibrium, at least for a given context, is a limit case of being resilient.

So much by way of elucidating the sort of explanation that the virtual demand for esteem will make possible in the scenario where it has never been activated. What now of the case where it has been activated in the past and where, even though it is no longer active, it has shaped the habits and motives responsible for the behaviour, it has ensured that they are such as to produce the behaviour in question?

In this case, as in the other, the reference to the virtual demand for esteem can provide an explanation of the resilience of the behaviour. But in this case there is also a separate aspect to the explanation provided. The demand for esteem explains, not why the behaviour occurs—the occurrence is wholly explained by the habits and motives at work—but why the only habits and motives around are ones that produce such behaviour: in particular, behaviour that gives the agent a certain level of esteem. This explanation is similar to selectional explanation in biology. The history of natural selection may explain why the only organisms around in a certain environment are those with such and such traits but it does not explain why the organisms have those traits (Sober 1984: 147–8). The history of the activation of the desire for esteem, in the scenario described, will do something similar.

One last word. We may seem to have suggested that the fact that the desire for esteem plays a virtual role means that it cannot also at the same time play an active one. But this would be a mistake. Consider agents who are subject to the virtual control of the desire for esteem, being disposed to revise and alter how they act in the event of its not delivering a certain level of esteem. Such agents may not have or display any active desire for esteem, conscious or unconscious, when things are going well. But equally they may. They may take a certain, perhaps modest degree of pleasure in acting virtuously, because acting in that way clearly brings them esteem; and as a result of this active concern for esteem they may not attain quite the level of esteem that would accrue to more saintly counterparts. There is no tension in the idea that the desire for esteem should have both an active and a virtual presence in people's psychology. When we speak in what follows of the desire for esteem playing a virtual role in people's behaviour, it should be understood that we are not ruling out the possibility that in some contexts it plays this sort of active role as well.

CONCLUSION

In the first section of this chapter we raised the question as to whether esteem is something in active demand among ordinary people. However attractive esteem is, and however far it depends on factors within an agent's control, it might not be rational for people to target esteem in the manner of actively demanding it: that is, to exercise control over relevant factors with a view to increasing their esteem. It might be self-defeating or counterproductive for them to do so.

A number of thinkers have argued that this is in fact the case, the pursuit of esteem being itself disestimable and the pursuit of esteem being something that it is difficult to hide. We pointed out that the challenge in question should not be overstated, since it only applies to the attempt to win esteem for being virtuous of disposition, not to the attempt to win esteem for acting virtuously—out of whatever motives—or for having the behavioural capacities of the virtuoso ballet dancer or mathematician. And we also observed that the attempt to win esteem is not very deeply disesteemed even in the case of virtue; most people would prefer an esteem-loving agent who behaves virtuously, for example, to a vicious one who is indifferent to esteem. But nonetheless there is a serious challenge here and we addressed this in the second section of the chapter.

We argued first that there are a number of concealment strategies, some personal, others of a more social variety, that people may use to target virtue-based esteem without suffering problems of counterproductivity. But we spent most of the time developing a model under which most people do effectively demand esteem—virtue-based esteem and esteem more generally—without demanding it actively under normal circumstances: that is, without targeting it as a goal, consciously or unconsciously; without exercising control over relevant factors with a view to increasing the esteem they secure.

The model postulates that though people's behaviour is driven in many cases by regular habits and motives, it may still be controlled in a virtual manner by the concern for esteem. It may be that the behaviour wins the agent a good deal of esteem and that if it failed to do so, the concern for esteem would be activated and would lead to the adoption of habits and motives that do produce satisfactory behaviour. In this model the concern for esteem is usually just a standby cause that does no work in producing behaviour but nevertheless it rides herd on behaviour; it is there, ready to be activated, in the event of the behaviour not serving the agent well in the esteem stakes.

If the concern for esteem plays such a virtual role in the control of people's behaviour, then it will raise no problems of counterproductivity. The reason is that people do not disesteem the existence of the concern for esteem as such, only the duplicitous and deceptive attempt, acting on that motive, to give the impression of being virtuous. And so the model described shows us how esteem may be effectively demanded among the populace at large, opening up the possibility of a genuine economy of esteem.

In drawing the chapter to a close, we looked at the question of how the desire for esteem is explanatory, under the model in question. We argued that even in the unlikely event that it happens never to be activated, the desire can be invoked in an equilibrium explanation of the behaviour it controls; that behaviour will represent a stable equilibrium so far as any departure would be corrected and the behaviour would be restored. And we argued that, in the case where the desire has been activated in the past and has removed itself later from the scene, it offers an additional explanation that resembles the sort of explanation provided by selectional theory. It explains why the only habits and motives around are such that the behaviour they generate serves esteem well, even if it does not explain the appearance of that behaviour itself.

3

The Supply of Esteem

We have seen in the previous chapters that esteem is a scarce commodity that everyone desires—scarce in the sense of requiring effort and scarce in the sense of prompting competition—and that everyone is in a position to demand and pursue it, at least in concealed or virtual mode. This is sufficient to establish that there will be an economy of esteem. People will compete with one another in the pursuit of esteem and this aggregate competition will shape the context in which they individually pursue it.

A system of competition that unintentionally generates aggregate feedback effects on the competitors involved is already a substantial sort of economy. It might be illustrated in the anarchic economy of miners who compete with one another for the gold in the mountain and make it progressively more difficult to find gold, say by forcing newcomers to dig shafts in difficult terrain. But normal economies are not mere systems of competition in the demand for certain goods. They are also systems of exchange in which people not only pursue certain goods in competition with one another but also compete with one another to provide those goods at favourable exchange rates. The community of people that the economy mobilises comprises suppliers as well as demanders or consumers of the goods in question.

The question to which we now turn, then, is whether esteem is a good—that is, a desired commodity—such that not only can people compete with one another in demand for the good, they can also compete in its supply. In this still richer economy, people would be able to compete for rewards associated with conferring positive esteem or withholding negative. They would try to undercut the rates at which they are willing to provide esteem, whether in exchange for reciprocal esteem or for other goods. They would be able to control the supply of esteem with a view to economic benefits, looking for the exchanges that serve them best.

As in the case of demand, there is a problem that may seem to make it impossible for people to supply esteem in the required manner. We outline that problem in the first section of the chapter and then argue in the second section that there is a way beyond it. The way in which people overcome the problem, managing to make esteem a matter of supply, resembles in a significant manner the resolution of the problem raised by demand. Thus the resolution postulates a virtual sort of supply and exchange, arguing that this is as effective in creating a full economy as an active pattern would be.

The consideration that gave rise to the problem discussed in the last chapter—the problem for demand—came to appear in the light of the resolution offered, not as a block to the economy of esteem, but as a constraint on how it operates. The argument of this chapter, as we shall see, supports a similar conclusion. The problem for the supply of esteem considered here turns out to reflect, not a block to a full exchange economy, but a constraint on the operation of such an economy.[1]

1   THE PROBLEM

The source of the problem

The problem that came up with demanding esteem—demanding it in the active sense of trying to exercise control with a view to increasing one's esteem—was that the activity of demanding esteem in that way is itself disestimable. It is disestimable, at least, in the case of seeking esteem for being virtuous of disposition. And the reason, plausibly, is that if one pursues virtue-based esteem in this way then one is acting out of one motive—the esteem motive—with a view to being thought to act out of another: the virtuous motive. One is being duplicitous and deceptive.

A parallel problem arises with the project of supplying esteem, in particular with supplying esteem for the sake of some targeted return, selfish or altruistic: in short, with intentionally supplying esteem. But the problem in this case is even more deeply rooted than the problem with demand. The problem is not just that trying to supply esteem voluntarily is likely to be counterproductive or self-defeating: that is, irrational. It is that the idea of supplying esteem intentionally is not even coherent.

---

[1] So far as esteem is supplied involuntarily, it is costlessly supplied. And that raises a distinct problem from that discussed in the text, since costless supply would seem to mean that suppliers will drive one another to supply at lower and lower prices or with less and less discriminating standards. But this appearance is misleading. Because esteem suppliers cannot appropriate any benefit from their involuntary supply of esteem, they have no reason to compete as suppliers and no reason, in particular, to compete by lowering their standards. And even if they could, the race to the bottom might be inhibited by the fact that the value or utility of esteem to those esteemed will be positively related to the standards of those who supply it.

Esteem is an evaluative attitude, as we saw in the first chapter. But that means that I can esteem someone if and only if I believe there are reasons of fact—reasons based in the quality of their motivation or behaviour—that support a positive evaluation. One cannot esteem someone without believing that the facts support a positive evaluation. As an evaluative attitude, esteem has a mind-to-reality direction of fit; it comes or goes, when rationally held, with the way the agents and actions evaluated present themselves to the subject.

This means that while I may choose to pay evaluative attention to someone or not—to form an estimative attitude towards them or not—I cannot choose to evaluate them positively or negatively and I cannot choose to hold them in esteem or disesteem. I may choose whether or not to look at the evidence as to what sort of a performer the person is in this or that area but if I do look at the evidence, and it speaks for a certain evaluation, then that evaluation and the associated level of esteem will be wrung from me, willy nilly. If it is not, then to that extent I cannot be functioning in a fully coherent manner.

Not only is the problem that arises with the supply of esteem more deeply rooted than the problem raised with demand; it also applies across a wider range. The problem in the demand case comes up most straightforwardly in the case of people seeking to win esteem for virtuous dispositions, not for virtuous performances and not for virtuoso achievements. The problem in the supply cases comes up equally across the board. I cannot freely decide to think well of you in any area. I cannot decide to attribute virtuous dispositions like honesty or loyalty to you but equally I cannot decide to ascribe virtuous action or to see your performances in dance or chess or mathematics as examples of virtuoso achievement.

Esteem cannot be given as a gift

Given these basic facts about evaluation and esteem, a first result is that I cannot make a welcome gift of my good opinion or a poisoned gift of my bad. I cannot decide to think well of you, whether or not I wish you to know that, just because you are someone I like. And I cannot decide to think badly, just because I find you uncongenial. Gift-giving is a voluntary action. And I cannot represent myself—to myself, to you, or to anyone else—as voluntarily offering you my esteem. For that would be to suggest that the fact of my esteeming you is fixed by a free decision on my part. If it is fixed by a free decision on my part, then it is not fixed by how I believe things to be with you.

And if it is not fixed by how I believe things to be with you, then it is not an evaluative or estimative attitude.

That this holds true of esteem is a matter of mutual or common belief: everyone believes that it holds, everyone believes that everyone believes that it holds, and so on; or so on, at least so far as no one disbelieves at any level that the required belief holds at the prior level (Lewis 1969). That it is a matter of mutual belief shows up in the fact that you would assume that I must be joking or talking nonsense if I told you that I had decided to think well of you: to think well of you, not just to act as if I thought well. The way we commonly conceptualise esteem makes it impossible to offer it in the manner of a gift. Under that conceptualisation, indeed, not even the gods could make a gift of their esteem.

Esteem cannot be traded

As it is going to be impossible for people to make a gift of their esteem or disesteem so, for similar reasons, it is going to be impossible for them to trade in esteem. When I seek to trade with you I offer you something in return for that which I seek; I present it as a *quid pro quo*. I suggest that I will give you my offering if and only if you give me yours and I display the assumption that the same is true of you in reverse. But this suggestion and assumption make no sense if esteem is the good offered or sought. For whatever I offer you in the trade—sweet words perhaps—it cannot be esteem, and whatever I seek from you in the trade, it cannot be esteem either. Nothing that could be exchanged in the voluntary manner of a *quid pro quo* could have the character of an evaluative, belief-dependent attitude.

Just as the corresponding claim is a matter of mutual knowledge in the case of the gift, so this impossibility thesis is a matter of such knowledge too. That appears in the fact that it would make no sense for someone to offer their esteem in exchange for something another can give them, or to seek the esteem of the other by offering them something in exchange for it. No one could take such an offer or such an overture seriously; it could only seem to be a joke.

The upshot of all this is that though we are suppliers of esteem to one another, we are parametric suppliers who cannot help what we do and cannot seek strategic advantage from it. If I notice someone doing something or revealing themselves to be a certain sort of person, then I will more or less inevitably think well or badly of them (McAdams 1997). This will often be palpable to other people, in particular to the person esteemed or disesteemed, especially in the many contexts where I operate along more or less the same lines as they. Indeed, it will often be a matter of mutual belief among the parties involved, and any witnesses to the interaction, that I must think well or badly of the person in question. In such cases, I will supply esteem or disesteem in a bountiful measure. Yet I will supply it, willy nilly. I will not be in voluntary control of the esteem or disesteem that I provide for the other and I will be incapable of assuming voluntary control of the provision.

We emphasise that in these remarks we are talking about providing the attitude of esteem or disesteem, not providing marks of such esteem or disesteem; we come to those later. So far as the substance of esteem and disesteem go, we are to one another like the moon or the sun. We cast light or fail to cast light on others—and we thereby reward or penalise them—without being able to do anything about it. We cannot help but be sources of brightness or gloom in their lives. Short of shutting ourselves away from the company of others, or keeping our eyes cast forever downwards, we cannot help but see what they are; we cannot help but form an opinion about them; and we cannot help but form opinions that are more or less detectable to others.

Our position as providers of esteem for one another is, therefore, quite a curious one. The evaluations we form and the esteem and disesteem we provide thereby generate benefits or costs for those who are the objects of our evaluation, at least when we are relatively transparent. But these benefits and costs appear as externalities that we cannot internalise: we cannot bestow or withold them, depending on what those others offer us in return or depending on how we otherwise feel disposed towards them. So far as our evaluations and estimations go, we can only look on ourselves as mechanisms that give off those responses in a reflex, involuntary fashion.

Esteem cannot be transmitted

In the ordinary exchange economy, not only do people give goods of their own making to one another; they also pass on to one another goods that they have received in previous exchanges. The exchange economy involves the circula-tion of exchanged goods, not just individual incidents of bartering or swapping goods. It involves the transmission of goods from person to person, not just insulated trades.

As there cannot be any gifts or trades in the space of esteem, however, so there cannot be any transmission either. I may receive an important measure of esteem from person A and I may wish to pass on that esteem to person B, whether as a gift or a trade. But just as I cannot give B my own esteem at will, so I cannot give B some of the esteem that A gives me. The esteem with which A provides me sticks to me like mud; it is inalienable. That esteem is something that I can welcome—or in the case of disesteem deplore—but it is not something that I can voluntarily pass on to another, no matter for what reward.

The reason this is so goes back again to the evaluative character of esteem. If I enjoy a certain level of esteem in the mind of another person, A, that has to be because of how A takes me—takes me involuntarily—to be. But there is no possibility, then, of my voluntarily passing on some of this esteem to another person, B; it may be that A does not know B or even that A thinks ill of B. The block to the circulation of esteem is as absolute as the block to its being given as a gift or a trade.

2 TOWARDS A RESOLUTION

The problem just discussed constitutes a serious challenge for anyone who thinks that there may be a full, exchange economy of esteem at work in the social world. The problem is that esteem cannot be intentionally supplied by people to one another; its supply is, in the nature of things, essentially involuntary. It is not just that it would be self-defeating or counterproductive—that is, irrational—to try and supply esteem intentionally to others, as the teleological paradox suggests that it may be self-defeating or counterproductive to try and demand esteem in an active, targeted way. The very idea of supplying esteem on an intentional basis, whether as a gift or a trade, or by way of transmitting the esteem of a third party, is incoherent.

But though there is no possibility of exchange in the space of esteem, there is a possibility of exchange in the space, as we describe it, of esteem services. These services are voluntary acts whereby one person may raise the probability of another's enjoying esteem, whether for the presence of virtuous disposition, virtuous action, or the virtuoso display of talent. The acts have the effect of increasing the esteem in which another person is held, by the agent or by third parties. And being intentional services, they may lend themselves to being exchanged. Certainly they are not subject to the problem that bedevils the exchange of esteem itself.

We explore this possibility in two stages. First we look at the intentional sorts of activities that constitute esteem services, offering three major examples of the category. And then we show how these services may figure rationally in an exchange economy, arguing that their voluntary provision is not likely to be self-defeating or counterproductive.

Stage one: some esteem services

The fact that esteem cannot be provided intentionally does not mean that people are incapable of voluntarily providing services that will facilitate the appearance—and the appearance on an involuntary basis—of esteem. That is why the problem raised is not an insurmountable obstacle to the emergence of an economy of esteem. We mention three such services that a person can voluntarily provide, whether in the way of an exchange—though perhaps only, as we shall see later, a suppressed sort of exchange—or in the way of a gift.

The first service or courtesy that I can voluntarily provide is to give attention to agents after a pattern that they invite or endorse—to give attention, for example, to a domain or to performances where they shine—and after a pattern, therefore, that is likely to increase my esteem for them. No matter how well you perform, you will not win any esteem from me for your performance unless I am prepared to give it attention; and a corresponding message holds for disesteem. And because I may choose to give or not to give attention to your efforts after the pattern you invite, I am in the position of being able to offer or withold something that goes proxy for my esteem. I may choose to give or withold my attention either after a pattern that promises to increase esteem—say, a pattern that you clearly desire—or after a pattern that holds out no such promise: after a pattern, indeed, that threatens to arouse my disesteem. If you are a writer who is anxious to impress me, then I may choose to give attention to the works you would like me to read and judge you by; or I may choose to give attention to the juvenilia about which you are embarrassed.

The second esteem-related service that I can voluntarily provide for a person is closely akin to the first; it involves giving expression or not giving expression to an opinion of you and your work. The service or courtesy envisaged is that of testifying to a favourable opinion or not testifying to a bad opinion, whether those opinions be real or simulated; and the corresponding disservice is that of not testifying to a favourable opinion or testifying to a bad opinion—again, whether the opinions be real or simulated. No matter how well or badly you perform, and no matter how well or badly I think of you, your performance will not win as much esteem or disesteem outside our circle unless I am prepared to express an opinion of it. And so I can make a gift to you, or perhaps enter into an exchange with you, in regard to my testimonial activities.

The limit case of testimony-based esteem—and the limit of what I may confer via my public testimony—arises when it becomes a matter of common belief that you are esteemed. You may be known or believed to perform well in a given area by every member of the population whose esteem matters to you. And yet it may be that no one in that population is aware of the fact that this is so. Each thinks well of you and you are perhaps aware that each thinks well. But no one else knows that everyone thinks well of you. Each thinks well of you on the basis of their immediate awareness of your merits, no one on the basis of knowing that others think well: no one thinks well of you on a testimonial basis.

Common belief comes on the scene when not only is it the case that everyone thinks well of you; everyone also believes that everyone thinks well of you, everyone believes that everyone believes this, and so on in the usual hierarchy (Lewis 1969). When such common belief is in place everyone will have a testimonial reason for thinking well of you: the fact, registered in the common belief, that others think well of you. In one variant of such common belief no one may depend on that testimonial reason for how they rate you; they may each also have an independent basis in direct observation for thinking well of you. But in more likely variants this need not be the case. It may be that some or even all of the population think well of you, only because they believe that everyone thinks well of you and they take that believed fact as a testimonial basis for thinking well of you themselves. The phenomenon of informational cascades—rapidly developing bodies of shared opinion—explains how this sort of thing can develop (Bikhchandani, Hirshleifer, et al. 1992; Kuran 1998; Kuran and Sunstein 1999).

Where esteem goes to common belief in any such manner, then it is going to be particularly robust. You will enjoy the esteem on a testimonial base that is going to be very hard to disrupt; this is because common belief in general is hard to disrupt. We describe such commonly imputed esteem as fame, and the corresponding form of commonly imputed disesteem as infamy. Fame is akin to glory, as distinct from mere honour, in some traditional terms (Elster 1999: 203 ff.). Infamy amounts to stigma, as distinct from mere shame, in terminology that John Braithwaite (1989) has popularised (see too Ahmed, Harris, et al. 2001). We explore some aspects of fame and infamy in Chapter 8.

The problem raised earlier may rule out the voluntary bestowal of esteem, then, but it does not rule out the voluntary provision of services that go proxy for esteem. My favourable attention goes proxy for the esteem I confer on you myself, my favourable testimony goes proxy for the esteem that others can give you. But the exchange of esteem is blocked, not just in so far as I cannot intentionally provide my own esteem, but also to the extent that I cannot intentionally transmit to you the esteem that others give me. And there is a third, intentional service that goes proxy for such inherited esteem, in the way that attending and testifying go proxy for my esteeming you or others' esteeming you. I may associate myself with you in a way that reflects onto you the esteem—or of course the disesteem—that others give me. Or I may dissociate myself from you in a way that stops such reflection.

If I publicly identify with you in a certain way, say by inviting you to join a relevant network of colleagues or friends, then I can give you a share in some status, good or bad, that I enjoy. Or if I publicly disown you, say by imposing a sort of ostracism, then I can deny you any share in that status. Think of the power of a Nobel Laureate to attract colleagues or collaborators. Or think of the effect of an Academy Award winner when they name someone in particular as having been vital to their success. What they each offer is not just a favourable testimony—though they do offer that too—but a reflection onto the cited person of the honour that they themselves have won.

Stage two: the exchange of esteem services

What we have seen is that though I cannot intentionally confer or withhold esteem, I can confer or withhold certain esteem services. But the fact that I can intentionally withhold or confer these things does not entail, by itself, that I can rationally give them as a gift or use them in exchange, whether in exchange for similar services or for other sorts of goods. I may be able to give you something intentionally, without its being rational of me to give it; as with the active pursuit of esteem, it may be self-defeating or counterproductive to do this.

It turns out, as a matter of fact, that the exchange of esteem services does run into this sort of problem. The fact that esteem is an evaluative, essentially involuntary attitude means that the esteem services I provide can only serve as credible conduits of esteem—and can only provide rewards for your behaviour—in contexts where I am taken to be suitably sincere in expressing esteem. But the problem is that my sincerity will always be in question where there is a straightforward exchange involved.

Suppose I give favourable attention to your efforts, looking at all and only those aspects of performance to which you invite my attention. Suppose I offer favourable testimony as to your achievements. Or suppose that I confer a favourable form of association on you. These services will hold out prospects of bringing you esteem—mine or another's—only so far as I am taken to believe sincerely that what I pay attention to is typical of your performance and that what I say or suggest about your merits is true. But if I do these things in a situation where I manifestly stand to gain from what you give me in exchange, then it will be difficult for me to persuade anyone, least of all you, that I sincerely hold such beliefs. And so it will not clearly be rational of me to offer the services; they are not likely to secure for you the benefits that might trigger a return.

When I exchange one thing for another in the standard pattern, as we saw, then I offer my commodity or service or money in return for the other's in the manner of a *quid pro quo*. I suggest—indeed I take it to be a matter of common awareness—that I give you what I offer because and only because you give me what you offer; and I assume—again I take it to be a matter of common awareness—that you give me what you offer because and only because I give you what I offer. The exchange comes of a targeted attempt on the part of each to better their lot and it is conducted in a wholly open or overt manner: the motive and strategy on each side is a matter of common awareness.

Suppose now that I offer my favourable attention to your performance in a context where it is a matter of common awareness that I do so because and only because I take you to be offering me something in return. Or suppose that I testify to your merits where the exchange motive is equally a matter of common awareness among those others as well as between you and me. Or suppose that I offer you association with me, and reflected glory, in a context where the exchange motive enjoys the same general salience. It does not take a great deal of reflection to realise that in such situations the service I discharge may not bring off the desired effect in the domain of esteem. Depending on what I seek in exchange, the allegedly favourable attention, testimony, or association that I offer is likely to look insincere. And to the extent that it looks less than fully sincere, it will be incapable of credibly manifesting esteem on my own part or of generating the esteem of others for the person in question.

These comments may overstate the problem that affects the exchange of esteem services in one respect. We have been discussing the problem on the assumption that I offer an esteem service because and only because you offer me something in return: because you offer me something in return and for no other motivating reason, conscious or unconscious. Things are somewhat more complicated if I offer that service, in part because you offer me something in return, and in part because you are deserving of the service by my lights. If this is known to be the case, then my esteem service will certainly have some value—it will mark the fact that I take you to be deserving—but that value will be reduced by the fact that it also marks the fact that I take you to be someone who can offer me a profitable return. The problem in this more complex case may not be as severe as in the case of straightforward exchange but it remains a problem.

The difficulty in both cases stems from the fact that standard exchange, as we have been envisaging it, is active in character, like active demand. It involves targeting, exclusively or partially, the personal advantage to be achieved by means of exchange. But the problem is not insurmountable, for exchange can occur without such overt targeting, as demand can be exercised without overt targeting. And in non-standard exchange of that kind the sincerity problem does not cause the same trouble.

Just as the active demand for esteem may be concealed by personal or social strategy, so one way in which exchange may occur without the overt targeting of personal advantage is by means of concealment. I can hide from you the fact that my offering favourable attention is tied, wholly or in part, to an expectation of reciprocity—say, a desire to get you, without your realising why, to feel positively towards me—or I can hide from others the presence of such a motive for offering you testimony or association. And if the exchange of an esteem service can be concealed in this way, then there is no reason why it should fail through being taken as insincere; the insincerity won't be manifest. I may successfully give you the semblance of my esteem, if I can hide the fact that I am offering you only favourable attention because of the returns in prospect, or partly because of those returns. I can successfully earn you the esteem of others if I can hide the fact that I am testifying to your merits, or associating with you, largely for reasons of personal benefit. That, after all, is why sycophancy and flattery work.

But this mode of non-standard exchange is unlikely to be very robust, at least in cases involving personal rather than social concealment. People are just too good at detecting patterns, especially long-run patterns, of concealment. The more interesting possibility, as in the demand case, is that exchange can be non-standard through being virtual rather than active. We believe that this is not just a logical possibility but one that is routinely borne out in people's dealings with one another.

Suppose that I am in the habit of giving you favourable attention, testimony, and association, where this habit is motivated by the esteem that I feel for you and only by that feeling of esteem. Suppose, second, that I enjoy similar benefits at your hand—for the moment, let us assume that they are esteem services—and that those benefits are equally supported by the esteem you feel for me. And suppose, finally, that were you or I not to enjoy such rewards in return, then in that purely counterfactual scenario we would each be motivated to take our attention, our testimony, or our association elsewhere.

In this scenario the rewards that each of us enjoys at the hands of the other do not motivationally explain our giving that person attention, testimony, and association; those services are given because of the esteem we each feel for the other, and for no other motivating reason. But the rewards still exercise a serious form of rational control over our behaviour. They are virtual determinants of the interaction between us and they give it an exchange structure. Though I give you esteem services because of esteeming you, and you give such services to me because of esteeming me, it still remains that neither of us would provide the services did we not receive them from the other in return.

In standard trades I give you X because—and usually only because—you give me Y or I expect you to give me Y. In this virtual sort of exchange I do not give you X, even in part, because you give me Y or because I expect you to give me Y. While I may offer you the relevant esteem services only so far as I continue to receive a return in kind for such behaviour, my motive for offering them is not that I receive or expect such a return. I offer them because of being in the habit of thinking well of you, admiring this or that trait, and so on. The reciprocation does not motivate me to pay you favourable attention, or offer favourable testimony or association. But still it is true that were you to cease to reciprocate, then I would respond by locating my esteem-giving services elsewhere. And, in particular, I might so respond through becoming aware of not enjoying the reciprocation and through seeing the services I provide as unrewarded.

Think by analogy of friendship. We do not love friends, or give them gifts—not even in part, let us presume—because they love us; we love them and favour them, in the ordinary run of things, because we like and identify with them. But it may nonetheless be true that were they not to love us or favour us in return, then in that counterfactual event we would tend to invest in other friendships. We may be completely sincere and devoted friends, cherishing those we love. And yet it may be the case that our devotion would not be capable of surmounting the obstacle that lack of reciprocation would create. (It may even be the case, indeed, that were our devotion capable of surviving lack of reciprocation, then it would constitute something better described as servility than devotion.)

We think that a similar pattern holds with esteem services. We give such services, when we are sincere, because we find them well earned, and only because we find them well earned; that is the sum of our motivation. But we are not saints—if that is the word—and were an esteemed person not to display any esteem in return, then that would lead us to back off and locate our efforts elsewhere. Perhaps more selfless souls would do better in that counterfactual event. But selfless souls need do no better than us under actual circumstances. We may be just as exclusively motivated by the deserts of those to whom we actually attend, those to whose merits we actually testify, and those with whom we would actually choose to be associated.

The services of esteem will represent a pattern of virtual exchange if they materialise under conditions of the sort we have been characterising. They will not be motivated by reciprocation, even in part, but they will be sensitive to whether or not reciprocation occurs. Let the reciprocation fail and the exchange will fail too. But that is not because those in exchange are actually motivated by a desire for reciprocal benefit, only because they would be motivated by such a desire did reciprocation fail. And so the sensitivity to reciprocation does not provide any reason for why the services provided—attention, testimony, and association—are or should be seen as insincere.[2]

We said that the virtual demand for something will always explain the resilience with which that good is attained and that in the case where the demand has been activated in the past—and disappeared again from the scene—it will explain why the motives and habits in the agent are such as to produce that good. Something similar holds in the case of virtual exchange. Where such exchange occurs, one or perhaps all of the parties involved provides an esteem service. Even if the demand for esteem has never been activated in the past on the part of someone who is rewarded by such services, it will still explain the resilience in the person's life of relationships where those services are forthcoming as rewards. And where the demand for esteem has been activated in the past, it will explain why the relationships that actually survive in the agent's life happen to be ones where this is so.

In discussing the virtual model of esteem in non-exchange contexts, we mentioned that the desire for esteem may play a certain part in the active generation of behaviour at the same time that it plays the role of a virtual controller; and this, without being seriously counterproductive. The same is also true of the role played by the desire for esteem in the context of exchange. The desire for esteem may be in virtual control of certain relationships, so far as one or another party would not act as they currently do were the esteem service to cease. And yet at the same time it may be true that the desire for esteem also has a certain active presence, say as a partial motivator for the person in question. When we speak in what follows of the desire for esteem exercising virtual control over an interaction we do not mean to rule out the possibility that it also has such an additional, active influence.[3]

---

[2] There would be extra evidence of our sincerity, of course, if we gave attention and testimony in some cases where there is no reciprocation. And so we might cultivate the habit of doing so in a certain number of cases. Thus the fact that there is much virtual exchange in esteem services does not mean that all attention and testimony and association has to be virtually exchanged. It will be better for your value as a provider of esteem services—it will increase the demand for your services—if they are often provided in cases where there is obviously no prospect of reward.

[3] In n. 1 of this chapter we mentioned the problem that were esteem costlessly supplied then that would raise the spectre of a race to the bottom, with suppliers competing to supply it at lower and lower prices or with less and less demanding standards. Is this a problem with the supply of esteem via the supply of esteem

CONCLUSION

As there is a problem with whether people can actively demand esteem, so there is a problem with whether people can actively supply it. In fact the problem in this second case, so we argued, is more deep-running and more wide-ranging than in the first. It is more deep-running, because esteem is an evaluative attitude such that it isn't even coherent to think of offering it voluntarily, whether as a gift or a trade, or of voluntarily passing it on. It is more wide-ranging, because it arises as a problem, not just for the esteem attaching to virtuous dispositions, but also for the esteem that goes, independently of the disposition revealed, with virtuous actions and virtuoso performances.

We discussed this problem in the first section of the chapter and then argued in the second that it need not block the emergence of a full economy of exchange in which there is, not just the competitive demand for esteem, but also something approaching its competitive supply. As in the last chapter, the problem considered turned out to direct us to a constraint on how the economy of esteem operates, not to anything in the nature of a block.

The resolution of the problem involved two stages. First we identified certain voluntary activities whereby I can affect the esteem in which you are held. These include attending to all and only the aspects of your performance that you want me to attend to, giving testimony to your merits and failing to give testimony to your faults, and choosing to associate with you in some way. And then we argued that there can be a structure of exchange in such services, making for something like an exchange economy of esteem.

In any active, overt exchange of services, of course, the sincerity of the provider is bound to come into question, rendering the exchange relatively ineffective and making the pursuit of exchange more or less irrational. My offering positive testimony to your merits is not going to be very persuasive for an audience—it will look like a cynical, insincere exercise—if it is clear that I do so, wholly or in part, because of the return that you promise to give me. But this difficulty can be overcome, however temporarily, by concealing the exchange. And it can be overcome in a robust, reliable way so far as the exchange involved is virtual, not active.

In the virtual exchange of esteem sevices each party serves the other well because of genuinely esteeming the other. That is what makes the services credible and manifestly sincere. But it just so happens that were the one not to

services? No, it is not. For one thing, esteem services are actions and so are not costlessly supplied. And for another, the esteem service is dependent for its value on the esteem it carries; thus, it must not be driven by low standards, applied without discrimination, subject to doubt about its sincerity, and so on.

provide the other with esteem services in return, then neither party would continue to serve the other. The desire for that return controls such relationships, removing those that fail to make the grade, and it leaves in place only interactions in which there is suitable reciprocation.

4

The Economy of Esteem

In concluding our sketch of how esteem functions in human life, we should say something on the emerging possibility of an economy of esteem. We will be turning in the next part of the book to the analysis of some concrete patterns in that economy but it may be useful at this stage to explain why an economy should be forthcoming. We divide the discussion into two sections. First we show how our results so far guarantee, at a general level, that there will be an economy of esteem. And then we look at how that economy is likely to materialise in practice.

1   THE POSSIBILITY OF AN ECONOMY OF ESTEEM

The conditions that give rise to an economy of esteem

An economy arises only with goods that are attractive and scarce: they will be scarce in the generic sense that effort is required to attain them—they are not manna from heaven—and they may also be scarce in the specific sense of forcing people into competition, with the efforts of each making success more difficult for others. We think of an economy as a system of competition in the demand for such goods and—normally though not inevitably—in their supply; in particular, as a competitive system that generates certain aggregate effects that feed back onto the patterns of demand and supply. The standard example of an aggregate feedback effect will be the pattern of relative prices that we must expect to emerge, and usually to stabilise, as a result of such competition.

We have found reason to think that conditions of precisely these kinds are fulfilled in the case of esteem.

1. Esteem is an object of general desire that is in scarce supply, both in the sense of requiring effort to access and in the sense of occasioning competition.

2. Esteem is in effective demand among people in the sense that people can rationally try to increase their individual levels of esteem.
3. Esteem can be rationally supplied as well as pursued so that people can also resort to exchange in seeking to increase their esteem.

We saw in Chapter 1 that esteem is an object of desire—a good—that is scarce in supply. We saw in Chapter 2 that esteem is not only an object of desire but also something that people can rationally demand or pursue—the pursuit is not self-defeating or counterproductive—at least so long as the pursuit is concealed or virtual in character. And we saw in Chapter 3 that while positive esteem cannot be given at will, nor negative esteem withheld at will, esteem services like attention and testimony and association can be supplied on that basis; and, so long as the supply is concealed or virtual, it can be supplied within a practice of rational exchange.

These conditions being fulfilled, we must expect to find an economy of esteem at work among people. We must expect to find that, other things being equal, rational individuals will control the things that they do, and the relationships they form—in particular, the esteem services they offer to one another—with a view to promoting the esteem in which they are individually held. Specifically, we must expect that they will often exercise such control in a concealed manner or, much more typically, in a virtual as distinct from an active mode. And expecting this, we can hope to be able to identify aggregate feedback patterns that appear in consequence of competition in the demand for esteem and in the supply of esteem. We can hope to be able to chart a system of interaction that feeds back on itself in the distinctively self-organising manner of an economy.

Some simplifications of presentation

The economy of esteem that we hold out in prospect may not be insulated, of course, from the economy of commodities and services that is described in the textbooks. Attitude-dependent goods of esteem may rationally be substituted by individuals for such material, action-dependent goods, as when someone foregoes a larger salary elsewhere in order to remain attached to a more estimable organisation—an organisation that may be expected to give them greater personal standing than the alternative—or when someone forgoes such esteem for a rise in salary. And attitude-dependent goods of esteem—or rather the services that obtain them—may be rationally exchanged for action-dependent goods, as when people pay an agent to broadcast their reputable performances in some area.

Not only is the economy of esteem bound to be engaged in this way with the material economy. It is also bound to interact with the system of power that obtains in a given society. An individual may cleave to those who have influence or standing, offering his or her esteem services in the expectation, not of being served in the same way by them or even served in a material manner—they may receive nothing but derision in return—but rather of being kept as a camp-follower, with all the sorry attractions of that employment. In situations of asymmetrical power, the virtual exchanges that take place may be deeply warped by that asymmetry.

But while the economy of esteem may be expected to overlap in these ways with the material economy and the regime of power, it will be convenient for us generally to abstract in this book from that interpenetration of systems. We shall mainly be presenting the economy of esteem as if it were a relatively autonomous, independent system of competition. No harm will result, provided it is clear that this way of speaking represents a simplification and idealisation of quite complex social realities.

Speaking of the economy of esteem is a simplification in another respect too. It suggests that there is a single, interconnected economy of the kind that we might find in a small community where it is a matter of common or mutual awareness that everyone is concerned about the same dimensions of psychology and behaviour, that everyone endorses the same ideals of performance in those dimensions, and that everyone is in a position to form an estimate of the performance of every other. But that suggestion is entirely misplaced so far as the contemporary world is concerned.

Almost every society that we know is going to be diversified in a way that generates fractures in the economy of esteem. One source of diversity is that people in different contexts will be concerned with quite different dimensions of performance: here with performance at work, there with performance in sport, and there again with performance as a family member or citizen. Another source of diversity is that in any such context people may pay allegiance to different standards of performance: some workers may approve of shirking, for example, where others deplore it; some family members may frown on dishonesty, others approve of anything that benefits the family. Yet another source of diversity is that in a given context, and even with a given audience that shares similar ideals, the performers with whom a given individual is compared in the formation of attitudes of esteem and disesteem may vary; one group may compare the person only with those of a similar background, another with performers in that category generally.

Nor are these the only sources of diversity around. There are also differences across contexts and groups in how far people are aware of comparative performance, in how far people depend on testimony in forming their attitudes, in how far people care about being esteemed or disesteemed by those outside a certain favoured group, and so on.

Just as the economy of esteem is not insulated from the material economy or the regime of power, neither is it really a single, homogeneous system in itself. There will be many overlapping subsystems within the economy of esteem in almost any contemporary society. And almost every individual will belong to a number of those subsystems, having a stake in how he or she stands in each. The subsystems will compete with one another for the energy and time of participants. And they will often be in conflict, in the sense that a high performance in one will count against performing well in another. Teenagers at school will have a stake in how they are thought of by parents, teachers, and peers but will find, in all likelihood, that it is hard to do well simultaneously in each of those subcultures. Peers may deride them for a high standing in the other groups, for example, and may drive them into systematically underperforming on those fronts.

2   THE ECONOMY OF ESTEEM IN PRACTICE

Esteem-seeking strategies

If an economy is going to be predictable in any measure, then it must be possible to identify the broad strategies—better, perhaps, the margins of adjustment—that are available to rational agents within that economy and to discern the conditions under which those strategies will be activated. We may not be able to say what different agents will do in different conditions; we may not even be in a position to discern reliable, aggregate regularities in what agents are likely to do in specific conditions. But we must at least be able to say that given a particular situation, and given a stable pattern of behaviour in that situation, a certain change will tend to produce an aggregate adjustment in this or that direction—just as we can say that if other things are held fixed then a rise in the relative price of a good will tend to reduce the level of relative demand. We must at least be able to make comparative-static predictions and to offer comparative-static explanations.

What are the strategies available to agents within the economy of esteem for promoting the esteem in which they are held? What are the margins on which they may adjust their behaviour with a view to increasing that esteem? If we cannot identify the likely strategies then we can have no hope of being able to make any predictions about the adjustments that various shocks will produce in the economy.

The best way to introduce the strategies available to the rational esteem-seeker is to identify the variables that determine how someone does in esteem terms. There are four questions that we need to ask, if we are to know how an agent does in esteem terms, and each of these points us towards a pair of relevant variables.

1. What *location* or locations of action does the agent operate in and what *level* of performance does he or she achieve?
2. What matters at that location: what *dimensions* of performance are taken into account and what *ideals* are assumed in evaluating that performance?
3. Who matters in that location: what *public* will judge the performance of the agent and in relation to which *comparators* will they tend to judge it?
4. What will that public take to be the *average* performance among those comparators—this may refer to mean or mode or median—and how far will they have *access* to the agent's performance in comparison to that average; in effect, to the agent's standing?

These questions point us towards eight variables on which rational agents may wish to act in promoting their own esteem. Here they are, with the claims we make for each, when other things are equal and when the strategies described are feasible.

Location: people will specialise in those areas where they can expect to do best in esteem terms.

Level: they will seek that level of performance there that promises to maximise their esteem at acceptable cost.

Dimensions: they will highlight the dimensions on which they score well and downplay the dimensions on which they do badly.

Ideals: and they will push the case for the importance of those ideals or desiderata that they satisfy in best measure.

Public: they will select audiences from whom the esteem supplied is likely to be large and of most evidentiary, pragmatic, or inherent value.

Comparators: and they will frame their performance so as to ensure comparison with a maximally flattering reference group.

Average: they will propagate favourable information—or perhaps misinformation—about the statistical norms among comparators.

Access: and they will control the access that the relevant public has to their performance—say, increasing or decreasing those who will form an audience—so as to increase their expected esteem.

Illustrating the competition for esteem

There are many different strategies that agents may take on each of these different variables or fronts—many different margins on which they may adjust their performance—and examples will accumulate in Part II. For purposes of getting a vivid, immediate sense of the strategies available—and for later reference—it will be useful if we distinguish between three broad kinds. First there are performance strategies that work on the first two fronts, to do with location and level of performance. Second, there are the publicity strategies that work on the last two fronts: access to the agent's performance, and to the average against which they will be compared—access to their standing relative to comparators. And third, there are broadly presentational strategies that operate on the remaining four fronts. These are not so certain of being available as the performance and publicity strategies and what they have in common is that they are designed, for a given performance and a given degree of publicity, to determine how the behaviour will be cast or framed or presented.

Competition in performance will drive people to try harder within any domain to behave in an esteem-winning way or to try to locate their efforts in those domains of activity where they are most effective in attaining esteem. To take some academic cases as an example, we may expect students to try to win the admiration of their teachers, researchers to try to establish a position among their peer group, and academics each to try to locate effort in that area, whether of research, teaching, or administration, where the estimative returns prove greatest for them personally.

But apart from competition in performance, we must also expect competition for publicity in any domain. For example, people will presumably want as large and significant an audience as possible to recognise their merits relative to comparators and as small and insignificant an audience as possible to recognise their demerits; they will want the audience to share a common awareness that their relative merits are recognised in this way; and they will want those who think ill of them to be inhibited from speaking ill and thereby spreading the poison.

Thus, students and researchers will presumably want to ensure that their successes are noticed, their failures overlooked; that those who speak against them are challenged and perhaps discredited; that the patterns of voluntary association they form testify to their merit; and that the involuntary associations to which they belong do not impact negatively on their standing. One possibility that is particularly worth noting here is that of making their successes a matter of common awareness. In the community of students, teachers, and researchers, it should be obvious that any one of them will be glad of fame, since it will reinforce them in general esteem, and any one of them will shrink from the prospect of infamy, since that is going to reinforce them in general disesteem.

The third area where we may expect competition is in what we described as the presentation of performance. How someone is evaluated and esteemed for a given level of performance and publicity is a function of a number of things, as we mentioned. First the dimensions and ideals that are taken as relevant. And, second, the public who are given exposure to the performance, and the comparators in relation to whom they are judged. We may expect that if opportunities for adjusting those matters to their own advantage are presented to rational agents, then they will tend to exploit them. To quote the psychologists, Dale Miller and Deborah Prentice (1996: 807), in summary of a range of empirical findings: 'Individuals generally try to present themselves in the most favourable possible light.'

An example of competition in presentation is provided by a pattern of behaviour often found among academic faculty, particularly those who do not score very well in mainstream assessment. They argue for the importance of those dimensions of evaluation that flatter them most: teaching, not research; or research in their own special area, not the standard variety. They argue that among the standard dimensions, they should be evaluated by ones that happen to flatter them most, whether they be publication rates, citation rates, student reviews, or whatever. And they present themselves as part of that constituency among whom they can best shine: not among the high-scoring teachers in their own department, perhaps, but among academic teachers generally; or not among researchers in their discipline but only among researchers who take their particular approach or pursue their particular specialisation.

The competition in publicity and presentation will not be confined to competing within the academic context. We may also expect those who belong to academia long-term—researchers and teachers—to be anxious about the publicity and presentation they receive in the wider society. And here it is worth mentioning two different aspects of the project they are likely to pursue. They will individually seek to belong to those different institutions—high-ranking universities, distinguished academies, and so on—membership of which will signal that they are well thought of by their peers. And they will individually seek to promote the cause of the broader associations—say, that of academics generally—that they necessarily belong to as professionals. They can be expected to vary the voluntary groupings to which they belong, and to vaunt the superiority of their involuntary groupings, in a way that testifies to their individual merit. We devote two chapters in Part II to these associational strategies.

We do not say that in taking initiatives in regard to their performance, publicity, and presentation people in the academic world are overtly and cynically seeking to promote their own reputations; in any case that would not be a good strategy to adopt, in light of the teleological paradox. Most of the time we think that the competition for esteem has a virtual character. People take the different paths they take for a variety of reasons: they work hard for the pleasure and sense of achievement it gives; they seek an audience for their work, out of a conviction that the work is worthwhile; they criticise the sorts of ideals that would downgrade the work out of a passionate belief that those ideals are inappropriate. It so happens, however, that they are reinforced in these efforts by the fact that their esteem is thereby increased. And were their efforts not to prove rewarding in that way, then the chances are that they would adjust and adopt other approaches. Their behaviour is shaped to the contours of a competition for esteem but the shaping is mostly achieved without conscious direction.

The resort to exchange

In illustrating the strategies that rational agents may adopt with a view to increasing the esteem in which they are held, we have said nothing about the possibility of their resorting to exchange, in particular the exchange of esteem services. But it should be clear that such exchange may provide an important means whereby people can hope to be able to improve how they stand in publicity and presentational terms.

Consider the following cases where academics enjoy reciprocal benefits in the domain of esteem.

1. Two or more academic parties—individuals or groups—benefit from professional association with one other: each earns some reflected glory, while none loses; reflecting one's glory does not mean diminishing it.
2. A referee testifies to the merit of a student, or a fellow academic, and earns in return the reward of being seen to be able to place that student or associate in a post.
3. One person testifies to the merit of another's book by writing an endorsement for the blurb and earns in return the reward of being presented to readers as someone whose endorsement is worth having.
4. Two researchers each give favourable attention to the other's work, thereby enjoying the benefit of their manifest, mutual esteem.

5. The academics in a given institution seek to make appointments that will add to their own esteem, and those looking for appointments seek to belong to an institution that will give a positive signal about their standing.

It is perfectly plausible, and not necessarily cynical, to think that these forms of reciprocal benefit represent exercises in exchange, in particular the virtual exchange of esteem. The idea is that each party acts out of habit or conviction or a sense of duty, or whatever, in taking the course described but that as a matter of fact their so acting is rewarded by a reciprocal benefit; and that were it not so rewarded—in particular, were it to attract a penalty in the esteem stakes—then it would not be likely to continue. The reciprocation is controlled by the interest of each party in enjoying esteem but the control is wholly virtual in character. Each party's interest in esteem stands by, ready to adjust the behaviour in the event of the wonted rewards failing to follow, but normally it has no direct role to play and can languish in the background.

The claim that these forms of reciprocation represent virtual, not actively intentional, exchanges can be borne out by considering some contrasting cases. Suppose A offers to pay B for allowing A to gain reflected glory through association with B; or suppose that a publisher offers to pay a high-ranking academic to express a good opinion, real or simulated, of a book; or suppose that one researcher suggests to another—cynically, not out of a sense of joint worth—that they should cite and praise one another's work. Most of us, we suspect—and hope—would reject such an offer out of hand as being quite objectionable; indeed we would have good, self-interested reason to reject the offer, since the discovery that we had accepted it would be so costly in esteem terms. And for corresponding reasons most of us would find it implausible to imagine that such offers are commonly made. But no such implausibility, or objection, arises with the cases mentioned earlier.

An elusive economy

The points argued in earlier chapters make us perfectly confident that the economy of esteem has a powerful influence in ordinary life, as illustrated in this sketchy example, shaping people's individual efforts and mutual responses. We hope to substantiate that claim more properly in the relatively detailed studies of Part II. Notwithstanding this confidence, however, we think that in daily life ordinary folk are less likely to recognise the role of an esteem economy than they are, for example, to acknowledge the role of the market economy. There is a natural resistance in folk psychology, if not to the thought that people cherish esteem and shrink from disesteem, at least to the practice of applying this assumption in making routine sense of what individuals do and of how they interact with one another.

This should not be surprising. To recognise the role of the economy of esteem in our lives is to think that when people react to the situations in which they find themselves, one controlling factor will always bear on how their reactions will score in the esteem stakes. And there is a great deal of evidence from social psychology that we are disposed to neglect the role of variable, situational pressures like this in explaining one another's behaviour. The desire for esteem is situationally variable in the sense that it prompts different pressures and different responses under different circumstances. We are much more inclined to trace behaviour to stable, situationally invariable dispositions that generate more or less stable types of actions: to dispositions like generosity or cruelty, which generate recognisably generous and cruel types of action. We are naturally led by what psychologists call the fundamental attribution bias.

E. E. Jones (1990: 138) puts the point forcefully. 'I have a candidate for the most robust and repeatable finding in social psychology: the tendency to see behavior as caused by a stable personal disposition of the actor when it can be just as easily explained as a natural response to more than adequate situational pressure.' This finding—that people are deeply prone to the funda-mental attribution bias—supports the idea that, even while they are conscious of their own sensitivity to a force like the desire for esteem (Miller and Prentice 1996: 804), people will be loathe to trace the behaviour of others to such a situational pressure. They are much more likely to explain the behaviour by ascribing a corresponding behavioural disposition to them. And that being so, presumably, they are likely to expect others to explain their own behaviour in those terms.

Suppose, for example, that people generally behave generously under the virtual control—partial or total—of the desire for esteem. That sort of behav-iour wins esteem for them and did it not do so, then they would tend to move away from it; the desire for esteem is not active in producing the behaviour but its presence ensures that the behaviour will satisfy it. Would the discovery that the desire for esteem plays this role be likely to lead people to explain generous behaviour, and to expect others to explain it, by reference in some part—in the part played by virtual controllers—to the motive of esteem? Not if the psychological research on the attribution bias is sound. Unlike the motive of generosity—a stable personal disposition—the desire for esteem requires no recognisably similar pattern of action across different situations and so is not the sort of factor that we are inclined to invoke in explaining one another's doings.

To the extent that the fundamental attribution bias has a firm grip upon our mental habits, then, the economy of esteem is bound to be something of an elusive reality (Brennan and Pettit 2000). Now we will see it, now we won't. Now, in moments of theoretical reflection, it will prove unmissable; now, in the immediate experience of others, it may fade into invisibility.

Perhaps we shouldn't deplore this blindness in folk psychology to the place of the economy of esteem in our lives. Suppose it became a matter of shared awareness that people's behaviour is virtually and deeply shaped by the fact that they are participants in a competition for esteem—an arms race for reputation. That ought not strictly to make any difference to people's pursuit of esteem—in particular, the pursuit of a name for virtue—since the virtual pursuit of esteem is consistent with being actually moved by virtue, and so they might still expect to have their doings ascribed to virtuous dispositions. But the line between virtual and active control is a fine, theoretical distinction, not a garden-variety divide, and it might well be lost in the popular awareness. And so the common recognition of the economy of esteem might damage that very economy by leading people to explain all virtuous behaviour as the active product of esteem-seeking. This would damage the economy of esteem, because no one could expect to be thought virtuous on the basis of acting virtuously; people could only expect to have the behaviour explained, to their reputational disadvantage, as an attempt to win esteem.

Arthur Lovejoy (1961: 98) thought there was a real problem here and suggested, by way of remedy, that we ought not to disapprove of the desire and pursuit of esteem—we ought to praise the habit of approbativeness, as he called it. 'Disapprobation of approbativeness or of the candid manifestation of it, ought, I suggest, to be disapproved.' We suspect that calling for disapproval of the disapproval of the pursuit of esteem, at least in most areas, is whistling in the wind. But we do not believe that the problem is a serious one, since people's habits of explaining behaviour—people's disposition to display the fundamental attribution bias—will inhibit them from explaining much behaviour in terms of the desire for esteem. In this respect, the error may be a happy fault.[1]

---

[1] There may be a certain cunning in this feature of folk psychology. The folk-psychological explanations that we provide of one another's behaviour, and the explanations therefore that we expect to attract from one another, serve as important regulators and stabilisers of our behaviour (McGeer 2002; McGeer and Pettit 2002). We learn, not just that we human beings are often moved by the desire to be fair or kind or friendly, but that we will be blamed for not being so moved, that these represent ideal motives which we should aspire to have; and this being so—as indeed the desire for esteem explains—we try to display such motives. The

CONCLUSION

The previous two chapters showed that the way is open for the presence of an economy of esteem in our social lives. In this chapter we sought to vindicate and illustrate that claim. The first part of the chapter was given to showing why an economy of esteem is possible and the second to illustrating the working of the economy of esteem in practice.

We argued for the possibility of an economy of esteem by identifying certain conditions that are sufficient for the emergence of quite a rich economy and by then showing, on the basis of earlier chapters, that those conditions are going to be fulfilled for the economy of esteem. Esteem is an object of general desire which is in scarce supply. People are in a position rationally to demand or pursue esteem for themselves. And equally people are in a position rationally to supply and exchange esteem with one another. Thus people are rationally bound to compete in both the pursuit and the exchange of esteem, thereby generating aggregate effects that feed back on their own choices.

We illustrated the economy of esteem in practice, first, by identifying the different variables on which rational agents can act with a view to promoting their esteem and then by giving examples of the broad strategies available in respect of those variables. We argued that the variables that determine how someone does in esteem terms are the *location* and *level* of performance; the *dimensions* of performance that are taken into account at that location and the *ideals* that are assumed in evaluating that performance; the identity of the *public* who will judge the performance of the agent and the identity of the *comparators* in relation to which it will be judged; the *average* performance imputed to those comparators and the *access* that critics have to the agent's performance in comparison to that average.

The broad strategies available to agents in respect of those variables are those of performance, publicity, and presentation. Rational agents in pursuit of esteem will look to where and how they perform: that is, to location and level; to how far their relative performance and standing gets publicity: that is, to how well they compare with presumed averages; and to how favourably it is presented: that is, to how it does on the remaining fronts—with what dimensions and ideals to the fore, and with which public and comparators in view.

We illustrated these strategies of performance, publicity, and presentation in relation to an academic community of students, teachers, and researchers, looking at the ways in which they may pursue esteem, and exchange esteem

importance of folk psychology may derive as much from this regulative function, as from any predictive utility. And it will serve that function, reliably only so far as it follows the patterns associated with the fundamental attribution bias (see, too, Pettit 1978; Macdonald and Pettit 1981).

services, in line with these strategies. In doing this, we emphasised that we are only committed in general to the belief that such agents will virtually pursue esteem, not to the belief that they will often actively do so. This fits with the argument in the previous two chapters.

The chapter concluded with a brief excursus on the fact that the economy of esteem does not have the salience of the ordinary market economy and that people may be resistant to recognising it in practice. The elusiveness of the economy in this respect may be due to the fact, as social psychology documents, that ordinary people are wedded to the practice of tracing behaviour to personal, situationally invariable dispositions on the part of agents, not to the different situational pressures that the desire for esteem is likely to prompt. This elusiveness may be a blessing, however, as it can guard people against being overimpressed by the ubiquity of the desire for esteem in their lives and so against undermining the economy of esteem itself.

PART II

WITHIN THE ECONOMICS OF ESTEEM

Introduction

If the arguments of Part I are sound, then social esteem is a good in pursuit of which people compete and a good that they even manage in some measure to exchange. That means, in effect, that there is every reason to think that there will be an economy of esteem. There will be a pattern emerging from the efforts of individuals in the domain of esteem that itself affects the efforts they should rationally make. There will be an aggregate-level system detectable in the motley of individual-level action and adjustment.

We turn in this second part of the book to try to vindicate the reality of the economy of esteem, and to give a sense of how analyses of effects in that economy are likely to go. Where Part I took us from the psychology to the economics of esteem, Part II is designed to take us right into the economics.

It is important not to give a false impression, however, of what we try to offer here. First, we do not mean to outline in a systematic way the various effects that materialise within the economics of esteem; that would be much too ambitious for a pilot study of this kind. Rather we attempt to illustrate some of the promising lines of inquiry that open up, once we recognise the reality of the esteem economy. And, second, we do not mean to subject the effects we mention to the full dress of technical economic analysis. We try to present accounts that will catch the eye of economists without becoming inaccessible to those in other social sciences.

There are eight chapters in Part II, and they divide into three major sets. Chapters 5–7 look at the economy of esteem with an eye to various simple sorts of equilibria that may emerge there. Equilibrium outcomes are patterns that leave no one with an individual incentive to break away and it is striking that under various assumptions there are equilibria in prospect within the economy of esteem. This feature should attract the eye of economists, since equilibrium analysis is such a well-entrenched aspect of their discipline.

The equilibrium results of Chapters 5–7 assume that there is no variability in the extent to which publicity is available on two fronts: in respect of the performance of individuals and in respect of the social standards underlying esteem. Chapters 8–10 look at the effects of lifting those assumptions. Chapter 8 looks at the effect of variations in contextual arrangements for providing publicity on individual performance. Chapter 9 looks at the effects of publicity about the general level of compliance with the ideals accepted in the society. And Chapter 10 looks at the effect of variations in individuals' efforts to control the publicity their own performances receive.

The equilibrium results of the first set of chapters assume, not just that publicity on these fronts is constant, but that the ways in which people associate or are associated with one another do not enter into the picture. This further assumption is lifted in Chapters 11 and 12, which complete Part II. Chapter 11 examines the ways in which people may seek to associate voluntarily with one another—or to avoid such association—out of a concern for their own social esteem. And Chapter 12 looks at how people may respond to the discovery that the ways in which they are involuntarily associated, say in ethnic or cultural minorities, affect the beliefs and expectations that others in the community form of them and so, ultimately, the esteem in which they are held.

We distinguished in the last chapter of Part I between three strategies—three margins of adjustment—which people may rationally explore within the economy of esteem: these relate, respectively, to performance, publicity, and presentation. In the studies sketched here in Part II we concentrate mainly on strategies of performance and publicity. Chapters 5–7 bear explicitly on performance and Chapters 8–10 on publicity. The final two chapters, on associational effects, bear on some questions of presentation but connect mainly with a mix of issues in performance and publicity.

5

A Simple Equilibrium in Performance

1 PERFORMANCE EFFECTS

The point of departure for the analysis of the esteem economy is a two-person interaction. In that interaction, esteem for actor A is obtained from observer B by virtue of A's level of performance in some arena of action, X. The simple first-round behavioural impact of esteem is to induce A to perform X at a higher level than A would otherwise do. Esteem here acts as an incentive, much like a conventional economic incentive, and has similarly predictable behavioural effects. Such effects are what we call performance effects. These represent the focus of attention for the next three chapters.

Although the two-person case has its uses as a point of departure, we will be assuming, unless the contrary is explicitly stated, the more typical case in which there is a community of individuals, all of whom act simultaneously as both esteem-recipients and esteem-givers. It will still be useful to distinguish between individuals' actions as demanders of esteem on the one hand and as suppliers of esteem on the other. But there will be many actors aspiring to be esteemed; and many potential observers all of whom will supply esteem or disesteem as they perceive it to be merited.

When we talk of performance effects, it may seem as if we are focusing unduly on cases where esteem is assigned on the basis specifically of actions. And many of our illustrative examples are of that kind. That fact might be taken to suggest that we are ignoring the cases where esteem is awarded for a disposition rather than for an action. But this would be a misinterpretation. The term performance here is intended to capture whatever it is that is the basis for esteem. In the dispositional case, just being an honest or benevolent or courageous person is the performance in question.

In the analysis that follows in the first three chapters of Part II, there are two different cases that arise. One is where performance in the relevant domain can come in greater or smaller amounts—more or less honesty; more or less bravery; more or less accomplished piano playing; and so on. The other is where performing means acting in a certain manner (or not), where there is no place for degree of performance. The role of the esteem incentive in the first case is either to encourage performance at a higher level or among a greater number, whereas its role in the second can only be to increase the number of those who perform appropriately. The first case figures here and in Chapter 6, the second in Chapter 7.

The particular focus of attention throughout this chapter is the presence of feedback loops between the levels of performance that the quest for esteem induces on the one hand, and the standards on the basis of which esteem is given on the other; standards reflect ideals in a way explained in Section 4. Those feedback loops create a logical connection between the individual responses to the social environment that individuals find themselves in and that social environment itself. Specifically, individual performances and prevailing standards for the award of esteem are jointly determined in equilibrium. Our object in this chapter is to derive that equilibrium, demonstrate the interdependence between performance and standards, and examine some of the more interesting properties of the equilibrium so derived.[1]

The argument is laid out as follows. First, we focus on individual performance level in the presence of a given standard. Our aim here is just to establish the general structure of the individual esteem-based incentive. This occupies us in Section 2. Then in Section 3, we show how individual performance connects to changed standards. Section 4 discusses the determination of standards and the interdependence between standards and average performance. In Section 5 we establish a kind of 'general equilibrium' in the performance domain and conduct some simple comparative static analysis and in Sections 6 and 7 we look at some interesting general features of the equilibrium.

As we indicated in Part I, the likely effect of esteem on behaviour—the 'esteem-related incentive', as we shall refer to it here—is a function of the size and quality of the (expected) audience. In Chapters 8–12, we shall examine the effect of changes in audience size and quality, and the incentives that agents themselves have to influence them. For the purposes of this chapter, however, we shall abstract from such effects. We shall simply take audience size and quality as given.

---

[1] A quite similar analysis to the one developed here is elegantly developed in Hollander (1990) though his treatment is somewhat more technical, and deals with a slightly narrower application—namely participation in the voluntary sector. Our own model was derived independently, and we only discovered Hollander's paper very late in the final stages of preparation of this book.

2 THE INDIVIDUAL CASE

Consider a single representative individual A performing at some level in the domain, X. The performance in question can be better or worse in terms of prevailing standards. A can, that is, exhibit more or less X—more or less courage or generosity or academic conscientiousness or professional competence. If A's performance is at a sufficiently high level, A will earn esteem from observers; if that performance is below a certain level, A will earn disesteem. And initially we shall take the simplest possible case in which the positive and negative esteem ranges exhaust the domain. That is, there is a point in the X-domain, which we denote S, which earns zero esteem and zero disesteem. Performance above S earns esteem; performance below S earns disesteem. (We shall interrogate this assumption and relax it somewhat in the next chapter: however, it is useful at this point to focus on the simpler case.) In fact, in the spirit of simplicity, we take it that esteem earned is a simple linear function of performance level. So:

$$E_i = a [X_i - S] \tag{1}$$

where E_i is the esteem that accrues to individual i, X_i is i's X-performance, and a is a constant. We can, without loss of generality, specify the units of esteem such that a takes a value of unity; and we shall make that assumption in what follows.[2]

We can depict equation (1) diagrammatically in Figure 5.1a. In this diagram, the level of X-performance is shown along the horizontal axis; and the esteem value associated with X-performance at various levels along the vertical axis. Disesteem is depicted just as negative esteem. The line DE shows the esteem that accrues at various levels of X-performance. It is upward-sloping from left to right and cuts the horizontal axis at S. The line $e'e$ shows the marginal level of esteem—that is, the additional esteem earned by improving X-performance a little at various levels of performance. By construction, marginal esteem is the same at every level of X-performance, reflecting the fact that equation (1) is

---

[2] This model presupposes that there is a cardinal metric of performance. In other words, it makes sense not only to say that Bjorling is a better singer than Wunderlich, but also that the difference between Bjorling and Wunderlich is the same (or greater or less than) the difference between Sutherland and Callas. That such a metric exists may rather strain the imagination. It is one thing to say that singing is such that some singers are better than others and quite another to say that the relevant differences can be compared. However, the model here is used for illustrative purposes only. And all the functional forms assumed between the relevant parameters are chosen for reasons of simplicity not plausibility.

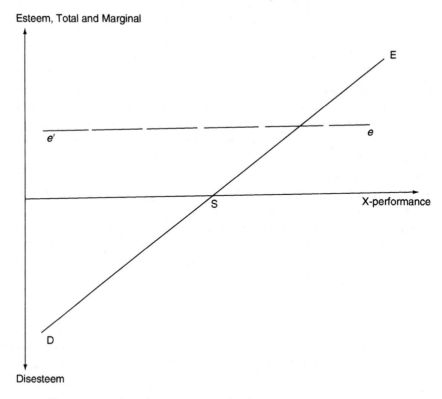

Figure 5.1a. *Relation between esteem and performance level—total and marginal.*

linear in X. Note that marginal esteem is positive even in the range where esteem itself is negative. A small improvement in X-performance can increase an individual's total esteem by reducing the level of disesteem suffered.

The additional esteem on offer from improved X-performance will have a utility that will depend, among other things, both on A's demand for esteem, and the amount of esteem that A already has from other sources. Both of these factors can, of course, vary between different performers. But let us suppose that the demand for esteem is identical across agents, and that X is the only source of esteem (or equivalently that the amount of esteem derived from other sources is the same for all actors). Then everyone's esteem-related demand for X will be the same and will have the shape given by $a'a$ in Figure 5.1b. This $a'a$ curve will be downward sloping as shown because the underlying demand-curve for esteem itself is downward sloping. Like all other goods, the more esteem you have, the less an additional unit is worth. In that sense at least, esteem is taken to be no different from any other object of desire.

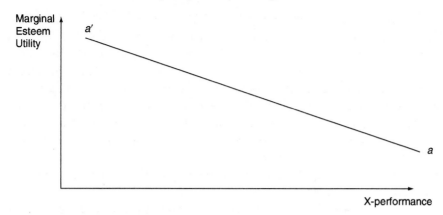

Figure 5.1b. *Marginal value of esteem for X-performance.*

The $a'a$ curve depicts the 'marginal esteem utility' to A of X-performance. Thus, $a'a$ is just like A's demand curve for X, except that it reflects only the esteem-utility of X to A. A may value X for reasons in addition to its being a source of esteem—say, because X-activity is enjoyable in its own right, or because it is instrumental in obtaining other goods. Or perhaps X is such that in the normal conduct of life A will be called on to exhibit it at some level that will reflect A's particular inclinations and capacities—as might be the case with honesty or cleanliness. In any event, at whatever X-level A happens to perform, there will be an additional 'esteem incentive' encouraging A to lift performance. And A's final personal equilibrium in the X-domain will reflect the influence of that esteem incentive. This is the sense in which it is reasonable to think of esteem as constituting an incentive much like a financial reward. Provided only that A has any desire for esteem at all, and that such additional esteem can be garnered by increasing X-performance, A's final choice of X-performance will be higher than it would have been in the absence of esteem-related effects.

3   THE RELATION BETWEEN INDIVIDUAL PERFORMANCE AND STANDARDS

In order to derive a full equilibrium in the X-domain, it is necessary to explore how the individual would respond to a change in the prevailing standard, S. So suppose that, for some reason yet to be explained, the standard were to increase. That is, the S point in Figure 5.1*a* moves to the right. If A were not to change her X-performance, then A would find herself with lower esteem. There would, under our simple construction, be no change in the marginal esteem that A derives, because marginal esteem is constant. But the fact that A would have less esteem than A had before means that the utility of esteem increases at the margin: there would be an increase in the marginal utility of the esteem. This increased utility of esteem gives A reason to increase X-performance somewhat: the esteem incentive has increased. That, at least, is our general claim—namely, that prevailing standards and A's performance are positively related. If the standard were to decrease, A would enjoy higher esteem at A's prevailing level of X-performance and the esteem-related incentive would correspondingly fall.

On this basis, we can derive a reaction curve that shows the relation between the prevailing standard, S, and the individual's performance of X. Such a

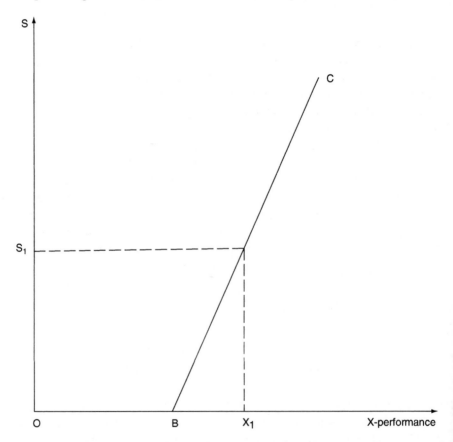

Figure 5.2. *Individual reaction curve.*

reaction curve is depicted in Figure 5.2 by the line BC. In that diagram, we depict along the horizontal axis the X-performance of our representative individual, A, and on the vertical axis the prevailing standard in the X-domain. The line BC traces out the level of performance that would be induced from the representative person by various levels of X-standards. So, if the standard were zero, the representative individual would choose to perform at X-level given by the distance OB. She would receive a positive level of esteem for that performance, because it is higher than the prevailing standard (zero at this point). And the fact that such esteem is on offer is part of the reason why her performance level is as high as OB. If the standard were to rise to S_1, then a performance level of OB would no longer generate as much esteem. In fact, if S_1 is more than OB, a performance level of OB would generate disesteem. In the face of this new standard, A would choose a level of X-performance that is somewhat higher than OB. Specifically, denote the new level of performance as X_1. Under our assumptions, it turns out that the increase in performance associated with the increase in standards from zero to S_1, $(X_1 - OB)$, is itself less than S_1. In other words, the BC line is upward sloping from left to right and has a slope greater than one—this is derived in the more technical appendix following. In Figure 5.2 the reaction curve is shown as a straight line but that is simply for geometric convenience.

APPENDIX TO SECTION 3

The fact that the reaction curve BC in Figure 5.2 is upward sloping from left to right with a slope greater than unity is an important piece of the analysis. The economist reader may be reassured to verify that this property of the reaction curve follows fairly immediately from the standard construction of individual preferences, familiar from basic microeconomic theory.

Consider the representative individual's indifference map between X, including its esteem value, and all other goods, Y, as depicted in Figure 5.3a. Initially, let the standard be zero. Then our representative individual will face a budget constraint of LM, reflecting the fact that X and Y have to be traded off at terms that are determined by, say, the amounts of time and energy that X and Y each require. When $S = 0$, the amount of X is OX_0 as in Figure 5.3a.

Now, from (1) above, with units of esteem chosen so that a = 1, we rewrite (1) as:

$$X_i = E_i + S \tag{2}$$

As standards, S, increase from zero to S_1, the consumption possibilities curve, LM, shifts inwards in parallel fashion to $L'M'$, where $M - M'$ is S_1. Standards change the amount of esteem associated with any level of X but they do not alter the relative trade-off between X and Y. At any level of X-performance, the esteem accruing is reduced by S_1. Providing both goods are normal in consumption (that is, consumption of both increases as total income increases) the new equilibrium will be at a point like B1. The corresponding level of X-performance will be such as to secure esteem level at E_1, where E_1 is equal to $X_1 - S_1$. Esteem will be reduced, so:

$$E_0 > E_1 \tag{3}$$

But from (2) above,

$$E_1 = X_1 - S_1$$
$$\text{And } X_0 = E_0$$

It follows from (3) that:

$$X_0 > (X_1 - S_1)$$

Or equivalently, that:

$$S_1 > (X_1 - X_0) \tag{4}$$

Given that Y is not inferior,

$$E_1 > (E_0 - S_1)$$
$$\text{Or } (X_1 - S_1) > (X_0 - S_1)$$
$$\text{Or } X_1 > X_0$$

So from (4) above:

$$S_1 > (X_1 - X_0) > 0 \tag{5}$$

The inequality in (5) tells us that the increase in A's X-performance is positive but less than the increase in standards that induces that increase in A's

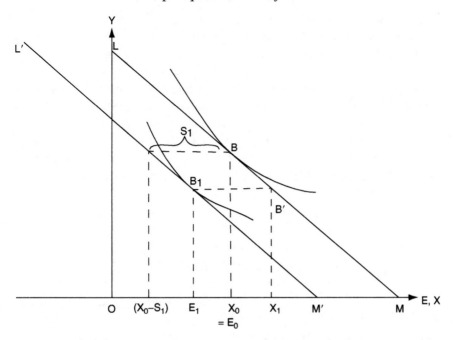

Figure 5.3a. *Indifference map between esteem and other 'goods'.*

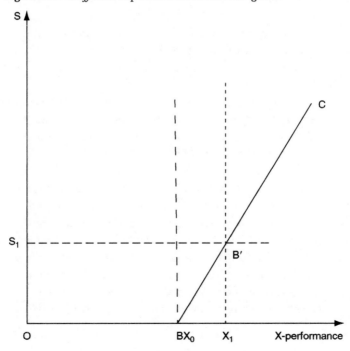

Figure 5.3b. *Corresponding reaction curve.*

X-performance. Individuals respond to increased standards by increasing their efforts, but not by so much as to increase the amount of esteem they enjoy. In other words, the reaction curve does indeed have the shape depicted in Figure 5.2: in fact, we can derive the reaction curve directly from Figure 5.3*a*, by mapping the levels of X against the corresponding standards that give rise to them. That mapping generates the reaction curve indicated by Figure 5.3*b*— which is essentially the same as that in Figure 5.2. In particular, the reaction curve is upward-sloping from left to right from some positive point on the horizontal axis, and has a slope in excess of unity. That property follows from the fact that both esteem and other goods are 'normal' in consumption.

4   THE RELATION BETWEEN STANDARDS AND AVERAGE PERFORMANCE

So far, we have treated the location of the standard that divides positively esteemed performance from negatively esteemed as exogenous—something that the agent takes as given and determined entirely independently of his own performance. That is true for each individual; but it is not in general true in aggregate. To complete the construction of equilibrium in the economy of esteem, we need to specify where the relevant standard comes from. To do this, we need to take some time out from the analytics to discuss the issue of standards in more general terms and return to matters raised in Chapter 1.

It is clear and unexceptionable that esteem and disesteem are assigned to performers by observers on the basis of how good or bad the performance is perceived to be. The goodness and badness in question involves an appeal to standards. And those standards are social constructs. They are so in two different senses which it pays us to distinguish.

In the first place, if there is to be any behavioural effect deriving from the desire for esteem, actors must have some knowledge of what the normal observer will think of different performances. If fear of shame is to drive my conduct, I have to have some reasonably clear sense of what others would consider shameful. Equally, if a desire for positive esteem is to spur me on to greater efforts, I have to have a clear sense of the direction in which my greater efforts are likely to be best deployed. The economy of esteem is in this sense dependent for its operation on a substructure of widely acknowledged values or ideals.[3] It is important to underline this assumption because it immediately establishes one difference between the economy of esteem and the economy of goods. The economy of esteem is evaluatively charged in a manner that the economy of goods is not.

There is, however, a second and even more important sense in which assessment standards are socially constructed. To focus on this second sense, begin with the following simple observation. Typically, when some observer evaluates an actor's performance, the evaluation is made by reference to the average level at which others in the relevant class of comparators are taken as a matter of common belief to perform. We might call this the perceived average level of compliance, emphasising the role of common belief, but we can often omit the word 'perceived', because in the cases we examine initially—and indeed in most of the cases we consider—we assume that perception is correct. The point to notice now is that standards are a function, not just of ideals, but also of perceived average compliance.

Consider a simple example. The ideal of truth-telling specifies complete honesty as the practice required or recommended. But if 'to be honest as this world goes is to be as one picked out of ten thousand', as Hamlet claims, then someone who tells the truth most of the time will surely be esteemed for her relative honesty. The measuring rod for evaluation will be influenced, even where it is not totally determined, by the perceived practices of ordinary performers in the relevant class.

In the interest of clarity, then, it is useful to distinguish between:

- The ideal performance, I, which we take to be that performance that fits the relevant ideal as perfectly as practical.
- The perceived average performance, X, which is the perceived average of the performances of all the agents in the relevant class.
- The standard performance, S, which we define to be the reference point on the basis of which esteem or disesteem is given.

For the purposes of this chapter, standard, ideal, and expected performance are all taken to refer to a level of performance within the X-domain. As we shall see in Chapter 7, all could equally be interpreted in terms of the proportion of

---

[3] In the discussions that follow, we shall mostly take those underlying values or ideals as given. In fact, the processes by which these values and the standards of behaviour that depend upon them come to be socially accepted is not necessarily entirely independent of the forces of esteem. At one or two points in later discussion, the question of the effects of esteem on value formation will occupy our attention. But for the purposes of the discussion in this chapter at least, we shall simply take the underlying values as given, and more or less a matter of common knowledge.

the population that complies with the ideal, when the ideal has an on/off character. But for the time being, we take it that S and I refer to levels of performance; and expected performance is just the statistical mean of the levels of individual performances (denoted X_i, for individual i).

In this setting, the crucial claim we make is that the standard, as defined, is determined as some kind of weighted average of the ideal and the perceived average performance. That is, if α is some constant, $0 \leq \alpha < 1$,

$$S = \alpha I + (1 - \alpha)X \tag{6}$$

In short, we are taking it here that the esteem or disesteem that any individual receives is determined by how the agent's performance compares with the standard, S, so defined. If A's performance lies above the standard, A gets positive esteem; if it lies below the standard, A gets negative esteem. That is the stipulation that equation (1) above articulates: $E_i = \alpha[X_i - S]$. What equation (6) tells us is the role that prevailing practices play in determining that standard.

5   EQUILIBRIUM IN THE ECONOMY OF ESTEEM

We are now in a position to derive the full equilibrium in the economy of esteem. We shall do so initially in the simplest possible case; and then relax some of the simplifying assumptions in the next chapter, showing to what extent the simplifications affect the central claims. The main simplification at stake immediately is that we shall assume that the standard as defined in the foregoing section is just average performance: ideal performance is taken to play no role in esteem. Equivalently, the α of equation (6) takes a value of zero. This assumption is made for purposes, as we say, of simplification. But it is not, we think, totally implausible in all cases. In the tax-compliance case, for example, although paying one's full tax, without any attempt at tax-minimisation, might be a notional ideal, it could be that positive esteem is applied to anyone who pays more than the average for a person with similar income and opportunities for evasion. However, we set plausibility issues aside to focus on the derivation of equilibrium in this simple case.

In section 3, we derived the reaction curve for a typical individual, showing how that individual's performance responded to alternative possible levels of the standard, S. All individuals will exhibit the same sort of response—and indeed, we can take our representative individual A as being precisely the average individual. So, A's performance at any level of S is just the average

performance. Reconsider now the reaction curve diagram, which we repro-
duce as BC in Figure 5.4. We need to add a further line showing the relation
between standards and perceived average performance expressed in equation
(6) above. This relation is depicted by the line OS′ in Figure 5.4; and given the
simplification already mentioned, where $\alpha = 0$, that line is the 45° ray from
the origin; for any level of average performance, measured on the x-axis, this
gives the same level for S, measured on the y-axis.

The line OS′ shows how the prevailing standard adjusts to changes in
average performance. The line BC shows how the average performer adjusts
her performance level to changes in standards. The point Q at which these
two lines intersect represents the equilibrium in this esteem economy. That

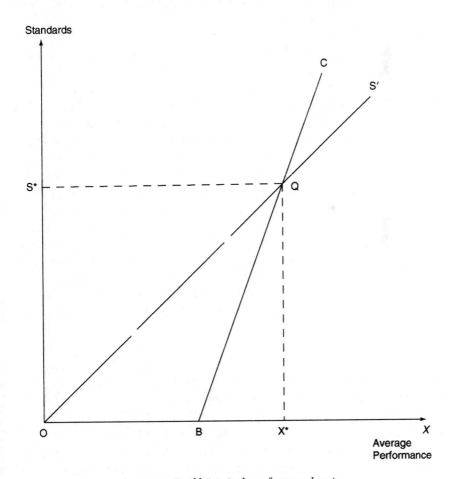

Figure 5.4. *Equilibrium in the performance domain.*

equilibrium is characterised by the pair $(X^*; S^*)$. When average performance is X^*, the prevailing standard, as derived from equation (6), will be S^*. Equally, when the prevailing standard is at S^*, the average performance induced by the esteem incentive will be X^*. In that sense, X^* and S^* are mutually compatible: Q does indeed represent the (unique) equilibrium in this esteem economy.

A multiplier effect

In exploring the nature of this equilibrium, it is useful to appeal to a little comparative static analysis. So consider what happens when an equilibrium of the kind exemplified in Figure 5.4 is subjected to some exogenous shock. Suppose X is tennis performance, and that a new tennis player comes to town. The new player turns out to be pretty good—certainly rather better than the town average. In all other respects, though, this new arrival is much like the original inhabitants—and in particular in respect of his desire for esteem. The first effect that the newcomer will have is that he will increase standards a bit. Players who were previously playing at the prevailing standard are now somewhat below. Now they are disesteemed: the quality of their playing is mildly shameful. Equally, those who hitherto enjoyed positive esteem will find that they enjoy rather less esteem. This loss of esteem among the original inhabitants will induce them to practice a little longer, and take a few extra lessons, and read a few more books of the 'How to Win at Tennis' genre. Their playing will improve as each tries to regain some of the esteem he has lost. But this will serve to raise standards for everyone—including for the new arrival himself. So everyone, including that new arrival, will need to improve performance slightly if they are all not to lose (further) esteem. And so on. Eventually a new equilibrium will be reached, with everyone—including the new arrival—playing rather better, but with much the same distribution of esteem and disesteem as prevailed immediately after the advent of the new arrival.

The diagrammatics can help illustrate the claim. Consider Figure 5.5. The effect of the new arrival is to shift the reaction curve outwards from BC to B'C'. Average performance will be just that much better than before simply because an above-average performer has been added to the sample. Accordingly, the equilibrium performance level will shift from that at Q (with average performance X^* and standard S^*) to that at Q' (with average at $X^{*\prime}$ and standard at $S^{*\prime}$). The new equilibrium will be achieved via successive rounds of the interaction between the average individual's performance and the prevailing standards. Now, it seems most plausible to assume that standards adjust more slowly than

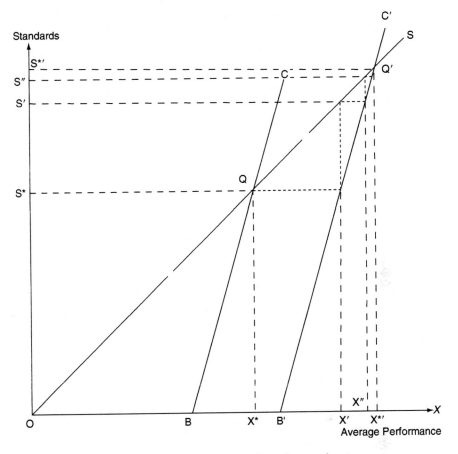

Figure 5.5. *Comparative statics in the performance domain.*

does average performance. On this basis, the first round effect is just that average performance increases to X'. But now standards will shift from level S* to S'; and this increase in standards will induce a shift in performance to X", which will in turn raise standards to S" and hence lead to a yet higher performance level; and so on. Eventually, the new equilibrium will be reached at Q'. The saw-toothed line from Q to Q' illustrated in Figure 5.5 shows the path that the community of performers will follow to the new equilibrium.

Notice that the final change in equilibrium performance is greater than the initial change attributable to the new arrival as such. In the terms of Figure 5.5, X*X*' exceeds BB'. There is involved here a kind of multiplier effect, whereby the initial exogenous change is multiplied in achieving the new equilibrium.[4] This multiplier effect reflects the positive influence of changing standards on performance and of changing performance on standards. As we indicated in our tennis story, it is not just that existing players are induced to improve their game in the equilibrating process: the new entrant who caused the initial increase in the prevailing standard is himself caught up in the process. He too will have reason to up his game before all the effects of the process are finally worked through.

This multiplier effect is worth underlining because it reflects a certain tidal character in the esteem economy. When performance by one or another individual increases exogenously, all the performers in the community will lift their games, securing in the process a new equilibrium. And this fact means that the final equilibrium changes in performance will be larger than the initiating changes.

Of course, we could conceive the comparative static experiment in terms of a reduction in the performance of some subset of the population. The new entrant could be a worse performer than the original average. In this case, the initial fall in the performance of some agents will create a correspondingly larger reduction in performance by all. The tide that rises may also fall.

To the analyst, it is clear that, in a global sense, all esteem-seekers are in competition with all others. But there need be no consciousness of this fact among esteem-seekers themselves. To them, it will seem as if the standards are fixed exogenously—much like prices in a competitive market. The effect of any one actor on standards will, in the typical large number case, be negligible. Accordingly, while the process of esteem-getting is competitive in aggregate, there need be no explicit rivalry. There is, in particular, no directly positional aspect to esteem in this model. People do not get esteem by being best in X-performance; and in fact, in the model as stipulated, one's place in the ranking of performances is strictly irrelevant to the esteem one accrues. Esteem is given solely on the basis of absolute performance—more X-performance means more esteem, more or less independently of what any other individual may do. But what all individuals in the aggregate do is relevant to the determination of the standards that apply. There is a feedback loop between average performance and standards.

As noted in Chapter 1, esteem might in particular cases be awarded on a positional basis—awarded, that is, according to where in the ranking of performances one comes. But this is a contingent, not a necessary, feature of esteem. And it is not a feature that we think is necessarily all that common.

---

[4] The multiplier effect in play here is analytically identical to that familiar from Keynesian macro-economics, whereby an initial increase in consumption expenditure is transformed into a final increase in equilibrium income/consumption that is larger than that initial increase.

Certainly, the feedback loops between average performance and standards that are the focus of this chapter are independent of whether esteem is given on the basis of ranking or of absolute performance level.

6 AGGREGATE ESTEEM IN EQUILIBRIUM

There are two related features of the equilibrium we have isolated that merit special attention. One relates to the implications for the total amount of esteem on offer. The other concerns the normative status of the equilibrium. We deal with these aspects in turn in this and the next section.

In the simplified model we have used, where standards are determined exclusively by average performance, there is no esteem enjoyed in aggregate. The average performer receives no esteem at all, and the pursuit of esteem is a strictly zero sum game: an increase in esteem for one person always involves a reduction in esteem for someone else. Consider the simplest case where everyone is identical. Each will have a positive marginal esteem incentive and will rationally improve X-performance in order to achieve esteem. But no one will actually be successful in achieving higher esteem. The final equilibrium will be one in which everyone is performing identically at a higher level by virtue of their demand for esteem—but there is no giving and no getting of esteem. An external observer won't observe any esteem or disesteem applied to any individual: but this does not mean that esteem has no influence. On the contrary, the desire for esteem has indeed improved X-performance. Moreover, esteem and disesteem will lie in the shadows and will be evoked as and when any one agent distinguishes herself, whether negatively or positively, from all the rest. In particular, one individual might recognise that all her efforts in the pursuit of esteem have been to no avail—that she might as well have saved herself the trouble. But if in the esteem equilibrium she were to reduce her X-performance, she would immediately suffer disesteem. She can only save herself the trouble of extra effort in the X-domain if she can organise everyone else to do likewise. And of course, there is no reason why she should even be aware that universal collective action of this kind would have the desired effect. All she knows is that she has laboured hard to get esteem, and that standards have risen in such a way that she hasn't been successful.

The case in which everyone is identical is of course a limiting case. More typically, there will be a distribution of performances, and so there will be esteem on offer to the high performers and disesteem for the lower performers in that distribution. Nevertheless, the total amount of esteem is fixed at zero;

and any one person's gain in esteem is always at the expense of the esteem accruing to some other person or persons.

In the shift from one equilibrium to a higher-performance one, there could be net positive esteem enjoyed as the equilibrating process works its way through to a new equilibrium. If, as seems plausible, standards respond more slowly than do changes in average performance, then average performance can lie above the standard for some time, until standards adjust. Obversely, in the shift from one equilibrium to a lower performance one, there will be increased disesteem. At best, then, aggregate esteem for the relevant constituency can be positive only in transition to a higher equilibrium; and these transitional effects will be correspondingly negative in any shift to a lower equilibrium.

This zero-esteem property is perhaps depressing, and may be puzzling. It is puzzling because we do not seem to have the analytic resources to speak of one community being a high-esteem community and another a low-esteem community, except where those communities are subsets of some larger community. There simply does not seem to be anything the community as a whole might do to increase esteem overall. Accordingly, it is worthwhile emphasising the features of the model on which that conclusion seems to depend, if only to see whether the model might be modified to generate a more congenial conclusion.

Four considerations occur to us as worth mentioning in this connection. The first involves a distinction between discretionary and non-discretionary performances. Consider the discretionary case—the case where individuals can opt out of X-performance if they choose to. Lots of activities that attract esteem/disesteem are like this. People can simply refrain from playing tennis or singing in public or going disco dancing. In such cases, suppose that standards are driven, not by the average performance of actual performers, but the (imagined) average of everyone whether they are engaged in X-performance or not. Then it is clear enough that aggregate esteem can be positive, both for any activity and for any individual. Most people who play tennis, or join the choral society, are people who believe that their tennis playing or singing is somewhat above average. They are probably right. So, most of those actually observed will obtain esteem. And of course people will have an esteem-based incentive to engage in those activities where their performance is best. This maximises their esteem overall. And when everyone does this, total esteem aggregated across all activities and all persons can easily be positive. It is a trivial observation that people are attracted to those activities in which they have some talent. It is worth emphasising that this fact is a puzzle in any account of behaviour that leaves esteem out of account. There is no obvious reason why people would happen to have a preference for some activity that they are tolerably good at, if preferences were just an unmediated matter of tastes. People tend to like the activities for which they have some talent because they do not like to make fools of themselves! Or, equivalently put, because those activities are ones in which they can expect to earn (positive) esteem.

Of course, not all performances are discretionary in this way. Many of the estimable dispositions that we have mentioned in our examples are such that people cannot avoid being judged in respect of them—traits of honesty or benevolence or courage. And some activities in some contexts are non-discretionary in a parallel way. In a system in which education is compulsory, for example, one cannot just opt out of revealing one's scholastic abilities. In these cases, the logic of the model as presented holds good: the total amount of esteem derived from such activities across all individuals is likely to be zero. So, whether an activity is discretionary or non-discretionary is important in determining the amount of esteem available in the aggregate.

The second consideration to be borne in mind is our assumption that the relation between performance and esteem, as depicted in equation (1), is linear. This assumption certainly simplifies the analysis, but we have not provided any substantive defence of it and in fact we think it somewhat implausible. That assumption is one we shall modify in the next chapter in what seems to us to be a plausible way. Intuitively, it is likely that in the absence of linearity, the precise distribution of individual performances will influence aggregate esteem—and that indeed turns out to be the case under our reformulation.

The third point involves our simplifying assumption that standards are determined exclusively by average performance. That is clearly an assumption that we shall want to relax; and we shall do that in the next chapter. However, as we shall show, doing so actually makes the picture rather bleaker and in that sense still more implausible. For when ideal performance figures in the determination of standards, aggregate esteem seems most likely to be, not zero, but negative.

The final relevant point involves emphasising that we are here treating audience size and quality as exogenously fixed. If the individual can adjust audience size and quality in order to maximise the esteem she enjoys, then aggregate esteem might be positive even for activities that are themselves non-discretionary. Again this is a matter to be taken up later, and in Chapters 9 and 10 specifically.

7 THE NORMATIVE STATUS OF EQUILIBRIUM

Is the equilibrium at Q Pareto optimal? On the face of things, and in the light of the foregoing discussion, apparently not. The point is clearest in the case of identical actors when standards are a matter exclusively of average perform-ance. In that special case, each performs at the average level. As we noted earlier, no one enjoys any esteem or suffers any disesteem in equilibrium at all. Nevertheless, all performers are performing at a higher level than they would if there were no esteem or disesteem in play. But this just means that they have all increased their X-performance for nothing. They would all be better off if they all chose a level of X-performance that abstracted entirely from any esteem effects.[5] Put another way, there exists an *n*-person exchange in which each performer agrees to moderate his X-performance in return for all others doing the same: that *n*-person exchange would leave all performers better off. Of course, any such arrangement is vulnerable to individual defection: if all agreed to reduce performance in order to establish a lower standard, any one of them could secure esteem, at the expense of others who abide by the terms of that agreement, by increasing his X-performance unilaterally. The outcome at Q is the outcome of an entirely familiar, *n*-person prisoners' dilemma; the equilib-rium represents the aggregate effect of each individual responding atomistically to the incentives she faces. In this sense, the model of esteem presented here is analytically akin to a model of road congestion or environmental pollution. The action of each individual produces an outcome that is worse for all of them than some other outcome that could in principle be achieved.

But though akin to the road congestion case, the esteem case is not the same. There is an extra normative complication in the esteem case that is crucial. Recall that esteem accrues to actors by virtue of observers having particular evaluative attitudes to X-performance. Those evaluative attitudes cannot properly be ignored in normative assessment of the outcomes of the esteem process. This general claim is one that we shall take up again in Part III but it may be useful to comment on it here.

The evaluative attitudes signal the presence of some kind of externality generated by X-performance—an externality that underlies the positive evalu-ation of X that is abroad in the community. Why is it, we might ask, that X is widely regarded as a good thing—an activity properly worthy of esteem? Note the direction of this question. We are not asking why performers want to perform X. We have taken it that that is a matter of the esteem that attaches

---

[5] In the case of identical actors, where the demand for X is driven exclusively by the desire for esteem and standards are driven exclusively by prevailing practice, the best outcome for the actors taken together is obviously when X is zero. Once actors recognise that the quest for esteem in the world of identical individuals is a hopeless quest, they will see that zero X is the best outcome. Note that the same general result holds even without identical individuals. All can secure the amount of esteem they enjoy (or disesteem they suffer) with less effort in X-performance and/or more of other valued activities if they can secure a coordinated equal reduction in everyone's performance.

to X-performance. Rather, we are asking why it is that observers place a positive evaluation on X-performance. For it is to be emphasised that the esteem supplied to those whose X-performance is good and the disesteem supplied to those whose performance is bad depends critically on observers valuing X-performance.[6] The presumption here is that X is a source of positive general benefits to observers, whether such benefits are to be understood as purely psychic or as grounded in something more real. If that presumption is accepted, then such general benefits ought to be included when the true Pareto optimum is calculated. So, for example, if volunteering for military service provides general benefits to the community to whose defence the volunteer contributes, the presumption is that that general benefit explains why volunteering is a source of esteem, and failing to volunteer a source of disesteem.

On this reading, the gains from exchange that seem to be on hand when performers get together to manipulate the prevailing standards are rather like the gains that are enjoyed by members of a monopoly cartel. The benefits the parties to the cartel enjoy are bought at the expense of the consuming public at large. Equivalently, in the esteem case, the benefit that seems to be on hand among the performers as performers, is also a cost to those same individuals in their role as observers. To make this claim is not to establish that Q is, after all, Pareto optimal: Q might involve too high a level of X-performance, even when the externality is taken into account (see Heckathorn 1989). But equally, Q might involve too low a level of X-performance, notwithstanding the fact that the forces of esteem internalise the externality to a considerable extent.

Our point here is not to establish any *a priori* presumption in favour of the optimality of the esteem equilibrium, but rather to rebut what might seem like the opposite implication. On the basis of the analysis in this chapter, one might be disposed to conclude that any esteem equilibrium is presumptively inefficient, and that all would be better off if the desire for esteem were less intense. No such conclusion follows. On the contrary, there is some presumption that the esteem incentive will work towards the internalisation of externalities that are reflected in the values on which esteem depends.

Whether ultimately the construal of observer values as a form of externality exhausts the normative content of those values is a question that we shall leave open at this point. Our basic claim is just that no proper normative evaluation of outcomes within the economy of esteem can leave out of account the

---

[6] Tyler Cowen (2002) claims that in a roughly analogous case the degree of norm adherence is inevitably suboptimal. His argument seems to suppose that the 'externality' associated with 'public goods provision' and the externality associated with the esteem relation between performer and observer are independent and that the latter could be internalised by an entirely separate set of exchanges. We think that that discussion fails to take sufficiently seriously the severe limits on the direct exchange of esteem that we discuss in Part I.

prevailing values on which esteem itself depends. However, there is some force to the observation that the quest for esteem is in aggregate counterproductive for those who seek it. For in any case where esteem is based on observer values that turn out to be of no normative significance, the quest for esteem should not be allowed to proceed unchecked (see e.g. Congleton 1989).

CONCLUSION

The object of this chapter has been to take some first steps in exploring performance effects in the economy of esteem. By performance effects, we mean the effects of the desire for esteem on the level of estimable activities and estimable dispositions. We examined these effects in a large-number setting, focusing on the interdependencies between individual performances, the creation of relevant standards, and the amount of esteem or disesteem on offer at different performance levels. Esteem incentives operate in a context where there are feedback effects between individual action and the social context within which such action is pursued. The performance level of each individual contributes to the standards by which each performer is assessed. Accordingly, there are, as we might put it, unintended consequences in play in the economy of esteem. To appeal to the terminology of Schelling's (1978) book, micro-motives create macro-behaviour patterns that are not simply a direct magnification of the individual case. Throughout this chapter, we stuck to the case in which performance is continuously variable. There can be more or less courage or benevolence or cleverness or artistic accomplishment and higher performance in such cases was taken to generate higher esteem (or less disesteem) continuously throughout the entire range.

We considered the simplest case in which the relation between performance and esteem is linear. In that setting, we developed first, in Section 2, a simple model of the individual's esteem-based incentives. Then in Section 3, we derived the relation between individual performance and the prevailing level of standards by which esteem is assigned. Section 4 examined the question of the relation between prevailing standards and actual practice. Our claim there was that standards are dependent both on ideal performance, some absolute reference point like telling the truth in the honesty case, or paying one's full tax liability in the case of taxpaying, and on prevailing practices in the relevant domain. The weight that each element contributes may vary; but it is the prevailing practice aspect that creates the feedback loop between performance and standards. It is that feedback aspect that forms the basis of the equilibrium analysis.

In Section 5, we derived the performance equilibrium and conducted some simple comparative static exercises. Several features of that equilibrium were the subject of special attention. One feature was the tidal effect of esteem; when performance improves it tends to improve together across the whole set of performers. When performance deteriorates, it induces a general deterioration across the whole community. The magnitude of this tidal sweep is captured by a multiplier which indicates for any initiating change in performance the (larger) final change in performance that will emerge in equilibrium.

In Section 6, we directed attention to the implications of the model for aggregate esteem across the whole community. An implication of the model, as applied to non-discretionary activities, is that aggregate esteem in such cases is fixed; and, in what turns out to be the best case where standards depend exclusively on average performance, aggregate esteem is zero. This aspect of the model's implications is rather bleak, since it implies that there is nothing a community might do to increase its overall esteem levels, and also somewhat implausible. There certainly do seem to be societies where on balance most people enjoy positive esteem, without this being at the expense of a few significantly disesteemed souls. And this prevails with respect to non-discretionary as well as discretionary domains of activity. The question therefore arises as to what modifications of the basic model might be required to avoid the zero sum result. We shall explore some of these modifications in subsequent chapters.

Section 7 examined the normative implications of the basic model. We pursued this aspect briefly here, because it is a matter to be pursued again in Part III of the book. We drew attention to two aspects of the model:

- First, the relation between performers is such that there exists a possible trade among them that would leave them all better off.
- And second, because that trade occurs exclusively within the set of performers and excludes specifically the values of observers on which esteem itself is based, nothing of ultimate normative significance can be adduced from the existence of that potential trade.

The more general conclusion is that in any proper normative assessment within the economy of esteem, there are two elements that must be weighed. One is the value that observers place on the object of esteem in question. The other element is the alternative valued activities that performers forgo in their pursuit of esteem in all cases where that pursuit is collectively futile.

6

A More Complex Equilibrium in Performance

In the previous chapter, we derived an equilibrium in performance for the economy of esteem, in which the feedback effects that connect performance levels and standards were a critical feature. Our more general object was to demonstrate that the economy of esteem exhibits a property that characterises most interesting models of social interaction—namely, that individuals both react to and create the social context in which they operate. We developed our argument by appeal to the simplest possible model, in which esteem was taken to be linearly related to performance, and standards were taken to be determined exclusively by average performance.

In this chapter, we want to generalise that simple model in two ways. First, we want to allow explicitly for a role of the ideal level of performance in determining standards. That is, we want to illustrate the equilibrium in the case where the parameter α in equation (6) lies between zero and one. Our purpose in doing this is just to verify that the central features of the model are unaffected by the earlier, zero α case. This task will occupy us in Section 1.

The second generalisation is more significant. We want to consider the implications of treating standard performance not as a point but as a range. This task will occupy us in Sections 2, 3, and 4. In Section 2, we lay out the modified model. In Section 3, we examine the implications for the likely distribution of performances and for aggregate esteem. And in Section 4, we examine the effects of these modifications for risk-taking and risk-loving behaviour over various ranges of performance, and try to indicate why and under what circumstances such effects might be significant.

1 STANDARDS AND IDEALS

The points we seek to make in relation to the role of ideal performance in determining the standard by which esteem is given can be made most easily by reference to the diagrammatics introduced in the previous chapter. In our earlier derivation of the performance equilibrium, we focused on the zero α case. In this case, the locus of possible equilibrium standards in Figure 5.5 is given by the 45° ray from the origin. It is a simple matter to replace that line by its analogue when α in equation (6) takes some positive value—say, $\frac{1}{2}$. In such a case, standards for the assignment of esteem will be the simple mean of ideal and average-prevailing performance levels. The relevant locus of possible equilibrium standards is then given in Figure 6.1 by the line $S'S$. Equilibrium in the performance domain will be at Q^* in Figure 6.1. At Q^*, the level of average performance, X^*, is exactly that required to sustain S^* as the standard; and with S^* as standard, X^* will be the average level of performance forthcoming.

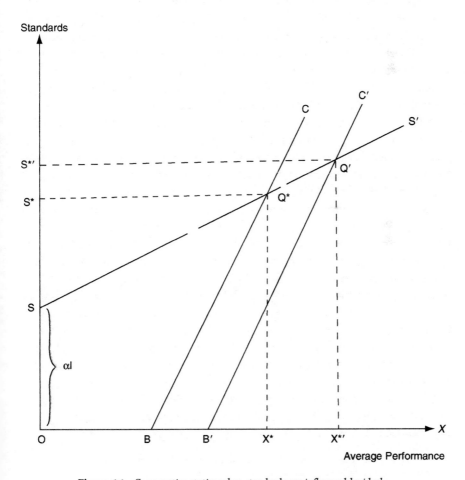

Figure 6.1. *Comparative statics when standards are influenced by ideals.*

We could now conduct a comparative static experiment like that which we undertook in Chapter 5. That is, we can suppose that the reaction curve BC shifts outwards to B'C' and examine the properties of the new equilibrium Q'. It is clear that the same general multiplier effect is present: the final equilibrium change in performance, given by $X^{*'}X^*$, is greater than the initiating change in performance, given by B'B. The equilibrium in that sense exhibits the same tidal character as in the earlier version. The multiplier is not however as large as in the case examined in the previous chapter—and clearly would disappear entirely if standards were determined by ideals alone.[1]

Allowing for a non-zero value of α serves to admit a wider range of possible comparative static experiments. We could examine the effect, for given α, of changes in the prevailing ideal, holding α constant. A change to a more demanding ideal would involve an upwards parallel shift in S'S, and create a final equilibrium combination involving a higher standard and higher performance. There would also be a multiplier effect in the shift to this new equilibrium. That is, the ultimate equilibrium standard would exceed the initial standard by more than the initial change in the ideal, reflecting the higher average performance that the higher ideal would induce.

It is worth noting that comparative static exercises might be pursued in relation to exogenous changes in all the parameters of the model. As we have just seen, ideals may shift—due to a collective effort at preaching perhaps, or the widespread promulgation of a new and more demanding code of ethics. Or the relative role of prevailing practice and ideals (the value of α) may alter, due perhaps to information about prevailing practice becoming more salient.[2] Or average performance may change, due to the introduction of new performers or exogenous improvements in the performance of existing players. What seems true in general in all these conceptual experiments is that the final equilibrium change will exceed the initiating one: the tidal character of equilibrium in the performance domain will be preserved. The reason for this tidal character lies in the positive relation between standards and performance— both at the level of individual behavioural response, and at the level of the determination of the prevailing standard on the basis of which esteem is assigned. In short, the basic conclusions of our earlier, somewhat simplified, model seem to be quite robust.

One specific aspect of the model that we explored in the previous chapter was its implications for the aggregate level of esteem available. We showed that for non-discretionary activities—those such that opting out of the activity is

---

[1] In that case, the locus of possible equilibrium standards would be a horizontal straight line. The feedback loop between average performance and standards would disappear.

[2] We shall explore that possibility in a rather different aspect in Chapter 8.

either infeasible or disestimable—the total amount of esteem available was zero, given that standards were determined by average performance alone. In the case where ideals as well as average performance influence standards, what is the situation for aggregate esteem? It is in the nature of ideals that they typically lie above average performance: they tend to be levels of aspiration, at least for most ordinary mortals. And if this is so, the aggregate level of esteem will be negative. And aggregate esteem will be more negative the greater the weight that ideal performance has in setting standards. The bleak conclusion, discussed in the previous chapter (Section 6) in the context of the simpler model, remains, and is indeed yet bleaker.

Finessing that bleak conclusion is part of the motivation for our further modifications of the simple model—modifications that we lay out in the ensuing sections. But bleak conclusions are not to be ruled out on account of their bleakness—only on account of their implausibility. And increased plausibility is the chief ground for the modifications we explore in the remainder of this chapter.

2   STANDARD PERFORMANCE AS A RANGE

In the simple version of performance equilibrium laid out in the previous chapter, we made the assumption that the relation between esteem and performance was linear. That assumption is captured in equation (1) and has the effect that as performance increases we move seamlessly through the range where disesteem applies to a range where positive esteem applies. This fact gives the standard a kind of knife-edge quality that we consider implausible. We want to explain why we think that quality implausible, and how the assumption might plausibly be modified.

Take some estimable activity or disposition like courage or benevolence. When we think of the people exhibiting possible performances in those domains, we might think of them as being either courageous or not courageous—either benevolent or not benevolent, and so on. There seems to be no necessary implication that someone who isn't courageous is therefore timorous, or that someone who isn't benevolent is necessarily mean. They might be. But they might also just not register as being especially one thing or the other: not benevolent, but not malevolent either—just normal over the dimension of performance in which benevolence and malevolence represent the extremities. It seems quite natural to think that, in lots of cases where performance is continuous, the way in which performance will map into esteem will not be continuous. The notably good will receive esteem, and will receive more esteem the better they are. The notably bad will be disesteemed and will receive more disesteem the worse they are. But lots of performers will be neither notably good nor notably bad—just... well, standard. In such cases, standard performance becomes a range—a range specifically in which neither positive esteem nor disesteem apply. To the extent that we need a specific point along the spectrum of possible performances to isolate as the standard, we shall just select the mid-point of this normal range.

A good way in which we might think about the standard-range assumption is to appeal to general uncertainty as to where the knife-edge standard falls. In the previous chapter, and generally throughout Section 1, we took it that the prevailing standards were common knowledge across the community of performers. In fact, as we have argued, this common knowledge assumption has two elements—either of which might strain reality in particular cases. Performers have to know what the prevailing values or ideals are. That is, they have to know the relevant domains in which esteem might be obtained and disesteem suffered. And they also have to know what the average performance is.

The first of these assumptions seems plausible in most cases. Though we can easily imagine examples where the extent and/or intensity of support for a particular ideal will be a matter of some speculation—cases, say, in which values are contested—the situation in the majority of cases will be clear enough. Professional probity and competence is positively valued; professional laxity and incompetence are to be deplored. And so on.

The second aspect, however, seems quite demanding. Even in cases where there is no doubt as to what kind of performance is ideal, there will often be considerable uncertainty as to what prevailing practice actually is—or, more specifically, where average performance lies. And when I am uncertain as to where exactly the prevailing practice lies, it is difficult to see how I could have much confidence in my judgement about whether I will be esteemed or disesteemed for a given performance—unless my performance is a clear outlier. The same applies if I believe that others are unlikely to know what average performance is, even if I have considerable knowledge myself. How can I rule out the possibility that some observer might find my performance disestimable even when I know it to be entirely standard? It may even be that a performance that is somewhat below what I take to be the standard, will be applauded by some observers. Different observers will have predictably different perceptions of the relevant standard. Moreover, observers themselves will have less confidence that esteem is merited except when the performance is clearly estimable. Expressing approval when other observers consider it inappropriate may itself be a cause of disesteem—a sign of lax standards, for example. If having appropriate values is itself an object of esteem, then the forces of esteem might well moderate any expression of our evaluations in all cases where prevailing standards are unclear.

In the neighbourhood of the standard performance S, observers will be individually less confident and even if esteem or disesteem is forthcoming performers can reasonably expect the positive and negative effects roughly to cancel out. As performance moves away from S, the verdict will become more unidirectional. Those agents whose performances lie below S will find that they are more often disesteemed than esteemed. And the reverse will apply for those whose performance is above S. But provided the performance does not stray too far from the standard, the effect will be small and within a range of standard performance negligible. It is only as performance moves into a range that is manifestly sub-standard by any lights, as we might put it, that disesteem becomes systematically mobilised in substantial degree. Equally, only as performance moves into the range of outstanding performance by any standards, will positive esteem become a systematically potent force. In short, plausible assumptions about what observers and performers can reasonably know provide support for a three-range model, in which we admit specifically a category of being neither estimable nor disestimable.

The central analytic point, as it relates to our current concerns, can be captured neatly in a simple diagram. Throughout Chapter 5, we assumed the relation between esteem and performance to be like that indicated in Figure 6.2a by the line E'E. In fact, we think that a more likely representation is that depicted by the line FNMF'. The range NM is taken to lie symmetrically about the point standard, S, by an amount k. Only performances outside the k-neighbourhood of the point standard, S, are esteem-affected: outside that neighbourhood, disesteem and esteem incentives become operative in more or less the linear way we earlier assumed.

This three-range formulation clearly has implications for the way in which esteem incentives operate at the individual level. Note that marginal net esteem—the extra esteem to be achieved or the extra disesteem to be avoided by increasing one's performance at the margin *ceteris paribus*—is a piecewise constant function of the kind shown by UV and WZ in Figure 6.2b. Recall that this function shows the esteem gained or disesteem avoided by a marginal increase in X-performance. It does not show the utility of that marginal esteem to the actor. To show that utility, we would need to include the individual's demand for esteem. A typical such demand curve would be expected to exhibit the familiar downward-sloping shape, so the marginal esteem utility of X can be represented in Figure 6.2b by the piecewise segments DD' and D"D. The conspicuous feature of 6.2b is the discontinuity over the range NM in the marginal esteem (utility) schedule. This discontinuity reflects the simple fact

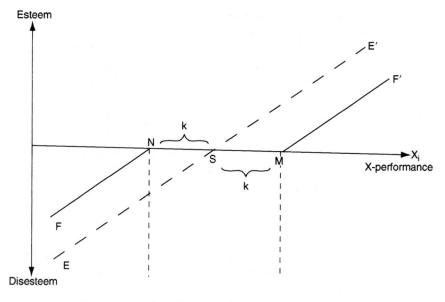

Figure 6.2a. *Relation between performance level and total esteem.*

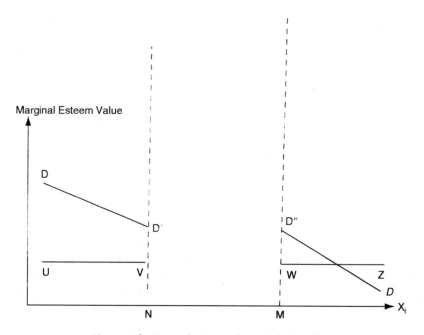

Figure 6.2b. *Marginal esteem and marginal value of esteem.*

that no esteem or disesteem accrues over the NM range. Esteem considerations simply do not bear on decisions about X-performance over that range. In what follows, we seek to spell out some of the implications of this discontinuity.[3]

3   EQUILIBRIUM IN THE THREE-RANGE MODEL

What are the effects of adding this third range of normal performance? There are four kinds of effects we want to isolate. One is the effect on the likely distribution of performances. A second is the effect on aggregate esteem. A third is the effect on the significance of esteem-related incentives generally. These three effects will occupy us in the present section.

The fourth effect of interest arises in cases where there is uncertainty about whether an action that might garner esteem will prove successful. In the presence of such uncertainty, the discontinuity in the esteem incentive, characteristic of the three-range model, generates different responses, according to where in the distribution of performances an individual happens to lie. Positively esteemed performers will tend to be risk-lovers and disesteemed performers will tend to be risk averse. But we postpone consideration of these risk-related consequences and their possible significance to the next section.

The distribution of performances

In order to isolate the effects of the third range on the distribution of performances, we proceed in three steps. First, we posit a distribution of X-performance in the absence of esteem effects. We then compare this initial distribution with the one that prevails when all esteem-related effects have been incorporated, under the conditions where there are only two relevant ranges— the case assumed in the previous chapter. We then do a similar exercise of adding esteem effects under the assumption that there are three relevant ranges. By comparing the second and the third distributions we are able to indicate the implications of the three-range case for the likely distribution of performances. Note that this exercise is a purely conceptual one. There is no

---

[3] We should acknowledge that economists have a general distaste for discontinuities. But the points to be made in what follows would also apply if the discontinuities were smoothed out and the piecewise linear version of the marginal esteem schedule were to be replaced by a continuous function with the same general shape. In the current context, it seems conceptually clearer to make the points about the esteem function by reference to the three categories of performance. We let the analysis stand on that basis.

actual distribution of X-performance in the absence of esteem effects that could ever be observed. However, this conceptual exercise suggests certain empirical implications—ones that could in principle be tested and that can certainly be confronted by our intuitions.

In order to elucidate this series of comparisons, it is helpful to consider Figures 6.3*a* and 6.3*b*. Suppose that the distribution of X-performance in the absence of esteem effects would be uniform across a given range—from J to H in Figure 6.3*a*. The uniform distribution is taken here for illustrative purposes only: nothing of significance hinges on that choice. The first question we pose is how that distribution would shift in response to the esteem incentive in the two-range case examined in the previous chapter. Answering this question is effectively a matter of summarising the conclusions from the preceding chapter, with one modest wrinkle.

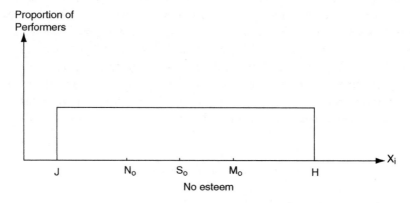

Figure 6.3a. *Distribution of performances without esteem effects.*

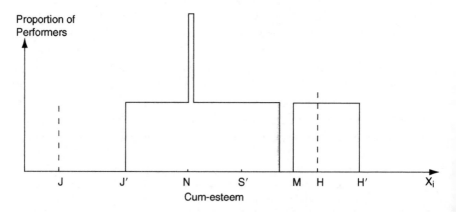

Figure 6.3b. *Distribution with esteem effects.*

We know from the previous chapter that:

- The esteem incentive will cause an increase in performance across the range. This is the direct effect of the esteem incentive.
- Further, we know that that increased performance will give rise to a higher standard on the basis of which esteem will be assigned. This is the standards effect.

Then the effect on the distribution of preferences when all esteem effects are included, given that there are two ranges of performance—the positive esteem range and the negative esteem range—is to shift that distribution to the right. There is a small complication, however. Because the marginal utility of esteem is diminishing, the effect on performance will be predictably smaller at the upper end than at the lower end of the distribution. Individuals at the lower end have less esteem and so are likely to value an additional unit of esteem more highly, *ceteris paribus*. Put another way, reducing disesteem is likely to be a more potent incentive than gaining a larger amount of positive esteem. That is just an implication of the downward-sloping demand-curve hypothesis, applied to esteem as a good. Accordingly, if the initial distribution of X-performance is JH in Figure 6.3a, then it would move to a uniform distribution of the form J'H' in Figure 6.3b, where JJ' exceeds HH'. This shift is taken to include both direct and standards effects.

Let us now allow for the no-esteem range in the neighbourhood of standard performance S: the area in 6.3b between N and M, where $N = S - k$, and $M = S + k$, as in 6.2a. Our claim is that the distribution in the presence of esteem effects will not be strictly uniform. It will exhibit two distinctive features:

1. a clustering of performance just above N—that is, at the lower end of normal performance $[N = S - k]$;
2. a hole in the distribution in the neighbourhood of M—that is, at the upper bound of normal performance $[M = S + k]$.

We discuss these features in turn. Consider the cluster effect first. For individuals whose performance would otherwise be just below N in Figure 6.3b, there is an incentive to increase performance so as not to endure the disesteem associated with performance that is sub-standard. But there is nothing to be achieved in esteem terms by pushing performance beyond N. At N, the marginal esteem incentive just disappears. Equally, individuals whose performance levels lie just above N have no incentive to alter their perform-ance, for there is no disesteem associated with a performance just above N, and no positive esteem either. Movements beyond N just shift one within the range of normal performance. Everyone close to N from below will shift to N, but those who would choose a performance level at N in the absence of esteem will stay put. Accordingly, we would expect a clustering effect in the distribution at or just above N.

Now, consider individuals whose performance in the absence of esteem would fall just below M. These individuals can, if they improve their performance a little, reap positive esteem benefits. It will therefore be rational for them to do so. If they were to leave performance unchanged their performance would simply be normal, with no more esteem than any others in the NM range. All those just below M will therefore leap to just above M, leaving a hole in the distribution at that point. But those individuals whose performance lies in the normal range, considerably below M, will not find the positive esteem they receive a large enough reward for the significant performance improvement required. They will just stay put. Accordingly, the with-esteem distribution will have the shape depicted by the distribution from J' to H' in Figure 6.3*b*. That is, there will be a characteristic cluster above N and a characteristic hole around M. Simply put, within the range of normal performance the distribution of performances will tend to be skewed towards the bottom end.

We should perhaps note that this skewedness within the standard performance range is a result of the general relation between performance and esteem, and not of the underlying distribution of performances. The same general shape within the normal range would be observed whether or not the initial distribution were uniform and whether or not the relation between performance and marginal esteem was strictly discontinuous. The particular formulation we have chosen serves merely to illustrate the more general point.

Esteem in the aggregate

In Section 6 of the previous chapter, we discussed the issue of whether aggregate esteem could be positive in equilibrium in the esteem economy. The logic of the model suggested not. Under what seemed the most plausible formulation, the average performer was likely to be subject to disesteem.

Note that this is not so once we introduce the three-range formulation. Depending on the precise distribution of performances, it is conceptually possible for everyone to lie entirely outside the disesteem range. Of course, not everyone can be positively esteemed in any non-discretionary domain: but some proportion can be, while the remainder fall into the normal performance range. By analogy, there could also be cases where there are many individuals whose performances lie in the normal range, and a smaller number whose performances lie well below it. In such cases, there would only be disesteem: no one would enjoy positive esteem at all. And of course, aggregate esteem would be negative. These extreme cases are all somewhat implausible. But they serve to illustrate the general point that, in the three-range setting, the precise distribution of performances is important for the aggregate amount of esteem enjoyed in the community. And depending on the properties of that distribution aggregate esteem might be positive or negative.

Esteem incentives

If an implication of the three-range model is that large numbers of people involved in any estimable activity may face no esteem incentive at all, does that not mean that esteem is diminished as a behavioural influence? The three-range model seems to imply that many, perhaps most, individuals do not receive esteem or disesteem in the performance domain, either *in toto* or, more to the point, at the margin. The esteem incentive applies only for the outliers in the performance stakes. And this seems to imply in turn that the feedback effects between average performance and esteem incentives, which were our central concern in the previous chapter, are quite small.

We do not think this conclusion follows. First, in the case of all discretionary activities, the demand for esteem will tend to drive individuals into those activities where they can earn positive esteem. In that quest, most individuals will derive positive esteem and that fact will influence performance and standards in the way indicated in the previous chapter.

But second, even in the case of non-discretionary activities, the logic of the argument does not support the disappearance of esteem incentives or the removal of feedback effects between standards and performance. Consider again Figure 6.3b. The endpoints, J′ and H′, of the equilibrium performance distribution are determined by individuals who do face esteem incentives at the margin—and exactly the same esteem incentives as they would face in the two-range case. And it is the response of those in the disesteem and positive esteem ranges who will determine the standard range, and thereby the midpoint of that range. To be sure, the distribution within that standard range will be predictably skewed towards the lower end, but by definition performance within that range does not register in the economy of esteem and so does not register for the determination of the standard.

Of course, there is the possibility that everyone might fall into the standard range, so that there would be no incentive in play at all. But we think even this possibility is unlikely. For we are inclined to think that the size of ranges as well as the normal performance itself is likely to be endogenous. That is, what is taken by observers to be an esteem-significant difference in performance is likely to be influenced by the differences in performance that are commonly observed. We have not formally modelled this feature, but we would not expect the k parameter in Figure 6.2a to be independent of prevailing practice, any more than is the prevailing standard. Specifically, if most performers are to be found clustered around the standard, then observers will tend to make more finely grained judgments. For any non-discretionary activity, we might reasonably expect that about a third of performers would fall in each of the specified ranges. The effects on standards driven by exogenous changes in performance or in ideals or in perceptions of prevailing practice might in certain cases be somewhat moderated; but the logic of the model suggests that most such changes will continue to have significant effects.

4   PERFORMANCE AND RISK-TAKING

One interesting aspect of the three-range model relates to its implications for decision-making under one kind of uncertainty—uncertainty concerning the relation between an individual's action and the esteem generated from that action. The actor's uncertainty here may reflect either the standards of evaluation that an audience will apply, or the actual performance that a given action will produce. In this section, we want to focus on the latter case. We will take up one aspect of uncertainty about standards in Chapter 9.

When I as a concert pianist am to perform for a new audience, I must decide both on the program and, let us say, on the tempos at which I will attempt to play the chosen pieces. In these matters, I can be more or less ambitious. If I choose a difficult program, I am likely to perform the pieces less well than if I choose an easy program. The inadequacies of my performance may be recognised more readily than the ambitiousness of the program. On the other hand, if I choose a program of popular or easy pieces, I may disappoint the audience—and perhaps even earn their contempt—by playing only trivia. Here I have to guess the sophistication of the audience, in addition to running risks over my capacity to deliver good performances of more demanding pieces. The same sort of dilemma arises in setting my tempos. Choices have to be made; and different choices embody different levels of risk. I can play safe, as we might put it, or I can take the risks.

Take a simple case in which I am contemplating an action, A, that has two possible outcomes. If A works well, it improves my X-performance by amount h. If A works badly it leads to a deterioration in X-performance by amount h.

The two possibilities are, we suppose, equally likely. I have to choose between action A and another action, C, which will leave my performance unchanged. In other words, I am offered a choice in which my X-performance is either Z, or a fifty-fifty chance of $(Z + h)$ or $(Z - h)$.

If the discussion in the preceding section is right, what I am likely to do depends in part on where Z lies in the domain of likely performance—or equivalently in the domain of expected esteem. To see this, consider Figure 6.4.

Suppose for example that Z lies at C_1 just above M in Figure 6.4. Then consider what happens if I take the gamble, and choose action A. If I am lucky, then my performance will be at $C_1 + h$, and I will receive esteem at E^+ in Figure 6.4. If I am unlucky, then my performance will be at $C_1 - h$. In this event, I simply fall into the standard range. I will receive neither esteem nor disesteem. So the expected esteem associated with the risky action A is E_1, i.e. $\frac{1}{2}(E^+ + 0)$. If I stay put, I receive a level of esteem equal to $E(C_1)$ in Figure 6.4. Clearly, E_1 exceeds $E(C_1)$: this gamble is a good bet. And this result generalises for any location of performance within an h-neighbourhood of M. That is, the risky action, A, will have a higher expected return than staying put whenever staying put yields a performance that is appropriately close to M.

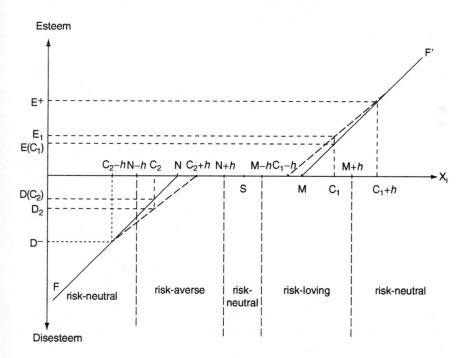

Figure 6.4. *Esteem and risk-in-performance.*

Now consider the obverse case where Z lies at C_2, just below N. At this level of performance I earn disesteem of $D(C_2)$. Suppose I undertake the risky action. In this case, if I am lucky, I simply move into the standard range: I derive no esteem or disesteem at all. Whereas if I am unlucky, and things work out badly, my performance will be at $C_2 - h$ and earn disesteem of D^-: my performance will be an object of derision. So the expected disesteem from the risky action is D_2. This is a bad bet, and I would be well-advised to choose the more conservative course. I should refrain from the gamble and just play safe even though I will earn mild disesteem from doing so.

Generalising a little, it should be clear that there are three ranges of performance where one will be risk-neutral. If Z lies near S then there is no advantage to be gained from the gamble. If I am lucky, then my performance improves—but not by enough to carry me out of the normal range. And equally, if I am unlucky then I lose no esteem because I do not fall into the disesteem range. I am indifferent between taking the gamble and not.

The same applies if Z lies above M by more than distance h. If I am lucky, I gain the same amount of esteem that I would lose if I were unlucky. There is no net expected gain in the gamble. The same reasoning applies if I am in the disesteem range below N by more than h. If I take the gamble, I stand to gain or lose in the esteem stakes by the same amount. So I will be indifferent between taking the gamble and staying put.

We can summarise this reasoning by appeal to Figure 6.4. Here, we show the esteem relation FNMF'; and for a given value of h, the various ranges over which the agent will have reason to be risk neutral, risk averse, and risk-loving in selection of action. Clearly, the larger is h the larger will be the regions on either side of M and N in which the agent will have reason to be risk-loving and risk averse respectively.

An example from academic life may help to make these points vivid. In the choice of research topics, there is an ineluctable element of risk. One may well devote much energy and time to a particular issue only to discover that there is nothing of interest to be said. There are what are widely regarded as hard problems in any discipline such that to solve them (or even throw new light on them) would be a notable accomplishment and highly estimable. There are also fairly safe problems such that to solve them would be quite useful but not particularly outstanding. In medical research, for example, there are what are held to be mainline avenues of enquiry, say in trying to discover causes or treatments of diseases, and also what are conceived as longshots—more specu-lative and perhaps unpromising lines that nevertheless may turn up something of major interest. Suppose then that we rank research universities into five classes, corresponding to the five divisions in Figure 6.4. As we understand things, mainline avenues of enquiry are pursued by the best research teams—those, as we may suppose, in the top of our five classes. In the next class of institutions, there are researchers who are known professionally as the maver-icks—those who pursue the high-risk long shots. Should any of these mavericks prove successful, they are then picked up by the first-rung universities and accorded the full range of academic honours that membership of the academic establishment affords.[4]

Taking this description at face value, the fact that high-risk research strat-egies are more to be found in second-tier than first-tier universities (the state of affairs as we understand it) is an interesting phenomenon that demands some explanation. Our conjecture is that the structure of esteem incentives has something to contribute here. We think that academics are, more than most, driven by a desire for esteem. And we think that academics in second-tier universities are, by the reasoning laid out here, more likely to be risk-loving in their choices of research topics than are academics in the first-tier places.

Such speculations may seem to be of interest only to academics. But there may be reasons why it might be desirable to encourage risk-taking in selection of research topics. It seems plausible that a system in which enquiry proceeds across a broad front may be superior to one in which all energy is directed at being the first to do what everyone else is trying to do. From the point of view of the system as a whole, it may be better to have scholars choose research agendas that are more speculative, and where the chances of each making a fool of herself (or simply wasting time, coming up empty-handed) are non-negligible. As far as the system as a whole is concerned, whether individual scholars make fools of themselves is of no account, providing that the overall expected return on the research enterprise is as high as possible. In other words, the system as a whole can pool risks that individual scholars may well find daunting. On this basis, there is a problem: individual scholars may choose research agendas that are on average too conservative. Or at least, most may do so. The mavericks would then be an exception. Accordingly, it may pay to spread research resources across the second-tier places where the maverick work is done. Or otherwise devise mechanisms to encourage more risk-loving research practices.

The foregoing example is an instance of a more general argument. Policy literature sometimes distinguishes between best-shot and weakest-link cases

---

[4] There is then a question as to their future conduct. If they are mavericks by disposition, they will continue to pursue high-risk research strategies as a reflection of their nature. But to the extent that, as we suppose here, they are mavericks by virtue of the incentives they face, the entry into the upper reaches of the performance range will tend to diminish their risk-loving propensities. Clearly, both dispositional and incentive explanations can exist side by side.

(see, for example, Hirshleifer 1983). In the former, the goal is to secure the highest performance across the set of performers. So, for example, in assessment of a country's performance in a particular sport, attention focuses on the best exponents—the fastest runners; the best football team; etc. It may be that the country with the highest medal count in the Olympic Games would not rate very highly on the basis of average performance across all the people in the country. But that fact is irrelevant. If the object is to do well in international competition, sports development policy ought to be oriented towards the top talent. Research strategy may be similar. So, arguably, in military settings.

By contrast, the weakest-link cases are those where the minimum of the performances is what counts for policy purposes. So, for example, in maintaining secrecy, policy needs to focus on the individuals who are least likely to keep silent. The classic example of this case is that of dyke maintenance: there is no advantage to increasing average dyke height or strength along some part of the river's course if along another part the dyke will give way under minimal pressure.

These policy environments have different implications for the desirability of individual risk-taking. In best-shot cases, risk-taking is desirable. In weakest-link cases, risk-taking by individuals is undesirable. The fact that esteem incentives induce risk-loving or risk-averse behaviour over different ranges becomes then a relevant fact in mobilising esteem incentives; and in the nature of the incentives so chosen. There is, of course, a great deal more to be said about the fine-tuning of esteem incentives in such settings. However, it seems intuitively clear that whether one is in a best-shot or weakest-link setting is likely to influence both where one focuses the spotlight of attention, and the nature of the rewards and punishments allocated.

When, for example, McDonalds chooses to reward the worker of the month by putting her photograph on an appropriately conspicuous plaque, it chooses to place incentives at the upper end of performances. McDonalds might have chosen to advertise its worst worker, thereby mobilising the forces of disesteem. Or it might have chosen to advertise its worker of the week or of the day or of the year. These policy dimensions engage issues of whether the esteem or disesteem margins are the more productive and indeed whether a small chance of a larger prize—being worker of the year—or a larger chance of a smaller prize—being worker of the week—creates better incentives. Analogous policy issues arise for professional bodies, for governments, for universities, for sporting clubs, for opera companies—for virtually all bodies that seek to influence the conduct of their particular constituencies. In that sense, the analysis of this section is, we think, almost certainly of wider application.

CONCLUSION

Our concern in this chapter has been to generalise the analysis of performance effects laid out in Chapter 5, and to meet what might be seen to be natural objections to some of the simplifications involved in the earlier discussion. The generalisations ran along two different lines. The first line involved the role of ideals in the determination of the standards that observers use in giving (and withholding) esteem and disesteem. We pursued that aspect in Section 1. Our aim in that discussion was to verify that the general conclusions of the previous chapter apply provided only that prevailing practice, as measured by average performance say, plays some role in the determination of standards.

The second line of generalisation involved extending the performance range for esteem purposes from two to three. Instead of assuming that performance passes immediately from the disesteem range into the positive esteem range, with standard performance representing a knife-edge, as we did in Chapter 5, we here treated standard performance as itself a range. The effect of having three categories of performance—a disesteem range, a standard range, and a positive esteem range—is to create discontinuities in the marginal esteem schedule. We explored in Sections 2 and 3 the implications of those discontinuities for various aspects of the equilibrium in the performance domain.

We drew three conclusions. First, the three-range model creates a presumption about the distribution of performance within the normal range—namely, that that distribution will be systematically skewed towards lower performance within that range. Second, the three-range formulation makes it much more likely that total esteem enjoyed across the community will be positive, something that seems almost impossible in the two-range case. Third, we explored the implications of adding the extra range for the impact of esteem incentives. On the face of things, the three-range version limits, possibly considerably, the number of persons in any domain who face a marginal esteem incentive in that domain. Our claim, however, is that esteem effects still play an extensive role, both in explaining the allocation of persons across activities that might be sources of esteem, and in disciplining poor performance and encouraging high performance in those domains that do not admit the possibility of exit.

The discontinuities in the application of marginal esteem incentives across the range of performances also have implications for attitudes to certain kinds of uncertainty. We explored these implications in Section 4. The chief conclusions were that individuals in the lower reaches of the positive esteem range would tend to be risk-loving in relation to esteem; while those in the upper reaches of the disesteem range would tend to be risk averse. This observation suggests a connection between esteem incentives under uncertainty on the one hand and various different kinds of policy problems on the other. To illustrate, we drew a distinction between best-shot and weakest-link contexts, because those contexts seem to call for different postures in relation to individual risk-taking.

7

Multiple Equilibria and Bootstrapping Performance

In the discussion of performance effects in the economy of esteem that has occupied the previous two chapters, we have been considering the case where estimable performance is continuously variable. That is, esteem was taken to be assigned on the basis of the perceived level of performance, along some spectrum from low performance to high. That case might seem to be rather special. After all, in lots of cases in which esteem or disesteem is given, it is given for some action that one either performs or does not perform. So, for example, in the New York public toilet experiment, subjects either wash their hands after going to the rest-room or they do not: there is no extra esteem on offer for more assiduous washing. Many cases are like this. There is a behavioural practice in place with which one either complies, or does not. Esteem can be operative in such contexts, providing incentives to comply. But we do need a slightly different model to deal with this kind of case.

In this chapter, we consider just such an alternative model. Our claim is that, though the details of the earlier formulation do not apply, rather similar sorts of conclusions follow. In particular, feedback effects between compliance levels and esteem incentives still arise. And it is still possible to derive an equilibrium level of compliance in the performance domain. In fact, under what we take to be the most plausible set of assumptions, it seems likely that there may be more than one such equilibrium. We shall assume that actual and perceived compliance levels coincide, except when otherwise specified.

The central idea is this. When the number of persons in a given population who comply is relatively small, there will be positive esteem associated with so acting. Then, as the number of compliers increases, the amount of esteem attached to so acting will decline and conceivably disappear. For example, when few people tell the truth, doing so will be remarkable and represent a potentially significant source of esteem. But when most people are telling the truth, truth-telling is unremarkable and its esteem utility on that account unlikely to be very high. However, this fact does not necessarily imply that, over the range where most people conform, esteem effects disappear. For, as it becomes a matter of course that people comply, it tends to become a source of disesteem to fail to do so. Accordingly, esteem-based incentives to comply with the norm are operative with varying levels of intensity more or less over the whole range.

At the same time, the level of compliance that is forthcoming will be a positive function of the amount of esteem attached. The larger the esteem reward for complying, and / or the larger the disesteem penalty for not complying, the higher the level of compliance is likely to be. On this basis, we have available all the pieces necessary to derive a compliance equilibrium in which the number of persons who comply and the esteem gained by compliance are jointly determined. In fact, the remarks that we have made so far are already sufficient to suggest the possibility of at least two equilibria—a positive esteem, low-compliance equilibrium; and a negative esteem, high-compliance equilibrium. This multiplicity of equilibria invites exploration of the possibility of a leap from the one of these equilibria to another. We shall term the movement among these possible equilibria the bootstrap effect—for reasons that we shall explain as we proceed.

Richard McAdams (1997) offers an example of a possible bootstrap phenomenon in relation to ideals of recycling. The story, as McAdams tells it, goes this way. Initially, recycling is a somewhat eccentric practice engaged in only by the environmental enthusiast extreme. Within that group, however, recycling gradually takes on the status of an appropriate ideal. And in the process, the practice accumulates an increasingly articulate normative defence. With that normative defence in place, those who recycle enjoy a certain level of esteem, at least from among the environmentally conscious. Recycling comes to signal a special environmental sensitivity that even those who don't practise it are increasingly inclined to applaud. More and more people recycle in response to the esteem attached to the practice—and gradually the practice becomes normal. Once normal, however, it no longer reflects any particular credit on its practitioners, so positive esteem evaporates. At the same time, those who don't recycle now begin to become conspicuous. Their conduct increasingly reveals an environmental insensitivity that is at first mildly irritating and then begins to seem, as it becomes rarer, positively intransigent. Eventually, an apparently stable equilibrium is reached in which the only non-compliers are the especially shameless, the determined anti-environmentalists, and those who like to offend. The practice of recycling has become established, bootstrapped up from an initial situation in which the practice was relatively rare.

1   SOME SIMPLE ANALYTICS

Our aim in what follows is to provide some simple analytics that broadly follow and somewhat generalise the McAdams example. The critical analytic element in this discussion will be the relation between the number of persons complying with a given ideal and the esteem-based incentive associated with compliance. This esteem-based incentive is composed of two possible elements: a level of positive esteem associated with complying; and a level of disesteem avoided by complying. Both elements may be operative at the same time; but we think it plausible that each will be predominant over a different range of aggregate compliance levels. In particular, once the practice is established, positive esteem will accrue over the range in which the number of compliers is relatively low. Furthermore, as the numbers of compliers increases, the amount of esteem that accrues to compliance will fall. Disesteem for non-compliance will come into operation once the level of compliance reaches some threshold level, and the level of disesteem that attaches to non-compliance will increase as the numbers who comply increase.

Again, some simple diagrams will be useful. Consider Figure 7.1. On the horizontal axis, we depict the proportion, n, of the population who comply with the ideal.[1] On the left vertical axis, we depict the amount of esteem that each complier enjoys for various levels of n, and on the right vertical axis the amount of disesteem that each complier avoids—each non-complier suffers—for various levels of n. Compliance is, we take it, an on–off matter. If one complies, one enjoys the esteem (if any) attached to compliance. If one fails to comply, one suffers the level of disesteem (if any) associated with non-compliance.

We consider four possible ranges of compliance performance. First, consider the range from 0 to A in Figure 7.1. Here there is virtually no compliance with the ideal. Indeed, the behavioural practice involved has not yet registered *as* an ideal—not even as something one might reasonably aspire to do. Clearly, over this range, the esteem incentive can play no role. Then over a second range of compliance the practice becomes established as an ideal, even though it is not very widely practised. This is the range from A to B. Over this range, there is positive esteem associated with compliance. However, there is no disesteem

---

[1] In the formulation adopted in the previous two chapters, it will be recalled that there was an issue about the metric of performance on the basis of which esteem was taken to be given. What exactly, one might ask, is the index of courage that would enable us to declare not only that A was more courageous than B but also whether the difference between A's and B's courage levels was greater than or equal to the difference between C's and D's. Here, no such issue arises: the proportion of persons that comply is a conceptually clear fact about the state of the world, even if we may have some difficulty in determining what it is in some cases.

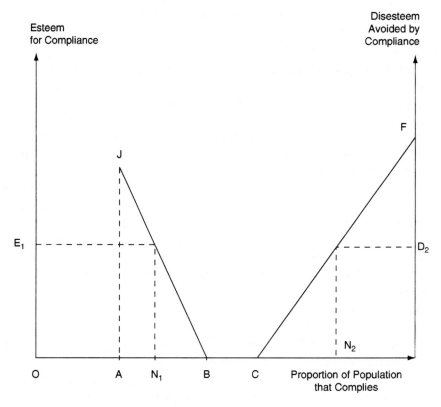

Figure 7.1. *Frequency and the supply of esteem.*

associated with non-compliance: compliance is not yet common enough for
failure to comply to be especially notable, and certainly not contemptible. The
positive esteem that accrues at each compliance level over this range is depicted
in Figure 7.1 by the line JB, indicating that esteem is positive but declining as
the proportion of the population that complies increases. If the number of
compliers is at N_1, for example, an amount of esteem given by E_1 is on offer to
all those who do comply. As the proportion of the population that complies
increases to B, the esteem to be achieved by compliance finally disappears. That
is, at B, compliance is sufficiently common to be unremarkable and hence no
esteem as such attaches to compliance. There is however a final range, from C
to 100 per cent, where despite the fact that no positive esteem attaches to
compliance, disesteem attaches to non-compliance. Over this range, most
people comply with the ideal and non-compliance becomes distinctive. The
disesteem attached to non-compliance increases as the numbers of compliers

increase over this range. Clearly, any disesteem attached to non-compliance establishes an incentive to comply no less than does the positive esteem operative over the range AB. For example, when the level of compliance is at N_2 in Figure 7.1, the disesteem avoided by compliance is D_2 and the esteem incentive to comply is exactly the same as that at N_1. The level of disesteem for non-compliance reaches its maximum at F, when compliance is universal.

As we have constructed Figure 7.1, C involves a higher number of compliers than does B. This means that there is a range between B and C where neither esteem nor disesteem accrues. It may be that no such range exists. It may be that both esteem for compliance, and disesteem for non-compliance, are operative simultaneously. In that case, B would lie to the right of C in the relevant diagram. In all cases however, it seems plausible to suppose that the relation between the esteem-based incentive to comply and the proportion of the population that does comply will have the general U-shaped form indicated in Figure 7.1. That is, there will be a downward sloping portion over the low-compliance range and an upward sloping portion over the high-compliance range.

The function illustrated by JBCF in Figure 7.1 indicates, then, the esteem incentive associated with compliance, at all possible compliance levels. In that sense, it can be thought of as somewhat analogous to a demand curve for compliance, with esteem as the currency of reward paid by observers. Clearly, in order to construct an equilibrium level of compliance in this setting, we need to ask also what the level of esteem forthcoming would have to be in order to secure compliance at particular levels. We have to construct the analogous supply curve of compliant behaviour. This is the task to which we turn.

To secure low levels of compliance, we take it that no esteem is required at all. We take it, that is, that there will be some proportion of the population that will behave in the relevant way whether there is any esteem reward or not. Suppose that that base level of compliance is given by the proportion V in Figure 7.2. In order to secure compliance from a higher proportion of population than that base level will require that compliers be subject to some incentive. And the required incentive will plausibly have to be larger and larger as the level of compliance increases. At very high compliance levels, in the neighbourhood of 100 per cent, there may, in fact, be no possible esteem incentive that would secure compliance at that level—the required esteem incentive would have to be virtually infinite. This is so because as we get close to compliance by all, compliance is required of those for whom it is most difficult. Moreover, there will be some non-compliers who are relatively impervious to disesteem—the shameless ones. For this latter group, there may be no esteem incentive imaginable that would secure any behavioural response. And there may be some residual group of countersuggestive souls who derive their esteem from flouting accepted conventions. The point here is that we should expect the esteem incentive required in order to secure compliance to be a generally increasing function of the compliance level, and to be more sharply increasing as the required compliance level becomes very high. We illustrate this curve by VW in Figure 7.2.

To determine possible equilibria in this extended example, we need to isolate those levels of compliance at which the esteem incentive required is equal to the esteem that is actually forthcoming. In order to illustrate such equilibrium positions, we put the two curves, Figures 7.1 and 7.2, together and focus on the points of intersection. These intersection points are represented by V, N^*, N_0^*, and M^* in Figure 7.3. All of these points are potential equilibria: that is, all these points are such that the esteem incentive required at that level of compliance equals the esteem incentive forthcoming at that level of compliance. However, as we shall see, not all of these potential equilibria are likely to be stable.

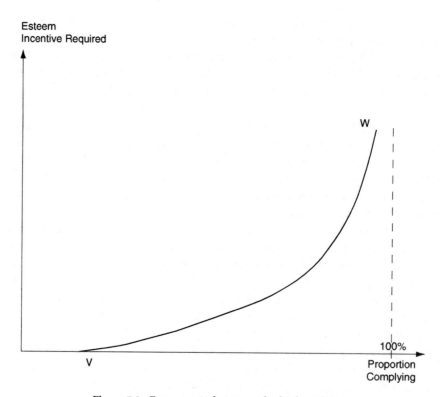

Figure 7.2. *Esteem required at various levels of compliance.*

Consider each of these points in turn. At V, agents act spontaneously as the ideal requires, not because of any esteem available but rather from pure inclination. And there is, in fact, no esteem or disesteem given at this level of performance. So V is a perfectly stable equilibrium. However, it is only stable locally; a shock to the system of an appropriate magnitude—say, the recognition of the behaviour as an ideal—could engender a shift to a new equilibrium. Suppose that the numbers of compliers were to increase to A. At this point, the behaviour comes to be countenanced as a plausible aspiration and esteem kicks in. Individuals now have an esteem-related reason to comply, and a process would immediately be set in motion that would shift the number of compliers to a higher level.

The second possible equilibrium position to be considered is at N*. Here, again, the level of compliance is such as to generate exactly that level of esteem-related incentive necessary to sustain compliance at the level N*. This too is a locally stable equilibrium. If compliance were to fall below N*, the esteem to be achieved by complying would increase and individuals would be induced to

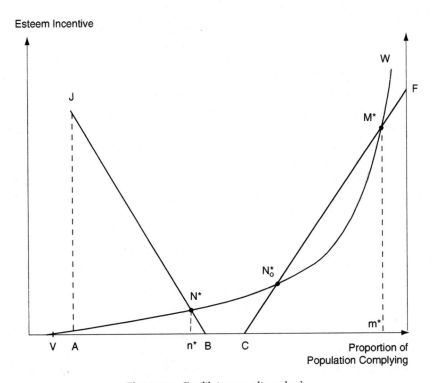

Figure 7.3. *Equilibrium compliance levels.*

restore their compliant behaviour. Alternatively, if the number of compliers were to increase above N^*, the esteem attached to compliance would fall below the level necessary to generate that number of compliers. The number of compliers would then fall until equilibrium at N^* was restored. We shall refer to N^* as the low-compliance or positive esteem equilibrium—at N^* all compliers receive positive esteem for their compliance.

M^* is the corresponding disesteem equilibrium. Here the proportion of the population who comply is rather higher than at N^*. There is no esteem to be derived from complying—compliance is, after all, what most people do. But there is disesteem for non-compliance. And the threat of that disesteem is what supports compliance at the observed level. The high-compliance or disesteem equilibrium, M^*, is also stable. Should compliance fall below M^*, the disesteem associated with non-compliance would be sufficient to induce more individuals to comply: compliance would be restored at the M^* level. And obversely if there were an increase in compliance beyond M^*, some individuals would find that the cost of compliance exceeded the cost of the disesteem they endured for non-compliance. So those individuals would cease to comply and the proportion of compliers would fall back to M^*.

Consider finally the potential equilibrium at N_0^*. This possible equilibrium is unstable. Although the esteem incentive required for a compliance level at N_0^* is exactly equal to the esteem incentive that is forthcoming, small changes away from N_0^* would be sufficient to induce larger changes in behaviour. Consider, for example, a reduction in the compliance level to somewhat below N_0^*. Over this range, the level of esteem forthcoming (given by the CF curve) is not sufficient to sustain that level of compliance (given by the VW curve). Accordingly, the degree of compliance will fall, until eventually a new, stable equilibrium is reached at N^*.

Obversely, an increase in compliance above N_0^* will give rise to a situation where the disesteem avoided by complying exceeds that required to sustain the level of compliance. This is shown by the fact that the CF curve lies above the VW curve over this range. More people will be led to comply and the esteem incentive will continue to rise until the equilibrium at M^* is reached. And as we have already seen, M^* is a stable equilibrium, so there will be no further movement beyond M^*.

2 BOOTSTRAPPING

There is special reason for interest in the fact of multiple potential equilibria. This is that there is the possibility of choice among those equilibria. In particular, there is the possibility of kick-starting a process that moves from a low-compliance equilibrium to a higher-compliance one. At V, for example, a small increase in compliance might get us into the range at or beyond A— in which case, substantial esteem incentives are brought into play and further compliance responses are induced. Likewise, in the neighbourhood of N_0^*, a small change in compliance from just below N_0^* to just above N_0^* transforms a process of declining compliance into one of increasing compliance and will be sufficient to place us in the range that leads to M^*. In this way, small strategic interventions in compliance performance can induce significant changes in the equilibrium level of compliance. As we have seen, those small-scale interventions are likely to be especially potent when compliance levels fall in particular ranges—the range just below V and the range just above N_0^*.

Of course, we can imagine that the relevant sequence of shocks necessary to produce the progress from the zero esteem equilibrium at V, to the high-compliance equilibrium at M^*, occurs through happy accident rather than deliberate manipulation. That seems to be the case envisaged, for example, by McAdams in his recycling example. It is therefore of some interest to enquire as to the circumstances under which such happy accidents are most likely to occur.

Note that the likelihood of a shift from one equilibrium to another is dependent on how close to one another the various equilibria lie. It may be, for example, that the stable low-compliance equilibrium lies quite close to the unstable N_0^* equilibrium—a case illustrated in Figure 7.4a. Here, only a small shock would be required to bootstrap performance to a new high-compliance equilibrium at M^*. For once the level of compliance moves beyond N_0^* in Figure 7.4a, the momentum will carry compliance all the way to m^*. Equally, however, it may be that N_0^* and M^* lie quite close together—a case illustrated in Figure 7.4b. In that event, only a small negative shock to compliance levels would be required to make the high-compliance equilibrium M^* unravel through N_0^* and shift the esteem economy back to the low-compliance equilibrium at N^*. The bootstrap that can be done up, as we might put it, can also be undone!

The bootstrap metaphor, however, suggests something rather more intentional than happy accident. In that spirit, suppose the government or some other large player in the system wished to secure a shift among equilibria, or perhaps more modestly, a shift in the prevailing equilibrium in the direction of greater compliance. What instruments might be available for such purposes, and what effects of such instruments should we look to? As the foregoing discussion suggests, there are really two issues at stake that need to be distinguished.

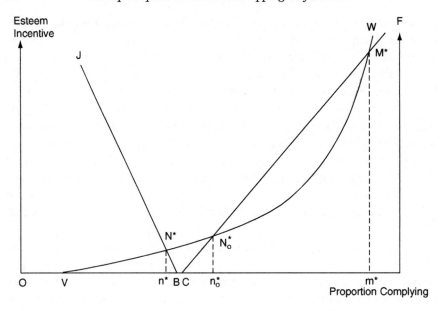

Figure 7.4a. *Low-compliance equilibrium vulnerability.*

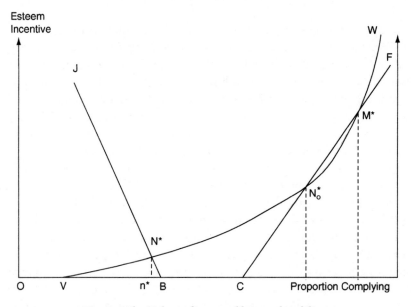

Figure 7.4b. *High-compliance equilibrium vulnerability.*

The first issue relates to the effect of the intervention on how close the low-compliance equilibrium is to the unstable equilibrium and on how far the high-compliance equilibrium is from the unstable equilibrium. Interventions that narrow the gap between the unstable and the low-compliance equilibrium will render happy accidents more likely; those that widen the gap between the unstable equilibrium and the high-compliance equilibrium will render unhappy accidents less likely. Both will be welcome, though for somewhat different reasons.

The second of the two issues mentioned relates to the effect on the particular equilibrium at which we happen to be located, bootstrap effects aside. This shows up in comparative static analysis of a kind entirely analogous to that pursued in Chapter 5. Here we want to pursue two such exercises.

The first comparative static exercise involves an expansion of audience size. As we shall argue in greater detail in the next chapter, increased publicity so understood seems likely to increase the esteem and disesteem associated with any level of performance. So, in the current case, the effect of increased publicity can be modelled as an increase in the esteem incentive in play, at any particular level of performance. Consider on this basis Figure 7.5. The esteem incentive at each level of compliance is increased by the same factor. So the esteem on offer when compliance is at A increases from J to J'; and the disesteem avoided when compliance is at 100 per cent increases from F to F'. Accordingly, the positive esteem, low-compliance equilibrium shifts from N^* to $N^{*'}$, involving an increase in the equilibrium level of compliance from n^* to $n^{*'}$. And the negative esteem, high-compliance equilibrium shifts from M^* to $M^{*'}$, involving an increase in equilibrium compliance from m^* to $m^{*'}$. Whichever of the stable equilibria is operative, compliance in equilibrium increases with increased audience size. Note further that the unstable equilibrium $N_0^{*'}$ also moves to a lower level of compliance. This has the effect of making the low-compliance equilibrium and the unstable equilibrium closer together; and correspondingly of shifting the high-compliance equilibrium further away from the unstable equilibrium. These shifts tend to make the high-compliance equilibrium more robust to random shocks, and makes the prospect of bootstrapping from the low to the high-compliance equilibrium more likely.

Consider now the second comparative static exercise; this will be of some specific interest in Chapter 9. Suppose that observers misperceive the level of compliance. Suppose that the actual level of compliance is higher than observers perceive it to be; so that, for example, at A, actual compliance is ten percentage points higher than is perceived. If this misperception were corrected then the level of esteem forthcoming at (actual) compliance level A would

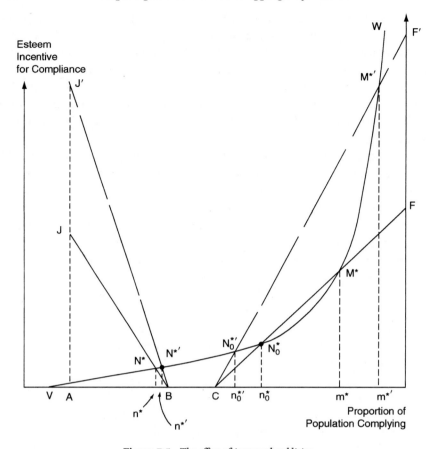

Figure 7.5. *The effect of increased publicity.*

decline. The curve JB would shift left to J′B′, as indicated in Figure 7.6. Equally, the curve CF would shift left to C′F′. For example, originally, at 100 per cent compliance, observers would believe the compliance level to be only 90 per cent. They would therefore assign less disesteem to non-compliers than they would were their misperceptions to be rectified. The level of disesteem at 100 per cent compliance would increase from F to F′, as shown in Figure 7.6. The effects of this correction of misperceptions are then threefold:

- To shift the low-compliance equilibrium at N^* to a lower level of compliance, at $N^{*'}$. This shift is attributable to the fact that what was previously perceived as a rather heroic level of compliance is now perceived as more ordinary: the esteem incentive has fallen and so equilibrium compliance falls.

- To shift the high-compliance equilibrium, M^*, to a higher level of compliance, at $M^{*'}$. This shift is attributable to the fact that the perceived level of compliance has increased and hence the amount of disesteem associated with non-compliance has increased. With that increase in disesteem, actual compliance levels rise.
- To shift the unstable equilibrium, N_0^* to a lower level of compliance, $N_0^{*'}$. The effect is to increase the distance in terms of compliance between the high-compliance equilibrium and the unstable equilibrium and hence render the high-compliance equilibrium more robust to random shocks.

In the bootstrapping spirit, we have deliberately constructed Figure 7.6 in such a way that the initial low-compliance equilibrium N^* involves a higher level of compliance than does the new, fully informed unstable equilibrium at $N_0^{*'}$. Now suppose we are initially at equilibrium point N^*. Then when misperceptions are corrected, the new esteem incentive at N^* will exceed the incentive required to secure additional compliance, and compliance will increase until $M^{*'}$ is finally achieved. Here then the bootstrapping process is secured by the intrusion of new information about prevailing practices.

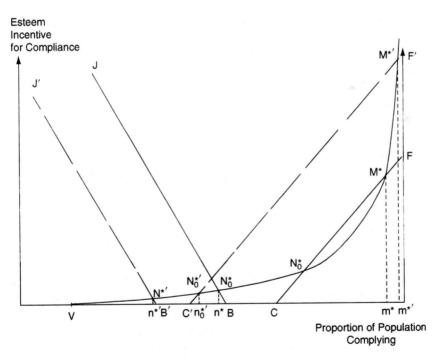

Figure 7.6. *Effects of changed perception of proportion complying.*

Other sources of external shock might be considered. But not every measure that secures additional compliance will necessarily be successful. For one thing, the initiating shock needs to be large enough in its compliance effects. But further, the efficacy of any measures introduced to stimulate compliance will depend on those measures not significantly moderating the operation of the underlying esteem incentives.

An example may help here. It is tempting to think that mandating compliance by formal law might serve the necessary function. The formal law will induce a belief among the population that larger numbers will comply with the ideal. In that manner, we might hope to kick-start a shift to a higher-compliance equilibrium. Moreover, that equilibrium would be such that the law itself needs minimal enforcement, because the forces of esteem (or disesteem, more accurately) may do most of the work in sustaining compliance. Perhaps. But there is a danger that once the law is in place, the esteem attached to compliance evaporates: individuals are now to be seen as complying not because of any moral sensitivities but because of fear of punishment. The general lesson we draw from this danger is that not all instruments of policy are esteem-friendly: some may crowd out esteem effects. Crowding-out, so understood, is an important issue; and we take it up in greater detail in Part III.

It seems clear to us that the foregoing analysis represents an analytically explicit account of the kind of mechanism that McAdams's account of the recycling ideal suggests. One virtue of going analytically explicit here is that we are alerted to the possibility of getting caught in a low-compliance equilibrium. McAdams's story does not actually mention the possibility of multiple equilibria: his discussion simply directs attention to the time-sequence of the phases in the emergence of the practice. On his account, the high-compliance equilibrium emerges by essentially spontaneous forces. However, in some other cases, those spontaneous forces may need a little assistance. The high-compliance equilibrium is an example of a quasi-invisible hand outcome in the sense that once reached it is likely to be self-sustaining. But the invisible hand here may need a bit of a hand to get it going in the first place. And it may need some independent support to prevent the bootstrapping process from reversing.

One final observation. In framing the discussion around the McAdams example, we may have given the impression that the high-compliance equilibrium is presumptively to be preferred over the low-compliance one. There are, to be sure, lots of cases in which we think that that is so, but as we made clear in our discussion in Chapter 5, the normative evaluation of alternative equilibria is a slightly tricky business. It is therefore worth noting a complication that arises in this connection that was not present in the performance model set out in the previous two chapters. This is that the low-compliance and high-compliance equilibria in Figure 7.3 differ with respect to the amount of esteem they give rise to. In the low-compliance equilibrium, all those who comply enjoy positive esteem. Those who don't comply receive no esteem benefit, but they don't endure any disesteem cost either. In the high-compliance equilibrium, no one receives positive esteem; but the residual non-compliers do endure disesteem. This observation seems to establish a (possibly weak) presumption in favour of the low-compliance equilibrium, other things being equal. Of course, other things are not equal in this case: no overall judgement can be made without assessing the normative significance of the activity with respect to which the compliance is defined. But if the activity in question happened to be one whose expansion we had no reason to promote, then the fact that compliers are made better off in the low-compliance equilibrium suggests a preference for that outcome.

CONCLUSION

Our object in this chapter has been to offer a model of the relation between compliance and esteem that is slightly different from that developed in the previous two chapters. As in those earlier chapters our focus has been on performance effects in the economy of esteem, but the context is one where performance is understood in terms of meeting, or failing to meet, the requirements of a norm, rather than in terms of a continuous metric of performance quality.

The analytic structure of the two cases is however very similar. The model of the esteem economy that emerges is one in which the level of compliance and the amount of esteem forthcoming for compliance are mutually determined. Here, however, the level of compliance is measured by the number of persons who comply rather than improvement in the level of performance by all individuals. On this basis, we establish an equilibrium in compliance, more or less analogous to the equilibrium in performance level derived in Chapters 5 and 6.

However, the analytics in this on/off case are interestingly different. The model is rather more like a simple demand/supply interaction. On the supply side, the relation between compliance level and esteem incentive required is much like the conventional upward-sloping supply curve of conventional economics: getting a greater supply of compliant behaviour requires an ever greater reward in terms of (marginal) esteem earned. The demand-side relation, on the other hand, is distinctive. The relation between the (marginal) esteem on offer and the compliance level is most naturally modelled as

U-shaped. The U-shape reflects the fact that the esteem incentive is composed of two elements, each of which comes into play over a different range of compliance. First, there is a positive esteem incentive that is most significant when compliance is not especially common. Then there is a negative esteem incentive associated with failure to comply when compliance is widespread.

The U-shaped demand-side structure is liable to give rise to multiple equilibria in performance—and in particular, to two potentially stable equilibria. One is a low-compliance, positive-esteem equilibrium. The other is a high-compliance, negative-esteem equilibrium. The question then arises as to whether it might be possible to bootstrap the economy of esteem from the lower equilibrium to the higher. Such bootstrapping may, in congenial cases, happen of its own accord. But that happy accident suggests a no less likely, unhappy accident, whereby exogenous shocks might cause a shift from the high-compliance to the low-compliance equilibrium. The bootstrap that lifts us up may also let us down. There is an interesting policy issue at hand here as to what measures might be put in place to kick-start the bootstrap (to mix our metaphors) and/or to hold the bootstrap in place against unravelling forces. We explored in some analytic detail one particular possibility, which we shall take up again in Chapter 9. This is the case where observers misperceive the extent of compliance, and therefore assign different amounts of esteem than they would assign if fully informed. Correcting a perception that compliance is lower than it actually is can either reduce compliance (if the low-compliance equilibrium applies) or increase compliance (if the high-compliance equilibrium applies).

The more general lessons we wish to draw relate to the power of equilibrium analysis, and to the general significance of feedback effects in interesting social processes. Whether individual performance is an on/off matter or is subject to a continuous metric, the attempt to derive an equilibrium in performance in the economy of esteem reveals the relevance of feedback loops between individual action and aggregate outcomes. Effectively, the rational response of each individual to the environment she faces contributes to the creation of that environment. This kind of social interdependence is as we see it part of what makes the economy of esteem an interesting object of study. This interdependence is also part of what makes the behavioural interactions generated by the pursuit of esteem an economy in a plausible sense.

8

Publicity and Individual Responses

The current chapter forms one of a trio, each of which deals with a different aspect of publicity. In the next chapter, we shall focus on the connection between publicity and standards. And in Chapter 10, we shall examine individual incentives in relation to publicity-seeking and publicity-shunning. In this chapter, however, we want to follow on directly from the models laid out in the earlier chapters. We want to treat publicity as an external factor, and examine the effects of publicity on performance behaviour.

The simplest way of approaching this question is to treat publicity as a matter of the size of the audience that directly observes a performance of some action. Our object in doing so is to investigate the effects of increased audience size on performance incentives. This will be our task in Section 1, focusing on the context where performers are anonymous. However, that case is just a point of departure. We want to generalise the conclusions of Section 1 to the case where performers can be reidentified, can accumulate reputations, and can become famous—or infamous.

In Section 2 we spell out what is involved in reputation and fame. Once agents have a recognisable name or face, they are reidentifiable and it becomes possible for esteem to accrue to them in a way that relies essentially on testimony. And equally it becomes possible for the esteem that the agents receive to be a matter of common belief, with nearly everyone esteeming them, believing that others esteem them, and so on. We explore various aspects of these possibilities in Section 2, associating fame and infamy with the case where esteem is given as a matter of common belief. We focus on the magnified publicity that goes with fame and infamy and we examine the implications for the motivation of the agents so esteemed.

In Section 3, we turn to a consideration of publicity policy. Part of the reason for our interest in publicity is that it seems to us to be the chief means by which the forces of esteem can be channelled and directed. By increasing the exposure afforded to performances, one can increase the associated esteem incentives without incidentally inducing changes in the basic operation of the esteem economy. Publicity is, in that sense, the main lever available for policy intervention. However, there are a large number of possible dimensions to publicity policy and our treatment will only take up one of these.

The issue we shall focus on is this: where, in the distribution of performances, should publicity be directed? Any particular publicity policy involves choices not only about how much light should be shed *in toto*, but also about where that light should be focused. Publicity is of interest because observer attention is a scarce resource. Accordingly, policy actions that serve to make some performances more conspicuous will usually serve simultaneously to make others less so. So, where should publicity be directed? Should publicity policy focus on excellent performances—say, by the award of prizes? Or should attention be drawn to the worst performances—say, by means of what we call 'dunce-cap' strategies? We attempt in Section 3 to set out the various issues at stake in making such choices and to explore some generalisations that seem to be on offer.

1   PUBLICITY AND THE NUMBER OF OBSERVERS

Other things—and in particular, the quality of the audience—being equal, it seems plausible to think that the esteem that an actor enjoys from a given performance, or the disesteem she suffers, is positively related to the size of the audience that comes to be aware of that performance. We want in this section to argue briefly for this claim and to explore the implications of the argument for the precise relation between audience size and performance incentive.

Consider the limiting case in which (external) audience is zero. Recall the Ring of Gyges fable. The ring served to make the wearer invisible. Its effects were precisely to challenge the strength of the moral principles the wearer claimed. Given such a ring, who could claim that his behaviour would remain unaffected? The prediction supported in the fable was that no one could safely chance the temptations that invisibility allowed. Everyone is likely to be affected by a relaxation of the discipline imposed by the scrutiny of others.

A contemporary vindication of that prediction is provided by an experiment conducted in New York public restrooms, which we mentioned in Chapter 1 (Munger and Harris 1989). The experimenter installed hidden cameras in the restrooms and observed the practices of the users in relation to washing their hands after use. In some of the bathrooms, it was arranged that someone else would be present—not explicitly monitoring conduct but simply present in such a way that the presence was detectable by the user. It was discovered that hand-washing was much higher when another party was present. The reported numbers are that 80 per cent washed their hands when the observer was present, whereas only about half that number washed their hands when acting totally in private. The mere possibility that one's action or inaction might be observed was sufficient to motivate a very considerable number of potential hand-washers. Note that the observer and the user were unknown to each other. There was no presumption that the user and the observer would even recognise each other in any subsequent meeting. There were no signals of disapproval or approval necessarily on offer. All that was at stake was the possibility that the failure to wash one's hands after use would be observed. Hand-washing is so widely taken to be an ideal that any observed failure will be expected to occasion a negative reaction in the observer's mind. That negative reaction is disesteem in our lexicon; and the threat of such disesteem is what we take to be the motivating influence in this case.

It might be thought that moving from an audience of zero to an audience of one may not generalise—that it is the fact of being observed rather than the number of observers that is relevant. Even were this so, numbers might still play a role. After all, to be observed in the relevant sense, it is necessary that the actor be noticed. The other might not actually detect your failure to wash your hands. Or perhaps she might see that you don't wash your hands, but fail to register the significance of that fact. Perhaps she is preoccupied with other thoughts. Perhaps this particular other isn't one who cares much about manual hygiene. All these are possibilities that are likely to diminish with the number of observers, up to the point where they get in one another's way and provide the agent with the safety of numbers. So the probability that performance will be detected in an esteem-relevant way increases up to that point with audience size. The general point here is that increasing public access to performance serves to increase the probability of being observed; and this increased probability itself powerfully mobilises the forces of esteem.

In addition, however, audience size as such seems to be an independent relevant influence. As you tee off for the first hole in your weekly round of golf, a solitary watcher does not have the same effect as a crowd of fifty or so. As numbers increase you become more nervous. More hangs on the shot. If there is only one observer you can ruefully shrug off your duffed drive. Before a substantial crowd, the effect is mortifying. And obversely for the case of a positive accomplishment. When you hit your hole in one, you rather wish there had been a crowd around to observe it. True, others in your foursome will applaud. But it would have been nice if there had been larger numbers to cheer the spectacle.

Simply stated then, we take the level of esteem or disesteem associated with a given act generally to increase as the size of the audience increases. There may be threshold effects in the relationship: one such threshold seems likely to apply in moving from zero to one (external) observer. And there may be a point at which additional numbers become irrelevant. But it seems clear that as the numbers of observers increases, so do esteem effects and the associated performance incentives. This effect on esteem we refer to as the 'publicity effect'.

The publicity effect is likely to interact with the level of performance itself in such a way that the effect of audience size will not be the same at all levels of performance. In particular, when the esteem or disesteem attached to a performance is itself low, the effect of increasing numbers seems likely to disappear at lower levels of audience size. But at the extremes of the distribution of performances—for performance that is outstandingly good or spectacularly bad—the effects of increased audience seem likely to extend into the large-number range.

A diagram may be helpful here in clarifying the effects we have in mind. Consider therefore the formulation of the relation between esteem and performance that we developed in Chapter 6. To focus on esteem-related incentives, however, it is helpful to consider marginal esteem—that is, the extra esteem that accrues for a unit increase in performance quality over the range. The marginal esteem for an initial low publicity level (one external observer) is shown in Figure 8.1*b* as the line segments AA′ and A″A‴ (exactly analogous to the UVWZ segments in Figure 6.2*b*). This marginal esteem curve is derived from the relation between performance and esteem depicted in Figure 8.1*a* (which corresponds to Figure 6.2*a*).

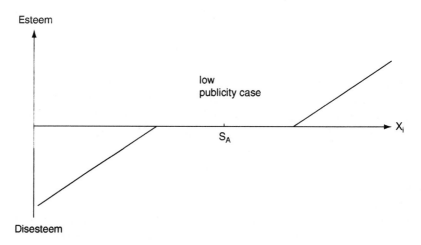

Figure 8.1a. *Relation between performance and esteem in the low publicity case.*

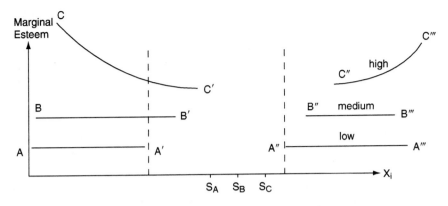

Figure 8.1b. *Marginal esteem curves for varying publicity contexts.*

Now introduce the first phase of additional publicity, increasing audience, say, to four observers. Marginal esteem rises over the entire range: there are now more observers to give esteem and there is therefore more esteem on offer. So incentives to improve performance increase at all levels where esteem/disesteem is operative. The new marginal esteem levels are given by the line segments BB' and $B''B'''$. Note that the prevailing standard has increased from S_A to S_B, reflecting the higher performance equilibrium that is associated with enhanced performance incentives. For the same reason, B' and B'' correspond to higher levels of performance than do A' and A'' respectively.

As a final step, consider the effects of the second phase of publicity, as audience increases say from 4 to 1000. Our claim is that this will alter the marginal esteem levels to something like those indicated by the line segments CC' and $C''C'''$ in Figure 8.1b, with the characteristic falling portion over the range CC' and rising portion over the range $C''C'''$. Again, C' lies beyond B', and C'' beyond B'', reflecting the effect of increased performance incentives on performance and therefore on standards, S_C (beyond S_B). However, here, the main incentive effects apply at the extremes of the distribution of performances—to the truly outstanding and the spectacularly disastrous.

The bottom line here is that publicity effects magnify esteem-related incentives, though the effect is unlikely to be uniform across the range of performances. Generally we can increase performance by ensuring that there is an audience and by increasing the size of that audience, other things being equal. What specific measures we might put in place to achieve this end is an issue we take up below in Section 3.

2   FROM OBSERVATION TO FAME

As the New York restroom example shows, it is not necessary that the observer know you or be likely to see you again in order for esteem effects to be behaviourally relevant. In particular, it is not necessary that your conduct influence the reputation you will carry into future transactions.[1] There can be no reputational effects if you cannot be identified in the future as the one who failed to wash his hands. You must be reidentifiable: you must be, not anonymous, but as we might put it, 'onymous'; you must have a recognisable name or, at the least, face.

But reidentifiability can do a lot more than just make it possible to aggregate esteem, positive or negative, across time. It can also mobilise two important social factors. First, it can enable people to testify to the negative or positive merits of the named person; it can introduce testimonially based, indirect esteem. And second, it can make it possible for people to form in common the belief that someone so named and identified is esteemed by all: to come to believe that everyone esteems the person, believes that everyone esteems the person, believes that everyone holds this belief, and so on.

The two factors that reidentifiability puts into play operate independently. Let the members of a group of people all esteem a given individual in a certain negative or positive manner. That esteem may be given without testimony playing any role, through everyone observing the agent directly and forming a direct appraisal. And whether given with testimony or not, it may be given with or without its being a matter to any extent of common belief. The possibilities are distinguished nicely in the matrix of Table 8.1.

Cases 1 and 2 in the first column both involve reputation, as we might say; people will have a good or bad reputation in a group, so far as each recognises

Table 8.1. *Esteem with reidentifiability*

	Without common belief	With common belief
Testimony not essential	1	3
Testimony essential	2	4

[1] It is important to make this point because agents' reputations are increasingly included in economic models of core market relationships, and it might be thought that that inclusion encompasses all of the effects of esteem that the economist would or should want to know about. For example, the work on iterated prisoners' dilemma interactions, and the closely related work on trust, recognises that it may pay a prudentially rational individual to develop a reputation for being co-operative or trustworthy. Such a reputation will lead the trustworthy individual to be attractive in the future as a trading partner. We do not, of course, deny that possibility. We do deny that it exhausts what is interesting and behaviourally relevant about esteem. Esteem can operate without reputational effects.

their merits or demerits, whether directly or in some part indirectly; and this can be so even if that fact is not in any degree a matter of common belief. Where there is common belief, however, as in cases 3 and 4, someone can be said to enjoy fame or infamy within the group; and this is so, whether or not testimony plays an essential role in generating the esteem that is a matter of common belief (see Cowen 2000).

Case 4 is of particular interest. Everyone knows that Einstein was a genius; that Caruso was a wonderful singer; that Arnold Palmer was a superb golfer; that Don Bradman was a great cricketer; or, to take more contemporary examples, that David Lewis was a brilliant philosopher, and John Nash a brilliant economist. Everybody knows these things even though perhaps only a small proportion of the population has actually read anything of Einstein's, or ever heard Caruso sing (even on record); or seen Bradman bat. Perhaps even among philosophers, few have read much of David Lewis. Many economists may never have read any of Nash's papers, even though 'Nash equilibrium' terminology is totally familiar to every economics undergraduate.

These examples are an instance of a phenomenon that has come to be described as an informational cascade (Bikhchandani, Hirshleifer, et al. 1992).[2] When a large number of people come to hold a particular belief in common— say, the belief that someone is estimable—that fact will tend to be salient in the community at large, so that others are given a testimonial reason thereby to adopt the belief themselves. And as more and more people join the ranks of the believers, the fact of their having that common belief becomes more salient still, thereby attracting yet others. The cascade may develop to the point where virtually everyone comes to share in the common belief.

We should take note of a particularly interesting possibility—the extreme case in which a person who is held in esteem or disesteem as a matter of common belief may not be appraised by anyone on the basis of direct observation and knowledge. It may be that all other members of the group form their view of the person on the basis of one another's testimony: on the basis, ultimately, that each believes that others think well or ill of that agent. Many, perhaps most, of those who believe that the famous deserve to be held in the high esteem that they are, ground that belief in the fact that others believe it. Some of those others, one assumes, will be direct observers. But it may be difficult to determine whether a particular person is a direct observer or not

---

[2] Under special conditions the Condorcet jury theorem would provide particularly powerful reasons for each to follow the crowd (see Black 1958; Condorcet 1976).

and, as it turns out, no one may form their esteem on a direct, non-testimonial basis.[3]

The possibility of indirect observation and common belief clearly adds hugely to the level of esteem that A can enjoy. Even though many esteem A only on a testimonial, indirect basis, the esteem is none the less genuine for that. If I genuinely hold the belief that A is worthy of esteem, then I will naturally esteem A, whether I come to the belief of her esteem-worthiness via direct observation of her performance(s) or via trust in the validity of the prevailing consensus.

The central point we want to underline here is that the prospect of becoming famous greatly magnifies esteem incentives. (We may stick for convenience to the case of fame rather than infamy.) For the purposes of calculating effects on performance incentives, the earlier treatment of audience size can be taken to apply whether the audience is composed of direct or indirect observers. And it is clear in that sense that the prospect of becoming famous serves as a huge boost to performance incentives. Let it be the case that A has that prospect in view; then the esteem stakes for A enter a new and much magnified dimension. And when we come to the very large audience case, as illustrated by $CC'C''C'''$ in Figure 8.1b, it is clear that the fame and infamy cases are those depicted at the extremes of the performance distribution, where the performance incentive is most intense. It is, perhaps, with something of this in mind that Hamilton refers to fame as 'the ruling passion of the *noblest* minds' (Madison, Hamilton, et al. 1987: LXXII p. 414).

But if fame can be a spur in the economy of esteem, it is essentially so only in prospect. Fame once realised is likely to be a significant brake on esteem incentives. The chief reason for this lies in the fact that fame is sustained by indirect observation and common belief, so that it is stable under small perturbations. We now proceed to argue this.

Let the proportion of direct observers, in the sense that we have used the term here, be p. These direct observers are the effective authorities on A's esteem-worthiness, but they need not be acknowledged experts or identifiable

---

[3] It is even possible, we should note, that there is a common belief that someone is estimable in a group, without any member of that group holding the person in esteem, whether on a testimonial or non-testimonial basis. Each may proclaim a belief in the merits of that person out of a desire for the esteem they think they will thereby win; they may expect to win esteem for displaying the belief so far as they believe that others see merit in the person. In this case we would have another example of pluralistic ignorance (Miller and Prentice 1994; Schroeder and Prentice 1998). Everyone has a false belief about the attitudes of others—in this case, their attitudes of esteem—and this leads them to behave in a manner which supports a pattern that no one individually endorses. Thus a famous person—if this is a case of 'fame'—may be esteemed by no one. The fame in this case will be very precarious, of course; witness the story of the Emperor's new clothes. But, as we shall show, it will also be precarious in the less extreme case covered in the text.

among the population at large. Indeed, it will be a difficult matter to determine who are direct observers and who are not. For it will not be particularly estimable for you to announce to the world at large that you have no reason for believing that A is estimable beyond the fact that everyone else seems to. The temptation will always be to invent some kind of rationalisation for one's belief. And given the demand for such rationalisations, it seems likely that it will be a matter of common belief not only, say, that Einstein is a genius but why he is. Most of us can utter the words 'special theory of relativity' and 'e equals mc squared' even if we don't really know what the words mean.

For this kind of reason, it may be quite difficult for individuals to know precisely how big p is. A necessary condition for me to follow the crowd in my beliefs as to A's fame-worthiness is that I believe p to be above some important threshold value. But that is true for all indirect observers, so once again I have reason to follow the crowd. If a critical mass of indirect observers believe that p lies above the required threshold, then I may have good reason myself to adopt the prevailing belief.

Belief in A's fame-worthiness has the character of a coordination game of the kind illustrated by the matrix depicted as Table 8.2. In that matrix, each clearly has an incentive to believe that A is fame-worthy—believe that a— if more or less everyone else does. And each has an incentive to believe the opposite if others happen to change their minds. Accordingly, the equilibrium in community belief has the same properties as a coordination equilibrium. The structure of belief has something of the same quality as decisions as to which side of the road one will drive on, or what language you will have your children learn, or what system of weights and measures you will adopt. That is, the prevailing belief is stable to small perturbations, but sensitive to large ones. I have reason to continue to believe while most others do; but reason to relinquish that belief as soon as a critical mass of others do so. Perhaps the small proportion of direct observers will not change their beliefs; but I will usually have no way of knowing that fact. I will simply observe that most people, many of whom speak with apparently great authority on relevant subjects, have changed their beliefs and this fact will give me reason to change my beliefs as well. And so for all other indirect observers.[4]

---

[4] Although the beliefs that support fame are rather like those that support fads and fashions, it would not be quite right to think of fame in such terms. With mere fashion, there is a presumption that the prevailing vogue will change; and indeed there are likely to be systematic forces in play that secure that change. Fame is more stable than fashion, in that sense. On the other hand, it is clear that fame can be vulnerable to perturbations that are large enough. History is replete with examples of persons who enjoy the status of 'once famous'.

Table 8.2. *Interdependencies of belief*

	Others believe *a*	Others believe not-*a*
Believe *a*	10	0
Believe not-*a*	0	10

Now this belief structure has implications for performance incentives. The capital nature that fame shares with reputation means that fame will not be very sensitive to further performance, once it is established. Each additional action becomes only one among a number of actions on which fame is based. And each additional action will add to your esteem only if it is superior to the average of your previous actions—only, that is, if it is above-average for you. Your previous performance becomes in that way a relevant standard for additions to reputation. Even if you generate additional esteem in the moment of action because your performance is appropriately better than the average of all others, you stand to lose overall esteem as observers come to agree that you are not the performer you once were!

If you are someone famous, the proportion of direct observers of any performance will be but a fraction of the total of the people who esteem you. So you can hardly expect to add much to your esteem by an additional performance. On the other hand, if some of those present announce, with an appropriate air of regret, that you are not the performer you once were, that belief has a chance of becoming part of the prevailing belief structure. This chance is a small one to be sure. The direct observers of your performance are a small fraction of the total set of those who believe you to be fame-worthy. On the other hand, if such an adverse rumour were to get around, there is only the tide of popular opinion to hold the belief structure in place—and that tide can turn. Moreover, the downside cost to you in esteem terms is quite spectacular. Additional performance, then, has little prospect of significant upside gain, but some prospect of significant downside loss. The esteem incentive here then favours inaction rather than action. If the domain in which your esteem has been won is a discretionary one, one that you can opt out of if you choose, then opting out seems like a good strategy. And even if the domain is a non-discretionary one, you might nevertheless seek to live a life of obscurity far from the gaze of possible observers. The object should be to reveal your qualities in the relevant domain of fame as rarely and with as small an audience as possible. In short, the famous have every reason to rest on their laurels.

It is, for example, not entirely unknown for sportsmen, singers, performing artists of all kinds, to retire at or near the height of their powers. Or for academics who showed enormous early promise and published major pieces in early career simply to cease to publish. Or to publish much less and only pieces of a less ambitious kind. Better to quit than to stay on, deteriorating until you become one of those slightly sad figures of whom the best that can be said is that they were great in their prime. Early death may, on this reading, be an asset in the acquisition of fame: it ensures that the performer exit before the performance has an opportunity to decline.

There are three effects that are worth distinguishing here and we label them:

- the capital effect;
- the risk effect; and
- the laurels effect.

The 'capital effect' refers to the fact that the beliefs supporting fame have a durable quality. Such beliefs are unlikely to be sensitive to further observation of performances, so the incentive for further effort is diminished: the esteem benefit from further outstanding performances is likely to be even smaller, by virtue of the stability of beliefs about fame-worthiness. The 'risk effect' refers to the downside prospect of one's own actions upsetting the fame that one currently enjoys. If one's possibly bad performance were to affect popular beliefs negatively, the loss from performance stands to cost more in esteem terms than any gain from good performance. This looks like a bad bet. Why put one's esteem at risk when the possible gain is small and the possible downside loss is very large? The 'laurels effect' refers to the diminished demand for esteem as one becomes more highly supplied with it. One who is already famous has less reason to pursue esteem than one who aspires to be famous, just because the demand for esteem is like all other valued objects, subject to diminishing marginal utility. In the fame case, all three effects are potentially operative. And all serve to inhibit esteem incentives in the performance domain.

The situation with infamy is a little different. Clearly, in the infamy case, there is no risk of things getting worse—no risk of destroying a great reputation. And there is no diminishing marginal utility of esteem kicking in to discourage action. On the contrary, the infamous person has every *incentive* to rehabilitate himself in the eyes of the world. But there is one feature that is common between infamy and fame. And that is the relative impotence of the actor to do very much to alter the state of affairs even if she wanted to. The famous do not want to. The infamous *do* want to. But because their infamy has taken on a life of its own, largely detached from the actor's performance and from direct observation of it, there is little the infamous can do.

In the infamy case, then, only the capital effect is operative. In that sense, fame undermines esteem-related incentives more than does infamy. But the capital effect may be so powerful on its own that incentives for the infamous to try to redeem themselves in the eyes of the public are considerably muted. Moreover, unlike fame, infamy may well undermine self-confidence in one's capacity to perform in a manner that would change observers' perceptions. Fame might give self-confidence; infamy seems unlikely to do so. The point here is that it is the prospect of fame and infamy that is to be properly identified as 'the spur'—whether to the noblest minds or otherwise. The realisation of fame (or infamy) serves on the contrary to dull the impulse to honourable action.

3   PUBLICITY POLICY

As we have made clear, one motive for writing this book is an interest in the normative implications of esteem-seeking. This normative aspect has a number of dimensions. In the first place, we want to draw attention to the economy of esteem so that policymakers will not witlessly inhibit or destroy its operation. In the second, we want to emphasise the desire for esteem as a possible resource in institutional design. And at the more direct policy level, we want to know how the forces of esteem might be mobilised more effectively in cases where its effects are desirable, and obversely how those forces might be suppressed in any cases where the effects are malign.

In this latter policy connection, publicity presents itself as a natural policy instrument. It operates to augment esteem incentives without any apparent incidental effects that might interfere with the independent operation of the esteem economy. In this chapter, therefore, we need to say something about publicity policy in relation to esteem.

Policies designed to increase publicity can take a variety of forms, and can operate in a very wide range of contexts. There can, for example, be provisions against secrecy. Freedom of information legislation exemplifies. So do requirements that various kinds of meetings be open; or requirements that decisions, and perhaps the reasons for them, be promulgated in particular forums and in appropriate forms. We can also imagine the collective provision of information. An academic department might require its staff to publish annually a list of their publications appearing in that year. Hospitals might be required to publish survival rates for various categories of their patients. Or the government may itself collect and publish information of various kinds: lists of persons convicted of drunk-driving; or lists of persons that did not vote; or statistics about performance in various domains. Corporations may give medals for good workers. Wine-growers associations may give prizes for best wines—or have a worst-wine-of-the-year award that they independently publicise.[5]

The various dimensions of these possibilities and the range of contexts in which they might be applied are bewilderingly extensive, and we do not here intend to try to cover much of that ground. Our strategy instead is just to focus on one particular aspect: that of where in the spectrum of performances esteem incentives should be focused.

The point of departure here is that publicity is valuable because observer attention is a scarce resource in limited supply. This scarcity property means that directing attention to one aspect of performance virtually always implies drawing attention away from another. Think of publicity as a spotlight in a field of dusky grey. The operation of that spotlight serves to isolate various parts of the total terrain: the very act of making some parts more salient renders other parts more difficult to discern. Where should the spotlight be focused? And given that operation of the spotlight is independently costly, how much spotlighting should we do?

Consider yet another academic example. Suppose we are to evaluate the research performance of academics within a particular university or across a university system—perhaps academics generally or those within a particular field. Here are three different pieces of information we might make public:

- The names of the academics who have failed to meet certain base criteria (e.g. published an article in a refereed journal or a book with a reputable publisher in the last three years);
- The names of those academics who achieved eminence (e.g. have annual citation levels in the top 5 per cent within their field worldwide);
- The names of those academics who have performed at the average level—however exactly measured.

The different measures of performance isolated in this academic example correspond directly to the focus of attention across the distribution of performers. The question posed by the choice among them is this: if we are to highlight the performance of agents in a particular range which range should we choose? It seems self-evident that there is not much point in focusing attention on the average performer. As our earlier discussions have indicated, the average or

---

[5] In an earlier piece that turned out to be somewhat provocative we argued the case for open voting in idealised democratic settings—following, as we discovered in the process of writing, the views of the later Mill (Brennan and Pettit 1990). The argument there is one based on the role of publicity in mobilising the discipline of esteem and it is discussed briefly in Chapter 15.

normal range is one in which there is unlikely to be much esteem on offer at the margin. Expanding the effective audience in this range will have a negligible effect on esteem-based incentives, because such incentives are weak in that range anyway.[6]

We do better to focus attention towards the extremes of the distribution—either by honours for the best, or badges of shame for the worst. There is an issue here as to whether there should be a single prize or prizes for first, second, and third or equal prizes for the top n, where n is a small fraction of the total. Or obversely, graduated penalties at the lower end. There is analysis to be pursued on this question, but we do not pursue that aspect further here.[7] Our concern is rather with the issue of whether the focus of publicity should be on performances at the top or bottom of the distribution.

We shall denote publicity policies that focus attention on the lower end as dunce-cap policies; and those that focus on the upper end as honour-roll policies. Clearly, the dunce cap focuses incentives on those who perform at the bottom end. Individuals strive to avoid the ignominy of being identified as the dunce, the last in the race (provided that that performance is indeed shameful). But for those who do not expect to be in the bottom range, pressure is diminished. In a world where being not the worst is all that matters, there is no recognition for being best and so little incentive to try and be the best. Alternatively, if the policy is an honour-roll one, if all attention is focused on top performers, the pressure is taken off those who might be judged weakest, or indeed even those judged merely mediocre. Only those who might reasonably aspire to the prize(s) are subject to the augmented publicity effects: others have the pressure of esteem reduced.

Can we say anything systematic about whether dunce or honour-roll strategy is to be preferred? In fact, there are a number of considerations that weigh here. We shall direct attention to five, which we denote:

- the goal specification aspect;
- the incentive aspect;
- the distribution aspect;
- the standards aspect; and
- the utility aspect.

---

[6] Providing information that shows that performances in this middle range are higher than generally thought may well have an effect on standards, and hence on performance incentives. This is a complication we take up in the ensuing chapter.

[7] Whether the relevant performers are likely to be risk-loving or risk averse seems likely to be relevant. See the related, though brief, discussion in Chapter 6.

The goal specification aspect

In Chapter 6, we drew a distinction between best-shot and weakest-link policy situations. We used that distinction to make a point about policy design—a point that is as simple as it is often overlooked—that a first step is to seek clarity about what exactly the policy goal is. The best-shot/weakest-link distinction is especially useful in pointing up issues in publicity policy, and especially in relation to the choice between dunce-cap and honour-roll policies. So let us return briefly to that distinction.

Let the set of individual performances of X be denoted:

$$X_1, X_2, X_3, \ldots, X_n$$

Then as before we can isolate best-shot, weakest-link, and normal cases, according as the policy objective is associated with:

$\max \{Xi\} - $ —the best-shot case;

$\min \{Xi\} - $ —the weakest-link case;

$X_1 + \ldots + X_n$ the normal case.

There are clearly many other possibilities that one might plausibly construct, but we shall just focus here on simple cases.

Clearly, the precise goal will influence where the focus of publicity should lie. There is little point in exposing the inadequacies of the worst performers if the primary performance incentive should be located at the upper end (as it should be in best-shot cases). Obversely, if the problem to be guarded against is say police corruption, medals for police bravery will not direct attention (or esteem incentives) at the appropriate point in the distribution of performances. There is a good deal more to be said on this general issue. It is remarkable how often policy discussions will specify the general domain of policy concern—police issues, or academic performance, or defence capacity—with a very loose specification of the precise aspect of the distribution of individual performances that is relevant. In some cases, to be sure, this is not an important issue. Sometimes it is crucial.

The incentive aspect

Once the goal is specified, we will want to locate the publicity at the appropriate point. There are several considerations in play here. In best-shot and weakest-link cases, the goal specification aspect will almost certainly be decisive. But let us suppose that the case at hand is a standard one where what we want to do is just to get the biggest impact *in toto*. As we noted earlier, performers in the normal range will be relatively impervious to publicity effects; so it will not pay to focus publicity there, however large the numbers in that range. Because publicity incentives are stronger at the extremes of the distribution, we will still have a choice between dunce-cap and honour-roll approaches. Are there any general presumptions that weigh in making this choice?

Note that, other things equal, esteem means more to those who have less of it. That is a result of the diminishing marginal utility property of all goods, which property we take to apply no less to esteem than to other things. So other things being equal, agents will work harder to avoid disesteem than to gain positive esteem: shame is the stronger force for anyone who cares about esteem.

Other things are not necessarily equal, of course. Perhaps not everyone has the same demand curve for esteem. Suppose there are some who do not care about the esteem of others at all. We might expect that such persons will be disproportionately represented at the bottom end of the performance spectrum, because these persons have no esteem incentive to spur them on. Equally, such persons will be relatively impervious to the dunce-cap possibility. Provided that there are any persons who care deeply about esteem, there will always be competition to receive a prize; whereas if there are some who care little for esteem there may be no competition to avoid being at the bottom. If everyone has a more or less equal desire for esteem—if that desire is a more or less uniform feature of the human species, as Adam Smith supposes—then the diminishing marginal utility property will predominate and the presumption in favour of the dunce-cap stands. But if there is considerable variance among agents as to the extent to which they desire esteem, then that consideration would argue in favour of an honour-roll focus.

The distribution aspect

Clearly, when one is concerned with aggregate response, much will depend on the precise distribution of performances. If there is a larger number of actors at or near the top end of the distribution than near the bottom, it would be better *ceteris paribus* to focus attention (and reward) at the top. A suitable measure of the relevant magnitude might be the proportion of the total population of actors who fall within a given (not too large) neighbourhood of the top, and of the bottom. *Ceteris paribus* one should choose the top or the bottom—honour-roll or dunce-cap—according to which has the larger such measure.

The standards aspect

Strategies with respect to publicity are likely to have a systematic effect on perceptions of others' performances and hence on standards. A dunce-cap strategy serves to make lower performances salient, and hence reduce standards against which everyone is evaluated. Most people look tolerable compared to the worst. In that way, the dunce-cap strategy tends to lead to lower effort, and lower performance across the range. By contrast, the honour-roll strategy makes the best performances salient—that strategy tends to elevate standards, and to make everyone have to work a little bit harder to keep up. We shall take up the connection between standards and publicity in greater detail in the next chapter. It seems intuitively clear however that drawing special attention to poor performance is likely to lower perceived standards and drawing attention to excellent performance to raise them. On the face of things at least, the standards aspect favours an honour-roll over a dunce-cap publicity strategy.

The utility aspect

The primary object of normative concern throughout this discussion is to secure more of the highly valued X-performance. We are not primarily concerned with just making the performers feel good. As we have already noted in Chapter 5, the effect of esteem is to make all performers work harder in X-performance than, as performers, they would collectively like. In that context, we have already argued that such considerations are by no means decisive. The direct effects on performers' utility are of minor normative significance. But that fact does not make them irrelevant. And it is these secondary effects that the utility aspect is designed to capture. There are two dimensions here. The first picks up on the obvious fact that when a prize is awarded the recipient is made to feel good. By contrast, when the dunce-cap is assigned, the recipient is made to feel miserable. This consideration is, other things equal, a count against the dunce-cap. The second dimension appeals to a presumption, which we shall explore in greater detail in Chapter 11, that observers prefer to witness attractive rather than repulsive performances. It is pleasant to witness an outstanding or admirable performance; it is unpleasant to witness a repulsive or shameful one. So if we are going to increase the number of observers of some performance or another, there is something to be said for choosing a performance that will be attractive to observers.[8]

The bottom line?

Putting these various aspects together, what is the final verdict over the issue of dunce-caps or honour-rolls? As we see it, much of the issue is likely to be decided by the proper goal specification. If weakest-link or best-shot categorisation applies, that is likely to settle the issue in favour of dunce-cap or honour-roll publicity respectively. But if it is aggregate X-performance that is the object of policy, then we think that the balance of considerations favours the honour-roll strategy.

Obviously, the discussion here has been conducted at a considerable level of abstraction. It would clearly be useful to take some specific cases—that of courage, or trustworthiness, or cleanliness—and attempt to characterise these valued dispositions as mainly best-shot or weakest-link or whatever. We might then be able plausibly to explain why we observe mainly honours in the academic cases, and both honours and dunce-caps in the military cases (medals and dishonourable discharges are both in play), and mainly shaming activities in the cleanliness case. On the basis of more detailed argument, we might be able to devise suggestions as to more finely tuned publicity policies to fit these and other specific cases. But that sort of detailed work lies some distance downstream. Our chief object here has been instead to illustrate the sorts of issues that seem likely to bear in such cases, once the role of publicity in the economy of esteem is more generally understood.

CONCLUSION

Publicity, understood as audience size, is the fuel of the economy of esteem. As external audience size grows from zero to one to larger and larger numbers, both the quality and the intensity of esteem-related incentives change. Other things equal, and specifically for given audience quality (an aspect that we shall take up in Chapter 11), the more extensive the publicity, the more intense the esteem-based effects.

---

[8] There may be exceptions. Schadenfreude is not, after all, exactly unknown. And envy could lead me to prefer to witness performances that are not better than my own. Or, as a performer, I might just prefer to be relieved of pressure to increase my own performance.

Our object in this chapter has been to explore the implications of increased publicity. In Section 1 we focused on the relation between performance incentives and increased publicity at different points in the spectrum of performances. At low levels of publicity, esteem incentives seem likely to be increased proportionately; but at very high levels of publicity, esteem incentives seem to be affected mainly at the extremes of the performance distribution.

In Section 2 we turned to an analysis of reputation and fame, including infamy. Reputation and fame/infamy become possible once an agent can be reidentified, having a recognizable name or at least face. But reidentifiability makes it possible to mobilise two social factors: testimony and common belief. The esteem given to someone reidentifiable, then, may be formed with or without essential reliance on testimony, and with or without its being a matter of common belief. Where there is common belief, fame and infamy materialise. And the limiting case of fame and infamy is where someone is esteemed as a matter of common belief but not esteemed by anyone directly: he or she will be esteemed by each because each believes that everyone else esteems them.

Fame greatly increases the effective audience of the acts that produce fame. So fame in prospect enormously magnifies esteem-related incentives. But fame once achieved can seriously inhibit incentives for further action. The famous can rest on their laurels. And the infamous may find that, however hard they try, their bad reputations are relatively impervious to estimable action. In this sense, the connection between fame/infamy and esteem-related incentives is somewhat ambiguous; and towards the end of Section 2, we explored that ambiguity.

Section 3 of the chapter dealt with publicity policy. Policy for increasing publicity—either by inhibiting secrecy (i.e. increasing the likelihood of observation) or by providing information/exposure on a subsidised basis—is one of the readiest means by which the economy of esteem can be supported by explicitly collective interventions. Equally, policies that support secrecy or require privacy or otherwise inhibit the extent of exposure are a primary means for undermining esteem-related incentives. In our discussion of publicity policy, we were concerned in particular with the question of where the light of publicity might best be focused—on the kind of information about performers that might best be provided to the community of observers. This issue is by no means the only one that arises in relation to publicity but it enables us to deal with a range of questions that seem to us to be important from a policy viewpoint. We concentrated on this particular issue because it enables us to illustrate the kind of analysis that should be applicable to all aspects of publicity policy.

In dealing with this issue of where best to focus publicity, we distinguished between honour-roll and dunce-cap policies and drew attention to several considerations that are relevant in the choice between them:

- Goal specification considerations—that is, whether policy itself is directly concerned with performance at one or other end of the performance spectrum;
- Incentive considerations, including specifically the thought that fear of shame might be a stronger incentive than desire for positive esteem;
- Distribution considerations—that is, where the bulk of performances happens to lie;
- The effect of emphasising high as against low performance on perceived standards;
- The utility aspect—that is, the effect on both performers and observers of publicising poor or high performances.

We are inclined to think that the balance of such considerations establishes a weak *ceteris paribus* presumption in favour of honour-roll strategies; but we concede that that balance is likely to be highly sensitive to the details of specific cases.

9

Publicity and Accepted Standards

A significant feature of the basic model of the esteem economy laid out in Chapters 5 and 6 is the relationship between the behavioural responses that the desire for esteem produces and the standards on the basis of which esteem is supplied. In those chapters, we argued that these standards are established as some weighted average of ideal performance and average performance, establishing thereby an interdependence between equilibrium standards and the level of performance. The alternative formulation developed in Chapter 7 was characterised by a similar interdependence between esteem incentives and prevailing practice. In all these formulations, we took it that the relevant standards could be regarded as common knowledge within the community of actors. In this chapter, we want to modify that assumption.

Part of the object here is to provide scope for standards to change in response to publicity—publicity both in relation to specific performances, and more generally in relation to prevailing practices. We seek to create this scope in Section 1. But examining the effect of (credible) information about prevailing practices on the level of performance serves an incidental function: it provides us with an independent test of some of our general claims about the positive relation between standards and performance. We explore the relevant evidence in Section 2.

In Section 3, we examine the provision of information about standards as an independent strategy in the economy of esteem. If, as we believe, and as the evidence we cite seems to suggest, information about prevailing practices does influence behaviour, then provision of such information becomes a way of intervening in the economy of esteem. That scope for intervention, however, invites questions as to the incentives of those who provide the information—questions that all participants in the esteem economy are likely to ask. Information about standards can only have behavioural consequences if it is believed. And whether and to what extent it is believed depends on the sources from which it comes and the manifest incentives of the author(s). One possibility of some interest in this connection is that false perceptions as to prevailing practice may sustain higher performance in the estimable domain than would true perceptions. If so, and if higher performance is desirable, there is a case to be made for false beliefs. This fact invites discussion of issues related to public hypocrisy. We explore the same issues in a slightly different way in Section 4 under the rubric of the whistle-blower's dilemma.

1   HOW RELIABLE IS COMMON BELIEF?

The operation of the economy of esteem depends on a structure of shared belief across the community of actors—beliefs about what performances are esteemed; how much esteem attaches to different activities; and about what prevailing practices in relation to these esteemed activities are. To this point, we have taken it that all those beliefs arise as common knowledge within the community. Everybody believes the relevant facts; believes that everybody believes them; believes that everybody believes that everybody believes them; and so on.

But this is implausible. Some of the relevant facts are obscure. It is, for example, one thing to argue that ideal performance in a particular domain is a matter of common belief and, other things being equal, common knowledge. It is another thing entirely to argue that average performance is common knowledge. And without that knowledge, the prevailing standard in that domain must be a matter of some doubt. It is, for example, plausible to think that benevolence is a disposition that is positively esteemed, and plausible to think that everyone knows that this is so. But how are actors expected to know how well others on average actually perform on the benevolence scale? Each will have individual observations of the conduct of others, but these observations will in each case necessarily represent a small sample of the total. Perhaps, on average, the resultant perception errors could be expected to cancel each other out. However, even the recognition of such perception errors has implications. One element, for example, in our argument for the three-range model of the estimable domain (in Chapter 6) over the two–range version (in Chapter 5) depended on just such perception errors. More particularly, public information about the practices of others can play an independent role in shaping perceptions about prevailing standards and hence in influencing actual behaviour.

Furthermore, although it may be clear enough that particular activities are estimable, it may not be entirely clear just how estimable they are. Benevolence may be esteemed—but only mildly so. Perhaps in some eyes, benevolence is a sign of weakness and induces a mild contempt. When someone cooperates in a prisoners' dilemma setting, she may be regarded with approbation for defying her individual interests and acting in the common good. Or she may be identified as a sucker who doesn't possess the wit to recognise the setting she is in. Courage may be esteemed much more than benevolence—and more than many people think. Or much less. In short, the observers' values on which esteem is based are by no means invariably transparent. And this fact matters. For example, in making the relevant behavioural trade-offs between acts of generosity and courage, say, and/or in deciding which dispositions to cultivate (and hence which dispositions to leave to their own devices), the idealised rational esteem-seeker will need to know the relative strength of observers' values in these various domains. That information will not necessarily be freely available.

Quite apart from such natural uncertainty, as we might label it, there are systematic factors at work that may lead to biased estimates of what prevailing practice actually is. For one thing, there are asymmetries in the way in which poor performers and good performers respond to the possibility of observation—a matter we shall explore in some detail in the next chapter. A poor performer tends to shun the light—to hide his poor performance. He minimises the probability of being observed and/or the size of the audience to which he is likely to be subject. A good performer, by contrast, rather relishes the light. Of course, to pursue that light unashamedly may be a dubious strategy: if you always seek attention, as we saw in Chapter 2, you might be judged to be just showing off and that seems likely to cost you some esteem. Nevertheless, you will not be at all averse to having the light fall upon you. You will be in favour of general arrangements that increase the probability for everyone that their activities will be observed and/or widely publicised. And you will certainly not expend resources in attempting to keep your performance invisible, at least not unless you are unusually modest. For these reasons, the performances that are observed will tend to be a biased sample of the actual performances—with the bias tending to indicate higher average performance than actually prevails.

At the same time, the fact that this upward bias exists is itself likely to be common knowledge. So when cases of bad performance are discovered, they may well be afforded much more attention than cases of good performance. Instances of corruption among politicians, for example, might be rather more noteworthy than instances of non-corruption. Each such instance is taken to be the mere tip of the iceberg, precisely because the corrupt have reason to remain under water. Thus, cases of observed corruption can assume a special salience. They tend to be seen as evidence for a more widespread phenomenon. And it might easily come to be widely believed that corruption is the rule rather than the exception. Equally, in the tax evasion context, it may be that only the most egregious cases get reported. So the instance in which an extremely wealthy person is found to pay negligible taxes becomes newsworthy—whereas the large number of cases in which people of all kinds are totally compliant simply escapes notice. In this way, popular perceptions as to the extent of tax evasion, especially by the very rich, might come to be distorted. The truth of the matter is that, in most such cases, we simply do not know the truth of the matter. We don't know what prevailing standards actually are.

So the assumption that standards are common knowledge needs to be revised. Neither common practice nor the strength of observers, underlying values is totally transparent, and common perceptions may well be wrong. Further, because it is the actors' perceptions of the standard that drive behaviour, information about what prevailing practice in the relevant domain actually is, stands to influence that behaviour. New information about prevailing practice, if believed, will have a predictable effect on esteem incentives and therefore on performance, similar to that of the arrival in town of the new tennis player in the comparative static analysis presented in Chapter 5. New information about prevailing ideals or values will have a similar effect.

2 PERCEPTIONS AND PERFORMANCE

The foregoing observations offer us a means of testing our general claim about the positive relation between standards and performance. This claim played an important role in the analysis in Chapters 5–7.

Consider the core diagram laid out in Chapter 5. Suppose that, as in the simplest model, standards are given by average performance, but that perceptions of average performance differ from the true average—specifically, that the perceived average performance, denoted $P(X)$, is γX. Let us suppose that γ is 80 per cent, so that the perceived average performance is 20 per cent less than the actual. In Figure 9.1, we replicate Figure 5.4, except that the relation between performance and perceived standards is given by the line OM which lies below the true standards line OS, as shown. The average performer's reaction curve is given by BC. Because esteem incentives are driven by perceived rather than true standards, the resultant equilibrium will be at Q^*, with performance level at X^* and perceived standard of M^*. If however the misperception were corrected, so that γ took a value of 1, then the equilibrium would shift to T^*, with a higher level of performance at Z^* and standards based on a true assessment of average performance at S^*. An account of the move to the new equilibrium would involve, first the correction of the misperception, so that the perceived standard at Q^* would become S' (which equals actual performance, X^*, as required). In the face of this higher perceived standard, esteem assigned

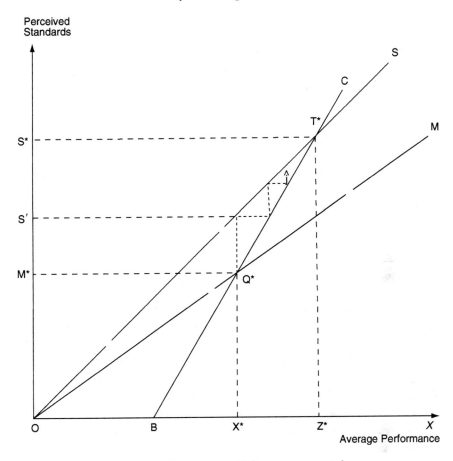

Figure 9.1. *Misperception of failing practice corrected.*

at current performance levels will decline and so actual performances will increase in pursuit of esteem. So average performance, and hence standards, will increase until finally the process comes to rest at T^*. Provided only that the individual reaction curve BC has the given shape, upward-sloping from some positive level of X-performance and with a slope greater than unity, then an increase in the value of the γ parameter will be associated with an increase in the equilibrium value of average X-performance.

In the alternative formulation analysed in Chapter 7, we examined explicitly the effect of changed perceptions of actual compliance levels. We showed there that an increase in the perceived level of compliance leads to an increase in equilibrium compliance if the high-compliance, disesteem equilibrium prevails—and to a reduction in equilibrium compliance if the low-compliance, positive esteem equilibrium prevails; see Figure 7.6 and surrounding discussion. In the discussion that follows, we assume that the high-compliance equilibrium is the one that prevails. That assumption seems consistent with the examples we use, but the lack of complete generality should be noted.

In short, then, information that changes common beliefs about performance levels will be positively related to actual performance. If actors come to believe in common that average performance is higher than they previously believed— if the perceived average rises—then their own performances will increase. If actors come to believe in common that average performance is less than they previously believed, then their own performance will decline. At the intuitive level, the postulated relation seems plausible enough. People will often offer as a rationalisation of their own dubious activities the claim that everyone else does it. If it becomes evident to all that everyone does not do it, then that rationalisation is clearly weakened.

The evidence on this matter seems encouraging. In the tax compliance case, for example, there seems to be some evidence of a positive relation between one's own non-compliance and the perceived non-compliance of others. (Song and Yarbrough 1978; Kaplan and Reckers 1985; De Juan, Lasheras, et al. 1994; Bosco and Mittone 1997). In laboratory experiments, Wenzel (2001) investigates subjects' attitudes to tax evasion and makes information about those attitudes available to subjects, with an eye to effects on compliant behaviour. His hypotheses were: first, that respondents would exhibit more intense support for a morality of tax compliance than they believe to be held by others; and second, that revealing the facts about higher ideals or values actually held by others—and so about the higher actual standards relevant—would lead to increased preparedness to comply. His experiments so far seem to indicate support for both hypotheses.

Similar results emerge in work on alcohol consumption by students (Prentice and Miller 1993; Schroeder and Prentice 1998). Students are, apparently, more disgusted by drunkenness than students commonly believe. And once this fact is made public among the student body, there tends to be reduced drunkenness.

The tax and alcohol cases are instances of a phenomenon that has come to be known as pluralistic ignorance (Miller and Prentice 1994). Each member of a plurality holds a certain attitude; each believes that all others hold a contrary attitude; that latter belief plays an important role in determining the behaviour of each; and that behavioural pattern appears to give observational evidence of the contrary attitude ascribed. The esteem perspective makes good sense of how one's behaviour may be shaped by beliefs about the attitudes of others. And it also suggests why false beliefs about others' values may be robust: this, because questioning prevailing values can itself be a source of disesteem. It would take us a little far from our main purpose to examine pluralistic ignorance in any further detail here; but some of the relevant issues appear in a different guise in what follows. Our interest here is just in the behavioural nexus between beliefs about prevailing standards and actual behaviour. Is it the case that when beliefs about prevailing practice are altered actual behaviour tends to change in the same direction as perceived prevailing practice does? The evidence developed in relation to pluralistic ignorance seems generally to support that proposition.

A connected example, professionally closer to home, involves an anxiety about the use of public choice methods in the study of political processes. The charge is that the ascription of simple wealth-maximising behaviour to all political agents can easily become a self-fulfilling prophecy. Steven Kelman (1987: 87) makes the point eloquently:

Cynical descriptive conclusions about behavior in government threaten to undermine the norm prescribing public spirit. The writings of journalists—and even the writings of professors—can decrease public spirit simply by describing what they claim to be its absence. Cynics are therefore in the business of making prophecies that threaten to become self-fulfilling. If the norm of public spirit dies, our society would look bleaker and our lives as individuals would be more impoverished. That is the tragedy of public choice.

The general claim that Kelman makes here is that beliefs about the behaviour of politicians and others in public life, promulgated by putatively irresponsible academics (among others), can influence the behaviour those commentators purport to describe. Good conduct is sustained in part by the belief that others act properly and expect that others will act properly. Our models of the economy of esteem suggest why that will be so.[1]

3   INFORMATION ABOUT STANDARDS AND THE INCENTIVES OF INFORMATION-PROVIDERS

Recognition of the behavioural impact of information about standards—either about underlying values or about prevailing practices—can create incentives for relevant players in the economy of esteem to provide information about

---

[1] One can, of course, accept this general proposition about the relation between such beliefs and behaviour, as we do, without necessarily thinking that public choice academics have much influence, or that academics and journalists should write anything other than the truth as they see it (see also Brennan and Buchanan 1988).

those values and practices. The University College Warden, who has to manage the conduct of a couple of hundred unruly undergraduates, will be delighted to find that a significant majority of students find drunkenness disgusting—or that widely reported stories of drunkenness being a way of life among undergraduates are just false. The Warden will have good reason to do a little empirical work on his own patch, and promulgate the findings widely if they come in as he hopes. Equally, if preliminary research indicates that taxpayers are on average much more compliant with the tax system than popular mythology makes out, the tax authority will want to make those findings public and will want to pursue further research along such lines. Once it becomes common knowledge that standards in the tax-compliance arena are higher than previously thought, the level of compliance can be predicted to increase still further.[2] And similar consequences follow, if the information that comes available indicates that attitudes to non-compliance are rather more negative than popular prejudice has it.

Lack of information concerning prevailing ideals and practices can, of course, cut both ways. Sometimes (as seems to be true in the tax case) general disesteem for non-compliance will be more intense and the general practice more law-abiding than common beliefs about ideals and practices would indicate. There can, however, be no general guarantee that perceived standards will always lie below the true ones. Suppose, for example, that the tax authority discovers that evasion/avoidance in some particular area is much more extensive than is commonly supposed. Then far from having an incentive to go public, this will be an item of news that the tax authority might well choose to withhold. For, once it becomes common knowledge that avoidance is more extensive than people believed, actual compliance may be expected to decline.[3]

There is an important general lesson here. The mirror image of the incentive to correct widespread misapprehensions is the incentive to suppress uncongenial information; and this incentive extends to supplying information that exaggerates the extent of compliance. Indeed, if the tax authority has an institutional interest in maximising compliant behaviour, it has a corresponding incentive to promulgate information about high compliance levels and general

---

[2] At least this is so if the tax-compliance equilibrium is one where there is disesteem for non-compliance rather than esteem for compliance. As we showed in Chapter 7, compliance response to an increased perception of compliance will reduce compliance if we are in a positive-esteem equilibrium.

[3] Again, the possibility of a positive-esteem equilibrium is a complication. If in this low-compliance case, compliance is a source of positive esteem, then revealing that compliance is lower than people take it to be will tend to raise the esteem incentive. However, this complication does not vitiate the general claim that incentives to reveal information are influenced by the effects that information is predicted to have.

taxpayer indignation about non-compliance, whether that information is true or not. And taxpayers can come to recognise these incentives, so that even where the tax authority provides accurate information, it may not be believed. There is, then, a problem of credibility that confronts the tax authority and other analogous bodies (like professional bodies, which have an interest in the reputation of their profession).[4]

In the tax authority and analogous cases, it seems that one means of increasing credibility is to entrust the research activity and its promulgation to some arm's-length independent body. The credibility will be a direct function of the independence of the latter body. So, for example, funding a university department to do the work will make for more credibility than doing the research in-house. And endowing the university department with funds to conduct this work over a long future will be more credible than commissioning research on an annual basis, with the possibility of withdrawal of funds should the arrangement not work out. It is worth emphasising that the strategy of outsourcing the research here involves two elements. One is that the university department has little interest per se in the size of tax revenues or the extent of compliance. The other is that the university department's stake in maintaining its reputation for the integrity of the research it produces is independently valuable to the department. The success of the university researchers depends on their professional esteem and that esteem will be prejudiced if they are seen to be cooking the results. In other words, the fact that the university has an especially high esteem stake in the integrity of their research is part of the reason for the university's credibility. And this is in turn part of the reason why the tax authority can use the university to convey credible signals more or less on the tax authority's behalf. In other words, esteem plays a role here at a level other than that of substantive tax compliance.

The example of the tax authority extends to cover a wide range of organisations all of which have an incentive to provide information about prevailing practices, with an eye to the effect that such information will have on standards of conduct and thereby on performance. In some cases, as with professional bodies or universities, there is an additional consideration—namely, the esteem in which the profession or university itself is held. So the university has an

---

[4] This credibility issue is one that has attracted some attention among game theorists in a variety of settings, and is an area where the existing economic theory of reputation is of considerable relevance to the economy of esteem. There is a variety of models that may be of relevance here—the so-called 'cheap-talk' models and more general signalling game settings. There is a considerable literature in this area, of some degree of technical complexity. Standard references include Selten (1978); Kreps & Wilson (1982); Milgrom and Roberts (1982); and Vickers (1986).

incentive to play up the quality of the research its academics produce, both because that is good for the reputation of the university and because it tends to raise the perceived standards and hence performance within. The Firefighters' Association has an incentive to promote the courage and expertise of firefighters, both because that adds to the esteem of all their constituency externally and because it raises perceived standards within.

However, in lots of cases where standards are relevant, there is no single body which has special access to information about standards, or which might be thought to exercise special responsibility in collecting or providing such information. There will simply be individual citizens, whose moral (and esteem) concerns may include not just conduct in relation to the prevailing standards but also promulgation of information about compliance with those standards. Common beliefs about ideals and practices in such cases will simply emerge from the interactions among individual agents and will depend not only on what those individuals observe but also on which of their observations they report. For those individuals, sustaining proper standards will seem a proper moral object. If honesty, courage, and generosity are to be esteemed, they are also worthy of promotion. One way of promoting the value in question is via one's own performance and so far, we have focused entirely on that aspect and the esteem arising in relation to that performance. But promotion of the activity includes promotion of relevant standards, and one means of such promotion will be talking up standards. Such 'talking up' might include, for example, a refusal to promulgate stories of notable lapses. It might involve maintaining a resolute focus on the heroic end of the performance spectrum in what one reports. It might include clarifying and promoting relevant public ideals. All of these are activities consistent with the promotion of better performance in the associated domain. Moreover, such activities work to support higher performance overall even if the performance of the individual promoter falls well short of the ideal—and even of the average. That is, someone whose own performance in the domain of courage, say, is far from lustrous may well talk up the virtues of courage to his fellows; and, other things being equal, that person is arguably more estimable for doing so.

Any such divergence between conduct in relation to promotion of relevant standards and conduct in the arena of action itself might well be construed as a form of public hypocrisy; this contrasts with the private hypocrisy, whether 'simulation' or 'dissimulation', discussed in the Introduction. Such public hypocrisy is more than the compliment that vice pays to virtue: hypocrisy becomes part of the mechanism that supports such virtue as there is. Deliberate attempts to suppress information about bad performance, or to exaggerate accounts of good performance can, if successful, serve to raise standards, and thereby raise performance. Of course, hypocrisy dare not speak its name here. If it came to be widely believed that common talk about common practice could not be believed, then the effect of such talk on prevailing standards might be counterproductive. People could come to believe that things were much worse than they are just because common talk cannot be believed. And they would be inclined to adjust their performances accordingly. But a community that refuses to believe the worst is more likely to practice better—even if the prevailing beliefs are actually false.

It is worth emphasising that in referring to hypocrisy here we are not talking of an individual's pretensions to be better in estimable arenas of action than she actually is; that is why the hypocrisy is public, not private. Individuals do not talk up (or refuse to talk down) their own performances but rather performances in general. There is a fine line, of course, between the sort of cultivated generosity of spirit that refuses to believe the worst of others on the one hand, and collective self-delusion on the other. It is as if there were a social convention fostering the perception that standards are higher than they actually are. And this social convention is one that may itself be supported by the forces of esteem. Because one who is concerned to maintain appearances can be interpreted as supporting higher performances, doing so can be estimable.

There is a tension here for the operation of esteem incentives. A refusal to believe the worst of someone may serve to keep standards up, but it also involves softening the forces of disesteem that might otherwise fall on the outrageous performer. When the tax authority declines to expose an extreme case of tax evasion for fear that such exposure might erode public confidence in the tax system, esteem incentives for all who might be exposed are directly blunted. As emphasised in the previous chapter, the *ex ante* incentive to avoid shameful conduct is a positive function of the publicity that shameful conduct receives. A widespread practice of averting one's gaze in the face of shameful behaviour blunts that incentive. This is a cost with which any such culture of generosity ought to reckon.

4   THE WHISTLE-BLOWER'S DILEMMA

The focus of the previous section was the incentives of agents in providing information about standards. What emerged in this discussion was a possible tension between providing that information in particular instances and maintaining popular perceptions of prevailing standards of conduct. One way of illuminating some of the issues at stake in that tension is through an examination of what we here call the whistle-blower's dilemma.[5]

When we talk of whistle-blowing here, we have in mind going public—that is, reporting the situation to external bodies that might be expected to publicise the putatively outrageous conduct to the community at large. Some of the issues we shall be concerned with arise also in reporting the conduct to relevant internal authorities, but this internal reporting is not what we have in mind. Whistle-blowing is what one does when the internal remedies are ignored—perhaps because they have been tried and have failed. Whistle-blowing, in this sense, is to be seen as operating against a background of institutional secrecy.

One of the notable features of many whistle-blowing episodes is the fact that, when public exposure is finally achieved, it is only after what *ex post* seems like an unconscionably long time. In the process of the revelations, it often becomes apparent that many people on the inside had known what was going on or had very strong suspicions but had said or done nothing. What is exposed is not just a set of incidents but also an apparently appalling culture of silence. In the case of child molestation within the church, for example, it now seems that in many cases there had been abundant evidence available to the ecclesiastical hierarchy—at least, a significant accumulation of complaints—and little had been done. Perhaps there had been a confrontation of sorts between the priest in question and his bishop. Perhaps the priest in question had been sent off on a retreat or had been obliged to receive counselling. Perhaps the offender had been moved from his current incumbency to another—perhaps one where there would be less temptation. But in case after case, it seems, the church establishment did its best to cover things up, to minimise public trouble, and move on as if little of consequence was really at stake.

There are three kinds of questions we want to ask about whistle-blowing, and its connection to esteem. The first two are purely explanatory. Why is it that whistle-blowing is seen to be so heroic an activity? And why does it seem to take a long time before practices that everyone *ex post* recognises as unconscionable see the light of day? The third is related to the first two but focuses on the directly normative aspect. Why might it be not only prudentially wise but also morally desirable for would-be whistle-blowers to be reluctant to blow the whistle?

Consider the purely explanatory aspects first. In lots of cases, it is clear that being a whistle-blower can carry penalties in conventional economic terms. Whistle-blowers can lose their jobs; and the amount of legal protection has

---

[5] The number of whistle-blowing and alleged whistle-blowing episodes is enormous, and growing. (See, for example, the extensive bibliography offered in de Maria 1995)

until recently been meagre in many jurisdictions. In cases like the Enron and Worldcom exposures, the exposed firms went bankrupt and the whistle-blowers' jobs disappeared as part of the fall-out.

But what of the implications for the whistle-blower's likely esteem? That, after all, is another important currency in our scheme of things. Note first that all members of an organisation or profession have an interest in the esteem with which the organisation or profession itself is held. If I am a priest in the Roman Church, my level of esteem as a priest is intimately connected with the esteem in which the Church is held. I am likely to believe strongly that priests can do some good, and that the good they can do is positively related to the authority within the community that they exercise. Equally, if the medical profession fell into sufficient disrepute that the ill were less inclined to go to their doctors or to take the advice of their doctors if they did go, doctors are bound to think that this is a bad thing. It will certainly be a bad thing for doctors' incomes and for doctors' esteem in the community. But it will also undermine the potential good that doctors are prone to believe doctors can do. Of course, when a doctor or a priest behaves outrageously, those who hold the values of the profession will be outraged. The perpetrator of the outrageous acts, the whistle-blowee as we might put it, must be the primary focus of professional contempt. But the instinct to kill the messenger is also likely to be in play. The profession will have a strong esteem-related interest in having the matter dealt with quietly—in having the problem handled without losing the general professional esteem that is currently enjoyed. Whistle-blowers may be acting to instantiate professional values; but they do so in a way that is likely to be costly to the profession. And professionals are likely to resent that cost. The esteem calculus is therefore ambiguous at best. Fellow-professionals are likely to esteem the whistle-blower's demonstration of values, and even the whistle-blower's courage. But they are not likely to esteem the act of whistle-blowing as such. Moreover, it is worth emphasising that if whistle-blowing is courageous, it is so precisely because the whistle-blower is likely to pay some cost for going public—and that cost is likely to be an esteem cost as well as a narrowly economic one.

Note too that there is a free-rider problem in place here. Pretty well everyone in the know may agree that the outrageous practices should stop. But not everyone will want to go public as the mechanism of securing that end. Those high in the hierarchy who have most at stake in the reputation of the profession may be expressly charged with the protection of professional reputation. They will therefore have most interest in trying to secure secret remedies. And even among the renegades who have less to lose, and who think that going public is the only reliable solution, each may well prefer that someone else blow the whistle. The structure of the interaction is illustrated in Table 9.1. Here, each believes that the whistle should be blown. So if I believe that no one else will blow the whistle, I will. In the final column (the 'no one else blows' column) the payoff for blowing, denoted 2, exceeds the payoff for not (payoff of 1). But each gets the highest payoff (of 4) if someone else blows. Note that the payoff matrix is devised to reflect the fact that there is strength in numbers: I do better if I'm not the only whistle blower. The payoff in the 'some others blow' column (of 3) exceeds that in the 'no others blow' column (of 2). Nevertheless, it is best for me not to blow if someone else does (4 is greater than 3). This is a game with a structure redolent of the familiar battle of the sexes or chicken. It has the 'I'll fumble, you pay' character of the faculty drinks session. Each is engaged in a strategy of implicit bluff in which each hopes that someone else will give in first. In lots of cases, however, this game can have players fumbling for a long time.

In short, we have reason to think that even those agents who are convinced that whistle-blowing is justified will be reluctant to blow the whistle. Moreover, we have reason to think that not everyone who shares the basic professional and organisational values will think that whistle-blowing is the most appropriate solution, or even an appropriate solution at all.

So we can explain, in terms of ordinary self-interest—with interests here understood broadly to include esteem-related considerations—why individuals will be reluctant to blow whistles. It is however notable that some of the considerations serve not just as explanations of reluctance but also as justifications. What is just a tricky decision-making problem for the whistle-blower in terms of prudential self-interest carries elements of a genuine ethical dilemma. What should the would-be whistle-blower do? And how if at all do the facts of the esteem economy bear on that more general ethical dilemma?

Some pieces of the answer to this question are already in play. It may be important for the good workings of society that citizens have confidence in social institutions. Exposure of some notable public institution—a notable case of corruption in the courts, or of medical malpractice, or of widespread tax evasion—may have an effect on public trust in those institutions (and actually

Table 9.1. *The whistle-blower's dilemma*

	All others	
	Some blow	None blow
Blow the whistle	3	2
Don't Blow	4	1

justified trust in some cases) that would be extremely undesirable. Equally, and in the spirit of the arguments in this chapter and the last, such exposure seems likely to have negative effects on the standards that prevail within the relevant profession.

On the other hand, if violations of professional ideals are not made public then the forces of esteem are not fully operative. If each knows that her professional lapses are likely to be covered up, then her incentives to improve her game are substantially reduced. How can the desire to avoid disesteem operate to full effect if a conspiracy of silence is maintained?

Suppose though that the whistle-blower turns out to be wrong. Conceivably, considerable damage will be done to the reputation of an innocent party, to the profession, and to the whistle-blower herself, who is now cast as an attention-seeking troublemaker. The downside risks are non-negligible, in both self-interest and ethical terms. Is there anything in the structure of the whistle-blower's dilemma, as set out in Table 9.1, that bears on this possibility? We think there is.

The reasoning, following lines discussed by Feddersen and Pesendorfer (1998; 1999) in connection with the unanimity rule for juries, goes this way. In lots of cases, I will not be the only person in a position to have information about a suspected case. In deciding whether to blow the whistle in such a case, I rationally focus my attention on the circumstances in which my action will make a difference. And the only case in which this is so is when no one else blows the whistle. For if someone else blows the whistle I don't need to. This fact gives me pause. Because there is, after all, some uncertainty about whether whistle-blowing is actually justified—uncertainty about the facts of the case, about the consequences of going public, and so on. And I realise that each other person is making an independent assessment of these considerations and that, in the only case that matters (i.e. where my action is decisive), none of those others has decided that the circumstances justify proceeding. Of course, they may be just free-riding. But I may think that most of them are persons of good conscience who would blow the whistle if they judged it to be ethically justified. In other words, the context that rational deliberation forces on me is one in which I have to make a judgement contrary to the judgement made by everyone else. I have epistemic warrant for doubting my belief that blowing the whistle is an appropriate action. And concomitantly, I have grounds for thinking that others will take my whistle-blowing to be unjustified and possibly contemptible.

The bottom line here is that a would-be whistle-blower has good reason to think twice. Some of those reasons are good only in a prudential sense. Life may go badly for me even if I am right as to the facts of the matter. But some of those reasons are good in a more explicitly moral sense. The defence of professional standards and of (justifiable) public confidence may legitimately counsel in favour of handling the matter internally. Unsurprising, then, if those who are most likely to be in the know prove reluctant to go public. The would-be whistle-blower should not be unaware of these considerations. She will need to be pretty sure of her facts and pretty confident about her motives. There is an onus of special care. She faces a dilemma—both as to whether whistle-blowing would be best for her, and as to whether whistle-blowing is justified more generally.

It does not seem likely that any general recipe for action apart from specific cases is going to be valid in whistle-blowing predicaments. In the economy of esteem, there is some presumption that sunlight is the best antiseptic. But there may be cases where that presumption fails. Recognition of this fact provides some possible justification for, as well as explanation of, the widely observed practice of organisational secrecy. It is against the background of that practice that whistle-blowing itself has to be understood and normatively assessed.

CONCLUSION

Our object in this chapter has been to explore a range of issues connected with the intersection between publicity and standards; and specifically with the effect of information about prevailing practice on esteem incentives and thereby on practice itself. The point of departure for this exploration has been the generally positive interdependence between performance and standards that we have argued is a characteristic feature of the economy of esteem.

In Section 1 we interrogated the common knowledge assumption about prevailing values and prevailing practices. Even where the values within a community are well established and widely acknowledged, there can still be considerable uncertainty about what actual practices are.

This uncertainty allows scope for provision of information about those practices and for such information to alter the practices themselves through the change in esteem associated with altered perceived standards. In Section 2, we briefly canvassed some of the available empirical evidence and found it to be broadly supportive of our claims about the positive connection between perceived standards and performance.

In Section 3, we examined the incentives in relation to the provision of information about prevailing practices to which this connection gives rise. Any collective body—a professional organisation, or a government, or a university, or a corporation—that has an interest in higher performance in a particular estimable domain has an incentive to subsidise the provision of data that suggest that average performance is high. The existence of that incentive is independent of the truth or falsehood of the data in question, though it is dependent on the credibility of the information-providing agent.

Many of the issues concerning the connections between standards and publicity are exposed in what we term the whistle-blower's dilemma, and Section 4 was devoted to a discussion of this dilemma. The puzzle that motivates the discussion is why, when the whistle is blown, it so often transpires that many people maintained silence in the face of suspicions or outright knowledge of the misdemeanours in question. In fact, of course, the very notion of whistle-blowing presupposes the existence of rather weighty forces for silence within organisations: going public would be unremarkable unless there were taken to be forces in place against doing so. In our discussion, we enumerated some of those forces:

- the organisation's own reputation, which those associated with it have an esteem-based incentive to defend;
- the effect of loss of reputation on standards within the organisation (effects on what we might think of as organisational morale);
- the 'I'll fumble, you pay' structure of interaction that gives each potential whistle-blower an incentive to refrain from blowing the whistle, in the hope that someone else will;
- the implications of that structure for individual beliefs about the evidentiary warrant for whistle-blowing. If each has reason to believe that all others think that whistle-blowing is unwarranted, she is prone to be inhibited herself.

The general message we draw from our discussion here is that the relation between standards and performance creates a complex connection between information about performance on the one hand and incentives in relation to the provision of such information, on the other. To be sure, the discussion here is preliminary: it is partial and somewhat speculative. However, we think there are interesting general issues to be disinterred in this general area; and our primary object in this chapter has been to indicate why we think that is so and why an explicit focus on esteem can illuminate those issues.

10

Seeking and Shunning Publicity

In Chapter 8, we examined publicity in its role as an esteem-magnifier in relation to individual performance. In that context, we took it that publicity was a matter of exogenous factors—a matter, that is, of prevailing publicity policies and institutions. In Chapter 9, we directed attention to publicity about prevailing performance and to the connection between changing perceptions of prevailing performance and esteem-based performance incentives, via the effect on standards. In both chapters, we abstracted from the possibility that audience size itself might be a matter of individual behavioural manipulation. In this chapter, we want to focus attention specifically on this latter question. We want, that is, to focus on individuals' publicity-seeking and publicity-shunning behaviour.

Clearly, individuals can to some extent choose the degree of exposure their performances receive. They can seek the light—or shun it. They can expend larger or smaller amounts of time, effort, and creative imagination in promoting their exposure—or, in the disesteem case, in securing their privacy/secrecy. They have reason to make these expenditures because audience size influences the amount of esteem received. So much is clear. But what are the implications of such activity for the operation of the economy of esteem—and particularly for the performance-centred effects that occupied us earlier? That is the main question we wish to address in this chapter.

In addressing this question, however, we want at the outset to acknowledge that sometimes—or for some people—publicity seems to be an object of desire in itself, quite apart from any role it may play in augmenting esteem. Some people seem to enjoy being in the limelight, apparently independently of any judgement that they will receive esteem by being so. Are appearances real here? Are people publicity-seekers independently of being esteem-seekers? And if so, what implications, if any, does that fact have for performance-related esteem incentives? More fundamentally, what does the desire for publicity, in and of itself, say about our construction of the nature of esteem? These questions are also ones that we hope this chapter will help answer.[1]

We shall begin by examining the implications of publicity-seeking and publicity-avoiding activities for esteem incentives in the domain of perform-ance. We shall conduct this examination in two settings. The first is where all publicity-seeking or -reducing activities are driven exclusively by esteem con-siderations. That case occupies us in Section 1. In Section 2, we allow for the possibility that publicity (or attention) might be an end in itself and ask what effect that complication might have on the earlier analysis. In Section 3, we explore some of the considerations that seem important in determining whether and when a desire for publicity in itself will be most important. This discussion takes us back to issues relating to recognition, a matter that we touched on in passing at the end of Chapter 1, and that we now need to pursue in a little more detail. Recognition turns out to be an independently significant element in the operation of the esteem economy and we discuss briefly the implications for institutional design of a desire to promote more extensive recognition.

In the analysis contained in Sections 2 and 3, we assume that attention-seeking is pursued via some means other than performance itself. But clearly, one way of attracting attention is through outstanding performance—out-standing in either a positive or a negative sense. We are especially interested in the negative case—what we term the *enfant terrible* syndrome. This case is interesting because it seems to represent a counterexample to many of the central claims of our analysis of publicity. It challenges, in particular, the idea that the desire for greater publicity is connected with better X-performance. We examine the *enfant terrible* case in Section 4. We think the analysis there suggests that the scope of such perverse cases is limited. These cases can plausibly be taken to be exceptional. And because they are exceptions, the general presumptions derived from our analysis can be allowed to stand.

---

[1] In posing questions about a possible independent desire for publicity, it is natural to think also about the possible independent desire for privacy. There are, however, limits on how far we should allow the scope of our discussion to range. We have already indicated at various points that the desire for privacy may have nothing to do with any desire to avoid disesteem. The relevant distinction here is between acts that are regarded as disestimable, whether or not they actually generate disesteem (and specifically whether or not they are actually observed), and acts that become disestimable (if at all) only when performed in public. Actions that are likely to prove offensive if undertaken in public, for example, might be objects of disesteem when so performed—but are widely regarded as utterly innocent and even appropriate when conducted in private.

1   PUBLICITY-SEEKING AND PUBLICITY-SHUNNING

Other things being equal, more publicity makes for stronger performance-centred effects—stronger incentives to behave in more admirable ways, or less contemptible ways. On the face of things therefore, we ought to encourage all publicity-seeking if we want to encourage X-performance. The relevant argument is most obvious in the case of disesteem. People who behave in ways that would be considered shameful under prevailing standards will have reason to avoid exposure. They will try to locate their action where exposure is less likely. That avoidance activity will not only diminish the disesteem they endure: it will also, incidentally, serve to blunt performance incentives. As bad performers locate in places where their actions are more likely to pass unnoticed, esteem-based constraints become increasingly ineffective.

Publicity policies over the range of lower performance, then, should be designed, not just to increase publicity as such, but also to inhibit publicity-avoidance activities that disesteem avoiders will rationally pursue. Put another way, policies that increase publicity over the lower ranges of performance cannot be merely passive. It will not be enough simply to permit greater publicity: it may be necessary to enforce it.

So, for example, the role of a free press and conscientious investigative journalism is commonly regarded as crucial to a free society. Freedom of information legislation has been introduced more and more widely as a discipline on the activities of government and professional bodies. Judges are made to defend their judgements in writing, in a form that is accessible to public scrutiny. Political decision-makers are made answerable to the community through channels in which spin and prevarication are made more difficult. Adversarial institutions are employed so that those who monitor and criticise the actions of others are those who have the greatest incentive to do so. All these publicity-promoting policies serve not just to make actions more public but also to block attempts by the actors themselves to make their actions secret.

There is, though, another reason why exposure avoidance might be undesirable. Exposure avoidance often absorbs time and energy that the performer might have used to improve her performance. If we imagine a situation in which the aggregate time and energy devoted to performance improvement and exposure avoidance is fixed, then all exposure avoidance is necessarily at the expense of performance quality.

Recognising this fact has implications for the design of anti-secrecy policy. Consider some such policy that serves to make exposure avoidance an extremely resource intensive activity. Suppose that notwithstanding the policy, lots of poor performers manage significantly to reduce exposure—though only at considerably increased cost in terms of time and effort. In that case the effect on performance in aggregate might turn out to be worse than if no policy had been introduced. The resources used up in publicity avoidance are resources that could have been used in performance improvement. We think that there is a clear presumption that policies making publicity-avoidance activities more expensive will improve performance. However, it is worth emphasising that this is not necessarily so. Policy design should attend not just to the effectiveness of alternative measures in increasing exposure, but also to the level of resources that may be used up in avoidance attempts.

If esteem incentives are to be maximally effective, the need for restrictions on publicity-shunning action over the disesteem range seems self-evident. But is the need for such publicity-enhancing policies restricted to the negative performance range? After all, in the positive performance range, individuals get more esteem the more publicity their performances receive. They have an incentive to pursue the limelight. And once they have placed themselves appropriately, the incentive to improve performance is augmented, not reduced. Nevertheless, even in the positive range, we think that there is likely to be a role for collective intervention to promote publicity.

There are two considerations here. The first we will call the inhibition effect. Blowing one's own trumpet can be a source of disesteem, as we saw in Chapter 2, even in cases where self-promotion adds to esteem on balance. In that sense, even high performers may be reluctant to place themselves in the limelight in any circumstance where they might be thought to be doing so deliberately. And they will be no less reluctant to create the limelight that focuses on their own performance. Better if they have exposure thrust upon them. Better, that is, for them and for the full play of behavioural incentives that surround esteemed activity.

An academic high-flier, for example, can fully support a general policy of public circulation of annual publication lists within her department—but might well be reluctant to circulate her own list in an environment where no such policy exists. Sending around her curriculum vitae is likely to strike everyone as mere self-aggrandisement. Publicity-seeking may then not emerge spontaneously, or where it does, it may not be pursued with as much vigour as would maximise esteem-related performance incentives.

Furthermore, even if the inhibition effect is not relevant or is less strong than we might suppose, there is a direct resource-related point here exactly analogous to that applying in the publicity-avoidance context. Call this the substitution effect. Consider a tolerably distinguished academic. She can spend her time pursuing her research agenda; or she can work at promoting herself and

her work through the accepted channels. That is, she can engage the confer-
ence circuit; she can accept all invitations to give seminars; she can arrange to
have academic visitors of eminence to her home institution and look after them
well; she can lobby to become an officer in her international professional
association. All of these publicity-oriented activities increase the exposure of
her work; but at the margin these activities are at the expense of the work itself.
It may be preferable, therefore, if individual efforts to pursue publicity are
constrained. We may certainly need policies that require esteem-relevant information to be publicly available—even publicly promoted. But it may well be
better if the amount of information to be circulated is collectively determined,
and set exogenously. Any effects that inhibit additional publicity-seeking may
actually be desirable, because they prevent wasteful status-seeking competition
among high performers. We want policies that require publicity. But once those
policies are in place, we may want to suppress publicity-seeking at the individual level—and this, even though the increased publicity augments performance
incentives.

The points at issue can be illustrated by appeal to a simple diagram. In
Figure 10.1, we show the trade-off between effort expended in performance
improvement and in publicity-seeking, with the former on the horizontal and
the latter on the vertical axis. Effective esteem for individual i, e_i, is given as
some product of esteem due to performance $(X_i - S)$ and audience size, P_i. So a
curve representing combinations of performance and audience size, with each
combination generating the same level of esteem, will plausibly have the shape
of a rectangular hyperbola of the kind illustrated by e_0 in Figure 10.1. If the
amount of effort to be assigned to the pursuit of esteem in total is fixed, then
we can depict a particular individual's option set as given by all points below
and to the left of the KL line. Then that individual's optimum will be at a point
such as U_0, where the e_0 locus is tangent to upper border of that option set, KL.

Now, suppose that some collective entity (the government, say) were to
provide a certain level of publicity directly, say by providing free to everyone
information about X-performances. The amount of publicity thereby provided
is given as P. This policy will serve to shift the individual's option frontier
upwards by P to $K'L'$, and give rise to a new equilibrium at U_1, with
X-performance at X_1 and total publicity at P_1. Clearly, X-performance has
gone up: $X_1 > X_0$. And individual publicity-seeking has gone down to
$(P_1 - P)$. In other words, the publicity policy has induced an increase in
performance effort and a concomitant reduction in individual publicity-seeking.

We have framed this illustration around the case of an individual who
earns positive esteem and is a natural publicity-seeker. The case of a disesteem
avoider does not admit an analogously simple treatment. In the disesteem case,

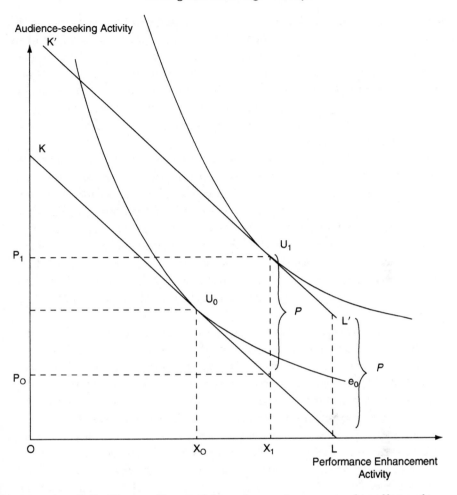

Figure 10.1. *Trade-off between effort expended in performance improvement and in publicity-seeking.*

the publicity thrust upon the performer serves to encourage him in greater publicity-avoidance activity. So in this case, policy should aim not just to increase publicity but also to increase the cost to him of publicity-avoidance activities.

2 PUBLICITY AS AN END IN ITSELF

Publicity-seeking can be explained as a means to higher effective esteem. Desire to minimise disesteem can also explain attention avoidance, a phenomenon that is also not exactly unknown. But what of a desire to be in the limelight in and of itself—and specifically, independently of any esteem that the individual hopes to obtain thereby? We do not want to deny that possibility; and we shall in the next section speculate a little about what may underlie it. We do think that it is rarer than might appear, and we shall try to argue for the rareness proposition in the ensuing sections. In this section, however, we want to investigate the implications of publicity as an end in itself for the issues examined in the previous section.

We can be brief here. As we argued, activities designed to manipulate audience size have two possible effects on performance incentives. One is the fact that audience size may be lower than desirable—either because of a desire for secrecy, as in the disesteem case; or because, as in the positive esteem case, of the esteem cost of appearing to be an esteem-seeker. The other effect involves a reallocation of effort away from performance enhancement towards publicity-seeking or avoidance. Its impact simply reflects the scarcity of effort, time, energy, or creative imagination that underlies all human activity. How would these two effects be influenced if there were a desire for publicity in itself?

It seems clear that the effects in relation to audience size would be moderated by a desire for publicity in and of itself. In the negative esteem case, any esteem-based desire for secrecy has to be set against the loss of publicity. Accordingly, the extent of secrecy-promoting activities is reduced. In the positive esteem case, the force of the inhibition effect has to be set against the value of the greater publicity that would otherwise be available. In both positive and negative esteem ranges, the desire for publicity serves to increase audience size and therefore moderate any tendency for audience to be too low.

In relation to substitution effects, however, the direction of the effect is different in positive esteem and negative esteem cases. In the positive esteem range, any desire for publicity in itself will exacerbate tendencies to substitute promotional for performance effort. In the negative esteem range by contrast, the resources that are redirected from performance improvement are oriented towards reducing audience size: a desire for publicity in and of itself will therefore moderate substitution effects in the negative esteem range.

These simple observations offer, in principle, an empirical test of the importance of publicity-seeking as an end in itself. To the extent that publicity does have independent status as an object of desire, we would expect high performers to invest more in attention-seeking than shameful performers invest in attention-avoiding, *ceteris paribus*. We have no direct evidence on this matter ourselves. But of course there is the simple observation that, if this desire for publicity in itself were sufficiently widespread and strong enough, then attention-avoidance would never be a problem. We would never require arrangements that inhibit secrecy, or discourage agents from pursuing it. Casual evidence suggests that such arrangements are indeed required. Attention-seeking may be widespread, but it is not strong enough to guarantee a minimal level of publicity, except perhaps for a minority of agents.

But there are some specific cases where there does seem to be a demand for audience and attention as such and we shall examine these in the remainder of this chapter. One case involves the conceptually important category of recognition, already briefly discussed in Chapter 1. The other involves an interesting, but we think necessarily unusual phenomenon—the *enfant terrible* syndrome. We consider these in turn.

3   FAILURES OF RECOGNITION

In normal circumstances of social life, it is quite difficult to be confident that the things you do will be unobserved. Unless you have deliberately worked to minimise the likelihood of external observation, the chance that you will be observed or found out if you do something truly shameful, or even mildly disestimable, is non-negligible. And in many cases, that non-negligible chance of observation is sufficient to make you refrain from the shameful action, or to engage in it less extensively.

But there are several ways in which, though you are actually observed, the observation does not register with the observer in the manner necessary for forming esteem or disesteem. We are concerned here with one particularly striking case. If you are to be esteemed, then observers must assign to you a certain status—that of being a proper subject of their evaluative capacities. The observers need to give you recognition, as we put it at the end of Chapter 1. We now want to take up the issue of recognition in somewhat greater detail.

Consider John Adams (1973: no. 5), describing the lot of the performer to whom attention is routinely denied:

He feels himself out of the light of others, groping in the dark. Mankind takes no notice of him; he rambles and wanders unheeded. In the midst of a crowd, at church, in the market, at a play, at an execution or coronation, he is as much in obscurity as he would be in a garret or a cellar. He is not disapproved of, censured or reproached: he is only not seen. This total inattention is to him mortifying, painful and cruel. . . . To be wholly overlooked and to know it are intolerable. . . . To feel ourselves unheeded chills the most pleasing hope—damps the most fond desire—checks the most agreeable wish—disappoints the most ardent expectations of human nature.

At least on the face of things, Adams's view is that attention as such is valued, independently of any esteem that such attention serves to magnify. There is, on Adams's account, a species of invisibility that is wholly repugnant to those who suffer from it. This is the involuntary invisibility imposed on people who are not identified as making any claims on the observer's evaluative attention. And Adams's view seems to be that this kind of invisibility is worse than censure. To be the object of disesteem, on this reading, is to have conferred on one at least the dignity of enjoying a certain basic recognition. Such recognition is a necessary condition for being disesteemed (or esteemed), and raises questions that are distinct from audience size. The fact of merely being in the potential observer's purview cannot generate esteem or disesteem if observers do not register a person's actions or attributes in the way necessary for the relevant kind of evaluative response. Perhaps observers look upon such a one as they might upon a rock or a tree. They may even evaluate his presence, as they might a rock or a tree, by reference to aesthetic criteria or with an edge of irritation that he is taking up space. But the kind of recognition necessary for the operation of esteem or disesteem is not forthcoming. The unrecognised is not invisible as an object, but is invisible in the social sense relevant for esteem or disesteem.

We might compare the person lacking recognition to another kind of failure of observation—that in which the performer is out of sight, say the case of Crusoe marooned on his island, before Friday appears. Crusoe too is unobserved. But there is a fact about his case that might be reassuring to Crusoe: namely, that while he is not recognised by others, this is because there are no others around; it is not because there are others around and they fail to recognise him. Though Crusoe lacks the pleasures (and moral restraints) of society, he at least has the satisfaction of knowing that others do not deny him the status of recognition. Crusoe's position is in this sense quite different from that of Adams's unrecognised actor.

We might represent recognition as an on–off thing on the grounds that, as we saw in Chapter 1, a person either falls within the scope of the observer's moral purview or does not. That is, recognition might be thought of as rather like legal standing: one either has it or one does not. We think that there is an element of truth in this representation but that it can be overemphasised. One might be effectively invisible, in the manner that Adams seems to envisage, but equally one might have only a degree of visibility. One might be recognised by some, not by all. Or one might be afforded recognition in some domains, not in every domain. A beautiful woman may, for example, be highly visible to male participants at a dinner party; but her contributions to the intellectual discussion may be treated as inaudible. Comments she makes may just be ignored—

not even registered by the male participants as having been made, as if presumptively unworthy of recognition. Or at a more finely grained level her remarks on certain subjects may be attended to, but not her comments on public affairs or political issues or the state of the economy. On those topics, whatever she may actually say, she is just not part of the conversation. Adams is surely right to see this condition as mortifying. To be truly seen; to be genuinely heard; to have one's actions noted in the observer's book; in short, to be afforded recognition, is something that is fundamental to our sense of worth.

Clearly, such recognition is connected to esteem in the sense that one cannot be esteemed without it. But recognition has an independent value that only becomes evident in the disesteem case. The desire for esteem carries with it the desire for recognition. Adam Smith's reference to 'man's original desire to please his brethren' can be interpreted as including the desire for recognition. But the desire to avoid disesteem and the desire for recognition are conceptually and practically distinct. Smith's claim in the same passage that 'disapprobation' is 'most mortifying and most offensive' has to confront John Adams's rival claim that to be morally invisible is worse, even, than disapprobation.[2]

The desire for recognition, so understood, might make it sensible for people to pursue the attention of others, even if that attention leads in some instances to disesteem. People who have very low recognition, or think they do, will, if they aspire to esteem, have reason to seek attention even if in that instance the attention does not generate esteem. Attention can be an investment in recognition. Attention-seeking may be best understood in such terms. What appears to be a demand for publicity independent of the demand for esteem is more likely to be a demand for publicity, independent of the esteem that accrues from the particular action for which the attention is sought. We think that what is sought in such cases is often recognition. And this recognition is sought, we think, because of the future esteem it promises. Certainly, no esteem can accrue without it.

[2] In fact, there is some ambiguity in Adams's formulation. One might think that the 'most ardent hope' that Adams refers to is exactly the longing for the approval of one's brethren. On this reading, it is the knowledge that, in the absence of recognition, one cannot ever achieve that approval, whatever one does, that 'chills the hope', 'damps the desire', 'disappoints the expectations'. The use of the terms 'hope', 'desire', and 'expectations' here may be instructive. Given the widely observed tendency of each to think better of himself than others do, each might imagine that, were he 'recognised', he would indeed enjoy positive esteem. The case in which he might be the object of disesteem simply does not occupy the imagination. Put the point more strongly. Suppose I know that I would be 'disapproved, censured, and/or reproached'. Would I then trade lack of recognition for censure? Adams's claim that someone in my position would do this may reflect his judgement of a natural optimism in the human spirit.

Recognition is often a matter of culture—of social practices and conventions, in which roles are differentiated and hierarchies established within roles. Many of the hierarchies in question may strike the contemporary eye as inherently morally objectionable and abhorrent on that account. Here however our interest is less in the intrinsic moral implications of the practice of treating others as (more or less) invisible, and more in the implications such practices have for how the economy of esteem operates.

Because publicity depends on recognition and because the intensity of esteem incentives depends on publicity, the economy of esteem will clearly work more effectively when there is more extensive recognition than when there is less. To the extent that we seek to mobilise the behavioural incentives associated with esteem, then, we should also seek to establish institutions that increase recognition, *ceteris paribus*. The same sorts of arguments that we outlined in Chapter 8 for publicity policies and institutions apply *pari passu* with respect to recognition.

In many cases, the institutions governing recognition are stable features of a prevailing culture and will not be particularly sensitive to external manipulation. Still, there is usually some scope both for individual action within, and for collective action external to, the culture's operation—which action can be mobilised in favour of greater recognition rather than less. So, for example, in connection with extending the franchise, what is often seen to be at stake is a matter of recognition of the voices that have hitherto been represented, at best, via the noblesse of others. Likewise, representative assemblies might be such that members of relevant groups are seen to be present and to speak for themselves as a means of symbolising the recognition that those groups are afforded.[3]

Recognition is not though just a matter of formal institutions. One who invariably treats the other with a kind of inattentiveness is guilty of failure to recognise by stealth. And systematic inattentiveness of this kind can arise as a kind of social habit. And can mobilise the same incentives on the part of the overlooked to secure proper recognition. Clearly, it is the systematic nature of the inattentiveness here that does the work. As we noted earlier, to be the object of occasional inattentiveness is just a fact of life. People have other things on their minds. To demand that others' attention always be focused on oneself is unreasonable and almost certainly disestimable. Equally however to find that one's potential observer is always looking away, always preoccupied with other things, invariably giving full attention to someone or something else—that is

---

[3] Ann Phillips's (1995) discussion of the structure of representation makes this kind of point eloquently—especially in relation to women and indigenous peoples.

an assault on one's recognition. That kind of treatment calls for measures to grab the other's attention, to seek the recognition otherwise denied.

One final point on recognition and its institutions. It may seem as if there is a scarcity constaint to be applied here, analogous to that which operates with publicity. Recall that in the latter context, we noted that focusing attention on one range of the distribution of performances serves to distract attention from other parts of the distribution. Attention we said is in limited supply. Is this not also true of recognition? We think not. The distinguishing feature of recognition is a preparedness to register performance if one observes it. Recognition simply involves the presumption that the other, whoever she may be, is a moral equal. This is a matter of attitude not action and we do not think that scarcity applies in this domain.

4   THE *ENFANT TERRIBLE* PHENOMENON

The *enfant terrible* phenomenon, as understood here, is characterised by the use of performance that is disestimable as a means of attracting attention. On the face of things at least, this case represents a counterexample to our general contention that publicity/attention is to be understood as instrumental to greater esteem. The *enfant terrible* deliberately courts disesteem as a necessary feature of his attention-seeking strategy. In other words, this case seems to attest to a demand for attention in and of itself.

However, as the earlier discussion suggests, there is no necessary conflict involved here. If the individual has low recognition and expects to have performances in the positive esteem range in the future, it could be entirely rational to invest now in higher attention in the future, even if that involves negative esteem currently. There are, however, several conditions to be filled if the *enfant terrible* strategy is to be explicable as part of a lifetime esteem maximisation exercise:

- Attention in future periods must be positively related to attention in the current period.
- The performer must believe that future performances will fall into the positive esteem range.
- The most effective route to attention in the current period must be via poor performance.

This last condition may need some explication. Clearly, there are a variety of ways in which a person might increase the attention she receives. Only one of those involves the quality of her performance in the estimable domain. The best strategy for esteem purposes would be to have her performance conspicuous in the positive range—to be conspicuously good, rather than conspicuously bad. That strategy must be inaccessible to her. But since the *enfant terrible* strategy involves negative esteem, it must also be the case that routes to attention other than through X-performance are relatively ineffective. What is characteristic of the *enfant terrible* case is that the route by which recognition is secured is precisely the same as that in which esteem is secured—namely, X-performance.

To the extent that these three conditions are met, the *enfant terrible* case can be explained as part of a long-term esteem-maximisation strategy. But we do not need to press an implausible line here: we do not necessarily deny that attention may be an object of independent desire. What we do want to argue is that the *enfant terrible* case can be best understood in the context of an analysis in which the implications of attention-seeking for esteem are explicitly included.

Consider, in particular, the individual optimisation exercise for some agent in a single period. We shall suppose that this individual has a demand for attention as such in this period, and leave on one side the question of whether that demand can be explained by a desire for future esteem. We might then formulate the trade-off between attention and esteem in terms of the overall value, V, that combinations of attention and esteem have for an agent, i.

$$V_i = \chi.A_i + A_i.E_i \qquad (10.1)$$

where A_i is the level of attention afforded the individual, $A_i.E_i$ the level of effective esteem, and χ a factor showing the importance of attention as such vis-à-vis esteem.

Now let A_i be a function of the form:

$$A_i = [X_i - S]^2$$

This form reflects the fact that as performance moves away from the standard the level of attention secured increases at an increasing rate. Doubling the distance from the standard quadruples the amount of attention received. Esteem is taken, as in the simplest form, to be a linear function of $[X - S]$, as in Chapter 5. So we have:

$$V_i = [X_i - S]^2.[\chi + (X_i - S)] \qquad (10.2)$$

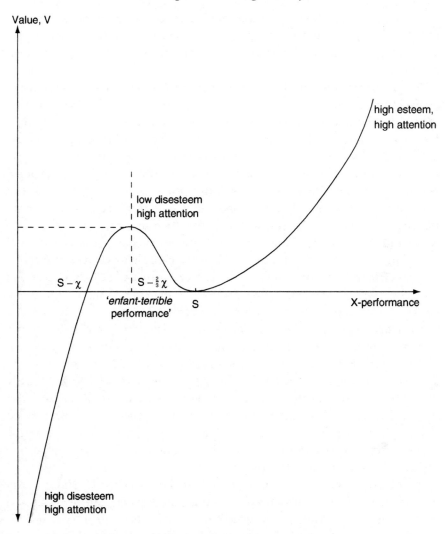

Figure 10.2. *The* enfant terrible *case.*

This function is a cubic in performance quality, X. And as such it has a characteristic shape, of the type illustrated diagrammatically in Figure 10.2. Note that V is zero at two points: one where $X_i = S$ and the other where $X_i = (S - \chi)$. Moreover, it is easy to show that the V-curve has two stationary values: a minimum at S; and a local maximum at $[S - 2/3.\chi]$. That local maximum lies to the left of S; it corresponds to the *enfant terrible* possibility.

What the formulation shows is that the individual can have more of overall attention/esteem value by lowering performance below the standard over some range. Note, though, how limited the *enfant terrible* possibility turns out to be.

At least under this formulation, the *enfant terrible* performance turns out to be well short of the totally outrageous. Beyond some point, the disesteem that the bad performance induces, overwhelms the positive effects on attention: as the curve indicates, net negative value accrues once performance falls below $(S - \chi)$. Provided that current esteem has any value to the actor at all, an attention-seeking strategy of wilfully bad performance will be its own undoing beyond some point. If successful in securing attention, the negative effects of disesteem will cut in. And the larger the attention secured, the larger the disesteem will be. The implication is then that the *enfant terrible* strategy is more likely to consist of minor acts of irritation, medium-level violations of prevailing standards—such as acts of rudeness and the like—than of spectacular acts of defiance. That conclusion is a direct consequence of including esteem in the actor's value function. In the absence of any such sanction, the *enfant terrible* would simply behave as terribly as possible.

But what might we adduce in defence of our claim that the phenomenon is best understood as one element in a longer term strategy which is itself esteem driven? There is of course the etymological evidence. The phenomenon is, apparently, one that is notable among *enfants*—not among *anciens*. Clearly those who are early in their esteem-seeking careers are more likely to make an initial investment in recognition, as part of a longer-term esteem-driven strategy. The *ancien terrible* would be a more serious challenge to our overall position and we have at least the conventions of ordinary language supporting the idea that the case is relatively rare.

In any event, there is reason to think that the *enfant terrible* strategy will be rare. If the object is to attract attention, the strategy can be successful only if it is not too widely practised. If many individuals were to act in this manner, the behaviour would lose its salience. And it would not draw the attention that is its object. Accordingly, we are inclined to think that the strategy only makes sense when there is only a small number of *enfants terribles* in town.

Finally, it is worth emphasising that, if our argument is right, the *enfant terrible* syndrome carries the seeds of its own redemption. Once a tolerable level of recognition is gained, once the individual can be assured of a certain threshold level of attention, the calculus of the *enfant* will change. If recognition is, as we think, a capital good, then once it is accumulated, raw esteem considerations tend to take over and the *enfant* will be led to behave like an adult![4]

CONCLUSION

In this chapter, we have examined individuals' rational responses to the opportunities they face to manipulate audience size. This has involved a shift of focus somewhat away from performance-centred effects, as we term them—though those performance effects have remained in the background as the main object of ultimate concern.

In Section 1, we focused on the implications of publicity-seeking activity for performance incentives. There are two elements involved here. One involves direct effects on audience size and therefore incentives to improve performance. So, for example, individuals at the lower end of the performance range will rationally pursue secrecy in their attempts to minimise disesteem. And *ceteris paribus* the reduced audience size will diminish performance effects. Equally, although individuals at the upper end will not rationally pursue secrecy, they may be inhibited from pursuing publicity to the extent that would maximise performance incentives. In both cases, then, interventions to increase audience size by direct regulation may be required. The second element involves substitution of publicity-avoiding or publicity-seeking activities for performance improvement activities. Any time and energy expended in manipulating audience size is time and energy that could have been used in performance enhancement.

In Section 2, we looked at the implications of the possibility that attention/ publicity might be an end to be pursued for its own sake, independently of its effects on esteem. Again, there is a distinction to be drawn between the high performance and the low performance end. At the high performance end, any such intrinsic demand for attention exacerbates the resource-using problem. On the other hand, at the low performance end, the intrinsic demand for publicity serves to inhibit the quest for secrecy and the resource-using problem concomitantly.

Whether there is a demand for publicity as such, and independent of esteem effects, is then a matter that has some consequences for our analysis, and for

---

[4] In Chapter 12, we examine another case in which there is an apparently perverse relation between disesteem and publicity—the 'coming out' case. In this case too the object could be thought of as attention-seeking. But in this case, the aim of action is to articulate one's conscientious objections to the values on which the disesteem is based.

the policy implications to be drawn from them. Accordingly, in Section 3 we attempted to trace the origins of that demand—if indeed such a demand does exist. This attempt led us back to some basic considerations in the nature of esteem, around the issue of recognition—an issue we mentioned briefly in Chapter 1. Our view is that the demand for recognition is real, that it probably springs from long-term esteem considerations, and that in the economy of esteem it explains the demand for attention and publicity. Recognition is a precondition for esteem and so we also examined institutional arrangements that seem to us conducive to broader patterns of recognition. Because recognition is attitudinal rather than action-based, recognition is not victim to the same natural resource constraints as is attention. In particular, more recognition for one group does not necessarily mean less recognition for another, however true that may be for attention.

In Section 4, we examined what might seem, in the light of our earlier treatment, to be a case that presents difficulties for our general treatment. One central claim in our discussion has been that actors who are likely to suffer disesteem will try to avoid publicity. That claim seems to be violated in what we call the *enfant terrible* case. We tried to show that this case can be explained in terms of a modest extension of our basic model. The extension in question includes long-term as well as instantaneous effects on esteem. In the *enfant terrible* case, performers are to be understood as investing in recognition. On balance we think that such cases are to be seen as exceptional ones that are broadly consistent with our overall intellectual scheme.

11

Voluntary Associations

In the previous six chapters, we have examined two general topics in the economy of esteem—the role of esteem in influencing performances in estimable domains; and the role of publicity, both in its effects on performance incentives and as a matter of interest in its own right. In this chapter and the next, we consider a third aspect of the economy of esteem—those forces operative in the economy of esteem as a result of people's voluntarily banding together, or being involuntarily thrown together, in what can loosely be described as associations. In this chapter we look at the esteem effects that materialise in voluntary associations, and in the next at those that transpire in associations of the involuntary kind.

There are two reasons why we are interested in voluntary associations. In the first place, recall that our general project here is motivated in part by a desire to explore salient analogies between the economy of esteem and the economy of goods. We want to take concepts that are familiar from traditional economics and see if those concepts have some counterpart in the economy of esteem. There are, for example, in traditional economics, collective action aspects on both the production side—as studied in the theory of the firm—and on the consumption side—as studied in the theory of public goods in its many variants. We want to explore in this chapter whether the kinds of centripetal forces that create firms and other similarly collective entities in the economy of goods are also operative in some form in the esteem case; and if so, what the distinctive features of the esteem counterparts are.

The second reason for our interest in voluntary associations is that, as we aim to show, collective action allows a form of exchange in esteem. In earlier discussion, particularly in Chapter 3, we emphasised that the economy of esteem is unlike the economy of goods in the crucial respect that the economy of goods is constructed on the basis of the possibility of exchange. Exchange in esteem is a barely coherent idea: B cannot offer some of her surplus esteem to A, either in exchange for goods or in exchange for some of A's esteem in another domain of activity. Nor can A add to his esteem just by buying approval from observers: any esteem that A derives is grounded in a belief that A is estimable, and that belief cannot be for sale. But though the exchange of esteem is impossible, the exchange of what we earlier described as esteem services is not. And voluntary associations bring many esteem services on stream.

In Chapter 3, we isolated three esteem services, which we described as attention, testimony, and association. The term 'association' in this context refers to the service whereby glory is borrowed—or, as in the negative counterpart, the disservice whereby ignominy is contracted. This service is often going to be ensured by the formation of a voluntary association, since those of us in certain groupings may derive esteem in the eyes of outsiders from the company in which we are kept. But voluntary associations will typically lead to the provision of testimony and attention as well. Members of certain groupings may give one another's performances a degree and kind of attention that they each seek and of course members may routinely testify to one another's merits.

In the discussion that follows, we shall be displaying a variety of ways in which voluntary associations facilitate the exchange of esteem services, and the macro-patterns to which they thereby give rise. We shall do so, not in the context of simple bilateral exchange, characteristic of the economy of market goods, but rather in terms of the kind of multilateral exchange more characteristic of so-called club goods (Buchanan 1965; Sandler and Tschirhart 1980). We develop our argument in terms of this larger-numbers setting because the esteem advantages of collective activity are in no way limited to the two-person case. The enhanced esteem that accrues to individuals by virtue of their forming voluntary associations accrues to all of them equally: the two-person collectivity is to be seen as a special case, of no particular significance.

In developing the arguments in this chapter, we shall direct attention to collectivities under their aspect as conduits of esteem. This is not because we think that other considerations do not enter into the formation of collectivities, or that esteem does not play an important role in collectivities that form for other reasons. Some of our examples will necessarily involve associations that form for many purposes, of which esteem is only one. Nevertheless, the analysis focuses exclusively on esteem aspects. We want to isolate the forces that make for the formation of collectivities within the economy of esteem specifically, and it is helpful in doing so to exclude any unnecessary complication.

The shape of the argument in this chapter is as follows. We begin by isolating the factors that make for forming voluntary associations in the esteem case. We think that there are two such:

- Economies of scale in publicity that make reputation-pooling a means of augmenting individual reputations. This directly associational aspect occupies us in Section 1.

- The construction of associations for mutual admiration. This aspect occupies us in Section 2.

These two considerations do not necessarily suggest associations of the same size or composition or structure of relationship. So in predicting the shape of esteem-based institutions, we need to examine the various trade-offs that members of collectivities will have to make. In Section 3, we speculate about the relative significance of these various factors under the rubric of choosing the right pond, following the title of Robert Frank's well-known book (Frank 1985).

In Section 4, we investigate whether esteem associations are likely to have any special characteristics. In this context we try to establish the distinctive advantages that such associations exhibit in overcoming free-rider problems. Esteem-generating collectivities are likely to be characterised by unusually strong group loyalty in the behavioural sense that members work reliably to promote the interests of the collective. Members may each provide testimony as to the quality of the collective, for example—and do so without incurring the disesteem they would court if they provided testimony to their own merits.

All of these arguments are designed to show how collective action can enable the exchange of esteem services among members of appropriately structured groups. What, though, of the room to exchange esteem services for other things—and thus incorporate the operation of esteem more generally within the market for goods? We examine aspects of this issue in Section 5. Our concern in this section is, though, quite limited. It deals mainly with the commercialisation of associations whose more obvious purpose is esteem-related. While at one level our interest is in the interface between the economy of goods and the economy of esteem, we approach that issue very much from the economy-of-esteem end.

1 EXTERNAL ESTEEM AND REPUTATION POOLING

A brief breeze through *Who's Who* reveals that what often identifies the 'whos' in question and justifies their inclusion in that august catalogue is their membership of particular associations. X was, for many years, the principal cellist with the Berlin Philharmonic Orchestra. Y is currently a Professor at Harvard. Z was a member of the 1947 Australian Test cricket team that was undefeated throughout the entire tour. W won the Nobel Prize for Chemistry. V was a member of rock group Abba. And so on.

In some of these cases, the esteem that such descriptions signify derives less from the individual's independent accomplishments and more from the accomplishments of the group of which she is a member. That is, the performance on which esteem is based is itself a team effort. The quality of an orchestra, a football team's record of success—these are not merely a matter of the qualities of individual performances, even if player quality is an important input into the team's success. Here then, though the collective may be an independent object of esteem, the collective's existence is not to be explained predominantly in esteem terms.

But not all cases are like this. Some of the designations pick out collective entities that are based solely on individual performances. And our interest here lies in those cases, because in those it is the esteem itself that constitutes the basis of the association. Consider, for example, the British Academy. There is no sense in which British Academy members produce some joint product, the quality of which is an object of esteem. Each of the members is esteemed by virtue of an accomplishment that is essentially her own. Yet each of them receives additional esteem from their membership of the Academy. And each of them contributes in some small measure to the esteem that the Academy *qua* Academy enjoys. The Academy serves to augment the esteem of its members—without the individual performances as such being in any way an aggregate. There are, as the economist might put it, economies of scale across persons in the securing of esteem.

Or consider the Nobel Prize. In accepting the award, each Laureate is associating herself with other winners. And the esteem she receives thereby is nothing more than a kind of amalgam of the estimable qualities of all the other winners. Of course, those estimable qualities may be largely presumed. The Nobel Prize may be famous in the same way that an individual may be famous. That is, very large numbers of people may esteem Nobel Prize winners without having a very clear sense of what the Prize was awarded for, or indeed of who else has won the Prize in the past. Still, the Prize only becomes famous because those who receive it are famous in the relevant circles. Ultimately, the Prize is nothing more than a badge of membership for the association of winners. The esteem advantages of the Prize are in that sense advantages attributable to a form of reputation-pooling. These are the advantages of association as we earlier defined it.

As these examples show, the nature of the relationships within voluntary associations, as here understood, can be very thin indeed. Members of such an association need never meet. They need have nothing to do with one another at all, beyond the requirement that they be associated for esteem-relevant purposes in the popular imagination. Of course, what kinds of bonds need to be in place for individuals to be so associated is an open question. Perhaps they need to write joint papers, or sing duets, or be members of the same football team. But the relations they share could in principle be as spare as those that Nobel Laureates share; and Nobel Laureates do not need to meet in order to be associated.

What is at stake in the gains from reputation-pooling? How do they come about? One way of formulating these effects is to suppose that each performer has a direct audience, which we can designate $A\{X_i\}$, for performance of X by individual i. Then the direct audience for a group of individuals who amalgamate into an association is just the union of the sets $A\{X_j\}$ for all the individuals in that association. This means that as the membership increases, other things equal, so does audience size and hence publicity.

But there is a cost to this increased publicity. The perceived level of performance of the association is, we may suppose, just the average of the performance levels of association members. So everyone has an incentive to form an association with the highest performers in any domain. And up to a point, those highest performers will value such association because it adds to their effective audience. But only up to a point. Beyond that point, the deterioration in the association's perceived average performance will not compensate the highest performers for the increased publicity. The highest performers will veto additional entry into the association, or in the limit simply quit the association. Even the Nobel Prize would lose its lustre if the award began to be made to scholars who were widely perceived among the cognoscenti to be spectacularly mediocre.

These intuitive remarks suggest that there are two related issues involved in the formation of esteem associations—one relating to the composition, and the other to the size of esteem associations. We consider these aspects in turn. So, to fix on composition questions, take association size to be fixed. And suppose the association is trying to decide whether to admit A or B to membership in the last available slot. Assuming that A and B make identical contributions to audience size, there will be a unanimous decision on this matter: award membership to the higher performer. But this just means that the association that emerges will consist of the highest n performers. The association can always gain by replacing any member with one who has higher performance.

There might, of course, be more than one association in any domain. But the associations that form will be hierarchically ordered. The top n performers will be in the top association; the next n performers in the next association; and so on. At some point, the impulse to form associations will disappear. This point will be reached when average performance lies below the positive esteem threshold. Additional publicity cannot add to my esteem if the association I join has an average performance that does not generate esteem. Or at least this is so unless my individual performance generates negative esteem; and in that case the association would have no reason to admit me.

This general conclusion about the composition of esteem associations strikes us as significant. These associations exhibit an intrinsically hierarchical structure: they will form, as it were, from the top down. So, unless there is intervention from other factors, the best performers will congregate in the most prestigious associations, the next best performers in the next best associations, and so on.[1]

How big will such associations be? In general terms, it is clear that association size will be determined by the condition that the marginal esteem gain from audience expansion equals the marginal esteem loss from perceived performance deterioration. We spell out what is involved in this equilibrium condition in a little more detail in the appendix immediately following.

APPENDIX TO SECTION 1

Following the general spirit of the formulation introduced in Chapter 8, we take the simplest possible case in which esteem is just the product of audience size and performance quality. That is:

$$E_n = A_n.[X_n - S] \tag{11.1}$$

where E is group esteem; A is group's audience size; and X is the average group performance, for group of size n. This expression will be maximised when the marginal benefit in terms of proportionate increase in audience size equals the marginal cost in terms of proportionate reduction in average group performance.

So, consider marginal esteem gain from audience expansion. Suppose that the audience size for each individual is $p.T$ where p refers to the proportion of total population T that observes any individual performance. Suppose initially that the audiences vary randomly from performer to performer but that audience size is identical for each performer. Both of these assumptions are implausible because higher performers are likely to attract more attention,

---

[1] This fact has the incidental consequence that the equilibrium in the formation of esteem associations is not like an equilibrium in the formation of firms. The esteem associations in any domain, being hierarchically ordered among themselves, can never be in perfect competition. We touch briefly on that topic later in the discussion of the power of associations to expel individual members.

and the likely observers of the outstanding performers in any particular domain are likely to be positively correlated. But the total independence of individual audiences is a useful initial simplification. On this basis, p can be interpreted as the probability that each will be observed individually. Then $(1 - p)$ is the probability of being unobserved individually. And, given independence of the individual audiences, the probability of the association being unobserved is the probability that no one in the group will be observed—or:

$$1 - (1 - p)^n.$$

The expected audience for an association of size n is then $[1 - (1 - p)^n].T$. And the marginal change in audience size, ΔA, as we move from size n to one of size $(n + 1)$ is:

$$\Delta A = [1 - (1 - p)^{n+1} - (1 - (1 - p)^n].T$$

which simplifies to:

$$\Delta A = pT.(1 - p)^n \tag{11.2}$$

and since $pT = A$, then

$$\Delta A / A = (1 - p)^n$$

It can be seen by inspection that the larger is n the smaller is $(1 - p)^n$ and so ΔA gets smaller and smaller as n gets larger. The marginal benefit in terms of increased publicity is diminishing. The reason for this is that as size expands, so does the probability that someone in the association will be observed by any particular observer; hence, the smaller the pool of non-observers from whom additional observers might be added when group size is increased. Suppose we now add the consideration that the marginal member will have a smaller audience than infra-marginal members, by virtue of having a less distinguished performance. In particular, take the case where the highest performing individuals are already quite famous. Then the marginal advantages to forming associations with any except a small number of similarly famous performers will be quite low. In those cases we would predict that associations would be pretty small. Add too the fact that the individual audiences in question are likely to be positively correlated. Then, increases in n are likely to add very little to audience size beyond some finite point. On this basis, we can derive in

Figure 11.1 the marginal esteem benefit from expanding group size, *n*, as *n* increases. We show this as the line LM.

Given what we have concluded about composition, the decline in group performance as an extra individual is added is the difference between the average performance of the highest n performers and the average of the highest (n + 1) performers. That is,

$$\Delta X = X_n - X_{n+1}$$

$$\text{or } \Delta X/X = 1 - X_{n+1}/X_n \tag{11.3}$$

The expression (11.3) is the marginal cost of expanding membership, and can be depicted in Figure 11.1 by the curve JK. This curve seems likely to be roughly constant, and is drawn on that assumption. Accordingly, we can specify

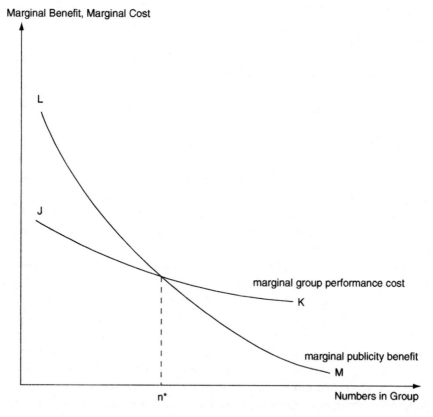

Figure 11.1. *Relation between marginal esteem benefit and expanding group size.*

the equilibrium size as n^*. And as indicated n^* is likely to be fairly small in any domain where the individual performers are likely to be individually relatively famous; and larger in any domain where even the best performers are relatively obscure.

One feature of the equilibrium size n^* is worth noting. That equilibrium is derived on the basis that the existing membership determines the size of the association: n^* is the membership size that maximises esteem for the existing members. But consider the $(n^* + 1)$th individual. He very much desires to join the association. Although he can join an association of lower rank, he will in that lower association enjoy much less esteem because the average performance in the lower association is lower. Moreover, the cost to existing members of the higher association in allowing that marginal non-member to join is actually quite small. If there were some currency with which this marginal entrant could pay existing members to allow him to join, it is highly likely that all those existing members could be fully compensated. In that sense, one might conclude that the association is too small, too 'exclusive'. Note though that if such a trade were arranged, there would be a cost to members of the next-level association, because their top performer had gone to join another, higher league. Of course, the relevant quasi-exchanges are limited here to those that can be transacted via esteem. Still, the conceptual experiment is interesting. From a utilitarian, and even a broadly contractarian perspective, associations may be excessively exclusive.

2   INTERNAL ESTEEM AND MUTUAL ADMIRATION

In the previous section, we considered the formation of associations—collectivities which serve to augment the esteem which members of the group derive by virtue of economies of scale in publicity. The additional esteem that is thereby generated accrues from the community at large. We call that external esteem. What, though, of the esteem that accrues from members within the collectivity—what we term internal esteem? Within a group, members are often privileged as observers of one another's activities. When I join Covent Garden as a principal, I shall certainly be more aware of the quality of the other Covent Garden principals than I was in my previous location in the Welsh National Opera. And they will be more aware of the quality of my performances. When I leave the University of the South and go to the University of the North, I will, among other things, change my internal audience. My immediate colleagues are those with whom I talk and try out ideas and who routinely hear my comments at seminars. And they will have to deal subsequently with the students who are products of my courses. Those immediate colleagues know a great deal more about my professional performance in these arenas than does the average academic in my field, to say nothing of the average person I meet. The members of groups to which I belong represent my local audience and become a primary source of my esteem—or disesteem.

Now, throughout the discussions of publicity in preceding chapters, we have assumed for simplicity that all observers can be taken as identical suppliers of esteem—that the esteem of any one observer is equivalent to the esteem of any other. In many contexts that assumption seems reasonable enough. In contexts where audience composition is essentially random (and where standards of valuation are common knowledge), it is the average observer whose esteem is relevant. But there are lots of contexts where the distribution of possible observers is skewed in totally predictable ways. In such contexts, the composition of the audience seems likely to make a very significant difference to the value I place on any esteem that is forthcoming, and therefore to the performance incentives that are in play. We shall focus here on four aspects of audience quality: alertness; relevance of attribute; discriminating capacity; and testimonial potential. Let us consider these in turn.

Clearly, some individuals are naturally more *alert* than others; they are intrinsically more observant. Sometimes this is artefactual. A paying audience at Covent Garden is less likely to sleep through your performance than the audience in an aged persons' home where you are providing a free concert, even if everything else is equal. Contexts where there is a dedicated audience are for this reason (and possibly others) presumptively more esteem-generating than contexts where the audience is randomly composed, simply by virtue of the fact that the self-selected audience attends to performances more intently.

Equally, an audience that shares a special concern for the *attribute* you are revealing is more esteem-relevant than an average audience, even where that average audience is equally attentive. It seems reasonable to suppose that an audience at Covent Garden will normally be particularly interested in singer quality. But suppose you are performing on a night when the house has been bought out by some corporate giant to invite its major clients. The esteem generated on such a night will be worth rather less, and your incentive to perform at your best moderated, just because that audience will predictably be less interested in the quality of the singing.

Some audiences are more *discriminating* than others even where all share a particular concern with the same dimension or attribute of performance. If you know that several bishops renowned for their preaching are in the congregation as you ascend the pulpit steps, this fact is inclined to add a special edge to your desire to preach well. If your old singing teacher is in the audience for your concert, you will want to sing especially beautifully. Giving a seminar at Chicago where the participants are well known to be especially smart and well-informed on your subject is a potentially more potent source of esteem (or disesteem) than giving a seminar at the nearby community college. Of course, discrimination, alertness, and attribute-relevance all tend to go together; but cases can easily enough be constructed in which one characteristic is present without the others and it seems useful to treat the aspects separately.

Finally, some audiences are salient in that they are especially well placed to offer testimony. On the opening night when the reviewers are present in force, a good performance is especially desirable—even if you consider them a mob of fools whose artistic judgement would benefit from serious enforced refinement. It is the fact that the critics' judgements are broadcast to the reading/listening public, rather than their being the arbiters of refined assessment as such, that lends them their special power. Equally, as an aspiring physicist, you may not think much of the judgement of a particular famous scientist, but recognise that her fame implies that her testimony counts for a great deal. If that person can be induced to write a favourable reference for you in job applications or give your work favourable citations or simply speak well of that work in public, this will be advantageous to you in augmenting your esteem from others. This fact makes her esteem (or disesteem) particularly potent. Again, testimonial potency seems likely to be correlated with alertness and attribute relevance and discrimination; but there is nothing logically necessary about the connections.

Of course, whether attentiveness, attribute relevance, discrimination, and testimonial potential are attractive characteristics in an audience depends on your location in the performance spectrum—and in particular on whether you expect to receive positive or negative esteem in relation to your performance. These features in an audience will be desired if you expect your performance to generate positive esteem. They might be desired, too, if you wished to put your performance to the test.[2] But setting aside uncertainty about the quality of your performance—assuming, that is, that your assessment of the valuations that others will place upon your performance is accurate—then if your performance is sub-standard, you will rationally shun attention from the best audience. Best to have no audience at all. Or if you must have an audience, better to have one that is inattentive, non-expert, undiscriminating, more interested in something other than your performance, and of negligible influence. In short, better performers will tend to seek a better audience. Worse

---

[2] The discussion about risk aversion and risk loving in Chapter 7 bears here. Whether you will be disposed to put your performance to the test depends *inter alia* on where in the distribution of performances you take yourself to lie.

performers will seek a worse audience in the sense that we describe it here—and at best no audience at all.

The foregoing considerations speak to the demand that performers have for an audience with appropriate qualities. But the construction of audiences has a supply-side dimension as well. Observers, as well as performers, must be in equilibrium. To this point in the argument, we have not said much about the motivations of observers. We have talked as if observers were available more or less gratuitously. And we have assumed that, although performers might manipulate the size of their audience to some extent, the audience itself plays an essentially passive role. It is now time to rectify this omission.

It is entirely consistent with the involuntary nature of observer evaluation that the observer may derive pleasure or pain from the act of observation. And in fact, it seems almost self-evident that this will be so. That is, the observer will delight in contemplating a fine performance and be repelled by a disastrous one in any estimable domain. In aesthetic contexts, for example, the contemplation of the beautiful, the admirable, the extraordinarily impressive is surely pleasurable for its own sake. Indeed, in the case of artistic performance or sporting prowess, we have the evidence that people are prepared to pay money (and often to queue for many hours) in order to be able to play the observer role. Similar considerations seem likely to be present in the case of moral attributes. We warm to the contemplation of generosity and kindness; we relish displays of courage and honesty and probity. It is pleasurable to us, absent perversions like sadism and voyeurism, to contemplate the best of human nature. And we are revolted by acts of cruelty and meanness and spitefulness. Or at a lower level, by conduct that is offensive or discourteous.

If this is accepted, then audiences will more naturally attend when there are estimable actions/attributes/dispositions on show than when there are disestimable ones. Alert, discriminating, expert audiences will tend to follow good performances and place themselves in environments where such good performances are more likely than not. So one of the benefits of being a Harvard professor is that you will attend a large number of truly excellent seminars—a larger number than if you had remained at your currently less distinguished institution. And this is something that you, if you are an astute and appreciative observer of others' work, are likely to especially value.

For convenience, divide performers into two sets: the high performers and the low performers. Let observers divide similarly into two sets: one alert and discriminating; the other non-alert and less discriminating. Then the former sets in each category will naturally desire to get together. Good performers will want an audience of good observers; and good observers will want to observe good performers. There is, though, a complication. This happy match can only work if the sets are composed of the same persons—operating now in performer, now in observer roles. Suppose, by contrast, that those who are good performers are bad observers, and vice versa. Good observers will want to congregate around good performers; but will find that so congregating involves their being surrounded by poor performers, because these poor performers are other good observers also chasing good performers. In short, if performance quality and observer quality are negatively correlated, groups that match good performers and good audiences are infeasible. Indeed, unless performance quality and observer quality are positively correlated, the possibility of groups forming specifically for the purpose of creating audience seems undermined.

It seems clear, however, that the positive correlation case is, in general, a fairly plausible one. One reason for thinking so is that in order to become a good performer in most fields, one must develop an alertness and sensitivity to one's own performance. Developing skills in any arena usually involves a certain amount of intelligent self-appraisal and a capacity to distinguish good performance from bad. Those same observational sensitivities will tend to spill over onto observation of others' performances almost automatically. Moreover, the testimonial value of good performers in any domain is almost certain to be worth more than the testimonial value of poor performers, just because good performers themselves have better audiences. So while it is not an analytic truth that good performance and good observer characteristics are highly correlated, we do think it is a reliable empirical generalisation. Certainly, it seems to be the case that most people operating in any domain value most highly the esteem of those who are already most highly esteemed in that domain.

And on this basis, we have a natural explanation of why associations might be formed with a view to promoting mutual admiration. Good performers attract good observers; and those good observers are themselves good performers. There is a mutuality of esteem available here that creates a natural cement in the formation of the group. These are mutual admiration societies in a purely descriptive sense. Perhaps that term has a slightly negative connotation, as if there is something contrived in the esteem that each supplies to each. We do not mean to support such a connotation. Groups of lustrous performers seem likely to form spontaneously in the economy of esteem, without any suspension on anyone's part of total propriety in action or in judgement. Each quite genuinely esteems her fellow members, is proud to belong to a group of such distinguished performers, and quite justifiably basks in the esteem that she receives, no less genuinely, from others in that group.

We should be clear though that this outcome is not merely a matter of a natural fellow-feeling among those with common skills and common values.

The pattern of association does depend on a contingent fact—namely, that performance quality and observation quality are highly correlated. We think that that is likely to be so; but things could conceivably be otherwise.

3   CHOOSING THE RIGHT POND

The esteem you derive from members in a mutual admiration society will depend not only on performance standards in the community at large, but also performance standards in that particular society. If you join a society where there are higher quality performers, you will get less esteem from members than in a society where average performance is lower. The esteem you do get in the high-performance society will probably be worth more to you, issuing as it does from a more estimable audience. But there is a trade-off here, and there seems to be no reason why that trade-off will be resolved in every case in favour of the higher performing group.

Now, if there is a trade-off between alternative mutual admiration societies, there will also be a trade-off between groups more generally. For, as we have noted, membership of any group will normally do double duty—the group will both provide an internal audience and a pattern of association with that audience on the basis of which the external community will assign esteem. Taking the various considerations into account, which ponds will people choose?

In engaging with this question, the focus will remain on those performers who are in the positive esteem range. These are the individuals who have an incentive to form groups, because the rationale for group formation is publicity of one form or another and publicity is something that only the positively esteemed desire. We shall continue to analyse the question in a context in which groups form essentially for esteem-related reasons. There may be other reasons for groups to form; and the composition of those groups will reflect those other reasons.

For economists, the question of choosing the right pond has a particular redolence. Robert Frank (1985), in one of the notable sources of esteem considerations in economics, develops an argument about the effect of the desire for local status—an esteem-based notion—on the distribution of income within firms. The argument goes that within a firm the higher-productivity/higher-income individuals enjoy more esteem, and the lower-productivity/lower-income enjoy less (or suffer disesteem). The lower-income persons have to be compensated for the ignominy of the diminished status they endure; the higher-income persons, because they receive the benefits of higher status, need to be paid less. Income differentials within firms are thus squeezed to compensate for the effects of esteem. The effect across the economy at large is a less dispersed income distribution than marginal productivity theory would imply. This argument is a fascinating and plausible one.

Frank's story is concerned essentially with the trade-off between internal esteem and income, as if internal esteem were the only esteem that counts. In the folk-tale account of choosing the right pond, by contrast, it is the trade-off between internal esteem and external esteem that seems to be central. 'Would I rather be a large fish in a small pond? Or a smaller fish in a larger pond?' We think that's a fair question—and one that does not admit an obvious answer. Here, we want to engage the question on its own terms, unencumbered by wage differential aspects, and explore the considerations that seem to be at stake.

You are to make a choice among ponds. You are an academic, let us suppose, and you have just received an offer from a more distinguished university than your current one. Will you accept? To simplify, suppose that the salaries in real terms are virtually identical. Only esteem considerations bear.[3] What will those considerations be? There are, it seems to us, five major ones:

- First, there is an association effect. You will be joining a more distinguished institution, and your esteem within the general academic community will increase by virtue of that fact. This is a consideration that clearly argues for accepting.
- There is also a within-group effect. Within your current university, you are among the higher fliers. You get lots of internal esteem from that fact. In the new location, you will be among the lower fliers. You will certainly get less internal esteem, and perhaps even be somewhat disesteemed by your immediate colleagues. This is an argument for staying put.
- Third, the esteem of your new colleagues, if you can earn it, will mean more to you. They are themselves highly esteemed across the profession and their esteem really means something. Moreover, they are pretty astute judges of academic quality.
- Of course, you would be able to increase your esteem by higher performance and the marginal esteem on offer for that higher performance may

---

[3] We do not suppose that universities form for the sole purpose of managing the esteem flows of their academic staff or students. We do though think that esteem is a major motivator in academic circles, and one which we can abstract from other complications in order to provide an example that might be vivid to our readership.

well be higher in your new location. But that too involves a cost. You will find yourself running faster, even if your esteem levels increase.

- The standards effect goes with a publicity effect. By virtue of the reputation of your new institution, more people will come to your seminars when you visit other universities; more people will read your papers. This raises the marginal esteem incentive: a good performance will be worth more and a bad performance will cost you more just because there will be more witnesses. Again, you will have to reconcile yourself to running harder.

We do not here want to offer an elaborate model to illustrate the calculus among these various effects, or a diagram to illustrate the model. Trading-off the various considerations seems to us to offer no simple answer. There are, though, things that seem likely to influence which way you might choose. If you are prepared to give up a good bit more time and energy to professional activities, you are more likely to accept. If your demand for time and energy is relatively inelastic (so that the response to greater marginal esteem rewards is likely to be small) you might do better to stay put. If your chief esteem constituency lies *outside* your local university—say, among a small group of scholars in a particular subfield—internal esteem is going to mean less to you than external esteem. You are then more likely to accept. Put another way, in the best places, we predict that the more mediocre scholars will tend to spend more time outside their institution, among the general professional community perhaps, and less inside among their colleagues.

Your judgement as to whether to move institution may also depend on whether you think that you will be in the top half or the lower half of your new institution. If the former, you will at least be positively esteemed, even within your new institution. You will get less internal esteem than you did before but it will be of higher quality. If the latter, you may well be somewhat disesteemed by your colleagues, since you fail to meet the average performance standards of your new place. You will have the satisfaction of knowing that you are somewhat disesteemed by judges of quality—but this is not in itself an obvious improvement.

We reckon that the balance of esteem effects for most persons will argue for accepting offers from more prestigious institutions. But there are considerations that point in the opposite direction, and these may prove decisive in some cases. If that is so, what would otherwise be an unrelieved hierarchy within the esteem economy is moderated. Some smaller ponds may have some very distinguished fish; and some larger ponds, some rather less distinguished ones. And where group membership is influenced by factors other than esteem—salary levels, location, family preferences, and so on—the natural tendency towards a hierarchy of groups may well be further modified. Nevertheless, in almost all cases, esteem factors will play some role; and the considerations we have outlined here will, to that extent, be in play.

4   ESTEEM-BASED GROUPS AND FREE RIDING

Esteem-based groups have some distinctive qualities. One of the most important, we think, is their capacity to finesse the free-rider problem. We believe that esteem groups will tend to be characterised by a high level of what we might call behavioural loyalty. That is, members will be observed operating in the interests of the group *qua* group, in the absence of any conventional economic incentive to do so.

In standard economic analysis, individuals are normally taken to be predominant egoists. Adding esteem to the set of desires that agents are presumed to have involves no necessary modification to this assumption. Each agent is taken to be primarily concerned with his own esteem—not with the esteem of others. So, on the face of things there is no obvious reason why esteem groups would be any different from other groups in relation to free-rider problems. Each member of the group will benefit most if others spend the time and energy necessary to advance the group's reputation, testify to its excellence, promote its accomplishments, and hide its failures. The claim that esteem groups are likely to be relatively successful in handling the free-rider problem is therefore hardly self-evident.

We consider in turn three arguments that give support to the claim.

The power to expel

It is a characteristic feature of the voluntary setting assumed throughout this chapter that the collectivities under consideration possess the power to exclude. Indeed, such power is necessary for the very possibility of voluntary esteem associations. If all agents have complete freedom of entry into any esteem association, then individuals would enter until the esteem value of belonging was driven to zero. In fact, we took it that the determination of membership size and composition was collectively exercised by existing members, and argued that there would be consensus among those existing members in relation to size and composition decisions.

If the group collectively possesses the power to exclude, it seems also likely that it will possess the power to expel. That is, if the membership of the group is collectively determined, then the group management will be able to threaten members with expulsion if members prove recalcitrant.

This power is non-negligible. As we emphasised earlier, the structure of esteem groups tends to be hierarchical. Unlike the economy of goods, exit is always presumptively costly. In the goods economy, we can imagine an idealised perfectly competitive setting in which all consumers can costlessly exit if any one firm fails to perform according to their liking. In this setting the threat of exit is what maintains firms' incentives to charge the equilibrium marginal cost price. Collectivities in the economy of esteem are not like this. There cannot be perfect competition in any analogous sense. All members derive marginal esteem benefits from the esteem-based collectivity to which they belong. So the power to expel which the collectivity possesses is a non-negligible power. Of course, to expel a member also costs the collectivity something in terms of that individual's contribution to the collectivity's overall performance. To replace an existing member with another, initially outside, will reduce average collectivity performance. So there is a kind of bargaining relation between member and collective, in which the collective does not hold all the cards. Still, the collective holds most of them. In particular, if members were to decide collectively to pursue some action in the interests of the group or association—say, some special act of promotion by individual members—the capacity of members to free ride will be inhibited by this threat of expulsion. That threat gives management the power to enforce collective decisions and to compel individual members to act in the collective interest.

The special significance of the power to expel in this setting is that it operates *ex post*. Individuals who join a group may, on entry, undertake to act in the group's interests, and agree to pay dues for the employment of those who will serve the group professionally and to obey various collectively made decisions. But when time for delivery on those undertakings arrives, the individual members may prove unwilling to fulfil those commitments. Threat of expulsion is a genuine discipline, in a way that *ex ante* undertakings are not.

Indeed, there is an asymmetry here, because expulsion is more conspicuous than merely not belonging. When a professional group de-registers an errant member, that fact is likely to receive additional publicity precisely because additional publicity is what the group provides. It is one thing not to be a member of the Master Builders' Association—supposedly a badge of competence and reliability in house construction. It is another entirely to have been expelled from the Master Builders' Association. The latter provides a significant negative signal. The former only indicates absence of a positive one.

Of course, we cannot assume that the power that the collective can exercise here will be invariably used for purposes that are in the interests of the group as a whole. Management of the collective might well be captured by individuals with purposes of their own. Esteem-based groups, no less than groups of other kinds, will have good reason to make constitutions which embody provisions for disciplining errant managers and competitive processes for the selection of their officers. Indeed, the very fact that it costs members something to be excluded suggests that esteem-based collectives might be especially prone to such problems. But these management issues do not seem likely to have a distinctive cast in the esteem context and we shall not address them further here.

However, it is worth noting that the threat to the managers of disesteem from their members is a special feature of esteem groups where the management is drawn from the membership. After all, a central role of esteem groups is to promote mutual admiration among members: members are especially sensitive to the possibility of disesteem from fellow members. The practice of appointing one's agents from within the membership, rather than from external professionals, is therefore to be identified as a means of mobilising esteem effects.

Internal disesteem and free riding

Members of a mutual admiration society in a given domain can be presumed to be both good performers and good observers in that domain. Their performances are such as to generate esteem; and the esteem derived from others in the group, the internal esteem as we call it, is especially worth having. Sometimes it is the only esteem worth having. That is why some societies are secret. But in all such societies, whether secret or not, the esteem of one's fellow members is of particular value.

Action undertaken in the interests of the group is one means of garnering this esteem. In some cases, the action may take the form of promoting the domain of activity that the group represents. Or it may involve doing chore work for the organisation—being an officer, or undertaking special tasks. Developing a reputation for being a good organisational citizen is a good way of garnering esteem in an arena where it really counts. And obversely, becoming vulnerable to the reputation of being a freeloader or a poor citizen is something that members will be reluctant to court. There is nothing particularly analytically interesting about these tendencies, and it would be unhelpful to overlay a simple point with unnecessary complication. But it seems clear that if esteem incentives are likely to inhibit free riding in general, as we believe, then those incentives are likely to be especially telling in the context of esteem-based groups.

Collective promotion and the inhibition effect

In our discussion so far, there is, as we have emphasised, no direct assault on the assumption of predominant egoism. No individual in the esteem economy has any incentive to promote the esteem of another, except where the esteem of others bears positively on his own. But of course the esteem enjoyed by others will bear positively on his own, when those others are fellow members of an esteem association. Furthermore, the incentive to promote the reputation of the association may be greater than the incentive to promote one's own reputation, even though the association's reputation is a collective good posing standard free-rider problems.

Recall that there are limitations on individuals promoting their own reputation. Blowing one's own trumpet is a source of disesteem in most cases, as we saw in Chapter 2, even if the net effect of the self-promotion is positive. If only there were some way, I might muse, in which I could arrange for others to blow my trumpet, that would be ideal. But there is such a way. If I form a group with others of similar performance, each of us can promote the accomplishments of the group without promoting his or her own performance as such. Here, the free-rider problem works in one's favour. Precisely because one's promotional efforts are dissociated from one's own narrow benefit, one can promote the group without any necessary implication that one is promoting oneself. Blowing the trumpet of the group can be a superior technology for pursuing esteem for each of the group members than the technology under which they each blow their own trumpet.

Consider a group of individuals all of whom are engaged in some activity in which they exhibit genuine talent. For those individuals to extol the significance and importance of that activity hardly strikes us as strange, still less disestimable. It might indeed appear strange if they were to do otherwise. For a physician to testify to the significance of healthcare is just a reflection of proper professional conscientiousness: it reflects the sort of seriousness of purpose and awareness of responsibility that we expect from our doctors. To be sure, in so doing, each physician is providing a public good for all the members of her profession—but such provision is so routine as not to occasion comment, and certainly not to induce disesteem. Now, narrow the focus a little. For a doctor to praise the virtues of the hospital of which she is part, or even of the particular oncology ward where she practises, is probably not disestimable in most cases. She can speak glowingly of her colleagues, take pride in the recovery rates the ward manages, and so on, without generating any particular negative response. In the same way, the Vice-Chancellor or President of a university may promote her own institution—is expected to promote her own institution—without any implication that she is involved in self-promotion. Yet it seems clear that the esteem in which that institution is held contributes significantly to the President's own esteem. The greater the esteem of her university, the more likely it is that she will make her way into the pages of *Who's Who*, be treated with enhanced respect on inter-institutional visits, and so on.

The relevant elements of the argument can perhaps best be captured by aid of a simple diagram (see Figure 11.2). In this diagram, we show the marginal benefit to the individual promoter from promotion/testimony on the vertical axis and size of group promoted on the horizontal axis. There are two considerations to be weighed. One is the esteem benefit to the agent from the promotion/testimony undertaken, setting aside who is doing the promotion. This benefit is largest when the object is the agent herself and reduces systematically as the size of the group increases. Consider the benefit from promotional activity accruing to a particular moral philosopher, Z. Promotion might focus on: just Z's work; the work of all moral philosophers in her university; the work of all moral philosophers in the county; the work of all philosophers in the country; philosophy as a field; all academics. Z's benefit in terms of the additional esteem enjoyed by virtue of the promotional activity declines throughout that range. This aspect is captured by the curve $B(n)$ which declines as n increases in the manner depicted in Figure 11.2.

Consider now Z as the agent who does the promoting/testimony-bearing. The disesteem he accrues by virtue of beating the drum is shown by the curve $D(\underline{n})$. As indicated, this curve increases from a minimum at $\underline{n} = 1$. If group-promotion is itself a source of in-group esteem, this curve may well become positive at a certain point. Or it may simply rise to zero, as the inhibition on group-promotion disappears. What is however central here is that when we add these two curves together, we obtain a net $(B - D)$ curve, which has its maximum at some level of group size, $\underline{n}$, which is greater than one. This group size, $\underline{n}$, is the optimal group size for trading-off the normal free-rider problems with the self-defeatingness of self-promotion. At $\underline{n}$, the net incentive for agents to promote the activities of the group is maximised.[4]

---

[4] The optimal size for maximising association-benefits from esteem which we derived in the appendix to Section 1 above is of course an entirely separate exercise.

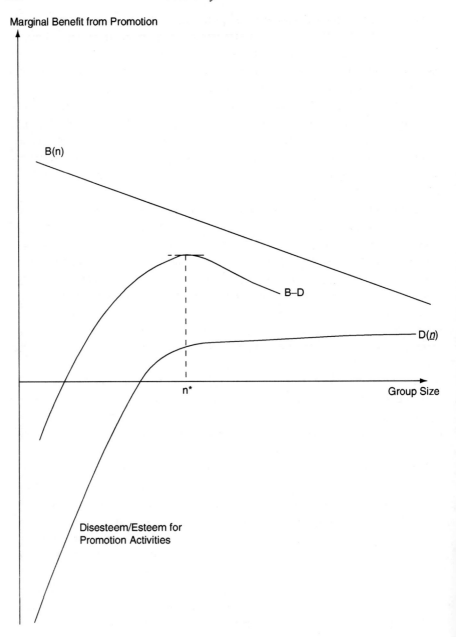

Figure 11.2. *Esteem-maximising group size.*

Now, it might be thought that the advantages of collective action in this context are illusory. If the teleological paradox is overcome exactly to the extent that the free-rider problem is operative, then the proposition that groups constitute a superior technology for promotion is strictly unproven: all that is shown is that group action is not inferior. It is therefore worth emphasising the points made at some length in Chapter 2. Most of those engaging in the promotion of the group's accomplishment need not be acting with self-promotion as a direct motive. The other motives that we have mentioned can all be in play. The point is simply that when individuals promote the accomplishments of the group, they will not be seen to be self-promoting and so will not lose esteem thereby.

We should finally note that this line of argument provides an independent reason for specifically collective action in the economy of esteem, to sit alongside reputation-pooling and mutual admiration considerations. The other two lines of argument canvassed in this section explain why associations and groups formed for esteem reasons might be effective in avoiding free-rider problems; but those considerations do not provide any independent grounds for the formation of collectivities. In that sense, the capacity of collective action to finesse inhibition effects in self-promotion has a distinct cast. Not only will collectives that are formed to provide reputation-pooling and mutual admiration be good at ensuring the collective provision of testimony, but the advantages of collective action in providing testimony will encourage the formation of collectivities even in cases where reputation-pooling and mutual admiration are absent.

5   QUASI-EXCHANGE BY ASSOCIATION

In isolating the economy of esteem from the economy of goods, we have sought to emphasis the relative autonomy of esteem relations. Esteem cannot be directly sold, as if it were just like any other commodity. I cannot purchase the good esteem of observers in any way other than via your coming to believe that my performances in relevant estimable domains merit your esteem. I cannot just reassign some of the esteem I enjoy to you in return for something else. And so on. So there are real limits to the extent to which esteem can be treated just like any other commodity.

Our object in this chapter has been to show that some kinds of exchange in esteem can nevertheless be secured, via the formation of collective entities of various kinds. Even so, the kinds of exchanges made possible involve exchanges essentially within the economy of esteem. That is, participants in trading networks exchange esteem for esteem. The question arises as to whether collective action might also create some scope for the exchange of esteem for goods.

Imagine an association formed for esteem purposes—something like a National Academy. Although we can predict that members will have reason to promote the organisation and contribute something to its maintenance and flourishing in terms of effort and energy, we might want to have officers who will take responsibility for certain core chores. To some extent, we can pay such officers in esteem terms. To be a Fellow of the British Academy is one thing; to be President is another altogether, and presumably carries rather more esteem. We may, in that sense, be able to ensure a satisfactory supply of officers of the association solely via the esteem rewards that office offers. But equally we may not. Perhaps the Fellows are so dedicated to their professional tasks that it is impossible to find Fellows prepared to stand for office and commit to the chore work involved. Or perhaps certain of those offices require special skills that are in short supply among the general membership.

Two solutions are at hand. One is to offer Fellowship status to persons with the requisite skills but not quite the academic lustre to be members on that basis alone, provided they agree to be appointed to the relevant office. Note that this transaction already moves us somewhat beyond the pure esteem case: existing Fellows are trading a little of their esteem in order to avoid administrative duties. Alternatively, the Academy could impose a levy on members, and use the resources to hire professional staff. Once this is done, however, it is possible to discriminate among the different Fellows, either by charging differential levies or providing differential services. Perhaps some members will be given life-member status and exempted from the levy. Perhaps an initiation fee will be introduced for new members. Perhaps certain members will be selected to enjoy the benefits of travel, or meals, or accommodation, and others not. One implication of having such a levy is that the association is encouraged to expand its membership beyond the limits that esteem maximisation alone would suggest. New entrants bring either special skills or extra cash—at the price of somewhat reduced esteem.

Of course, esteem effects do not entirely disappear. The Academy is likely to attract into the ranks of its professional staff those who especially value the association with the Academy. The person who is for thirty years Secretary of the Academy may well receive coverage in *Who's Who*; and there is surely some esteem on offer among one's friends for being on a first-name basis with Nobel Laureates and Regius Professors and others who occasionally get mention in the press. Any member of the general public who is at all disposed to esteem someone for being a Fellow of the Academy is likely also to esteem someone who routinely mingles with Fellows.

There are other ways in which the sale of esteem might be possible. A wealthy businessman may act as patron for a famous artist, and buy some esteem-by-association thereby. A famous sportsman may deliver television advertisements for a product, selling his testimony for a handsome fee and thereby cashing in on his esteem. And of course, since trade-offs have to be made between esteem-generating activities and other activities, it will be possible in principle to calculate the price for esteem in terms of other goods forgone at least for the average person. Other things being equal, high-esteem occupations, like the church in a bygone era or the arts or professional sport, will (in relevant expected terms) have to pay lower wages than low esteem occupations, like garbage collection or sewage cleaning. An orchestra with a high reputation will, on that account, have to pay less for equal quality players than a totally obscure one. A university with a very large cheque-book can buy a very prestigious faculty, and thereby a high reputation. And, following Frank (1985), lower productivity workers in a firm will tend to be paid above-marginal-product wages if low productivity is a source of disesteem, while higher productivity workers will tend to be paid below-marginal-product wages.

In short, there is no reason to expect that the economy of esteem will be totally impervious to conventional economic forces—any more than the economy of goods is impervious to esteem considerations. We certainly do not want to argue that the forces of esteem are irrelevant to the economy of goods. We see no reason to deny that influences run the other way. And it would be hopelessly implausible to do so. Our rationale for treating the economy of esteem as an autonomous entity is largely pragmatic. We think that in many cases the economy of esteem operates fairly independently and that it is analytically useful to focus attention on such cases. That strategy enables us to isolate esteem considerations from more conventional economic ones. But equally, in many cases—cases of considerable interest—the economy of goods and the economy of esteem interpenetrate and mutually constrain. Nothing in our treatment of the topic in this book should be interpreted as suggesting otherwise.

CONCLUSION

The central aim of this chapter has been to examine the centripetal forces operative in the economy of esteem—the forces, that is, that encourage individuals to band together in associations and groups for the sake of esteem. Our object has been first to isolate those forces, and then to describe the structure and character of associations to which those forces give rise. There are, we claimed, two primary elements at stake here:

- The economies of scale in publicity that make reputation pooling a rational strategy for esteem maximisation.
- The creation of audiences of especially good observers—those whose esteem is worth most to good performers.

We examined the first of these considerations in Section 1. We argued that the structure of associations will be hierarchical, with the highest-performing individuals forming the first association in any domain. In establishing association size, we posited a trade-off between the publicity benefits of expanding size on the one hand and the costs in terms of diminished average group performance on the other. We derived an equilibrium association size on the assumption that existing members determine that membership collectively.

In Section 2, we considered the role of groups in constituting audiences—in particular, the capacity of groups to put those with highest performance together with those whose esteem is worth most. We delineated those factors which seem to us to make for good observer quality, and argued that good performers generally make good observers. A positive correlation between the esteem A enjoys in domain X and the value of that A's esteem for others operating in that domain is necessary if mutual admiration societies are to be feasible.

In Section 3, we tried to put together the various elements in the trade-off between internal and external esteem via our own treatment of the choosing-the-right-pond predicament. We isolate five separate aspects of the choice:

- The esteem that each pond enjoys, as a pond.
- The chooser's standing relative to those within each pond.
- The quality of the esteem that fellow pond-dwellers give in each pond.
- The standards of performance that prevail in each pond.
- The publicity the chooser's individual performances will enjoy, by virtue of the particular pond association.

In Section 4, we argued for the proposition that esteem groups are relatively successful in securing loyal behaviour from their members. We see three separate considerations at stake in support of that claim:

- The capacity of the group to expel errant members.
- The internal esteem available to those who pursue group interests and the disesteem suffered by those who fail to pursue those interests.
- The advantages of collective vis-à-vis individual promotion of performance and domain, by virtue of esteem-related inhibitions in relation to self-promotion.

Section 5 involved the issue of exchange through patterns of association. We discussed there various more or less legitimate ways in which borrowed glory might become purchased glory. Patronage is one example; admission to esteem groups on the basis of services given rather than performance quality is another; sale of testimony by the famous is a third. But there is also the much wider range of cases in which individuals themselves make trade-offs between esteem and goods in choice of occupation, location of occupation, and so on. These latter cases do not establish a full market in esteem—they do not permit full exchange of esteem for money, but they may go some way in many cases, and a very long way in a few. We retain the conviction, nevertheless, that the economy of esteem is usefully analysed separately from the economy of goods. There may be leakage between the two economies, and the leakage may well be important to the operation of both. But there are genuine limits on the tradability of esteem, and those limits are conceptually significant. The economy of esteem stands as a distinct and somewhat independent aspect of the social order.

12

Involuntary Associations

In the previous chapter we examined associations and groups that form voluntarily. In this chapter, our focus shifts to the case of involuntary associations, in particular esteem-relevant associations that are thrust upon members rather than being objects of choice. Our questions here will be threefold.

- What are the defining differences between voluntary and involuntary associations?
- What are the implications of those differences for the way in which involuntary associations operate?
- Are there distinctive individual strategies or behaviour patterns that become operative when involuntary associations are in play?

We shall take up these questions *seriatim*. In Section 1 we briefly explicate what we take to be the defining differences between the voluntary and involuntary cases and we investigate the implications of those differences both for the macro-landscape to which each gives rise, and for the kinds of individual responses that involuntary association stimulates. As we shall show, the relation between voluntary and involuntary associations is not exclusively one of contrast. The voluntary case necessarily involves what we might think of as involuntary elements, by virtue of the capacity of members of voluntary associations to exclude non-members: denial of exit and denial of entry may have somewhat similar effects in some cases. Accordingly, in our discussion of involuntary associations, we shall take up a re-examination of the voluntary case, focusing on some of the implications of the characteristic limits to freedom of entry.

We turn in Section 2 to a consideration of the audience groups that are likely to arise in the presence of involuntary associations and their capacity to elicit group loyalty. And then in Section 3 we look at how involuntary associations can provide a motive for individuals to keep their membership of the relevant category secret and at the significance in the presence of that motive of members' going public.

1   ASSOCIATIONS, VOLUNTARY AND INVOLUNTARY

Involuntary associations arise where people in a particular category—defined perhaps by sex or race or linguistic group or ethnic origin—are esteemed or disesteemed by virtue of their membership of that category. In the limit, their esteem is totally determined by that membership: in less extreme cases, their esteem is merely influenced. Individuals are, as we might put it, associated for esteem purposes in the eyes of the general community; and are so, whether they wish to be or not. They are made members of an involuntary association.

The involuntariness in question operates both at the individual and the collective level for persons so associated. That is, not only is there no freedom of exit for individual members, but, in addition, the association considered as a collective does not exercise any power to deny entry, or to enforce exit, over its members: that power lies in the categorising practices of the community at large.

In these respects the involuntary association stands in stark contrast to the voluntary associations we considered in the last chapter. Those associations, as we argued, are characterized by: first, complete freedom of exit at the individual level; and second, a collective right of veto over the membership of the association.

Involuntariness has an important implication for the different macro-landscapes to which the two kinds of associations give rise. Everyone has full exit rights in relation to a voluntary association, and all associations that form for esteem purposes will have to augment the positive esteem of members. Associations that give rise to negative esteem can be ruled out. Moreover, because associations operate to make the positive performance of their members more salient, the macro-landscape is one dominated by esteem peaks. Almost all of the people whose esteem is promoted via assocation will be admirable, in one dimension or another; association effects will render the disestimable relatively invisible.

In the case of involuntary associations, by contrast, individuals can be caught in associations that cause them disesteem. They may earn borrowed contempt as much as borrowed glory. The structure of associations will serve as much to magnify negative as to magnify positive esteem. Of course, involuntary associations might be such as to confer positive esteem: A might be a national of some country that is generally held in high esteem and have that esteem thrust upon him by virtue of nothing more than his nationality. But negative-esteem cases cannot be ruled out. And it is that fact that makes the involuntary case distinctive. Any negative-esteem associations must be ones from which members cannot escape. If they could escape, they would. It is in this sense that the absence of individual exit rights is a crucial feature of the involuntary case. Accordingly, the macro-landscape in the involuntary case will predictably be littered with esteem troughs no less than peaks.[1]

In the later sections of this chapter we shall be looking at how the difference between involuntary and voluntary associations bears on the economy of esteem. But before coming to that topic it is important to recognise certain similarities between the voluntary and involuntary cases. These similarities arise because, as we have noted, the voluntary case necessarily implies the power of the association to exclude. This exclusion is involuntary for those so excluded, because those who are excluded would prefer not to be. We look now at two forms of exclusion to which voluntary groups give rise.

Default exclusion

In the pattern of associations described in the previous chapter, we took it that individuals would search across the set of estimable domains and the corresponding groups, and allocate themselves with an eye to maximising the esteem they enjoy. Most people, we took it, would find some group to belong to. Of course, where more than one group forms in a particular domain, all but those in the most prestigious group will confront limits on their freedom of entry: all but these would prefer to be in the more prestigious group. Nevertheless, in most cases limits on freedom of entry won't be total. Most individuals will be members of groups in a variety of domains, in each case augmenting the esteem they obtain in their various activities.

However, there may well be some individuals who are members of no such groups, and these individuals form a useful polar vantage point from which to explore the effects of exclusion. These individuals are such that their performances in every estimable domain are so lacklustre that entry is denied to them in relation to every esteem-based group to which they might aspire. Of course, these persons may join groups of other kinds—groups, that is, whose primary

---

[1] As we shall show, the difference in the macro-landscapes is a little bit more complicated than this simple contrast suggests. Even in the voluntary case, it is possible that disesteem associations may arise, for reasons we shall shortly explore. In a case we shall denote as the outsiders' predicament, the positive audience effects of a voluntarily formed group, if it emerges, will outweigh the negative association effects. Nevertheless, the general presumption remains that disesteem associations are much more common in the involuntary case. Effectively, the involuntary association context extends and makes much more general a phenomenon that in the voluntary association context is a limiting case—the phenomenon of negative-esteem associations. And because the negative-esteem case is much more common in the involuntary context, we shall in the discussion of involuntary associations that follows focus on those that involve disesteem. The examples of racial and sexual prejudice are taken, in that sense, to be more or less defining cases.

purpose is not esteem-related. We do not mean to suppose that such persons will be denied all aspects of sociality. But they will be denied entry to all groups whose purpose is significantly esteem-based. We focus in this section on these unfortunate individuals—these outsiders, as we call them. However few they may be, it will prove useful to think about how things appear from their perspective.

If our general assumptions about the structure of the demand for esteem are correct, the members of this outsider class share certain features. Precisely because they receive little esteem, they can be predicted to have an especially high (marginal) demand for it. Furthermore, precisely because groups serve to direct publicity to the activities of group members, the outsiders are backgrounded in the publicity stakes. Publicity, after all, is in limited supply. Even if, by some strange chance, one of these outsiders happened to perform at an estimable level, she cannot expect to enjoy a significant audience. The very fact that groups have formed makes her individual strivings in any estimable domain that much less visible. There will not be at hand members of her group to direct attention to her exploits. And she will have no group affiliation to point to as a means to establishing her estimable performance in that domain.

Now, a situation in which there is a category of persons with a very high unmet demand for esteem creates scope for a kind of values entepreneurship. Begin with the observation that, at the purely individual level, one likely response from outsiders is disengagement. Each outsider will, to the extent that her values and preferences are malleable, adopt the sour grapes strategy (Elster 1983). That is, she will find herself inclined to the view that the values that make for the esteem of others are wrong-headed or pretty silly or not to be taken too seriously. Or perhaps she will devalue the esteem that others derive, as based on misperceptions of performance or reflecting simply an overweening desire for esteem on the part of those who are successful in the esteem stakes.

But if this sour grapes attitude is likely to be a common feature among outsiders, then this common feature itself creates a basis for the formation of a fully fledged group. The belief that the successful others are ill-deserving, or that prevailing values are silly, can become the basis not just of shared belief but also of mutual esteem. In particular, should an explicitly countercultural group form, in-group esteem for exhibiting and/or promoting countercultural ideals and values would be available. Accordingly, in the voluntary setting examined in the previous chapter, the processes that are in play in the formation of groups seem likely to create a dynamic of values-resistance, culminating in the formation of countercultural groups. Within these countercultural groups, outsiders find their values shared and they can obtain the esteem they crave. In this sense, group formation in the voluntary case seems likely to give rise to an environment in which many of the prevailing values are contested. The emergence of countercultural groups is a natural outcome of the processes of voluntary group formation.

It is a characteristic feature of the outsider case that the in-group esteem that these countercultural groups generate for their members is likely to be those individuals' sole source of esteem. Members of such groups are therefore likely to exhibit many of the features of the involuntary associations that we examine below. To be sure, exit rights are not formally denied to members of such countercultural groups. But if leaving the group involves forgoing esteem entirely, and if the desire for esteem is as widespread and as intense as we have supposed, then exit will be very costly to any individual member. Equally, any countercultural group with the power to exclude members from the group exercises a kind of natural monopoly over its members; and the organisational structure of such a group will therefore have considerable capacity to enforce collective action.

To sum up the line of thought so far, there are three natural implications of our basic model of voluntary associations in the economy of esteem; these derive from the capacity of voluntary associations to exclude some individuals from membership. The implications are:

1. Processes of voluntary group-formation are likely to give rise to counter-cultural groups.
2. These countercultural groups will be largely composed of individuals whose access to esteem in more conventional arenas is extremely limited.
3. Peer pressure—and capacity for centralised control—will be most intense in groups of this kind.

These implications just fall out of the logic of voluntary group formation. They are in that sense part of the voluntary association story. But they are highly suggestive for the analysis of the involuntary case, and we draw them out here for precisely that reason. Besides, they add a slightly different colouration to our macro-picture of the voluntary case. It seems likely that there may be pockets of disesteemed groups spontaneously emerging within the esteem economy. These groups are characterised by significant negative esteem externally but no less significant compensating positive esteem internally. They are groups that are explicitly countercultural; and they are groups where peer-pressure is likely to be extremely potent.

We have framed the discussion of countercultural groups in terms of the extreme case of outsiders. Countercultural groups can of course also be domain specific. They need not be composed solely of persons who get access to no other esteem group at all. Where persons are denied access to esteem groups in any domain, there will be something of the same incentive to form a countercultural group in that domain. So, in the academic context, groups for the promotion of unconventional methods in various disciplinary fields are hardly uncommon. To a considerable extent no doubt, these groups owe their existence to serious intellectual misgivings about the predominant method. But the fierce rivalry and often mutual disdain that such groups exhibit towards the mainstream (and vice versa) is partly a result as well as partly a cause of the fact of exclusion. The outsiders case is a polar one in that the esteem derived from the countercultural group is the sole source of esteem for outsiders. In domain-specific countercultural groups, members might well be members of externally esteemed groups in other domains. Still, if the domain is an important one to the members, or if the domain is a non-discretionary one, or one that individuals find costly to leave for non-esteem reasons, then countercultural groups are likely to form and will exhibit much the same properties as outsider groups.

Discriminatory exclusion

The general picture of association in the voluntary case involves membership on the basis of performance quality in the relevant estimable domain. If X-performance is a significant source of esteem, then individuals who are high-performers in the X-domain will become members of the X-association. But in the presence of pre-existing involuntary associations, individuals may be excluded from membership despite the fact that their X-performance, considered on its own, would qualify them for membership. Suppose that individual A is a member of some category, Z, which suffers general disesteem. That disesteem may derive from the fact that members of the Z category are (believed to be) on average poor X-performers. Or it may be that category Z is just generally disesteemed, for reasons that have nothing to do with X-performance at all. In either case, A may find herself systematically excluded, on the basis of her Z-ness, from esteem groups for which she would otherwise qualify.

It is worth noting that existing members of the excluding group may not themselves be mistaken about the quality of A's performance. They may know even that A's performance is sufficiently distinguished to justify membership. But recall that the role of groups is to enhance esteem via expanded publicity. If A carries a certain disesteem within the wider community by virtue of her membership of category Z, then including A is likely to involve some loss of out-group esteem for the group. That loss, if large enough, will be sufficient to explain A's exclusion, even though the group members themselves might not endorse either the underlying judgement or its validity in this particular case. Group members are, after all, assumed to operate to maximise esteem in the light of prevailing beliefs and values. They have no necessary incentive to correct prevailing prejudices—even in those cases where members know the prejudices to be unjustified. It is, however, to be emphasised that the desire for esteem plays a critical role here in encouraging the exclusion of those who are categorically disesteemed: members' esteem will suffer if they are associated with the disesteemed![2]

In this way, category Z individuals may find themselves systematically excluded from esteem-enhancing groups. Individuals like A may thoroughly endorse the relevant group values, and be thoroughly estimable performers according to those values, but may still meet exclusion at every turn. Were it possible, A might well repudiate her classification—simply exit from the Z association. But such exit is, by hypothesis, not possible: A is identified as a Z and no attempts by A to deny that categorisation are relevant. In this sense, the case of discriminatory exclusion is properly to be seen as a case of involuntary association, where Z is the involuntary association in question. Examples of Z-like categories have abounded in human societies. At one or another time being a woman or being black, being Jewish or being Catholic, has played the required role; and the pattern, of course, continues in many societies, both for these categories, and for others.

It is notable that members of category Z are in a somewhat similar predicament to that of the outsiders, referred to in the previous section. We say somewhat similar because there are significant differences. For one thing, the Z members are actually accomplished at many of the activities that the general public regard as estimable. The Zs have no reason to repudiate the specific values that underlie the economy of esteem: the Zs simply desire what, in terms of performance level, they deserve—namely, access to the publicity that group membership affords.

---

[2] There is a contrast here with the statistical discrimination literature associated most notably with E. Phelps (1972). In the employment context to which the theory is most typically applied, there is an automatic economic cost involved in any systematic misperception. If an employer happens to know that the marginal product of a particular individual representative of the class or race or sex is higher than average for the category, that is information that the employer would not want to discard. There would be economic costs from doing so.

Unlike the outsider case, then, there is no need for the Z-group to be countercultural across the set of generally prevailing values. Instead, the Zs have reason to form a set of rival groups along essentially the same lines as the groups already extant in the esteem economy. So, for example, Women's Intellectual Clubs form where women are denied access to intellectual or academic associations. Black Athletics Clubs develop where blacks are excluded from athletic associations. Papal Knighthoods are assigned in Protestant monarchies where such honours are routinely denied Roman Catholics. And so on. Within such groups, there is no commitment to alter prevailing values—except in respect of the *discrimination* involved in their exclusion from other groups. The value of the relevant activities—intellectual pursuits, particular sports, etc—is accepted and endorsed. What emerges is a kind of parallel culture of esteem associations—this, by contrast with the counterculture in the outsider case—where the determination of members is to show that the excluded group can do better at the relevant activity than the non-excluded others. Thus the Harlem Globe Trotters were by common consent the best basketball players— and African Americans took justified pride in the fact—through a period in which blacks were excluded from the National Basketball Association in the United States.

Unlike outsiders, Z members share something beyond the fact of their exclusion: they are already an association of a minimalist kind in the eyes of the general community. That associational pattern encourages the creation of Z-groups, even if there were no such groups before. In other words, moving from category to group does not require the kind of entepreneurship that is needed in the outsider case.

If, for example, the Zs have certain common cultural or religious or ethnic or linguistic or other characteristics, these characteristics may well also be invoked as significant as the group structure comes into being. After all, the same forces that induce outsiders to become countercultural will encourage Z-category members to make a virtue of their Z-ness. In short, there will be forces in play encouraging what might otherwise have remained merely a Z-category to become an encompassing Z-group. And in the process, features of Z-group members that might otherwise have been individually insignificant to many of them become lodged within an esteem structure that strongly reinforces those features. In this sense, the Z-identity may be as much a creation of the fact of exclusion as it is of some pre-existing social facts. In the case of discriminatory exclusion, there must be some pre-existing social furniture; but the operation of esteem as a force for association certainly seems likely to reinforce and embed that furniture.

2   INVOLUNTARY ASSOCIATIONS AND LOYALTY

Let there be a category (denote it Z) such that it is impossible for any Z-member to be recognised as anything other than a Z-member. And suppose further that Z-ness is sufficient to exclude individuals so categorised from virtually all other esteem associations. What actions are available to a person (involuntarily) assigned to a negatively esteemed association of this monopoly kind? At first sight, the answer seems to be—not much. The individual behavioural incentives that occupied us in Chapters 5, 6, and 7 and the corresponding incentives to pursue or eschew publicity that were the focus of Chapters 8, 9, and 10 are all essentially irrelevant. There may seem to be nothing that the individual can do by way of individual performance or publicity manipulation to alter the esteem in which she is held. Disesteem, it appears, is thrust upon her by virtue of her association, and she must simply endure the disesteem that falls to that association.

This, however, is mistaken. There are two broad strategies available. One is to keep one's membership of the category on which the association is constructed secret. Clearly, that is an option more readily available in some cases than others—almost impossible in cases where the category is based on clearly identifiable physical features like skin colour, but quite feasible for categories like sexual preference or perhaps racial origins where these are not readily detectable. We shall examine secrecy in the next section.

The second option is to act as advocate of the association. The kinds of strategy we have in mind here emerge fairly naturally from our earlier discussion. They involve efforts at two margins—a modification of the values themselves (the countercultural element); and talking up the exploits of Z members in arenas that are already established as objects of esteem (the parallel culture element). So 'black is beautiful' and 'plump is sexy' are examples of the first. Promoting the exploits of category members in intellectual or musical or sporting or military contexts exemplifies the second.

Both kinds of promotional activity, if pursued with any degree of seriousness, could prove quite costly. The Museum of Polish Intellectuals or the Black Athletes' Hall of Fame do not come cheap. And of course, any effect on the esteem of her involuntary association is a public good to all members of that association: best for the would-be promoter if those other members work to promote the esteem of the association while she saves her efforts for privately more productive things. Now, we argued in the previous chapter that this free-rider problem may not be so significant in the case of esteem associations as it is in other settings. However, one important element in the voluntary context is missing here. The association has no capacity to expel members, and cannot use the threat of expulsion to secure compliance to collective decisions. Is there then any reason to think that the free-rider difficulties in promotional activities in the involuntary case might not be crippling?

We think that there is. If, as postulated, the association has a monopoly status in determination of members' esteem, then the only means by which a member's esteem can be increased in the community at large is via promoting the association as a whole. In a conventional public good case—law and order, say—incentives to free-ride on public provision are exacerbated by the fact that there are private alternatives to the collectively provided service. One can instal locks and guard dogs, or employ private security services. Where no such alternatives to the collectively provided service are available, incentives to free-ride are moderated. In more technical terms, the individual demand curves for the public good of category promotion are likely to be highly inelastic. This fact does not avoid the free-rider issue; but it does very substantially ameliorate its effects.

Again, a simple diagram will assist in making the relevant point. Imagine a group of n identical persons all of whom have a demand curve for a public good, P, that is highly inelastic. That is, it takes the steep shape illustrated by D'D in Figure 12.1. The optimal supply of P will occur where each individual faces a price-per-unit for P of mc/n, where mc is the marginal cost of P and n is the number of persons in the group. The optimum is thus P* in Figure 12.1.

The aggregate level of individual contributions in equilibrium in this case will be at M—lower than the optimal P*—where each individual demand curve (identical by assumption) cuts the mc curve. If less than M were to be produced, it would be individually rational for any individual to provide more. The cost of units of P is less than the marginal benefit over the range to the left of M, as indicated by the fact that D'D lies above the mc line. But because the demand for P is so inelastic, M and P* are actually quite close together. There are mutual gains from trade to be obtained from expanding P production from M to P*; but those gains are not particularly great, vis-à-vis the benefits that derive to individual category members over the range up to M.

The crucial assumption here is that D'D is likely in the case stipulated to be very inelastic. Clearly if the individual demand curve were rather more elastic, (say, D'''D'' in Figure 12.1) the amount of P that anyone would provide unilaterally might be quite small. With D'''D'', that amount would be M'', which is small vis-à-vis the optimum P*. Or indeed, no individual might find it in his interests to provide any of the good—category promotion—at all. The degree of failure attributable to free-riding would be very large. Our argument then hinges on the claim that individual demand curves for association-promotion activities in the case of monopoly associations are likely to be very inelastic.

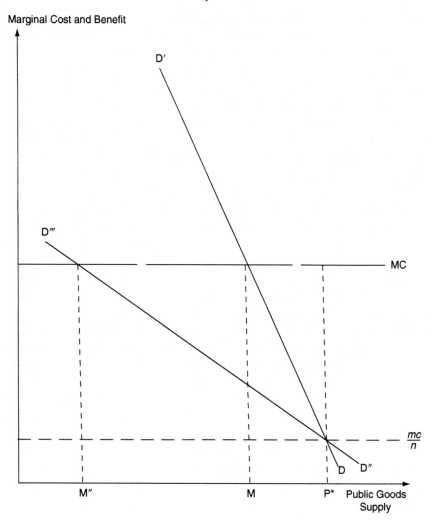

Figure 12.1. *Free-riding in promoting one's association.*

Our reason for thinking this is simply that there are no alternative mechanisms by which association members in such cases can derive esteem. More or less standard economic apparatus explains why individuals will act as if extremely loyal to the interests of the category—and specifically in the arena of category promotion within the wider community.

Note that any success achieved through such endeavours operates via changes in the perceptions of the external constituency: the primary addressee of such efforts is the community at large, rather than other members of the category. These are, in the terms of our earlier categories, attempts to secure associational benefits rather than audience benefits. But audience effects are not by any means ruled out for members of involuntary associations: the problem is rather that the choice of possible groups to join is restricted to members of the disesteemed association. Just as in the outsider's predicament, the incentive to create such a group—or to join such a group if it already exists—is extremely strong. All members of the association crave esteem, and one means for garnering that esteem is through creating an audience. That audience will however be restricted to those who are members of the involuntary association.

Two separate kinds of groups might be on offer. One kind is based on some independently esteemed activity. It seeks to create a mutual admiration society out of those members of the involuntary association who are good performers / observers in that activity domain. In this way, what emerges out of the involuntary association is a culture parallel to, rather than operating against, the mainstream. This seems likely to be an outcome restricted to those cases where the involuntary association is large. And even in this case, it is a significant fact that all members of all such groups share certain things in common—namely, the linguistic, ethnic, religious, racial, or whatever property on the basis of which the involuntary association is formed. Unlike the outsiders, who have nothing in common but the fact of their exclusion, members of involuntary associations have in common the feature that is attributed to them in the associative process.

It might not be surprising therefore if a single group were to form directly out of the association. Even where the alleged basis of the association is quite thin, lying largely in the prejudices of the general community, nevertheless the group that forms is likely to develop a distinctive character. It is likely to come to esteem the very properties on the basis of which its members have been excluded from other esteem-related associations and groups. If there are group-specific ethnic, linguistic, or cultural elements, these will tend to be disproportionately significant in earning in-group esteem, just because those particular features are predominant within the audience of observers. The effect of involuntary association is to differentially empower group-members as audience of other group-members. And this in turn differentially empowers those sources of esteem that are relatively significant within that group.

It is sometimes posed as a puzzle why it should be the case that groups seem especially to flourish when they are objects of persecution. Israelites in exile in Babylon discover there a new sense of who they are. Colonial regimes that rigorously discourage fraternisation with the local population can thereby support the flourishing of local identity—not just in the negative sense of non-corruption of the original culture, but more particularly in the positive sense of enlivening a dormant sense of distinctive native identity. Thus, the forces within the community at large that partition society into involuntary associations can actually be promoting the associations so formed. The wall that keeps people out also locks those people in—into the very associations that are objects of disesteem within the larger community.

In particular, once groups form, then they will possess a collective structure that has, among other powers, the power both to exclude and expel (from the group, if not from the underlying association). And as we saw previously, this power to expel carries with it the capacity to enforce behaviour that is in the group's collective interests. We do not mean to suggest by this observation that establishing such a power structure is a likely motive for establishing or joining such a group: we would look directly to the desire for esteem to explain the group's emergence. But it is an important incidental fact about such groups that they are likely to be well placed to solve free-rider problems, and hence to solicit action in the group's interests from their members.

Note further that the power to exclude is likely to be especially potent in the monopoly case. Where the group that forms is a category-wide group, that group is the only group to which members are likely to have access. When the category is large enough that a parallel culture emerges, then the effect of being excluded from any one group in the array is less devastating. If you are excluded from the Black Basketballer's Association, there will always be the prospect of joining the Black Baseballers, or Black Rollerbladers, or whatever.

The central point here is a simple one. When a group forms directly out of an involuntary category, one effect is to provide further resources for enforcing collective decisions. The prediction is that such groups will be especially effective in self-promotion

3 INVOLUNTARY ASSOCIATIONS AND SECRECY

Up to now we have taken it that members of involuntary associations are readily identifiable. In lots of cases, that assumption is valid. But in some cases, it is not. That is, there might be some associations whose membership is not transparent in this way. Associations based on sexual preference are an example that we have already mentioned in this connection. Or it may be that though the category is transparent for most members, it is not for all. Some who would be classifiable as black in genetic terms (say, because they have at least one black grandparent) may not have dark skin or the facial features that are taken to be characteristic of African races. In contexts where the category is an object of disesteem, these non-transparent members would be disesteemed were their membership of the category manifest: but it is not.[3] For this sub-set at least, there is a voluntary element to their membership: they can choose whether they declare their category membership or not.

In all such cases, there will be some incentive for unrecognised members of disesteemed associations to acquire the attributes that would tend to identify them as members of the general community, and therefore independently estimable. Such assimilation strategies are well known. Where the relevant category is ethnic or linguistic, one might remove oneself from the relevant ethnic neighbourhood; or change one's name; or cultivate the establishment accent. Even perhaps, ape the discriminatory attitudes of the general community. The ex-Australian academic in Oxford might, having honed his accent to acceptable Winchester tones, deplore with special vigour the low-level habits of visiting colonials. Gerald Finzi, son of Ashkenazy Jews, might become among the more aggressive proponents of the English watercress school of composition—of which he himself was an example. It is not to be thought that there is anything necessarily duplicitous about the exercise of choice of association here. One might simply think that one's identity is, or ought to be, a matter for individual choice. Or that membership of the relevant underlying category is a private matter, or that the attitudes toward that category are defective or improper. And one might take the latter view without wishing particularly to make an issue of that impropriety.

Nevertheless, the exit from the association that is available is so only because of the possibility that membership is not detectable. Or not detectable easily. In such cases, non-disclosure is an option. And it is an option that esteem considerations may promote. Those considerations will be most relevant when the individual otherwise receives considerable esteem—where performance in various estimable domains is at an appropriately high level. In such cases, the individual would lose much of that esteem were the association to become common knowledge. The incentive not to disclose, and indeed, where there is risk of discovery, to suppress the information, must be strong. On the other hand, secrecy can be a risky strategy esteem-wise. For, were the truth revealed, then not only would one lose most of the esteem that one enjoyed in the general community, but one would also be likely to endure the disesteem associated with duplicity—and this not least among the other members of the disesteemed association. One who is construed to have denied her Z-ness can

---

[3] It is conceivable that, in some cases, what is disesteemed is the characteristic of the category rather than the category itself. If so, then the efforts of individuals to divest themselves of that characteristic might be doubly esteemed. But this is not the case we have in mind here.

presumably expect little esteem from within the Z-community when her Z-ness is uncovered.

On the other hand, the very possibility of secrecy also allows the possibility of self-declaration. One whose membership of some disesteemed category is not a matter of common knowledge has the option of going public. We might describe this case as involving the coming-out effect. The term here is a reference to the practice of closet homosexuals publicly declaring their sexual identity, but it clearly has much more general application.

In Chapter 10, we examined the *enfant terrible* case as one of possible perversity in publicity-seeking, because individuals were seen to be acting (at least in the short run) to increase the disesteem they suffered. The characteristic feature of that case, as we interpreted it, is that the *enfant* in question embraces disesteem in order to obtain something that is yet more fervently desired— namely attention or publicity. We used that case to explore the question of whether publicity is an independent object of desire, over and above the esteem which publicity often serves to promote. In the coming-out case, something of the same perversity seems to be in play. There is a manifest embracing of disesteem; and because an important aspect of the exercise is to attract attention, there is a sense in which the more disesteem one attracts, the better.

But the motivation for the violation in the coming-out case is distinctive. In the *enfant terrible* case, the object is to draw attention to the actor—with an eye, we have conjectured, towards accruing greater positive esteem in the future. In the coming-out case, by contrast, the object is to induce observers to reappraise the ideal on the basis of which disesteem is assigned. The strategy achieves this reappraisal in two ways. One involves drawing attention to the prevailing ideal, with an eye to exposing its deficiencies. The other involves using the weight of the declarer's independently derived esteem, as a counter to any disesteem that may attach to the ideal under contestation. Coming out is most effective, then, when perpetrated by one whose esteem levels are independently already high. Violation of the prevailing ideal will cost the actor esteem, at least in the community at large—and this loss of esteem is an essential element of the strategy. The actor is effectively declaring that disesteem on the basis of this ideal is something that the actor relishes. Coming out is an act of conscientious objection in the esteem domain.

Even if the act of coming out in a particular instance is unsuccessful in significantly altering the ideal, it may serve a salutary function for others who share the actor's views—perhaps members of the disesteemed group, but not necessarily those alone. Coming out may even become an ideal and a standard for the disesteemed group—perhaps along the lines of the treatment of bootstrapping set out in Chapter 7. Each out-comer may obtain esteem at least from other members of the disesteemed group, and this in-group esteem may induce yet other members of the group to come out, and so on. The cumulative effect of this sequence may indeed ultimately change the underlying values. At the very least, it will alter the perceived standards and thereby reduce the disesteem in which members of the disesteemed group are held (along the lines outlined in the basic model in Chapter 5).

To the extent that the underlying values are altered, there are likely to be substantial esteem benefits on hand for the pioneers—those heroes who came out first. We do not claim that that prospect of esteem is what primarily motivates most—or perhaps any—of the original out-comers. But if the out-comer is successful in changing prevailing values, then there will be esteem attached to being a hero/pioneer; and the prospect of that reward is hardly going to be irrelevant.

The coming-out and *enfant terrible* cases are different in a further respect. In the *enfant terrible* case, the strategy is one of behaving badly so as to secure attention and/or recognition. That strategy is something that cannot be general. The strategy is bound to fail in its purpose if too many others adopt it. Best for you if you are the only *enfant terrible* in town. The coming-out case is precisely the opposite in this respect. Success is achieved when the flood of violators becomes so significant that the community cannot help but rethink its values.

All the same, the coming-out and the *enfant terrible* cases share the feature that they represent an exception to one of our general propositions—namely, that people will try to reduce their audience size when they face the prospect of disesteem. We think that these two cases are exceptions. And it is important to note that the incentive to reduce audience size remains. It is precisely because secrecy is attractive that the act of voluntary declaration carries force. The person who is incidentally discovered to be a member of the relevant disesteemed category or group does not come out; such persons are merely uncovered. Such discoveries might have an influence on prevailing standards, and thereby on compliance, but those so uncovered cannot plausibly derive esteem for such effects. The esteem on offer for coming out depends both on the paradoxical fact that coming out costs something in esteem terms, and on the contingent fact that continued secrecy is likely to be feasible.

CONCLUSION

Our object in this chapter has been to explore the role of involuntary associations in the economy of esteem. In Section 1 we focused on the contrasts and similarities between voluntary and involuntary associations. Unlike voluntary associations, involuntary associations cannot be explained by reference to esteem considerations. But individuals' responses to being involuntarily associated can be so explained, and exploring those responses was our prime objective here.

Members of involuntary associations cannot individually exit. Nor can they collectively choose who else will be a member of the association. These differences immediately create an important point of contrast between voluntary and involuntary cases: namely, that all associations in the voluntary case will augment positive esteem. The involuntary case will admit disesteem associations—and indeed most of the analytic interest derives from the disesteem case. This contrast can be spelled out in terms of the different macrolandscapes to which the voluntary and involuntary cases give rise. Voluntary associations go with a landscape of salient esteem peaks. Involuntary associations allow lots of esteem abysses.

Members of disesteem associations not only enjoy less esteem by virtue of their membership of those associations: they also tend to be excluded from positive esteem associations. Accordingly, we can learn something about the effects of (involuntary) disesteem associations by examining the effects of exclusion—effects that arise in the voluntary case as well, because the power to exclude is a necessary condition for voluntary associations forming. We examined two types of such exclusion, default exclusion and discriminatory exclusion, and drew out the implications of each for the likely structure of groups in the involuntary case.

In the previous chapter we argued that voluntary esteem associations and groups are likely to be able to finesse the free-rider problem: members of such associations and groups will often be observed acting to promote the esteem of the collective, or otherwise working in the collective interest. In Section 2 we argued that this attribute generalises to the involuntary case, though it operates through slightly different mechanisms. In the involuntary association case, there is no collective power to expel—which we noted is a formidable power in the voluntary case. But the fact that each member's esteem is uniquely tied to the fate of the association means that each member may be led to act in the association's interests, even though doing so creates equal benefits for other members.

In Section 3 we explored implications of the fact that membership in involuntary associations will not always be transparent. All Zs may be disesteemed by virtue of their Z-ness, but whether a particular individual is a Z or not may be unclear. In such cases, secrecy, or non-disclosure, is an option. In that sense, there is a limited element of voluntariness. The possibility of secrecy raises the issue of voluntary disclosure and led us to a brief discussion of the coming-out phenomenon. Like the *enfant terrible* case examined in Chapter 10, coming out seems perverse in the sense that it looks like a positive embracing of disesteem. Unlike the *enfant terrible* case, however, which might be construed as one element in a long-term esteem-maximising strategy, coming out is better thought of as an act of conscientious objection in the esteem economy.

PART III

EXPLOITING THE ECONOMICS OF ESTEEM

Introduction

This part of the book is designed to underline the potential uses of the economics of esteem in drawing up guidelines for institutional design and policymaking. Assuming that people are concerned about the esteem of others, and that this concern gives rise to the sorts of patterns reviewed in Part II, the question is whether it can be made to work for good, as most of us will see it, not for bad. We think that the economy of esteem can work for better or worse and that there is some prospect of our being able to shape it so that it works for better. The economics of esteem can have a normative as well as a positive aspect, directing us to lessons in institutional design and policymaking.

The case for this view is set out in these final chapters fairly abstractly, since the empirical groundwork for a more detailed programme in institutional design is just not available. We describe the economy of esteem, when it works for good, as an intangible hand that operates in parallel to the invisible hand of the market and the iron hand of the state. In Chapter 13 we make the case for thinking that intangible-hand regulation promises to be a particularly attractive and effective way for society to arrange its affairs. In particular, it promises to be more attractive and more effective in a number of respects than the more familiar alternatives.

We try in the remaining chapters to offer some more concrete vindication of that claim. Chapter 14 argues that the intangible hand is distinguished by the way in which it gives rise to social norms, distinguishing these from the laws that the polity coercively supports and the regularities that emerge spontaneously from the operation of the market. It critiques a well-known argument that norms are not going to be available when they are needed—in particular, when they are needed to help people escape collective predicaments—and it illustrates the many different ways in which norms may emerge and be sustained under the influence of esteem forces.

Chapter 15 tries, finally, to illustrate ways in which the intangible hand might be made to work for good, nurturing socially desirable norms and weakening socially undesirable ones. It will work for good so far as people are predisposed to be influenced by the desire for esteem; so far as the options before them are presented in a way that bends the desire for esteem in desirable directions; and so far as the regime of publicity under which they operate makes it likely that the desire will be effectively mobilised. The chapter illustrates these themes by identifying a range of cases where existing arrangements may jeopardise the potential of the intangible hand on these three fronts.

13

The Intangible Hand in Profile

1 THE NOTION OF THE INTANGIBLE HAND

The discussion so far has made it evident that people's desire for esteem can induce them individually to adjust their behaviour so as to increase the esteem they enjoy and can lead them in the aggregate—usually without their recognising the fact—to establish quite determinate patterns of behaviour and relationship. The patterns so established will be unintended consequences of their individual adjustments to the rewards of esteem and the penalties of disesteem. Sometimes those unintended patterns will be benign from the point of view of people generally, and sometimes they will be malign. The patterns will be benign and make people better off on the whole—better off by more or less accepted criteria of evaluation—if they involve an increase in what we tend to describe as social or pro-social behaviour. They will be malign and make people worse off on average if they involve an increase in anti-social behaviour: this can happen as the esteem available in a subculture induces members to act in a way that is hostile to the interests of outsiders.

This talk of people aggregatively generating unintended consequences, in particular consequences that constitute benign patterns, is reminiscent of the notion of the invisible hand launched by Adam Smith in his work on *The Theory of the Moral Sentiments* in 1759. Smith introduced this notion to characterise the way in which the rich spend money on luxuries, having had their fill of necessaries, and thereby enable others to have enough to purchase those necessaries for themselves.

They [the rich] consume little more than the poor, and in spite of their natural selfishness and rapacity, though they mean only their own conveniency, though the sole end which they propose from the labours of all the thousands whom they employ, be the gratification of their own vain and insatiable desires, they divide with the poor the produce of all their improvements. They are led by an invisible hand to make nearly the same distribution of the necessaries of life, which would have been made, had the earth been divided into equal proportions among all its inhabitants, and thus without intending it, without knowing it, advance the interest of the society, and afford means to the multiplication of the species. (Smith 1982: 184–5)

The invisible hand contrasts with the visible hand of law and regulation and management—for short, the iron hand—in so far as it involves the non-intentional as distinct from the intentional imposition of rewards and penalties on people; in particular, rewards and penalties that work to elicit an overall outcome that is, by received criteria, good for the society as a whole. Thus in Smith's example, the rewards that the poor give the rich who employ them—the gratification of their 'vain and insatiable desires'—elicits a pattern of redistribution whereby the necessaries of life become available to all. And those sanctions operate without the poor intending them as sanctions and without anyone, rich or poor, having to be aware that the sanctions operate in this way. This invisible hand contrasts with the attempts that the state might have made to secure the same result by resorting to the intentionally imposed sanctions of law and regulation: by exercising the iron hand of political power.

The esteem-based mechanism is like the invisible hand in one respect but it is unlike it in another. It involves non-intentional sanctioning, as the invisible hand does. But the factors that non-intentionally sanction agents in this case are not things that other people do—not the actions of the poor, for example, in securing the conveniency of the rich—but rather attitudes that they form in response to the deeds or dispositions of those agents. In order to mark this contrast with the invisible hand, we describe the esteem-based mechanism as an intangible hand (Pettit 1989; Brennan and Pettit 1993; Pettit 1993). Talk of an intangible hand is appropriate, because the attitudinal reward associated with having the esteem of others is intangible in comparison to the material goods and services that characterise the invisible-hand case.

It is common nowadays to recognise that as an invisible hand may work for overall good, so an invisible backhand—or, as it is sometimes called, an invisible foot—may work for overall bad (Hardin 1982). This happens, for example, when the free-riding motive leads people to exploit the fact of not being noticed or punished by others to behave in a self-serving but anti-social manner: say, to exploit a common resource at a generally unsustainable level. We hasten to say that equally the desire for esteem may often work to an overall malign effect. It may constitute an intangible backhand or an intangible foot (see Ellickson 2001: 30–6). For example, the intangible hand can lead those in a particular group to earn credit with one another by behaving in a manner that is detrimental to the population at large or to other groups (McAdams 1995; Dharmapala and McAdams 2001). Moreover, the sort of behaviour that is esteemed—say, that of seeking revenge for any harm to one's person or family, or that of vindicating one's honour in duelling—can propagate a mutually destructive general pattern (Elster 1990; Hardin 1995; McAdams 1997).

Nor are these the only ways in which an intangible backhand is likely to materialise in a society. We saw in Chapter 12 that the opinion formed of people is often dictated by the involuntary associations to which they are party. It may even be in such cases that no matter what individuals do in a certain domain, they will be esteemed—or more to the point, disesteemed—on the basis of an involuntary identity, say as belonging to a certain ethnic or religious group, or as being of a certain gender or age. This pattern can make for an overall outcome that is not only bad for the people suffering such discrimination but for the society as a whole. Again, as we noted earlier, there may be a systematic divergence between each individual's attitudes of approval and disapproval and the attitudes he or she ascribes to others; there may be pluralistic ignorance, as it is known (Prentice and Miller 1993). When this occurs on a large scale it may also give rise to an overall pattern that everyone has reason to deplore.

There is some irony in introducing the intangible hand on a model provided by the invisible. For we saw in the Introduction that it is almost certainly because of the rise of invisible-hand thinking that faith in the intangible hand, even a recognition of the intangible hand, declined. The invisible hand suggests that we may be able to arrange things to social benefit, not only without people's being particularly virtuous, but also without their being moved by the desire to be thought virtuous: that is, without the desire for esteem being called into operation. That must have appealed on grounds of economy to social thinkers of the late eighteenth- and early nineteenth-century Enlightenment. It must have reassured those who thought, as clearly some did think, that ordinary folk would be insensitive to considerations of honour. And it must have held out the refreshing prospect of a mode of ensuring social order that did not have any whiff of hypocrisy. We reviewed all these considerations in the Introduction.

But it is worth emphasising that prior to the appearance of the invisible hand in human thought, and indeed for some little time afterwards, it was a matter of common recognition, not only that people desired esteem, but also that this desire could work or be made to work to the benefit of society generally. This had been a recurrent theme, indeed, right back to Plato (Kamtekar 1998). Some more or less randomly chosen quotations should help to make the point, reinforcing our claim to be rediscovering an older tradition of thought rather than initiating a new one. We list them in the same spirit, and subject to the same qualifications, as the quotations we gave in Chapter 1, when we were urging the claim that esteem is attractive, disesteem unattractive, to most people.

Pierre Nicole (1676): In our present state of weakness it is therefore useful that we should be removed from vices not only by charity, but also by the kind of *amour-propre* that is called honour, so that when charity slackens, this honour may support the mind, and prevent it from falling into dangerous excesses. (Nicole 1999: 17)

John Locke (1690): For though Men uniting into Politick Societies, have resigned up to the public the disposing of all their Force, so that they cannot employ it against any Fellow-Citizen, any farther than the Law of the Country directs: yet they retain still the power of Thinking well or ill; approving or disapproving of the actions of those whom they live amongst, and converse with: And by this approbation and dislike they establish amongst themselves, what they will call Virtue and Vice. (Locke 1975: 353–4)

John Ray (1713): I cannot but admire the wisdom and goodness of God, in implanting such a passion in the nature of man, as shame, to no other use or purpose, that I can imagine, than to restrain him from vicious and shameful actions. (Lovejoy 1961: 165)

The Baron de Montesquieu (1748): Honor, that is, the prejudice of every person and rank, supplies the place of the political virtue of which I have been speaking, and is everywhere her representative: here it is capable of inspiring the most glorious actions, and, joined with the force of laws, may lead us to the end of government as well as virtue itself. (Montesquieu 1977: bk. 3, ch. 6)

Samuel Johnson (1751): Wise men differ about the love of fame. Some think it vain as, after death, it cannot benefit us. Others reply that it is a noble ambition, implying a resolution to merit the praise received and an aspiration to be of help to future ages. In truth, the love of fame is to be regulated rather than extinguished. It should not be the predominant passion—unchecked it may lead to ruin—but may serve as a useful adjunct to moral and religious motivation to goodness. It is the only recompense which this life offers to virtue. (Lovejoy 1961: 137)

Bernard Mandeville (1757): Men are better paide for their Adherence to Honour, than they are for their Adhrence to Virtue: The First requires less Self-denial; and the Rewards they receive for that Little are not imaginary but real and palpable. But Experience confirms what I say: The Invention of Honour has been far more beneficial to the Civil Society than that of Virtue, and much better answer'd the End for which they were invented. For ever since the Notion of Honour has been receiv'd among Christians, there have always been, in the same Number of People, Twenty Men of real Honour, to One of real Virtue. (Mandeville 1971: 42–3)

2 DEPLOYING THE INTANGIBLE HAND

Given that the intangible hand can and does often operate to good, the question naturally arises as to whether we may be able to design institutions and policies so as to increase its impact—and, on the other side, decrease the impact of the intangible backhand. We argued in earlier discussions that people adjust the margins of their behaviour so as to achieve greater positive esteem and, so far as possible, reduce any disesteem they may suffer. The question which arises now is whether things may be arranged so as to affect those margins of adjustment and improve the prospects for producing social good.

The margins of adjustment available to individuals in the pursuit of esteem are various but involve three broad categories, as we saw in Chapter 4: performance, publicity, and presentation. People may increase the prospect of esteem in different ways: by lifting their overall performance; by manipulating the publicity given to their performance relative to others, showing their better sides, and hiding their worse; or by manipulating presentational variables to their advantage. The presentational variables, as we saw, are the ideals or dimensions with reference to which people are judged; the public who will do the judging; and the comparators in relation to whom they will be judged.

The question that concerns us now is whether things can be organised in terms of publicity and presentation so as to increase the chance of improving—by whatever criteria are thought relevant—the performance that people generally display. And the answer, clearly, is that they can. Parents and teachers routinely try to arrange things so that the child's natural desire for esteem is put to what they see as good use. They hold out ideals in the light of which it is clear that the child will be judged in any area and they ensure, so far as possible, that its performance in respect of those ideals will be a matter of public awareness within the relevant group.

Nor is this pattern of mobilising the intangible hand confined to the domain where adults seek to train children. Consider, for example, the way that a business inducts its staff into what are seen as the appropriate ideals of employee performance and how it arranges to have the performance of staff monitored and reviewed. Or consider the manner in which a professional body articulates ideals for its members in explicit codes of ethics and relies on insider signals of performance, as well as on reviews occasionally triggered by complaints from outsiders, in order to ensure that performance levels are matters of relative publicity. Or consider how churches and some other voluntary associations promulgate the ideals that members are expected to embrace, and deploy mechanisms of shame and honour in the attempt to keep members in line.

Or consider, finally, the ways in which the state organises its business so as to muster the forces of the intangible hand and employ them beneficially. Politicians are provided with electoral incentives to invoke various ideals by which their behaviour should be governed and to seek publicity for their own achievements and for the failures of their opponents. Judges are provided with professional incentives to pay deference to the ideals of legal understanding and equity and they are forced to give reasons for their judgements that will ensure publicity for how well or badly they live up to those ideals. The different media organisations pronounce on the standards that ought to prevail in public life—no doubt, with differences in matters of emphasis and detail—and are poised to expose anyone who fails to comply. And of course the government in any society relies on the law to signal the expectations of the citizenry in general and on the effect of legal incrimination, not just in punishing offenders, but also in exposing them to the forces of shame (Braithwaite 1989).

All of these initiatives are capable of being more finely tuned. Governments or other collective agencies may explore new ways of ensuring publicity for the performance of agents and new ways of structuring the information publicised. That information may be focused on the highs or the lows of the agent's performance, for example; on the absolute level of each individual's performance or on the agent's position relative to others; and it may ensure just a widespread awareness of the performance of the agent or a strictly common awareness of that performance: that is, an awareness that involves everyone being aware that everyone is aware of it, and so on.

Similarly, new approaches may be taken to the shaping of factors that impact on the presentation of that performance. The ideals in the light of which the performance is judged may be spelled out explicitly, for example, as distinct from being left in unarticulated, implicit form. They may be reframed so that there is greater emphasis on what makes for good performance rather than on what makes for bad. They may be ideals that are focused on action, or ideals that are focused on disposition. And they may be ideals of absolute performance or ideals of relative score. In the same way, the group of comparators in relation to whom the performers will be judged may be shifted, as attention is given to a narrower or broader reference class. And so on.

Given earlier discussions, there is every reason to think that such variations will make for differences in the impact of the intangible hand—or backhand—and in the way, ultimately, that people behave. The intangible hand is not just something that we are invited to sit back and admire. It represents a social pattern that can to some extent be brought under intentional influence and that can be reoriented with a view to securing yet greater social benefit.

Apart from institutional initiatives that affect the publicity and the presentation given to people's performance, there is a third broad front on which a group or society might hope to foster the benign working of the intangible hand among its members. We describe this as the predisposition of those members to be moved by motives of virtue and esteem. It may be in a given case that other motives are in play which render the forces of esteem less powerful than they might be and that a good way in which the operation of the intangible hand can be promoted is by acting so as to remove or reduce the presence and impact of those countervailing motives. We discuss a variety of ways in which this may come about in the final chapter.

3   THE CRITERIA FOR GUIDING THE INTANGIBLE HAND

We have been speaking of the social benefits that can in principle be secured by the intangible hand. But what are the criteria by which it is determined that certain results are indeed benefits, others not? Rightly or wrongly, this question is not generally regarded as troublesome in the study of the material economy; mainstream economics claims to need only a thin, uncontroversial theory of the good. So what is the situation with the economy of esteem?

In mainstream economics, it is generally if not universally taken for granted that the preferences that lead people to demand and supply commodities and services in the material economy are beyond the threshold of criticism. Economic arrangements are assessed for how well they do in satisfying those preferences—that is, for how efficient they are in catering to the preferences—without any question being raised about the status of the preferences themselves. One economy does better than another, it is said, so far as it satisfies given preferences at lower cost: that is, at lesser cost to the satisfaction of yet further preferences. And one economy does better than another, it is proposed, so far as it better satisfies the preferences of some people, while not doing worse by the preferences of others.

Such principles are taken as completely uncontroversial, so far as they do not require the normative adjudication between different types of preference or between the preferences of different individuals. Mainstream economics does not have to judge on the merits of the preferences or the individuals in play; it simply works with the assumption that whatever people's preferences in the sphere of the material economy, it is better to have more preference satisfaction than less. In that sense economics operates with a thin theory of the good: it does not introduce any exogenous or thick criteria of assessment. We do not necessarily endorse the idea that such a thin theory is adequate for mainstream economics but we shall not be questioning that claim here.

There are some grounds on which we can make assessments of the economy of esteem that do not introduce anything more than a thin theory of the good. Suppose that people seek to satisfy their desire for esteem by competing with one another in the pursuit of publicity or in pursuit of a favourable presentation for their performance; they may expend great personal efforts, and exhaust many of their resources, in this competition. It is quite possible in the wake of such competition, as indeed we have seen, that everyone will enjoy roughly the same level of esteem that they had beforehand and yet that the competition will have cost them dearly in other respects. There is a powerful case to be made, just on the basis of a thin theory of the good, for discouraging this form of wasteful competition. It is likely that the people in the group could collectively ensure, at much lesser cost, that each will get a level of publicity and a variety of presentation that secures the same distribution of estimative rewards. And, other things being equal, everyone should prefer that sort of dispensation to the competitive one described.

Can the thin theory of the good serve the economics of esteem—that is, guide the deployment of the intangible hand—in any other ways? Since people are averse to disesteem, and are attracted to positive esteem, there are relatively uncontroversial grounds for preferring arrangements under which there is less shame suffered generally by people, and greater levels of positive esteem secured. Or at least there are relatively uncontroversial grounds for preferring such arrangements if other things are equal: that is, if the two sorts of arrangements have the same net effects on how people behave and relate to one another.

But at this point the thin theory of the good ceases to be of much service in thinking about how to organise or reorganise the economy of esteem. For in the ordinary run of cases a shift in the way the rewards and penalties of esteem accrue to people is almost certain to make for a marginal difference in how they behave. And while the shift may mean that people individually do better in the realm of shame and honour—they suffer less shame, for example, and enjoy more honour—it may generate an aggregate pattern of behaviour that they value less and that answers less well to the aspirations they have over how people in general should behave.

Recall at this point that the esteem and disesteem with which we regard others reflects the evaluations that we make of that behaviour, and of the disposition that produces it. If I esteem you, it is because I see value in how you act; if I disesteem you, it is because I see disvalue there. The value or disvalue may derive from the way the behaviour personally benefits or harms me, where the benefit or harm is one that I can acknowledge as relevant in other cases too, or the value or disvalue may be sourced in more impersonal, presumptively defensible views about what is good for the society as a whole. Where I see value, I will to that extent prefer that people generally, myself included, should perform those actions; and where I see disvalue, I will to that extent prefer that they do not perform those actions. Thus none of us can be indifferent to the behavioural effects of shifts in the economy of esteem. Even if those shifts may make for a greater satisfaction of our personal preference for receiving positive esteem and against receiving negative, it may make for a lesser satisfaction of those general, value-based preferences over how people should behave that lie at the origin of our estimative responses.

The upshot is that if we are to give countenance to all the attitudes involved in the demand and supply of esteem, we cannot limit our attention to people's preferences over the esteem they personally receive, as we try to evaluate different ways in which the economy of esteem may be adjusted or, equivalently, different ways in which the intangible hand may be deployed. We are bound to introduce thicker criteria of evaluation than those that are typically applied in the normative assessment of the material economy. We are bound to consider people's valuations of how people in general behave.

The criteria we introduce, however, need not be more or less arbitrarily imposed from outside. There is a source available within the economy of esteem itself for outlining the sorts of criteria that ought to be relevant. Take the way the economy of esteem may work among the teachers in a school. Teachers may wish to suffer as little disesteem as possible at the hands of their colleagues and to enjoy a maximum of positive esteem, and their preferences over the distribution of esteem are certainly relevant to the assessment of the economy as a whole: better, other things being equal, to have less disesteem suffered, more esteem enjoyed. But teachers have other preferences too that are manifested in esteem-related attitudes. The pattern in which they confer esteem or disesteem on one another—the pattern in which they may also invoke one another as models for emulation or avoidance—shows that they also want teachers in general to be conscientious, considerate, insightful, and the like. Without going beyond the community of teachers, then—and clearly in a proper assessment we should go further—we can see that it would be perfectly proper to invoke such value-based preferences or aspirations in judging how well the economy of esteem works at eliciting the sort of pattern desired. It would be perfectly proper to go to a thick theory of the good, not just the traditional, thin variety, in devising criteria for the evaluation of the economy.

One complexity here is worth noting as we pass, though it takes us into deep waters. Value-based preferences of the kind that lead us to esteem or disesteem others—or indeed ourselves—are different from the taste-based preferences generally considered in mainstream economics. It makes sense with taste-based preferences to imagine someone agreeing to let others frustrate his or her preferences, provided compensation is paid; or even to imagine the person paying others not to frustrate the preferences. But this scarcely makes sense with value-based preferences. Suppose I prefer that you be a conscientious teacher: because the alternative offends against my sense of value, whether as a fellow-teacher or as a student whom you serve badly, it arouses my indignation or resentment. The idea of your paying me in compensation for frustrating that preference, or of my paying you compensation for the cost to you of not frustrating it, would make little sense in this case. Certainly it would do nothing to allay my sense of indignation or resentment.

This observation opens up a number of questions about the status of value-based preferences but we will not be pursuing them here. Our concern in the present context is just to note that in adjudicating between arrangements for the distribution of esteem and disesteem, we may go beyond people's taste-based preferences for having more esteem and less disesteem, or for paying a lower price for the level of esteem they enjoy, without having to invoke exogeneous and inherently controversial criteria of assessment. We may go beyond the thin theory of the good without assuming the position of self-appointed judges. In assessing different arrangements, we can have recourse to the value-based preferences that people themselves display in the patterns of esteem and disesteem that they adopt.

This means that there is room for a principled consideration with every case that arises for adjudication as to what, intuitively, are appropriate criteria to invoke. The adjudication should take into account the value-based preferences—if you like, the aspirations—displayed in people's estimative responses, not just the taste-based preferences that they have over the responses they themselves receive from others. And, if relevant, it should go beyond the valuations displayed among those interacting agents, to take into account the preferences displayed in the estimative responses of the wider community.

How to weight those different preferences, of course, may often raise a tricky question. We may wonder as to how far the value-based preferences of adults should be taken into account, for example, in assessing the arrangements whereby the behaviour of teenagers is sustained by the economy of peer esteem that operates among them. We have nothing useful to say about that sort of issue in the abstract; it is one of those questions that can only be given proper consideration, case by case. That means that the assessment of the economy of esteem cannot be practised in the mechanical manner in which—rightly or wrongly—the assessment of the material economy is generally conducted. But neither does it mean that the assessment of the economy of esteem is to be driven only by arbitrary, theoretically imposed ideals.

4 A THIRD WAY IN REGULATION

With these points made, we hope that the intangible hand may begin to present itself as a medium of regulation that holds out very attractive prospects for anyone concerned with how best to design the institutions that operate in our society and to develop more detailed, collective policies. The different domains of social life are inevitably regulated by the various protocols and expectations that rule there, though in some domains the regulation may take the form of letting agents pursue their own ends within fairly comfortable constraints. What the discussion of the intangible hand makes evident is that people's desire for esteem represents a resource that no regulatory regime should neglect.

It is common to assume nowadays, as mentioned earlier, that there are only two ways of regulating actors in the social world. One is by means of the market, the other by means of a monitoring regime that holds out the promise of rewards for those who perform up to or above standard or the threat of penalties for those who fall below. Where the first involves the invisible hand of the market, the second deploys the iron hand of the state.

The assumption that these are the only regulatory alternatives is salient in the way governments often conceptualise the choice of regulatory regime in education or health provision or even in the organisation of traditional bureaucracies and agencies. The standard suggestion is that government has to assure itself in such areas that the taxpayers' money is well spent—it cannot blandly assume that those paid to provide the service will be virtuous and conscientious—and that there are only two ways of doing this. One way is by privatising the enterprises involved, letting the invisible hand of the market ensure that only the efficient providers survive. The other is by subjecting the providers to a regimen of scrutiny and sanction, requiring them to account for every hour on the job and every penny spent in pursuit of it.

The points made about the economy of esteem, and about the intangible hand to which it directs us, show that this dichotomy is not exhaustive. There is also a third possibility. We agree that government should indeed try to assure itself that the taxpayers' money is well spent in any areas of public activity. Even if there is virtue in plenty available in those areas, it is important that the public can have confidence that should virtue fail or lapse, still the officials involved will have incentives for performing to standard. But we do not think that the only ways of planning for a suitable level of performance are by resorting to the discipline of the competitive market or the discipline of the powerful overseer. There is also the possibility, so it seems to us, that those who operate in such an area will be disciplined into maintaining a decent level of performance—and disciplined into doing this, even when spontaneous virtue wilts—by the fact of being exposed to the bad opinion of others in the event of not keeping up to the mark and of being in a position to earn their good opinion in the event of meeting or surpassing the mark.

Contemporary critiques of the market-or-manage dichotomy often argue that those who work with that bifocal vision fail to recognise that much of life is played out under the gentle but still controlling influence of civil society, not under the harsh disciplines of market and management. We entirely agree. Civil society materialises as people relate to one another, and rely with confidence on one another, in domains where there is no question of market pressures or management responses dictating what people do. It materialises most dramatically when even strangers can succeed routinely in establishing such a relationship and such a mode of reliance, despite the fact that there is no question of personal attachments or anticipated consequences affecting what people do (Selznick 1992; Putnam 1993). We think that as the invisible hand controls what happens in the economic world, and the iron hand what happens in the world of law and management, so the intangible hand is the most plausible mechanism to invoke as the engine that drives civil society. In civil society people will behave most of the time out of a sense of what is required of them culturally and morally; the same indeed is true of how people behave in other domains too. But the force that is most plausibly given the role of virtual, backup controller in this area is the intangible influence of people's desire not to be ill-considered by their fellows, and if possible to enjoy positive, high regard.

The most important lesson that we draw from our reflections on the economy of esteem is that it is straightforwardly mistaken to think that as we consider how best to have different social domains regulated, in particular those domains that may be subject to political control, the only options available for our consideration are those of the invisible hand and the iron hand. That presumption prevails in much regulatory thinking and does so as a direct result of the neglect which the economy of esteem has been allowed to suffer since about the time that economics began to develop as a discipline. It is of the first importance, we think, that this neglect is put right and that regulatory thought is informed once again with a full sense of the possibilities available (see Pettit 1997: chs. 7 and 8).

The dichotomous view of regulatory possibilities has had a very bad impact on the behaviour of states in a number of areas. It has particularly affected the attitude taken to the various autonomous and quasi-autonomous bodies that belong to civil society but that states are politically required, at least in a certain measure, to support or subsidise. We are thinking of hospitals, schools, universities, research institutes, broadcasting stations, public utilities, women's refuges, consumer bodies, indigenous people's commissions, and the like. How can we throw public money at such bodies, so those in government reasonably ask, unless we assure ourselves that the public is getting value for its dollar? And then, under the influence of prevailing orthodoxy, the conclusion is drawn that government should impose a tough and uncompromising regime of management.

But the strategy of tough management is all too likely to be counterproductive. Think of the likely effects on teachers, for example, if they are required to record and account for how they spend every hour, if they are under constant pressure to establish a satisfactory performance relative to abstract indicators, if they are given little or no discretion on curricular, disciplinary, or other fronts, and if they generally have to live under the presumption of being lazy unless proven productive. Where teachers will usually take pride in their effort and achievement, and enjoy the rewards of a corresponding status in the local school and community—where teachers will usually be susceptible to the influence of the intangible hand—the tough-management regime is likely to diminish the prospect or importance of these rewards and to diminish the teachers' spontaneous civility. That this is so indeed is borne out in much recent empirical research (Frey 1997; Frey and Jegen 2001; Guerra 2002).We do not say that management is not important. But an appreciation of the role of the intangible hand makes it clear that tough management can often be bad management.

5   THE MERITS OF INTANGIBLE-HAND REGULATION

We shall be considering some ways in which the intangible hand is and might be used in regulation—some of those uses are intentional, some not—in the next two chapters. But before coming to that topic it may be useful to underline the attractions that are available by resort to the intangible hand for anyone concerned with regulation, whether that concern be the general interest of the social and political theorist or the very focused worry of the person who is looking for the best institutional pattern to establish, or the best line of policy to pursue, in some specific area. We mention three broad respects in which the intangible hand should prove extremely attractive. These are: that it is an inexpensive mode of regulation, an effective mode of regulation, and one that is hospitable to the presence of virtue—if you like, virtue-compatible.

An inexpensive form of regulation

Taking the expense issue first, the most striking merit of the intangible hand is that it represents a way in which people may police one another into a certain pattern of behaviour—a socially beneficial pattern, so we may assume—without those who do the policing having to make many intentional efforts or to suffer many voluntary costs. All that is required is that, while being presumptively conscious of relevant ideals and comparisons, people are there to observe—and to be observed observing—one another's behaviour. That is enough, all on its own, to ensure that the observees will be subjected to the regulatory discipline represented by the expectations of the observers. The observers may not like the lot that befalls them: envy may make them averse to witnessing fine performances, embarrassment to registering second-rate efforts. But normally there will be little they can do about it. Willy nilly, they will be there to impose sanctions on those they observe and to enforce the ideals that happen to be relevant to the behaviour of observees.

This is a great merit in the intangible-hand form of regulation, because it means that the intangible hand costs little to deploy. But not only does this form of regulation impose no costs on the enforcing agents themselves, so it also imposes few costs on those in more centralised positions who may make institutional arrangements or pursue specific policies with a view to facilitating that form of regulation. The governors of the system, as we may call them, will often have to make adjustments of the kind described earlier, of course—say, adjustments that ensure publicity for how well or badly people perform in a given domain—in order to ensure that the intangible hand works to best effect. But having set the mechanism in motion—having set up arrangements for the regular monitoring and reporting of people's performance, for example—there may be little they have to do in order to keep it going and to keep it working to good effect. The economy of esteem that they plan for may operate on a more or less routine basis. Like the invisible hand, it may approximate a perpetual motion machine that requires little fuel and maintenance. It may not be self-starting but there is every reason to think that in at least some areas it will be relatively self-sustaining.

An effective form of regulation

So much for the inexpensive character of the intangible hand. The second merit we see in this form of regulation is that it also promises to be highly effective. We say nothing more on the intensity with which people pursue the positive esteem of others and shrink from their disesteem. We assume that this desire is firmly entrenched in the make-up of most human beings and that the rewards and penalties on offer promise to be relatively powerful determinants of behaviour. But we have something more to say on two other respects in which the intangible hand promises to be an effective regulatory device. The first is that it copes in a distinctive manner with what we may describe as the detection problem; the second that it copes equally well with the problem of who will regulate the regulators.

The detection problem that arises with any mode of regulation is that when an agent's behaviour is liable to escape the notice of sanctioners, the sanction in question, be it a reward or a penalty, is likely to be correspondingly less powerful. The agent will not confront the prospect of enjoying the reward or suffering the penalty in the event of behaving well or badly but the prospect, rather, of enjoying a certain chance of the reward or a certain chance of the penalty. And as the chance is greater or smaller, so it seems, the motivation provided by the prospect is bound to be correspondingly stronger or weaker.

A remarkable feature of the intangible hand, however, is that it appears to moderate this problem or that it does so at any rate in a number of contexts. For as the chance of being detected lessens in any instance, it appears that the reward that will be offered in the case of being seen to perform well, and the penalty that will be suffered in the event of being found to perform badly, both increase. And not only that: they both increase in a way that is bound to be salient to all, so that a decline in the probability of detection promises to be motivationally compensated for in some measure by a corresponding increase in the size of the sanction in question.

The idea is straightforward and intuitive. Suppose that a student reproduces an existing idea as if it were her own in a context where it must have been clear that she would have been found out. In that case we are prepared to think that a slip may have occurred and so to reserve judgement and censure. But suppose that the student does this in a context where there was little chance, and little chance by the student's lights, that we would discover the plagiarism. In that case we have little reason to reserve our opinion. We are quite likely to think that she showed her true colours—the colours of a cheat—in that situation; the temptation involved flushed them out. Or again, suppose that someone does something heroic or generous. If the situation is one where there was very little chance that they would be identified, then we think all the more highly of them for acting as they did, whereas if it is one in which the likelihood was that they would be known to have behaved well then we may not be quite so generous in the opinion we form of them.

As the detection problem is frequently invoked in critiques of regulatory regimes, so another problem that has long been introduced in these discussions —particularly, in discussions of the iron hand of the state—is raised in the old Latin question *Quis custodiet ipsos custodes?*, 'Who will guard against the guardians themselves?', 'Who will watch the watchers?' If a regime of regulation involves establishing authorities who are to run the system, then the problem is to explain how those authorities are themselves to be regulated. The suggestion is that if powerful regulators are established who are themselves beyond the reach of regulation then things may be worse than they would have been without any regulation being imposed.

Intangible-hand regulation is not very vulnerable to this problem. The form of control exercised by the intangible hand is decentralised and, notwithstanding various asymmetries that may arise, all of those who regulate in this mode will be regulated in turn by others. There are no regulators who are in a position to escape the sort of regulation they practise when they police others by the opinions they form of them. And so there are no regulators against whom regulatees may lack resources. In some domains of opinion, of course, there may be a coterie or elite that has such control over publicity that serious imbalances of power arise. But there is a much lesser prospect of the outright tyranny that is feared by those who are concerned about the *Quis custodiet* question. Notice that the intangible hand scores in this respect, not just over the iron hand, but also over the invisible. For invisible-hand regulation, at least in the central case of the market, requires a dispensation of property rights and an enforcing authority. Thus it too raises the *Quis custodiet* challenge.

A virtue-compatible form of regulation

A question routinely raised in economic circles is whether various social arrangements proposed are incentive-compatible: whether they are such as to survive the reality of human motivations and, in particular, the self-interested behaviour to which such motivations are often likely to give rise. But while that question is well posed, there is another question that ought just as insistently to be raised. This is the question of whether the proposed arrangements are compatible, not with the more or less self-interested motivations that human beings frequently display, but with the virtues that they may spontaneously manifest or be capable of learning from the example and teaching of others.

We can readily imagine a system of regulation being introduced that might do good by providing self-interested reasons for people to behave in a certain pattern but do bad—and overall, do worse—by undermining patterns of personal virtue that already served to support that pattern in a fairly reliable way. The example of teachers that we gave earlier will serve to make the point. If teachers are subjected to a regime of tough management that leaves them little autonomy or discretion, then any independent virtue they have is all too likely to be undermined.

Put aside for a moment the interest of the teachers in esteem. So far as virtue survives, they will be led by two pilots, one oriented to the desirability of doing well, the undesirability of doing badly, the other oriented to the rather more self-serving incentives, positive and negative, that are made available under the management regime. There is a large body of literature supporting the claim that where this sort of dual control is put in operation, then spontaneous virtue may be undermined.[1] Virtue may be driven or crowded out by the presence of extra motivation such as that which a prospect of independent reward or the threat of an independent penalty provides. The means whereby such crowding out can occur are various, including in particular the effect whereby those who develop the habit of complying in the presence of independent incentives tend to lose the habit of complying otherwise: they become, quite simply, less virtuous (Pettit 1997: 218–19).

The final merit that we see in the intangible hand is that unlike many other incentive systems, it promises to be relatively virtue-compatible. Where both the invisible and the iron hand tend to present agents with incentives that are quite independent of virtuous motives, the intangible hand presents them with motives that often reinforce the regime of virtue rather than working independently of it. If someone behaves well for virtuous reasons, then they get the extra reward of being thought to be virtuous. And that extra reward, so we surmise, is likely to have a reinforcing rather than an inhibiting effect. We do not go off our friends when we find that treating them affectionately, as our friendship inclines us to do, actually gives us a lot of pleasure; the pleasure serves to strengthen the friendship. In the same way the fact that behaving virtuously gives a person the pleasure of being well regarded ought not to draw them away from virtuous behaviour but rather to entrench them more strongly in virtuous habits.

---

[1] (Brehm and Brehm 1981; Bardach and Kagan 1982; Sunstein 1990, 1990*b*; Ayres and Braithwaite 1992; Grabosky 1995; Frey 1997; Frey and Jegen 2001).

Well, it ought to do so at any rate, short of certain limits. We can imagine two scenarios in which virtue might be eroded under pressure from the economy of esteem. One is the scenario in which the reputation for virtue is as easily, if not more easily, attained without the effort of being virtuous. And the other is the scenario where it becomes a matter of common assumption that a main reason why people behave virtuously is in order to secure such a reputation. In this second scenario, as in the first, the desire to avoid suffering disesteem may argue against being virtuous. It may lead the good swimmer not to rush to the aid of the child in difficulties, for example, out of a fear of being thought to be looking for attention and approval (Latane and Darley 1970).

These scenarios, however, are highly unusual and it is hard to think of many real-world cases where they commonly materialise. We are inclined not to worry much about them and to stick with the observation that in less far-fetched situations there is every reason to think that virtue and the desire to be thought virtuous will pull together. As Hume expressed the point, 'to love the fame of laudable actions approaches so near the love of laudable actions for their own sake, that those passions are more capable of mixture, than any other kinds of affection' (in Lovejoy 1961: 185).

The position we are taking is well supported by some empirical research on how virtue can sometimes be crowded in, rather than crowded out. Bruno Frey (1997: 16–17) argues, on the basis of his research, that there are three conditions under which extra motivation may support virtue rather than supplanting it. First, the motivation provided does not suggest that the agent needs to be controlled from the outside. Second, it does not reduce the agent's self-esteem. And third, it does not obscure the presence of virtuous motivation when the agent complies (see too Pettit 1995). These conditions are all fulfilled under the intangible hand.

In any instance where the intangible hand serves to motivate an agent, it operates independently of the will of the people providing the motivating esteem. Thus its operation in no way suggests to the agent that others are seeking control of his or her behaviour. Nor does the provision of the associ-ated esteem incentive do anything to reduce the agent's self-esteem; if any-thing, it presents a reason for increased self-esteem, as we argued in Chapter 1. Nor, finally, does it obscure the presence of virtuous motivation, when such motivation is effective; on the contrary, the esteem provided testifies to the operation of virtue.

The Aristotelian observation that we mentioned in Chapter 2 may also be relevant in this connection (Aristotle 1976). If the intangible hand can support the operation of virtue in the manner described, then it may serve to establish that sort of behaviour as a spontaneous habit—as a virtue in the Aristotelian sense—among the agents involved. If the intangible hand is compatible with the presence of virtue, as just argued, then it can be productive of ever more independent habits of virtue; it can constitute a support for virtue that gradually renders itself less and less necessary: a ladder to virtue that can be kicked away at a certain level of habituation.

An Intrusive, Homogenising form of Regulation?

In rounding off this discussion of the intangible hand, however, we should confront a question that will be of concern to some. Granted that intangible-hand regulation promises to be inexpensive, relatively effective, and virtue-compatible, doesn't it still represent a mode of social control in which people poke their noses into one another's business and push everyone towards a common mould? We saw already that the intangible backhand represents a problem that complements the promise of the intangible hand. But shouldn't we also recognise that even when the economy of esteem works for good—even when it offers a hand, not a backhand—it does so by means that are inherently unsavoury?

We concede that there are contexts in which the operation of the intangible hand, however benign in its ultimate outcome, might be intrusive and hom-ogenising. Consider a society where the prevailing standards are detailed in content, conformist in character, and almost universally shared. The society may be a small-scale community where almost everyone is known to everyone. Or it may be a large-scale, more anonymous society that just happens to be regulated by a particularly cohesive body of public opinion and expectation. In contexts of these kinds the intangible hand would weigh heavily on individuals—certainly it would weigh heavily on individuals of the kind that most of us are—and might leave them little room to forge their own identity.

It was a concern about imposing this sort of burden on the human spirit that led John Stuart Mill (1978) to rail against the potential tyranny of common custom and public opinion. He had embraced a philosophy of romantic, expressive individualism that would have been foreign to most writers in earlier centuries. And of course he lived in a period and a place—Victorian England—where custom and opinion were particularly firm and intrusive. While he thought that it might often be good to force people to face a critical public (Mill 1964: 306), he still came to the view that the force of esteem is, at the very least, a dangerous form of social control. Should we go along with Mill, then, and embrace the prospect of intangible-hand regulation only with the greatest reluctance, even perhaps distaste? We do not think so, for a variety of reasons.

One is that the society that Mill found in Victorian England is less and less common in the contemporary world, or at least in the advanced, multicultural democracies. While public opinion is a powerful force in all societies, especially given the investment of government and the media in driving opinion in this or that direction, it is rarely as intrusive or as homogenising as it appears to have been in Mill's world. The environment where it operates has many contours and corners and is capable of allowing everyone, no matter how great the differences among individuals, to find a niche among fellow-spirits.

A second consideration is that among the values that hold an important place in the culture of contemporary democracies is the value of personal autonomy. Democracy gives rise, in the nature of things, to divisive and adversarial debate and participants will be able identify with the regime only so far as they can tolerate and respect those who stand for other points of view, or at least for other points of view with which coexistence is possible. It would be amazing if in a democratic culture people did not recognise the value of autonomy and give kudos to those who display it. And so far as that value has a place in the culture, of course, the intangible hand will not be the intrusive force for conformism envisaged by Mill. Within appropriate limits, it will elicit self-assertion, not suppress it. This factor might of course be boosted by explicit, centralised attempts to promulgate the value of autonomy.

A third consideration is related to this. Given that autonomy is valued in the culture, the intangible hand can be mobilised by those who feel that it operates unjustifiably against them. We saw how this can happen when we looked in Chapter 12 at the phenomenon whereby practising homosexuals 'come out'. When people come out in this sense they flaunt a feature for which they were previously faulted. They present as a matter of pride a property that others may have thought was a matter for shame. And in doing this, they turn the intangible hand around. Where it may once have been a force for oppression, their defiance—in particular, their success in challenging and changing established standards—can transform the intangible hand into a force that supports and unifies them.

The upshot is that invoking the regulation of the intangible hand need not mean trying to sup with Satan. However powerful its effects in shaping the way we live our mental and social lives, the intangible hand does not always push us in the same direction; it may push us into asserting ourselves, not into assuming a preformed shape; and it may exert the sort of push that can be turned around and used to our own advantage.

CONCLUSION

In this chapter, we moved away from an examination of how far the desire for esteem rules in people's hearts, and from a survey of some of the aggregate effects of that desire, and began to look at how it may be harnessed to the promotion of overall social good. In the first section we compared the invisible hand that has been familiar since the work of Adam Smith and the intangible hand, as we describe it, that operates when a pattern that is thought desirable overall materialises as a result of people's seeking of esteem. The invisible and intangible hands contrast with the iron hand of management in deploying sanctions that are not imposed intentionally. They contrast with one another, so far as the invisible-hand sanctions are provided by actions, intangible-hand sanctions by the attitudes that people form in response to others.

In the second section we argued that the intangible hand, like the invisible hand, is capable in principle of being manipulated so as to produce a greater level of social good. The performance of relevant agents may be lifted by adjustments to the publicity that their relative performance and merit receives and to the presentation that it is given: that is, to the dimensions and ideals in the light of which it is seen, to the comparators in relation to whom it is judged, and to the public by which it is judged. And it may be lifted, finally, through things being arranged so that people are more readily predisposed to be moved by relevant considerations of esteem.

But what are the criteria of overall social good that have to be invoked in any such assessment of how an economy of esteem works? We pointed out in the third section that they are not just provided by the preferences that people have over the degree and kind of esteem that they personally receive but also by the preferences for how people in general behave that are reflected in the estimative responses they form. The relevant criteria constitute a relatively thick theory of the good as distinct from the thin theory that is usually thought sufficient in the assessment of the material economy. But it is a thick theory that reflects the attitudes of agents themselves: those which shape their estimative responses to others.

The fourth section presented the intangible-hand form of regulation in prospect as a third alternative to the dichotomous possibilities that rule most regulatory thinking. According to orthodox approaches, regulation has to be pursued either on the basis of invisible-hand arrangements or by recourse to the iron hand of tough and uncompromising management. We argued that this dichotomy has iniquitous effects in thinking about institutional design and that the intangible hand should be introduced as a further, routinely available alternative.

We ended the chapter with a section outlining the merits of the intangible hand. We distinguished three merits in particular:

- It is an inexpensive form of regulation, being self-sustaining if not self-starting.
- It is also highly effective, having the means to get over the detection problem and the problem as to who will regulate the regulators.
- It is virtue-compatible, mobilising a form of motivation that is likely to buttress rather than to undermine spontaneous virtue.

We concluded this discussion with a consideration of how far the intangible hand may be an unsavoury social force—as John Stuart Mill sometimes suggests—arguing that there are a variety of considerations in contemporary democracies that offer support for a more positive view.

14

The Intangible Hand in Practice

1   NORMS AND THE PLACE OF THE INTANGIBLE HAND

So much for the possibility and the promise of intangible-hand regulation. But the issue that arises immediately is whether it works well and widely in practice, at least under suitable conditions. We turn now to that question, arguing that there is considerable evidence to support the belief that in any well-functioning society the intangible hand is an important social control. The discussion will give us a more detailed sense of how the device works and will put us in a position to explore the possibility, in the final chapter, of mobilising the intangible hand to new and good effect.

Wherever the intangible hand is in operation, it will serve to generate an aggregate social benefit and do so without anyone necessarily intending or even recognising that that benefit will be generated. What sorts of benefit might the intangible hand support? Social benefits can be generated by the laws and related rules established in any society but, far from being the work of an intangible hand, these are the work of legislators and governors; they represent the iron hand of management. Equally social benefits can be generated by the operations of a free market in which everyone is driven to sell, and is able to buy, at the competitive price, but those represent the workings of an invisible hand. So where then should we look in trying to discern regularities that promote social benefits, like the regularities of the law and the market, and that are supported by the intangible hand?

We think that the obvious place to look is to the third category of social regularities that are often described as norms. Norms materialise as regularities in social life, because there is general approval for the pattern of behaviour involved, disapproval for the failure to elicit that behaviour, or the expectation of such general approval or disapproval. In this respect norms contrast with market regularities, which do not need to be approved—at least not as a matter of logic—in order to materialise. Yet norms need not be enforced by collective ratification in the manner of laws, even if they are occasionally buttressed by legal support.

Up to this point we have invoked two important, esteem-related elements: the ideals that lie at the origin of esteem, and the standards that socially materialise in the light of the general level of compliance—strictly, presumed compliance—with the ideals. Norms, as we shall use the term here, represent a third, related element. They are the regularities of behaviour in a society or grouping that emerge as a result, at least in part, of the standards that prevail there and of the patterns of esteem or approval associated with standards.

In familiar societies norms dictate the ways in which people relate to one another in discourse, generally embracing patterns of honesty, trustworthiness, and sincerity; the ways in which they otherwise seek to influence one another, eschewing resort to violence, theft, fraud, and coercion; the ways in which they commit themselves conscientiously to various collaborative causes, playing the part that is collectively required of them; and the ways in which they conduct their business and professional lives according to relevant codes of practice. By many accounts norms in this sense are the motors of civil society, leading people to deal well with one another, even when they are beyond the reach of the law, are unconstrained by the discipline of self-interest, and are free of the incentives provided by family and related ties.

We believe that the intangible hand is most saliently operative in social life so far as it serves to maintain normative regularities of this kind. But while holding by this claim, we recognise that not all norms are socially beneficial; some are going to be the product of the intangible backhand, as we described it earlier.

It may be useful to illustrate this backhand possibility. Some norms may serve subcultures well, while serving the society as a whole badly (McAdams 1995; Dharmapala and McAdams 2001). Some norms may have a mutually destructive effect as in the norms whereby it becomes obligatory for people to exact revenge in kind for any harm done to a member of their family (Elster 1990; Hardin 1995; Nisbett and Cohen 1996). Some norms may impose fashions and fads on people who would generally prefer not to be forced to embrace them by the desire for esteem; they represent a tyranny of majoritarian esteem (McAdams 1997). And some norms may operate against the interests of the members of involuntary groups, being grounded in opinions that are held about the group as a whole and being insensitive to the merits of particular individuals (Phelps 1973).

Nor is this all. There is also a distinct possibility, already mentioned, that norms which have ceased to be socially useful, and have ceased to be supported by esteem, may continue in place, due to people not recognising that others have ceased to think well of those who conform and/or to disapprove of those who don't. 'Social practices will stay in place long after they have lost private support because people do not recognise that their personal shift in attitude is shared by others' (Miller and Prentice 1994: 543; see too Nisbett and Cohen 1996: 92–3).

But while some norms may work against the general welfare, by received lights, it is clear that there are lots of norms, actual and potential, that work for good. There is a great deal of literature in recent social science, arguing for the importance of such norms. It is generally conceded, not just that norms prevail in a way that is not to be explained by the influences of market or law, but that the institutions of the market and the law themselves presuppose and depend upon a regime of robust, supportive norms. The experience in post-communist societies is that markets have routinely failed to achieve the non-coercive form that they have taken in many other places and this experience has emphasised the degree to which market behaviour needs to be shaped by the widespread acceptance of suitable norms: by a tradition of civic behaviour that will induce trust and trustworthiness among participants (Putnam 1993; Krygier 1997). And recent studies of the law have emphasised that the explanation for why most people obey the law has little to do with fear of legal sanction and much more to do with the fact that it is normatively unthinkable for them to contemplate law-breaking (Tyler 1990; Tyber et al. 1997).

If the claims in this literature are to be given countenance, which we think they should be, then the thesis that norms materialise in social life under the influence of a sort of intangible hand—the work of the economy of esteem—should serve to catch many eyes. Let the intangible hand be recognised as a device that gives regulatory support to social norms—a device that relates to norms in the way that the invisible hand relates to market effects—and there can be no doubting the significance of its place in the social world.

Our discussion in the remainder of this chapter is structured as follows. We look in the next section (2) at a problem that has persuaded many economists and rational choice theorists, notwithstanding the evidence to the contrary, that norms cannot be socially important; this is the so-called enforcement dilemma. In Section 3 we show that the enforcement dilemma ceases to represent a serious difficulty, once it is recognised that people reward and punish one another within an economy of esteem. And then in Sections 4 and 5 we look at how precisely the economy of esteem operates as an intangible hand, supporting socially beneficial norms, and at the extent to which that economy can be incorporated into a project of institutional design; it can be incorporated into that project so far as it points us to ways in which beneficial norms may be reinforced, and other norms weakened.

Before leaving this section, however, a word on the definition of norms. Our argument will suppose that norms involve patterns of more or less general behaviour that materialise in part—that emerge or are stabilised—by virtue of the fact that people generally approve or are expected to approve of others displaying that behaviour, and/or disapprove or are expected to disapprove of their not doing so.[1] This core supposition about norms puts us in agreement with most recent authors on the subject and ought not to generate any controversy (Hart 1961; Winch 1963; Coleman 1990*a*; Sober and Wilson 1998; Elster 1999). The picture is reasonably straightforward. A norm obtains in a society only if it is generally complied with; only if people generally approve of others complying with it and/or disapprove of their not complying, or are at least expected to do so; and only if this pattern of approval, real or imputed, is not incidental to the compliance: it is required in some part to explain the compliance, presumably because compliance is relatively burdensome. Other conditions might be added to this core set of stipulations, say a condition to the effect that it must also be a matter of common awareness that the core set is satisfied. But we need not go into questions of full-dress definition here (Pettit 1990).

2   THE ENFORCEMENT DILEMMA

Norms are likely to be relevant in the full gamut of interaction between people, whether in exchanges between individuals and individuals, individuals and groups, or groups and groups. But one context in which there is a particularly salient role for norms to play is provided by the collective action predicament in which self-seeking behaviour on the part of each will work to the disadvantage of all. Here the presence of a norm against such behaviour would work to aggregate benefit in the clearest possible way. While it would inhibit everyone from self-seeking, it would more than compensate each by the effect of its imposing a similar inhibition on others.

Take the free-rider problem that arises as a result of everyone in a certain community littering or polluting as suits them, or using a public resource like a grazing common or a fishing reserve as they will. Everyone is worse off as a result of each so acting than they would be if each exercised a certain restraint. Yet no one has a self-interested incentive to restrain themselves, for each may think: if others do their bit then I won't cause significant harm by free-riding; and if others do not do their bit then any restraint on

---

[1] The norm that emerges on the basis of pluralistic ignorance will not involve general approval or disapproval—at least not in the most straightforward sense—but only the expectation of general approval or disapproval. The need for this weakening is overlooked in the definition of norms in Pettit (1990).

my part would be to no effect; so either way I do better for myself by rejecting restraint. Here is a situation, then, in which those who believe in norms will surely want to claim that a suitable norm can save the community from self-damage. And they may do so, with some support, since the norms governing grazing on the commons did actually materialise in history (Ostrom 1990).

As against this claim on behalf of norms, however, a long and distinguished list of economists and rational choice theorists have argued that norms cannot do the work required.[2] They suggest that the belief that norms can resolve predicaments of this kind—a belief typical of non-economic disciplines such as anthropology and sociology—is like a belief in the fairy godmother who is ready to counter every danger and difficulty. Where there is a collective action problem for a norm to resolve, there will also be a collective action problem raised by the enforcement of the norm. The problem is given fairly typical expression in this passage from Michael Taylor (1987: 30):

The maintenance of a system of sanctions itself constitutes or presupposes the solution of another collective action problem. Punishing someone who does not conform to a norm—punishing someone for being a free rider on the efforts of others to provide a public good, for example—is itself a public good for the group in question, and everyone would prefer others to do this unpleasant job. Thus the solution of collective action problems by norms presupposes the prior or concurrent solution of another collective action problem.

The problem raised for norms is described by James Buchanan as an enforcement dilemma and we follow him in that usage. While the argument presented by different writers comes in different versions, it can be regimented for our purposes in the following steps.

1. Norms will be required to support cooperation in collective action predicaments only so far as people have a limited concern for the collective welfare and are not disposed to cooperate spontaneously.
2. Norms will be available to support cooperation only so far as people are prepared to display approval or disapproval of what others do and thereby to enforce the norm.
3. But displaying approval or disapproval is costly and like the cooperation it is supposed to support, it will fail to materialise so far as people's concern for the collective welfare is limited.
4. If norms are required to support cooperation, however, then by 1 there is a limit to their concern for the collective welfare.

[2] (Buchanan 1975, 132–3; Heath 1976, 156–8; Axelrod 1984, 1098; Taylor 1987, 30).

5. So far as their collective concern is limited in this way, people will not be prepared to display approval or disapproval—by 3—and by 2, therefore, norms will not be available for the support of cooperation.

6. Thus the very condition under which norms are required to support cooperation—that people have limited concern for the collective welfare—is a condition under which norms are unlikely to be available.

The thought behind this argument is, on the face of it, persuasive. Imagine that people are so indifferent to the public weal that they are not spontaneously disposed to stop themselves littering; they just drop their food wrappings and drink cans on the public streets. Can we imagine such people being disposed to tick one another off for littering, as they are apparently supposed to do if a norm against littering is to obtain and have an effect? Surely the very indifference that made littering a problem is also going to raise a question as to why these people can be expected to exercise such mutual sanctioning? As it is easier to litter than not to litter, so it is going to be easier not to do or say anything than to go to the trouble of identifying and rebuking offenders. Thus the very condition that gives rise to the problem would also seem to undermine the possibility that a norm might be successful in resolving it. There is an inescapable dilemma involved, so it appears. *Let enforcement be required and it is not going to be available; let it be available and it is not going to be required.*

The crucial premise in this argument is that the enforcement of norms—the display of approval and disapproval—is personally costly. One cost that is generally recognised is that which is involved in the expression of disapproval, whether the expression be purely communicative or also involve some penalty (Elster 1989: 131). But another potential cost is that which may be associated with looking out for offenders to rebuke, or indeed compliers to praise. James Buchanan (1975: 132–3) mentions both. 'Enforcement has two components. First, violations must be discovered and violators identified. Second, punishment must be imposed on violators. Both components involve costs.'

If the enforcement dilemma is supposed to show that norms cannot do the work required of them in the free-rider and in other predicaments, of course, then it is going to be necessary for defenders to explain how it is that in many cases people do seem to conform to norms. This requirement is addressed in recently fashionable attempts to show that we may often expect rational, self-interested agents to adjust their behaviour to patterns that give the appearance that people are governed by a social norm. These approaches suggest that while normative regularities do often appear in social life, they reflect only the sort of motivation and adjustment that is typical of market behaviour; they are not regularities that require explanation in terms of the approval given to compliance and the disapproval given to deviance.

Conventional regularities are now commonly taken to be the product of mutually advantageous adjustments whereby people resolve coordination predicaments: that is, predicaments in which each party has an interest in doing whatever the others do—say, driving on the left or the right—and no one has any strong preference over what in particular is done (Lewis 1969). The suggestion in these approaches is that a similar explanation is available for more properly normative behaviour, in particular for behaviour in which there is at least an occasional short-term cost involved in people's sticking to the pattern involved; it is not just a matter of coordinating with others, to unalloyed, mutual advantage

Thus Robert Axelrod (1984) has shown that in certain situations of recurrent, pairwise problems of cooperation it will be rational for each party to be prepared to cooperate on the first encounter with any other and in any later encounter to do whatever the other did in the previous round (see too Sugden 1986; Taylor 1987; Skyrms 1996). If people tit-for-tat in this way, then we can understand why in many situations they will behave towards one another as if a relevant norm were in control of their response: they will each give reliable information to the other, for example, as if the norm of honesty held sway over their interaction. The agents will really be acting in a directly rational manner, following a conditional strategy that promises to maximise their presumptively self-concerned desires. But it will look as if they are responsive to a norm that is supported by the approval and disapproval of others.

We do not think that this way of explaining normative behaviour—and, in effect, of explaining away the role of norms—is likely to work on a broad front. It is quite unclear how it might be extended to normative behaviour involving how people behave towards others generally—say in large-number, free-rider predicaments—as distinct from how they behave in pairwise interactions. It is unclear, for example, why a potential free rider in this general case would find the implied, tit-for-tat threat credible: why he or she should believe that just to punish and reform an isolated defector, everyone else would be prepared to defect in retaliation—and defect over an indefinite period—thereby imposing a massive loss on themselves (Pettit 1986).

Some more recent approaches have sought to improve on the tit-for-tat story. Eric A. Posner (2000) combines a signalling model with tit-for-tat: by incurring costs, say in retaliatory enforcement, the parties involved signal to one another that they have low discount rates and are prepared to hold out against defectors. Again, Paul G. Mahoney and Chris W. Sanchirico (2002) argue for a model in which parties do not just punish defectors but punish those who fail to punish defectors (see too Henrich and Boyd 2001). But if these approaches are extended to normative behaviour involving more than pairwise interactions, then it's not clear how they can avoid the sort of credibility problem mentioned. We need not dwell on such issues, however, since the esteem-based perspective suggests quite a different approach to the explanation of why norms appear and assume a stable profile; in particular, it shows that the enforcement dilemma is not the insurmountable obstacle it has seemed to be.

3   BEYOND THE ENFORCEMENT DILEMMA

It has sometimes been remarked that, strictly speaking, the enforcement dilemma does not establish the impossibility of norms. It leaves open the possibility that the cost associated with enforcement or sanctioning is less than the cost associated with cooperation and that people, therefore, may be more generally disposed to sanction one another—and thereby to police one another into cooperation—than they are to cooperate in the absence of sanctions. This loophole has been explored in a number of discussions (Ben-Ner and Putterman 1998; Anderson 2000).

Elliott Sober and David Sloan Wilson appeal to this loophole, for example, in arguing for the naturalistic possibility of altruism. They describe cooperation in the sort of predicament we have been discussing as primary altruistic behaviour, and the sanctioning of others with a view to cooperation as secondary altruistic behaviour. And then they ground the possibility of social norms in the postulate that secondary altruistic behaviour is not as costly as primary. 'In comparison with altruistic primary behaviours, which by their nature are costly if performed without associated rewards and punishments, secondary behaviours can often be performed at a low cost to the actor' (Sober and Wilson 1998: 146).

There are abstract arguments as to why this should be so, though they have not commanded general consensus (Henrich and Boyd 2001: 80). In practice, many writers, including Sober and Wilson (1998: 146–8, 166–8), rely on ethnographic evidence in support of the claim, in particular evidence on the low-cost nature of gossip and on the policing role it can play (Sabini and Silver 1982; Braithwaite 1989; Coleman 1990a; Cooter 1996).[3] But is the ethnographic evidence sufficient to counter the force of the problem raised by the enforcement dilemma? Not obviously. It is not enough to show that gossip is low-cost.

---

[3] This ethnographic evidence has some experimental support in the finding that increasing punishment possibilities leads to an increase in punishment itself (Fehr and Gaechter 2000).

There are two other conditions that must also be fulfilled. First, low-cost gossip must operate truthfully and reliably against norm-deviance, not being driven in a more wayward fashion by the forces of envy and malice. And, second, low-cost gossip must be generally *believed* to operate truthfully and reliably. For if most people think that people will speak badly of them regardless of what they do, then they will not be disciplined by the fear of being spoken of in that way.

But we do not need to rely on the sort of abstract argument or ethnographic evidence mentioned for arguing that secondary altruism is cheaper than primary. Nor do we even have to rely on the platitude that there are many expressions of approval or disapproval that are very cheap and often convincing: the voluntarily controlled look of disgust or admiration, the shake of the head, the thumbs-up, and so on. For secondary altruism need not involve behaviour of any kind—it may involve just the manifest or presumptive formation of attitudes of esteem or disesteem—and so it may be, not just cheaper than cooperation, but absolutely costless.

The enforcement dilemma looks persuasive only because it exploits an ambiguity in English usage and thereby hides the possibility of such costless sanctioning. When it is said that someone approves or disapproves of what another did, one or other of two quite contrasting things may be conveyed. The message may be that the first person commends or censures the action of the second, whether sincerely or insincerely. Or the message may be that, whether or not anything is done in expression of the attitude, the first person takes a positive or a negative view of what the second did: they think well or badly of the action performed. On the first reading, the words 'approval' and 'disapproval' have a behavioural meaning; they refer to a sort of commendation or censure that involves action and hence (opportunity) costs. On the second reading, however, the words have an exclusively attitudinal register, and refer to a costless process—costless, because involuntary—of thinking well or badly of what the agent did.

With this ambiguity in mind, consider again the argument for the enforcement dilemma. Norms are available only so far as people are prepared to display approval or disapproval of what others do in the relevant domain, so the argument goes, but this causes a problem because the display of approval or disapproval is costly. A little reflection on these claims, however, makes clear that the display of approval or disapproval that is required for norms does not have to be the behavioural, costly display of such attitudes; it may involve merely the involuntary but manifest formation of such attitudes (Pettit 1990; McAdams 1997).

What might it mean to display approval or disapproval? On an attitudinal reading it will mean: *to approve or disapprove manifestly*—that is, to form the attitude of approval or disapproval in a context where others are in a position to see or assume that you do so. On a behavioural reading, it will mean: *to manifest approval or disapproval*—to go through the required verbal or gestural or intentional motions—whether or not one actually has the attitudes manifested.

According to our account of norms, people must generally comply with any regularity that constititutes a norm and their compliance must be explained in some part by the fact that others approve of compliance and/or disapprove of deviance. But in this sense it will be sufficient for norms to exist that people manifestly approve or disapprove of relevant actions—that they manifestly form those attitudes—and that their doing so causes agents to adjust their behaviour accordingly. It will not be required that people manifest the approval or disapproval involved by actively commending or censuring relevant agents.

The enforcement dilemma holds that the approval and disapproval whereby norms are reinforced in this way is personally costly to the agents who manifest it. But when this point is defended, the focus shifts from manifestly approving or disapproving to manifesting approval or disapproval: that is, to something that involves, not the formation of an attitude, but—as it is in most cases—the performance of an action. And while the performance of such an action might inevitably incur certain costs—in particular, avoidable costs—the formation of an attitude will not do so.

Buchanan says that there are two sorts of enforcement costs that may be expected to inhibit the formation of norms: the epistemic cost of finding violators—or as it may be compliers—and the practical cost of censuring or indeed commending them. Even if sanctioning involves an intentional action there may be no epistemic cost incurred; there will be many cases where the sanctioner just happens to come across agents who comply or violate the normative regularity. But intentional sanctioning will always involve a practical cost, according to Buchanan, for it will mean at the very least that the person has to devote time and other resources to the exercise and in most cases it will mean that they have to incur the cost of alienating someone censured and the cost of embarrassment that will often be involved in going out of one's way to commend an agent. Things become even worse, of course, if the censure is associated with imposing a penalty or the commendation with conferring a reward but we need not consider those further complexities here.

If people can sanction others, however, just by manifestly—or indeed presumptively—forming reactive attitudes to what they do, and without having to do anything themselves, then there is no avoidable cost involved from their point of view. They may regret being in a situation where they manifestly approve or disapprove of what someone does, thereby incurring an unavoidable cost. Thus they may regret coming across someone, perhaps a stranger or a friend, in a compromising situation; they may wish that they were a million miles away. But with this cost sunk, they may have to do nothing—in particular, they may have to incur no further cost—in order to punish the person involved. Let the situation be one where they are seen to observe what the agent does, and presumed to disapprove, and the mere fact of their being there will be sufficient to ensure that the agent will be effectively punished. And as punishment may be automatically and costlessly dispensed in this way, of course, so too may reward be distributed in that fashion.

Is it plausible to think that people will manifestly or presumptively form evaluative attitudes—attitudes of esteem or disesteem—when they see someone behave well or badly? Is it plausible, for example, that on seeing others see me acting in such a manner, I should recognise that they will thereby be led to form a high or low opinion of me? Surely it is. I will be able to see that they form such an attitude, so far as I see that given the evidence of their eyes—and given the standards that we share—I would do so in their situation. I do not need to see what they do, then, before seeing what they think. Even if their facial and other involuntary expressions do not give them away, I will see what they think on the basis of my knowledge of their epistemic situation: 'research has shown that people are remarkably accurate at estimating others' knowledge' (Miller and Prentice 1996: 809).

Our discussion of the economy of esteem makes it unnecessary to document these claims in any detail. We are already familiar with the idea that we may be judged by those who say or do nothing as a result; that just being well or badly thought of by others can be a significant sanction for people; and so that without doing anything in particular people may police one another into certain patterns of behaviour. Adam Smith (1982: 116) put the crucial point forcefully, when he argued that we are mortified to be disesteemed, as we are pleased to be esteemed, even though 'that sentiment should never actually be exerted against us'.

In discussing the enforcement dilemma, James Buchanan acknowledges that if we can devise instruments for the automatic, intentionally costless punishment—or presumably reward—of agents then we can overcome the problem. And, thinking of the possibilities of electric fences and gun traps, he is prepared to be relatively optimistic on this front. 'We need not reach into the extremities of science fiction to think of devices that could serve as automatically programmed enforcers' (Buchanan 1975: 131). We agree that we need not reach into the extremities of science fiction in order to identify automatic enforcers, but we also think that it is unnecessary to go to the gruesome lengths represented by these technological devices. For it is in the very nature of human beings, as centres of mutual evaluation and esteem, to act as automatic enforcers of one another's behaviour. We reward and punish others not just by what we do to them but also by what we think of them: more strictly, by what we presumptively or manifestly think of them. And in this sense our thoughts, manifest or presumptive, are not subject to choice or control. We serve as one another's involuntary and often reluctant probation officers.

We shall be looking in the remainder of this chapter at how such involuntary regulation may give rise to norms, and sustain norms. But in emphasising the role and importance of such attitudinal regulation, we do not suggest that it is the unique source of conformity to norms. The regulation envisaged can only work so far as people actually tend to explain conformity by the presence of virtue—or what is thought to be virtue in the group in question—not by the desire to be thought virtuous; and people will tend to do this, arguably, only so far as there are at least some generally persuasive examples of virtuous people available. In any case, the most plausible motivational picture, as already suggested, is that the desire to be thought virtuous operates for most people as a back-up support—operates as a virtual, not an active controller—rather than as the sole generator of virtuous behaviour (Sen 1998).

We are inclined to agree with Robert Cooter (1994) that a rule of norms will be powerfully reinforced if people generally internalise the norms, so that for them conformity becomes second nature (Tyler 1990). It would have been ad hoc to postulate such internalisation as a response to the enforcement dilemma itself; it would have involved simply rejecting the assumption of rational self-interest on which the dilemma is raised. But given that the dilemma is not insurmountable even in its own terms—given that conformity to norms is not inherently vulnerable to rational self-interest—it is reasonable to conjecture that there are habits that work in tandem with self-interest to produce conformity.

This is particularly reasonable, of course, if one endorses the Aristotelian observation that the emergence of such habits is likely to be facilitated by the very conformity that the desire for esteem supports (Aristotle 1976). We shall not be considering Aristotelian habits very much in what follows, but we should not be thought to deny their potential importance. The normal course of development through childhood to adulthood, at least in the case of the well-raised member of society, is very likely to encourage the onset of such habits.

As we do not have to deny the importance of internalisation and the development of habits, so we do not have to deny the importance of a mechanism that has recently attracted much attention: the mechanism of group-selection, in particular group-selection based on cultural as distinct from genetic transmission. Imagine that some groupings, say because of operating within a suitable economy of esteem, give rise to socially better norms than others: to norms that generate a survival advantage over other groupings. And imagine that conditions allow those groupings to maintain their identities over time, even as rival groupings break up due to the burden of operating with socially inferior norms. In such conditions there would be a selectional pressure in favour of the sorts of norms envisaged. We do not have to make a judgement on whether this sort of selection is likely to have taken place in the history of human societies, as Sober and Wilson (1998) maintain. But we can certainly be open to the discovery that it has, as a burgeoning literature suggests.[4]

4   PREDICTING AND EXPLAINING NORMS

Our discussion so far has been mainly negative, serving to establish the possibility of norms in face of the difficulty raised by the enforcement dilemma. We turn in this section to sketch some conditions under which we might expect norms to materialise, in particular norms that serve to advance the collective welfare. And then in the next section we ask how the factors in play might be brought under some measure of control and the intangible hand that they represent be designed so as to work for better effect.

There are a number of conditions that we can identify in the abstract such that if these are realised in any group then we may expect, as by an intangible hand, that the forces of esteem and disesteem will support the presence of corresponding norms (Pettit 1990). In particular we may expect that they will support the presence of norms that operate in general for the benefit of members of that community. We mention four conditions in particular. We think that these are sufficient for the emergence or stabilisation of norms, though we do not suggest that they are necessary.

The first condition is that there is a type of situation, Z, such that people are generally aware in that situation that an agent may behave in one of a number of saliently contrasted ways. Taking the simplest case, they are aware in any case of Z that the agent may choose to take either option A or option B. Call this *the choice condition*.

The second condition is that people are generally exposed in situation Z to the possibility of having their choice noticed by others; and people are generally

---

[4] Robert Boyd and P. J. Richerson are responsible for an ongoing series of studies related to the possibility. See for example Boyd and Richerson (1996; 2002; forthcoming) and Richerson and Boyd (1998; 2001). See too Soltis, Boyd, et al. (1995).

aware in situation Z that this is so. We may call this *the perception condition*. It postulates that there is little or no chance of people getting away with doing A or with doing B, for example, without this being noticed by others, and that in situation Z they will generally be aware that that is so.

The third condition is that of the options in situation Z there is one such that people in that situation are generally disposed to disapprove of others not doing it; and, moreover, people are generally aware in situation Z that they are each so disposed. We call this *the evaluation condition*. The evaluation that people in Z are disposed to make, according to this third condition, may take the form of an egocentric or personal comment, as in the complaint 'That's damaging to me', so long as the base of evaluation is one that would apply equally to others in the agent's position. In order for the disposition to be evaluative in character, and not just to constitute a taste-based preference, the base must be of this kind. But the disposition need not be to condemn the action in a moralised way, say from the point of view of the society as a whole.

Why not alter the evaluation condition so that it requires either approval of conformity or disapproval of nonconformity, as in the definition of norms? As a matter of fact we think that when a norm begins to emerge, with a growing minority of people displaying the required behaviour, the approval of conformity will typically play an important role in reinforcing the efforts of pioneers, as in the recycling case discussed in Chapter 7, and that at that point there won't be disapproval attached to nonconformity. But equally we think that approval of conformity will wane as the behaviour becomes more and more common and begins to consitute a norm proper—conforming will then be in the normal range—and that the condition that will be crucial is that nonconformity attracts disapproval, again as in the recycling case. Rather than continue to mark this complexity, however, we opt for the simplicity of assuming in the evaluation condition that a failure to take the relevant option in situation Z will attract disapproval or disesteem from the start.

The fourth condition requires, not just that agents are aware that they will be seen to make a particular choice, and that they will be disesteemed if they do not do so, but that equally they are not so concerned with other matters that the desire for esteem will lose its normal hold upon them. It must be that they are susceptible in the ordinary way to the rewards of esteem, the penalties of disesteem. Call this *the susceptibility condition*.

Given the points made at length in earlier chapters, we think that the obtaining of these conditions will serve to predict and will help to explain the presence of corresponding norms.[5] In order to bear out the claim, we consider

---

[5] Gaechter and Fehr (1999) provide questionnaire data that suggest that cooperation triggers a high degree of approval in a social predicament, free riding a high degree of disapproval.

a very simple case. Suppose that in the situation where someone has a cold there is a salient distinction between the options of going into company with that cold or staying at home, and that almost everyone in such a situation will be aware of this. And suppose that the perception and evaluation conditions are equally fulfilled. In that situation everyone is aware that others will notice it if anyone joins their company with a cold; there will be little or no possibility of hiding the infection. And in that situation almost everyone is aware that others will disapprove of anyone with a cold joining them; there is a manifest danger in being exposed to the cold virus.

We think that in such a situation it is likely that a norm against joining the company of others in the event of having a cold will emerge among the people envisaged. And that likelihood will be greatly increased, if the susceptibility condition is fulfilled too. If it is not fulfilled, then while each will clearly have an incentive for conforming with that regularity—and have something like the approval-related incentive required for norms—other incentives may prevail over it. Suppose that the option of staying at home has serious costs, say in employment or educational terms, and that joining others in company is going to be hard or impossible to avoid. In such a case the norm may emerge only as a norm governing casual social life, not life in the school or workplace. If the option of staying at home from work or school has such serious costs indeed— if the susceptibility condition fails in such a measure—then the evaluation condition is likely to fail also. Where it is generally recognised in situation Z that a person with a cold, A, has little option but to join others in company, people are unlikely to disapprove of A's doing so; the excuse available for joining others will be palpable enough to preempt disapproval. There may also be considerable approval on offer, of course, for those who nevertheless do stay at home.

We said that fulfilment of the four conditions would provide a plausible explanation for the emergence of a suitable norm. If all but one of the conditions were satisfied then we would expect the fulfilment of the fourth to generate the sort of motivation and behaviour by virtue of which a corresponding norm would come into existence. Once the norm is in exist- ence, of course, then the continued satisfaction of the conditions will explain the survival of the norm and will also explain its resilience: that is, the fact, assuming it is a fact, that the norm is more or less proof against a variety of possible shocks (Pettit 1993: ch. 5).

This simple example is distinguished by the fact that it presupposes only the sort of disapproval involved in people's being personally averse to someone who puts them in danger of catching a cold. People may not entertain any attitudes of disapproval, or of course approval, on behalf of the society as a whole or on behalf of the abstract moral order; they may not extend their sympathies to others in that way and feel indignation in the name of all. What is required is only that they each feel resentment on their own behalf, and are disposed therefore to complain—or at least would be disposed to complain were it not too embarrassing or troublesome or whatever. It is not that they regard themselves as special, of course. They each register a feature in the action—the danger it represents—that gives them, and would give anyone in their position, reason to disapprove of it.

But the example involves not only this egocentrically shaped form of disapproval: the attitude involved may even fail to be general in a distinctive sense. Everyone in situation Z may be aware of the danger posed by someone with a cold and may disapprove of the person's joining them in company, but this awareness and disapproval may come upon them case by case—that is, in one instance after another of situation Z—without their ever forming a general attitude towards people who behave like that. With anyone who puts them in the relevant danger they may be disposed to disapprove of what that person does. But they may not be disposed to disapprove as a general matter of anyone who puts them in that danger. They may disapprove of such people case after case—*in sensu diviso*, to use the medieval tag—but not disapprove of them as an explicitly conceptualised class, not disapprove of them *in sensu composito* (Lewis 1969).

There is also a third limitation that we might notice in the example given. This is that not only is the disapproval involved unmoralised and ungeneralised, as we can say, it also occurs without its necessarily being a matter of common awareness that it occurs. Everyone in the situation may have to be aware of the choice involved, and of the perception and evaluation to which the relevant agent is subject. But it need not be the case that everyone is aware that everyone is aware of that, and so on in the usual hierarchy.

Although the example given is simple, nevertheless it still serves to exemplify a large class of norms that obtain in any society. They are the norms that most of us are barely conscious of taking our guidance from, since they are not often supported in a surrounding discourse of general commendation and critique and are not reflected in levels of common or mutual awareness. They may include the norms that govern turn-taking in conversation, the use of eyes in relation to others, the distance at which one stands when speaking to another, and a host of such unnoticed but not merely mechanical regularities.

Can we readily extend our explanatory and predictive story beyond the realm of such simple norms? We see no problem in principle. Let people be aware of a choice between certain options that recurs in a given kind of situation; let them be aware that what someone does in that situation will be subject to the notice of others; and let them be aware—and share in a common awareness—that the options in question are matters of general, moralised approval and disapproval in their society, not just matters that incur the personal complacency or complaint of others. The conditions involved here are rather more complex than the austere conditions in which we explain the emergence of the norm about colds; they postulate, without independent explanation, that people have attained levels of generalised, moralised appro-bation and have done so as a matter of common awareness. But if we postulate the required background of choice, perception, and evaluation, then there would seem to be no serious difficulty in explaining why general, moralised norms might emerge and stablilise as a matter of common awareness: norms, for example, like those of honesty and sincerity, non-violence and non-coercion, conscientiousness and loyalty. We can see why the forces of esteem and disesteem would generate and buttress such norms and would operate like an intangible hand in giving them such support.

The materials to hand, then, enable us to explain the emergence, survival, and resilience of simple norms on the basis of independently intelligible levels of awareness and types of attitude, and to explain the emergence, survival, and resilience of more complex norms on the basis of richer kinds of awareness and attitude. But the materials may well enable us to do more. They may help to explain why the richer forms of awareness and attitude can come to be accessible once people have already established certain simple norms. Thus they may show us how the explanatory gap between a regime of simple norms and a regime of more complex norms might be closed.

Suppose that the simple norm against going into company with a cold has been established among certain people. Almost everyone conforms to that regularity—they do so, at least in part, out of an awareness that otherwise they will incur the personal complaint of others—and people in general benefit from that public or shared good. But the obtaining of those conditions creates an opportunity whereby an enterprising member may now gain in the esteem stakes (Pettit 1990; McAdams 1997, 2000). For suppose that someone hits by chance or strategy on a sort of behaviour—say, verbal behaviour—that is seen as censuring a person who offends against the regularity for the danger they represent to others generally, not just to the speaker. That person is bound to enjoy the approval—perhaps just the egocentrically shaped approval—of those who are put in danger. 'Any behaviour that promotes a public good', after all, 'is itself a public good' (Sober and Wilson 1998: 144). Assuming, plausibly enough, that people will be aware of the approval thereby gained, we can expect the practice of moralising in such a manner to be reinforced in the person who initiates it and to be imitated by others. Given the way the economy of esteem works, there is no mystery as to how the practice might get established.

If the practice gets established, however, then there is an immediate prospect of moralised norms emerging. For if people become disposed to moralise negatively or positively about a certain sort of behaviour, and if this becomes a matter of awareness—perhaps generalised, and perhaps shared in common— then there will be room for presumptive patterns of moralised approval and, even more crucially, disapproval to police people into appropriate behaviour. People might begin to stay at home when they have a cold, for example, because they will otherwise incur not just the personal resentment but the moralised disapproval of others.

If moralised approval and disapproval can serve to buttress norms that already exist on the basis of more egocentrically shaped evaluation, then there is no reason why they should not come into play in support of novel norms. Let moralised desiderata become established in common discourse and thought, say under the influence of religious or political leaders, and moralised approval and disapproval will be enabled to generate and stabilise the corresponding norms. One particularly interesting example of how this may occur was presented in Chapter 7, when we considered how a norm of recycling might emerge and stabilise, under a bootstrapping set of pressures.

We mentioned earlier that some writers envisage a hierarchy of progressively less costly norms, involving the sanctioning of behaviour at a first level, the sanctioning of the sanctioning of behaviour at a second, and so on. We think that there is something in the hierarchical idea. The emergence of a regime of egocentrically based norms is fairly easy to explain, given it presupposes only independently intelligible types of attitude: aversion to what is personally damaging, attraction to what is personally beneficial. But one of the egocentric norms that we can envisage emerging is a norm of censuring those behaviours that are already outlawed under such norms and commending those behaviours that are enjoined. And once we envisage that sort of norm coming into operation, we can see why the way is opened for the emergence of more neutral, explicitly moralised norms. Those norms will often support or supplant existing, simple norms but they may also take on quite novel forms.

The idea that moralisation—in effect, moralising talk—should have the sort of effect postulated will strike some as surprising. It is received wisdom that words are cheap, after all, and it is a familiar, game-theoretic assumption— though not one that is particularly well supported (Sally 1995; Mackie 1998)— that allowing parties to communicate in social dilemmas ought not to have any effect on what they go on to do. But the importance of moral talk is quite explicable within the perspective provided by the economy of esteem. For such talk can serve to alert an agent to the standards that obtain in the local community, and can draw the policing, estimative attention of people generally to the success or failure of the agent to live up to those standards (Miller and Prentice 1996: 808). Moral talk of the kind envisaged may be cheap, or even profitable, but it is still capable of activating the powerful forces that drive behaviour within the economy of esteem.

5   SHAPING NORMS

We have been arguing that just as the iron, political hand may be responsible for beneficial laws, and the invisible, economic hand for beneficial market adjustments, so the intangible hand should be seen as a device that offers parallel support for those beneficial norms that rule in any well-functioning society. This is a significant result from the point of view of anyone concerned with institutional design. It will help to restore confidence in the reality and power of norms among any parties who may have begun, say because of the impact of the enforcement dilemma argument, to be sceptical. And even more important, it will represent norms as factors of the kind that it is right and proper for a society to rely upon in the course of institutional design.

One of the most widely accepted principles of institutional design is that we should not be overly optimistic about human nature (Brennan and Buchanan 1981). Hume and Mandeville maintained that we should only rely on institutions that are fit to survive the presence of complete knaves. As Hume (1875: 117–18) said, in 'fixing the several checks and controls of the constitution, every man ought to be supposed a knave, and to have no other end in all his actions than private interest'. Or as Mandeville (1731: 332) had earlier written, the best sort of constitution is the one which 'remains unshaken though most men should prove knaves'. These writers may well have gone too far with this principle, since institutions that are fit to survive knaves may equally fail to inspire those who are more public-spirited (Pettit 1996b; Le Grand 2000). But the general point is persuasive: we should not design institutions that will work reliably only so far as people generally prove to be virtuous. We should economise, so far as possible, on virtue (Brennan and Hamlin 1995).

This being so, the claim that we have defended in respect of norms is of the first importance. For what we have been able to show is that norms are not supported by virtue alone, but also by the interest that people have in the attitudes of others towards them, in particular the attitudes that they entertain of esteem and disesteem. If this is right, then it need not be utopian to look to a regime of norms to sustain one or another institutional pattern. Provided that we can see why those norms are likely to be kept in place by the forces of esteem—as by an intangible hand—we can reasonably invest confidence in them.

This is to say that in the course of institutional design or redesign we are entitled, where suitable norms exist, to rely on their continuing in existence and to build certain expectations upon them. Furthermore, the considerations mustered show not just that norms are reliable social controls, but also that they are subject to certain intentional shaping effects. We may hope not only to exploit existing norms in the course of institutional design, but also to be able to engineer changes in existing norms and perhaps even to engineer some beneficial norms into existence—or, equally, to engineer some destructive norms out.

This point will not come as a surprise. We saw in the last chapter that there are at least three ways in which people may seek to influence the way the intangible hand or backhand operates among them. One is to shape the degree of publicity to which agents are subject in any domain; a second is to try and control the presentation to which their behaviour will be subject; and a third is to attempt to increase the extent to which they are predisposed to be moved by motives of virtue and esteem. Henceforth we shall refer to these as, respectively, the publicity, the presentation, and the predisposition strategies.

These three approaches will apply straightforwardly in the case of norms, connecting respectively with the conditions of perception, evaluation, and suceptibility mentioned earlier. To pursue the publicity approach would be to seek to change the extent to which the relative performance of agents is exposed to the gaze of others. To pursue the presentational would be to try and influence the sort of evaluation to which they are subject in the minds of the others who become aware of that performance. And to pursue the predisposition approach would be to try and minimise the role of other motives that might undermine the impact on agents of the desire for esteem. We can expect to foster the emergence or stability of a given norm, not just by putting motives that support it into commission, as we do in working on publicity and presentation, but also by decommissioning any motives that may work against it. The norm against going into company with a cold would surely strengthen and spread, for example, if it became a matter of general assumption that no employer or teacher could legitimately complain about someone's staying at home in the event of having a cold.

It is not difficult to see how these strategies might be employed by the people in any group, perhaps via a centralised authority, to shape the norms that obtain among them. Let the members of a community want to reinforce a certain norm obtaining among them and we can see straightaway how they might employ each of the strategies in this pursuit. They might take steps to shape the publicity attaching to relevant agents, relying on presumptive patterns of approval and disapproval to police them into greater compliance with the desired norm. They might try to ensure that the behaviour involved is presented in the appropriate light by disseminating information on the benefits of the desired pattern, by articulating and codifying relevant ideals, or by giving salience to this or that model group of comparators. And they might try to predispose people to be moved by the desire for approval through removing or reducing the influence of other, contrary motives; they might act, for example, so as to eliminate any fear of intimidation by others.

The people in any community or organisation may hope to shape their individual behaviour, then, not just by relying on the fear of legal and related sanctions, but also by using centralised initiatives—perhaps even formal laws— to promote suitable kinds of publicity for potentially estimable or disestimable behaviour, to establish modes of presentation that will activate the required form of esteem or disesteem, and to ensure that people are predisposed to be moved by corresponding, esteem-related motives. They may hope to have a collective influence on what they each individually do, encouraging the formation and operation of suitable norms, and discouraging the appearance or survival of unsuitable ones. We turn in the next chapter to consider some detailed examples of what this may involve.

CONCLUSION

The iron hand can produce social benefit by establishing coercive laws and other initiatives, the invisible hand by giving rise to the adjustments of the competitive market and related domains. How is the intangible hand to serve in a corresponding role? We argued in this chapter that it typically does so by giving support to social norms that operate—as norms may not always do—for the general good. We associate norms with the domain of civil society and we took them to be regularities in behaviour such that almost everyone conforms, almost everyone approves of others conforming and/or disapproves of their not conforming—or at least is generally expected to do so—and this pattern of approval or disapproval, real or presumptive, plays some role in explaining the presence of the regularities.

In the early part of the chapter we considered an argument that has had enormous influence in economic and rational-choice circles, to the effect that norms in this sense cannot do any of the work expected of them; in particular, they cannot serve to rescue people from collective action predicaments. The argument is that if people are not disposed to cooperate in such predicaments—if they are too personally self-concerned to do so—neither will they generally be disposed to enforce a norm of cooperation; the enforcement of the norm by the display of approval or disapproval is liable to be personally costly, just as cooperation is personally costly. This argument invokes the so-called enforcement dilemma. Let a norm be needed and people will not be willing to enforce it; let people be willing to enforce it and the norm will not be needed.

We showed that this dilemma is bogus, however, drawing on materials from earlier discussions. Expressing approval or disapproval is one way of displaying approval or disapproval, and this is a potentially costly intentional act. But another way of displaying approval or disapproval is just approving or disapproving manifestly—that is, manifestly having those attitudes. Not being an intentional act, this sort of display does not involve voluntarily incurring any costs. We know from our exploration of the economy of esteem that people can be motivated to act by the desire for approval or by aversion to disapproval, even when those attitudes are not intentionally expressed, and so we can see that the enforcement dilemma does not offer an insurmountable challenge to those who believe in the potential of norms.

The last two sections of the chapter were given to exploring the explanatory and policymaking implications of this view of norms. The second-last section gave an account of how we might expect certain simple norms to emerge and stabilise in the absence of any moralising on the part of people generally; how it is intelligible that once such norms are established, a norm of moralising about them should also appear; and why we need not be surprised that with such a norm in place there is a range of norms that may be elicited on the basis of esteem-related motives.

The last section went on to connect this story about norms with some points made in the previous chapter. It showed that if norms are sustained on such a basis—if they can be regarded as the work of the intangible hand—then there are clear possibilities for a community to exploit them in the design of its own institutions and to engineer changes in the norms that are going to obtain. They may foster norms by recourse to a number of strategies: by promoting suitable levels of publicity for potentially estimable or disestimable behaviour; by establishing modes of presentation that will activate the required form of esteem or disesteem; and by trying to ensure that people are not subject to contrary pressures and are predisposed to be moved by corresponding, esteem-related motives.

15

Mobilising the Intangible Hand

1 TOWARDS REFORM

The ideal initiative at this point would be to outline a programme whereby the intangible hand might be put in service to the common good. The idea would be to identify those areas where the hand already works for good and to devise means of reinforcing it there; and equally to discern the places where it does more harm than good and try to inhibit its operation at those locations.

There are strategies available whereby we might seek to advance such a goal. As we saw at the end of the last chapter a goal of the kind described might be advanced through any of three strategies, or a mix of those strategies. The first involves changing the kinds or levels of publicity given to what people do or fail to do; the second adjusting the presentation given to their behaviour, making sure it is cast in a light that prompts the desire for esteem in the required way; and the third removing the obstacles that might affect people's predispositions to be moved appropriately by that desire; or through a mix of these strategies. We call these the publicity, presentation, and predisposition strategies.

But it is not going to be possible here to do anything like outlining a programme of reform. There are a number of considerations that make this impossible. One is that in order to advance that programme we would need to have an agreed specification of the common good that is to be advanced: an agreed sense of the criteria whereby certain forms of behaviour are to be targeted as desirable, others as undesirable. We might attempt to implement the programme, of course, on the independently defended assumption that the relevant ideals are of this or that form (see e.g. Pettit 1997: ch. 7). But there are two other considerations that present more serious obstacles.

Both of these considerations relate to the lack of crucial empirical information. On the one hand, we do not have the information we require on exactly how adjustments to existing practices and institutions are likely to impact on the manner or measure in which people are rewarded by enjoying esteem, or penalised by suffering disesteem. And on the other hand we do not have a developed sense of the different, novel institutions whereby the economy of esteem might be influenced; we do not have an empirically informed modelling of the possibilities available.

Those in the relatively distant past who embraced the economy of esteem and made institutional proposals for the redirecting of esteem to a good common purpose avoided these empirical difficulties by drawing copiously on history, and on the authority of the ancients. The work of the seventeenth- and eighteenth-century theorists of esteem was driven in great part, as was the work of Machiavelli before them, by reflections on the experience of the Romans, as recorded by the classical historians and in their own emerging historical studies. By contemporary lights, however, that is a very ad hoc channel of empirical information. We cannot claim credibility for any detailed programmes of reform without having available well-researched bodies of fact and well-tested models of feasible arrangements.

Consider some of the possibilities mooted as likely in earlier chapters, and as more or less tentatively supported by experience and research: that the entry of high-flyers to various esteem-sensitive domains will drive up the level of performance in certain ranges; that at certain margins people will prefer a small pond in which they shine to moving—with benefit in the esteem of outsiders— to a large pond in which they don't shine; that the introduction of non-estimative penalties or rewards may actually reduce overall performance, through inducing defiance in relevant parties and undermining esteem-related motives; that its becoming a matter of common belief that someone is esteemed or disesteemed can render them less susceptible to the attraction of esteem, or to aversion to disesteem; and so on. While these are very plausible effects, there is little prospect of building programmes of reform upon them, short of having evidence on their strength and on their sensitivity to contextual considerations.

But without outlining a detailed or even partial programme for the reform of existing practices, it is still possible to do something useful in connection with the question of how best to deploy the intangible hand. What we are in a position to do is to identify points on the fronts associated with the three strategies of publicity, presentation, and predisposition at which, plausibly, there are failures that might be rectified with benefit to people generally. This exercise can be thought of as a tentative prolegomenon to the development of reform programmes.

The discussion does not claim to offer an exhaustive list of failures, needless to say, merely a suggestive one. And the failures examined all bear on the performance of agents in a given sector (for example, in politics or the public service or civic life), not on the capacity of a sector to attract people who are independently disposed (say, because of their virtue or their concern for esteem) to perform well there. They are limited to failures to motivate or moralise the agents actually in a sector, and do not include failures to select suitable agents for the sector (see Brennan 1996).

We shall be looking at the failures with a view to strengthening the intangible hand, rather than with an eye to weakening the intangible backhand. This limitation, however, need not be a source of particular concern. The failures identified as problems for the intangible hand point us towards phenomena that we might hope to eliminate. But they point us at the same time towards devices by which we might hope to inhibit the intangible backhand. If a given factor serves to stop the operation of an intangible hand, after all, then it will equally serve to stop the operation of an intangible backhand. We will move that lever in one direction when we seek to promote beneficial effects; we will move it in the opposite direction when we seek to block effects that are harmful.

2   THE TARGET OF REFORM

Before looking at the ways in which failures plausibly occur, however, it will be useful to remind ourselves about what any reform in the economy of esteem—in the working of the intangible hand—is going to target: what it is going to try and change. Such reform will start, as mentioned, from some specification of how social life can be improved. It may start from a specification at the level of the aggregate outcome of people's behaviour: it may take it as given, for example, that a certain organisation should achieve various ideals—say, that the state should operate by the rule of law—and that individuals, therefore, should behave in a manner consonant with that aggregate goal. Or it may start from a specification at the level of individual performance, assuming that it is desirable that individual parties generally, or those in a particular domain, satisfy certain constraints or promote certain states of affairs. Or of course it may start from a specification of how social life can be improved that involves a mix of such patterns of organisational and individual adjustment.

But however the improvement to be achieved is conceptualised, any programme of reform has to be focused, ultimately, on the shifts that it seeks in the behaviour of individual people. No institution or organisation changes without the individuals who give life to it changing; that is what institutional and organisational change consists in. And so for any programme of reform there has to be a representation of the changes that it seeks at the level of individual motive, habit, and action.

The reform programme won't be targeted on particular individuals, at least in the normal case, but rather on the patterns sustained in typical perform-ances, whether on the part of people generally or on the part of those who operate in a certain domain. It will look for shifts in the regularities of behaviour that such people embrace as ideals and more or less routinely fulfil. It will seek to establish in the habits of those parties the dispositions to act in fidelity to the regularities, this fidelity being reinforced by a susceptibility to pressures of esteem and disesteem, approval and disapproval.

Imagine now that a reform programme is fully successful in establishing general conformity to a certain regularity among the relevant parties; and, for simplicity, suppose that this is achieved without anyone forming false expect-ations of the kind associated with pluralistic ignorance. Most of the people involved will conform to that regularity, given the hypothesised success; most of them will be disposed to esteem such conformity in others, or to disesteem failure, given the means whereby the success is sought; and that pattern of approval will help in some measure to sustain the pattern of conformity, given that resort to those means was necessary and effective. And so the regularity established will constitute a norm, by our earlier account of what norms involve. It will attract general conformity and general approval, and the approval will help to explain the conformity.

This observation means that wherever an esteem-based reform programme is set up, the aim can be characterised in such a way that full success involves establishing or reinforcing a certain norm or norms among people generally or among people in the relevant domain. Of course, the programme in some instances may involve the elimination of certain norms—say, norms of a subcultural kind that are to the detriment of society generally—in order that the desired norms be put in power. And, equally, the programme may not require that the desired norms be fully or properly established—be established with more or less universal conformity in the relevant sector—in order to be successful in its own terms; those implementing it may be content to establish the norm only in a measure that increases overall conformity. But nonetheless the aim of esteem-based reform can be characterised, without distortion, as that of putting certain norms in place among the population generally, or among those in the population who operate in a certain domain: say, in politics or business or public service.[1]

---

[1] We need not think of the process whereby norms are put in place as a mechanical pattern of induction or conditioning whereby people are brought to sustain appropriate dispositions. The process envisaged may be dynamic in character with the norms that are put in place having to be continually maintained and negotiated, say in conformity to higher-order norms of discussion and interpretation (Ayres and Braithwaite 1992; Black 1998). For ease of presentation, however, we shall not be giving this aspect of things the attention it deserves.

The norms that most of us will want to see in place are going to include examples like those mentioned in the last chapter. Norms that govern the ways people relate to one another in discourse, embracing patterns of honesty, trustworthiness, and sincerity; norms that constrain the ways in which they otherwise seek to influence one another, eschewing resort to violence, theft, fraud, and coercion; norms requiring that people commit themselves conscientiously to various collaborative causes, playing the part that is collectively required of them; and norms that enforce codes of practice for the conduct of their business and professional lives.

The norms we seek in esteem-based reform may also include norms that govern, not a given, presumptively attainable sort of behaviour such as these examples illustrate, but rather the behaviour of trying to do one's best in a certain domain. They may include norms requiring people to seek certain aspirational goals—these may be positional goals which it is logically impossible for all to succeed in attaining—as well as norms requiring them to comply with clear-cut, universal constraints. In the aspirational case the reason for wanting the norm to be in place may be, not the benefit of everyone's making an effort as such, but rather an associated gain. The associated gain may be the benefit secured by that person or those persons who come out at the top; the general research norm of aspiring to be first to establish any scientific result may benefit research, fostering earlier rather than later breakthroughs. Or again the associated gain may be the benefit secured as a side-effect of the expenditure of effort; a general norm of aspiring to win academic prizes may benefit the society through raising the overall level of numeracy and literacy in the population.

To sum up this line of thought, then, wherever an esteem-based reform programme is introduced the aim can always be characterised as that of establishing or reinforcing certain desired norms—and, no doubt, weakening or disestablishing others—and the norms targeted for implementation may be norms of compliance or norms of aspiration. There are other distinctions too that might be made among those norms. Some of the norms will be related to general roles, for example, others to particular relationships. And some will be symmetric in character, applying equally to different people in their dealings with one another, while others will be asymmetric. But exploring those distinctions would take us too far afield.

These preliminaries covered, we now turn to look at some salient ways in which an economy of esteem, by our analysis, may fail to deliver goods that by everyone's lights are attractive. We mentioned earlier that the intangible hand may fail to deliver certain goods—in our current terms, the economy may fail to establish or reinforce desirable norms—so far as it does badly in giving publicity to how people perform, or in shaping the presentation of what they do, or in managing those factors that might affect their predisposition to be moved by the forces of esteem. We shall consider those possible varieties of failure in reverse order, looking first at failures to shape people's predispositions, second at failures to shape the presentation of their performance, and third at failures to shape the publicity given to performance.

3   FAILURES TO SHAPE PREDISPOSITION APPROPRIATELY

Three dangers to predisposition: the jury case

One of the oldest, most venerable institutions in western society is that of the jury. While the institution of the jury may often fail in a more or less scandalous manner, most of us put a great deal of faith in juries operating conscientiously according to their brief (Abramson 1994). Have we any good reason, however, to invest this confidence in juries? Or does our faith spring from a credulity that just happens, as luck would have it, to be on the mark?[2]

A basic consideration which supports a certain confidence in juries is the fact that people who are selected for the discharge of a public duty, and who are clear about what is expected of them, will generally find themselves moved by a more or less virtuous disposition to do their bit: in the jury case, to be conscientious in looking at the evidence and in determining, say, whether it establishes beyond reasonable doubt that the defendant is guilty. But this consideration will not operate on its own, as our explorations in the economy of esteem should make clear. For if it is a matter of common knowledge among jurors that they are each expected to be conscientious in the weighing of evidence—as the judge's instructions will have made clear—then each will have an auxiliary motive for behaving honourably. Honourable behaviour will reward them with a degree of honour or esteem among their fellow-jurors or

---

[2] We abstract here from the danger for unanimous jury voting identified in Fedderson and Pesendorfer (1998). For the record, however, we think that the forces of esteem may help to counter their problem. The alleged danger is, roughly, that each will think he or she should only worry about how to vote in the event of being decisive: that is, when the eleven others take the defendant to be guilty; that in that event the evidence of how the others go should be reason enough to vote 'guilty' oneself; and so that each may vote 'guilty' without really thinking about the matter. Were someone to take this line, then under plausible assumptions about detectability, they would incur or at least expect to incur a lot of disesteem. And that being more or less obvious, the forces of esteem may help to explain why, as it seems, jurors do not generally free ride in a manner that would endanger the institution.

will at least avoid the penalty of being thought to be dishonourably indifferent to the requirements of the procedure.[3]

Will these motives of virtue and esteem be reliable sources of conscientious performance among jurors? The institutional and legal tradition appears to suppose that so far as the jurors are not subjected to pressures that diminish or destroy their predisposition to be moved by motives of virtue and esteem, those motives will prevail. For the striking thing about the tradition, at least in its more recent formulation, is that it dictates steps for reducing the likelihood that countervailing pressures will operate and, so it seems, for encouraging the rule of virtue and esteem.

The tradition identifies and tries to moderate three sorts of pressures. The first is the special interest that may lead jurors to vote for a particular result— say, the discharge or the conviction of the defendant—independently of the evidence. The practice of vetting jurors, while it is often used strategically for other purposes, can be seen as an attempt to guard against this; the idea is to filter out any jurors who have a personal interest, one way or the other, in the result. The jurors dismissed may be friends or enemies of the defendant, for example, or people who are likely for other reasons to identify emotionally with, or be alienated from, the defendant.[4]

The second pressure targeted in the tradition is the inhibition, even the intimidation, that jurors may feel so far as the way they deliberate or vote is known to outsiders, in particular outsiders who have a strong desire for a particular result. The tradition guards against this danger so far as it tries to ensure the confidentiality of jury proceedings, shielding jurors from outside scrutiny.

The third danger identified in the legal tradition, particularly in recent times, is that jurors may feel pressured to conform to the views of the others on the jury, if they come from a similar background to those others—they constitute something like an in-group—and that background makes a particular finding presumptively salient or attractive for those in that group (Sunstein 2002). This

---

[3] This line on juries (defended in Pettit 1990; Brennan and Pettit 1993) would not work, of course, if esteem were valued only as a proxy for consumption goods. Thus consider Robert C. Ellickson's (2001: 22) comment on the implications of such a view, as defended by Eric A. Posner (2000). 'Posner's theory suggests that the contemporary jury is an ill-advised legal institution, at least if the major function of a jury is to bring contemporary social norms to bear in a legal proceeding. In an urban setting today, jurors are strangers with scant prospects of further interaction once the group has disbanded.'

[4] One danger against which there may not be adequate protection, of course, is the desire of jury members not to be delayed too much by the court proceedings. In 1714 Alexander Pope (1971: Canto 3, l. 21) marked it nicely. 'The hungry judges soon the sentence sign, | And wretches hang that jury-men may dine.'

danger is mitigated by the recent practice of trying to ensure that the jury is representative of sociologically distinct groupings, with a mix among jurors of Blacks and Whites, Catholics and Protestants, men and women, and so on.

If these observations are sound, then our institutions are designed, more or less effectively, to shape the predisposition of jurors to be moved by motives of virtue and esteem in a manner conducive to their fulfilment of their duty. By the very fact of doing this, however, those institutions draw attention to a way in which the economy of esteem may fail in other arenas. They direct us to three factors that the institutions in any area should try to moderate, if the economy of esteem is to operate there for the advancement of the general good. The three factors indicated are: special interest, outside inhibition, and in-group loyalty.

The danger of special interest

The danger of special interest undermining the way that the economy of esteem may work for good is obvious in a variety of circumstances. The context where it is easiest to illustrate the danger is probably the political one. Consider the members of parliament who are given charge of redrawing electoral boundaries, where their desire to be seen to have done this fairly—and thereby to win esteem within the general community—will have to compete with their desire to promote their chances of re-election. Consider those in government who have to make a certain decision that will impact on a company which has provided substantial campaign finance and the temptation, regardless of the cost to the common good—and to their own reputation—to keep such a supporter sweet. Or consider the minister who has a decision to make that will benefit one or other of two constituencies and the attraction of benefiting the more marginal and electorally more important seat, quite independently of which it is better and more estimable to benefit.

These are cases where our tradition has not been as assiduous as it has been in the crystallisation of jury practice, allowing a special interest to remain in place where, manifestly, that interest will jeopardise people's predisposition to be moved by relevant motives of virtue and, more importantly, esteem. They represent a very salient way in which, from the point of view of institutional design, the current economy of esteem often fails.

The authors of the *Federalist Papers* were very alert to the danger of special interest and argued at length about how to guard against it. Their recipe, roughly, was to have a vetting procedure in the first instance that would filter out those who might prove incapable of living up to the demands of office, even under the ministrations of a desire for esteem; and in the second to design affairs so that interest is bent to the service of duty—a design in which the desire for esteem bulks large (White 1987). The theme, which surely retains its relevance today, is sounded nicely in this passage: 'The aim of every political constitution is, or ought to be, first to obtain for rulers men who possess most wisdom to discern, and most virtue to pursue, the common good of the society; and in the next place, to take the most effectual precautions for keeping them virtuous whilst they continue to hold their public trust' (Madison, Hamilton, et al. 1987: 343).

The danger of outside inhibition

The second danger, no less salient than the first, is that the economy of esteem should fail to reinforce appropriate norms in a given area, because of a certain inhibition or even intimidation that the agent or agents may feel. Just as jurors might be inhibited from behaving conscientiously through their deliberations being known or knowable to certain others—however much esteem conscientiousness would earn among their fellows—so there are many other areas where similar inhibitions block the economy of esteem from producing goods that most of us would applaud.

Consider a case that will now be familiar to anyone who has recently been asked to write a confidential reference for a student or employee or associate. It is in the general interest—so at least we may assume—that referees are forthright and honest about the merits of those for whom they write; they may not be expected to expatiate on faults but they are expected to be realistic in ascribing merit and in making comparisons. But much recent freedom of information legislation has failed to protect letters of reference and referees now face the prospect in many countries that what they write will not be seen just by committees of appointment and relevant authorities but will also be available to candidates, should they seek it. No depth of insight is required to see that this can be a serious inhibition on referees, undermining norms of forthright honesty. And no power of prophecy is needed to predict that this may lead to a situation where confidential opinion is sought through informal channels, so that those applying for posts become more vulnerable to personal prejudice than they were before freedom of information laws were enacted.

The danger of inhibition from outside that is illustrated by this case, or by the case of the jury whose deliberations are not protected, raises a general and difficult question for a society in which transparency and openness are prized, and prized with good reason. That question arises also for every committee that is given a brief to do with appointments, or promotions, or the award of contracts or prizes, or just routine issues in which the interests of others are in any way at stake. Should the dealings of the committee be locked in confidence, thereby allowing the intangible hand to reinforce norms of conscientiousness: or to do so, at least, so far as the other dangers of special interest and in-group loyalty are avoided? Or should they be accessible to certain members of the public, thereby expressing our natural preference for the open over the closed? Or should some intermediate arrangement prevail?

The line of thought in this book is that the headlong pursuit of openness would be a great mistake, encouraging a resort to the informal and the non-procedural of the kind illustrated in the referee case. There is a need to guard against the dangers of the closed room, with the possibility that the rule of hint and innuendo and intimation may do harm to the interests of those outside. But the sorts of measures already in place with juries—formally if not always effectively in place—should go a good distance towards providing that protection. And in any case the protection can be increased, without damage to the way the economy of esteem may be expected to work, by allowing for possibilities of appeal and confidential review. Such possibilities should be much more attractive than a reckless resort to public scrutiny.

The danger of in-group loyalty

But perhaps the most salient danger that jury arrangements alert us to is that of in-group loyalty.

What are we to expect of Catholics on an ethics committee that is debating a question on which their church has ruled? The honourable line to take, and the one encouraged under the economy of esteem, must be to go with the arguments and vote conscientiously. But the temptation for any such church-goer to keep their religious identity intact—and to show other Catholics, especially others on the committee, that it is clear—must be enormous.

What are we to expect, again, of the faculty members of a university who have to advise high-performing students, when these students ask about where they should do postgraduate work? In particular, what are we to expect if the university is busily encouraging and rewarding organisational loyalty, and perhaps explicitly advising faculty to try to build up their postgraduate numbers? The professionally honourable line—and the one that will attract esteem over the long haul—will be to advise students in their own best interests. But loyalty to the local organisation, especially given the palpable rewards of loyalty, may easily undermine that.

These problems of in-group loyalty are often issues where the esteem-based pressures that we would like to see at work—those supporting conscientiousness on the committee or in the profession—are outweighed by esteem-based pressures of a different, more factional kind: ones supporting fidelity to the church, or favour for the home organisation. They operate, needless to say, across an enormous range of cases. The bodies cast in a rival position may be any corporate organisation on the one side and a broader profession on the other, whether the organisation be a commercial business, a law firm, a media organisation, or whatever. And of course they may also be the political party on the one side, with its own electoral and related interests, and on the other the state or society and the more inclusive interests with which it is associated.

Like the problems of special interest and outside inhibition, in-group loyalty has long been recognised as a force that may upset the capacity of the intangible hand to institute socially desirable norms and thereby promote the common good. David Hume, one of the most astute observers of political reality, put the point very keenly in a comment on how the economy of esteem may operate among the members of parliament. 'Honour is a great check upon mankind: But where a considerable body of men act together, this check is, in a great measure, removed; since a man is sure to be approved of by his own party, for what promotes the common interest [of the party]; and he soon learns to despise the clamours of his adversaries' (Hume 1994: 24).

4 FAILURES TO SHAPE PRESENTATION APPROPRIATELY

Given a fixed predisposition to be moved by motives of virtue and esteem, the extent to which agents are indeed so moved in a certain domain will be a function of the publicity given to their relative performance there and of the presentation or framing of that performance among the relevant public. We look in this section at how that presentation may be shaped in suboptimal ways: in ways that unnecessarily reduce the capacity of the intangible hand to bring about what most will see as benefits.

How the performance of agents in a certain domain is presented is a function of a number of factors, as we saw earlier: the dimensions and ideals that are taken as relevant in the performance; the public which is placed to assess the performance; and the comparators in relation to whom agents are judged. While it is possible to have failures in relation to almost any one or any mix of these factors, we do not intend to review those possibilities in turn. Rather we try to identify some particularly salient but still remediable failures that are likely to threaten in any society; these all involve one or more of the factors mentioned. We consider, first, a set of failures involving, respectively, the deactivation, the destabilising, and the eclipsing of virtue. We then examine a failure that we describe as the masking of attitudes. And we take note, in conclusion, of a number of cases where it is hard to rule on whether there is failure or not.

The deactivation of virtue

One sort of failure in presentation occurs when people are not clear about the relevant ideals or standards in the community. Consider in this connection the way that smoking in the presence of non-smokers has declined as it has become established in common knowledge, at least in many societies, that secondary smoking is a health hazard for those who are exposed to it (Ellickson 2001: 27–9). The decline in smoking under these conditions is undoubtedly correlated with an overall decline in the number of people smoking in any context, and with the introduction of laws that prohibit smoking in certain surroundings. But we believe it is highly plausible that even allowing for those effects, the common belief that secondary smoking is dangerous has had an independent impact on smoking in the presence of others.

To smoke in the presence of others, even in a situation where there is no law or convention against it, is now manifestly to invite their disesteem. This was not true twenty years ago, when only a routine courtesy prompted people to ask others if they had any objection to their smoking. At that time it was just not clear that secondary smoking was harmful; the reports to that effect were not established in common acceptance. And so there was no powerful motive to avoid smoking in company. Now that the harm of secondary smoking is well established, however, even to make an inquiry as to whether others object to one's smoking can attract disesteem, putting pressure on others to agree to something that they must be presumed independently not to approve.

It is worth noting in connection with the smoking case, that it illustrates the role that the law can have, not just in penalising a certain sort of behaviour, but in having that behaviour presented as something that is disesteemed, and known to be disesteemed, in a society. It illustrates the expressive as distinct from the sanctioning role of the law. While the law may hold out a sanction sufficient to reduce or remove smoking in certain public places, it can serve the incidental purpose of indicating the disestimable aspect of smoking in company and of activating the desire for esteem in the cause of reducing smoking in other social contexts. As Richard McAdams (2000: 340) explicitly argues, 'law changes behavior by signaling the underlying attitudes of a community or society. Because people are motivated to gain approval and avoid disapproval, the information signaled by legislation and other law affects their behavior' (see, too, Sunstein 1996; Dharmapala and McAdams 2003).

Smoking in company is a case where the clarification of relevant ideals, or of how they engage with behaviour, has triggered a new, higher level of performance. But there are many other cases where, by almost any lights, the lack of information on such ideals, or on how they engage with people's performance, continues to represent a failure in the economy of esteem: a failure to activate the intangible hand so as to secure what almost everyone would regard as socially beneficial behaviour.

An example that has been documented empirically—we mentioned this in Chapter 9—concerns alcohol consumption by students. In a study of attitudes towards alcohol on a college campus, Prentice and Miller (1993) found that most students thought that the average attitude towards alcohol abuse was more tolerant than their own. As a result, the relevant community ideal—or the ideal seen in light of general practice—was less demanding than it would have been had there been a better sense of what each felt. Had students only been aware of their fellows' attitudes, then presumably the esteem-related norm would have been more demanding and there would have been less abuse of alcohol overall.

The remedy in cases like these—or at least a first step in that direction— must be to establish ideals of performance in common consciousness, not just allow them to languish in obscurity. We might hope that the recent drive towards the codification of ethical standards in different areas may be a very positive development on this front. But there remain some cases where there is little or no prospect of relevant ideals being allowed to crystallise.

The most obvious example here arises, once again, in the area of public representation and service. For one endemic problem in current systems of democratic representation—one of many, as it happens—is that, whatever they say in the abstract, elected representatives will find themselves continually tempted in specific cases to adopt an approach that leads to the obscuring of ideals, or of the relevance of the ideals to their own behaviour.

Let a new party in government announce proposed guidelines by which representatives should be judged and should therefore be exposed, as we might hope, to the pressures of esteem. A first problem is that they will find it hard to get support from the parties in opposition, who will want to deny the governing party the kudos of establishing such a new code. And even if they do succeed in gaining all-party consensus, the members of the different parties will very quickly differ on questions of interpretation and adjudication, as they find themselves driven by electoral motives to attack their opponents for every suggestion of a breach and to defend any party colleagues who are exposed to such attack. It will not take long for the smoke of political battle to drive the crystallising ideals back into confusion and obscurity.

The failure here is, in our view, one of poignant proportions. Suppose that there were clear ideals ruling in public life, and a procedure for interpreting them and for adjudicating performance that kept the demands of those ideals clear and convincing. In that case the public as a whole would gain enormously in their democratic power. For those in parliament and government would not only be exposed to the discipline of having to secure re-election the next time around. They would have to live with the associated discipline of needing to avoid forms of behaviour that prompt public censure and of wanting to display behaviour that attracts esteem. They would be subject to the control of people, not just on the occasions when they go to the hustings, but at every juncture where their standing in the public eye is at stake. Assuming that no other failures got in the way, the natural power of scrutiny that the people have over their representatives would be considerably enhanced. Just by being there, attentive to the doings of those representatives, the people would constitute a more powerful presence in political life.

The eclipsing of virtue

We have been discussing a first way in which the failure to present behaviour appropriately may reduce the capacity of the intangible hand to work for good. A second such failure, now well documented (Frey 1997), occurs when people's level of performance in some area is reduced by the appearance of an extra motive to perform well: say, a motive deriving from the prospect of a new reward or the threat of a new penalty. The natural explanation is that when the extra motive comes on stream, it becomes obvious that agents now have that motive for acting in the desired manner, so that it becomes less likely that their performance will be put down to the presence of virtue and less likely that it will attract the esteem of those who observe it. The new motive can be so salient that it will eclipse any evidence of virtuous motivation. And this being something that agents themselves are in a position to recognise, we can see why their motivation to act as desired might decline rather than increase.

When virtuous motivation is eclipsed in this way, and overall performance declines, the failure occurs at the level of presentation. Things shift, so that the behaviour in question is now seen, not as an exercise of presumptive virtue— not as a performance fit to attract esteem—but rather as a rational response to the rewards or penalties that have been put in place.

The eclipsing effect, and the crowding out of virtue that it prompts, is easily illustrated (Pettit 1995a). Suppose that those who work in a company or organisation are not checked for how far they put in the required hours on the job, or for their rate of productivity, but are generally in the habit of working those hours, and perhaps beyond, at a high level of productivity. The scenario is quite plausible, considering the familiar levels of performance among teachers or social workers or researchers in public service, or executives and professionals in private business. And now imagine that, perhaps prompted by the wish to deal with an exceptional but outrageous case, the directors of the operation in question decide to introduce a system of clocking in and clocking out, and an arrangement whereby everyone has to report on how they use their time. It should be obvious that in introducing new, associated penalties, such innovation will make it harder for people generally in the organisation to be recognised as virtuously motivated, whether among colleagues or superiors, and to win the esteem that goes with that recognition.

Not only is it easy to imagine ways in which virtuous motivation may be eclipsed and the associated level of performance reduced. It is also easy to see that managers in public and private life will often be subject to pressures that induce them to take steps that eclipse virtuous motivation. The common demand that managers manage, maintaining control of how those in their charge perform, extends naturally into a demand that they be seen to do something about managing. And the desire to be seen to do something can lead them, if they are not alert to the way in which the economy of esteem works, to take steps that are counterproductive in the aggregate.

Won't the counterproductivity of the steps they take be more or less obvious to those concerned, be they electors or shareholders or whatever? Not necessarily. For the bad impact is likely to become salient only over the longer haul, not the shorter, and by the time it becomes salient it may be very difficult to turn things back. In particular, it may be difficult for managers to do this, since turning things back—putting their faith in the virtue of the workforce—will seem to involve an abdication of responsibility.

The destabilising of virtue

Bad management may also be responsible for another, related failure in the presentation of behaviour and in the activation of esteem-related motivation. Consider a now familiar pattern in the way in which government takes funding initiatives in relation to research. In one year, funding is distributed according to how well different proposals score against received criteria, as judged by a more or less independent body. But the pattern is not consistently maintained over time: in other years the system is shifted so that now one area of research is given priority, now another; or the criteria relevant are recast so as to reflect the views of the minister in charge or a broader political pressure; or the system is put on hold, at least for a time, so that some allegedly national priority can take its place; or the research to be funded has to have some industrial or commercial backing or relevance; or whatever. This sort of instability is easy to explain, given the pressures on those in government—the relevant managers—to be seen to be doing things. And the instability is paralleled in private funding bodies, as new executives find themselves motivated to make their own mark in the only way they distinctively can: by introducing yet another reform.

The instability envisaged here is bound to have a counterproductive effect in the economy of esteem, so far as it renders it extremely difficult for researchers to know what projects will catch the eye of funding bodies in the future, and what therefore will win esteem. A culture in which scholarship and productive science was rewarded, subject perhaps to marginal adjustments, on the basis of how far it meets traditional, well-established criteria of merit would clearly give scholars and scientists reason in esteem to work as hard as possible at living up to those criteria. But a culture in which the criteria are continually put in question by shifts in the funding and ranking basis is bound to undermine the presentation of performance in the consistently evaluated way that is required for the intangible hand to be effective. The culture will prompt a different kind of performance instead; say, one in which researchers are invited to second-guess the areas where funding will next be located and to risk all on that conjecture.

By way of analogy, consider the sort of performance associated with the received parody of Paris intellectual culture: a culture, according to this parody, in which the opinion-forming press moves according to blind fashion—or perhaps a love of the improbable and spectacular—holding up one style of research for applause in one season, and a quite different style in another. It should be clear that in such a culture the desire for esteem would not be allowed to work in a sustained way for the advance of any particular sort of work—say, traditional scholarship and investigation—but would be rendered useless by the fact that no one could know what would next catch the eye, and attract the approval, of the cultural authorities. Each might hope to take a line that would put them at the front of the herd in the next rush of fashion and such risk-taking would become the order of the day.

The masking of attitudes

While the deactivation, eclipsing, and destabilising of virtue are clearly problems in the economy of esteem, there is a further cultural possibility that
represents a more sinister danger. This is the possibility that due to a widespread fear of saying something that is not approved by certain repressive or
oppressive authorities, no one can be sure that others are sincere in what they
praise or deplore and no one can know what others are thinking when they
keep their peace; their attitudes will be effectively masked (Pettit 1994).

The economy of esteem can only operate effectively, whether for good or ill,
if it is clear to people that others will think well of them for doing this or that,
badly for doing something else. In particular, it can only operate effectively in
so far as this is true even when others say nothing. In order for people to be
policed in the quiet, effective way characteristic of the esteem economy they
must live in a social world in which the attitudes of others are scrutable. But the
world will not ensure such scrutability of attitudes unless people have had
the opportunity to learn from the remarks made by others that their thought
runs on certain lines. Let forthright speech be a rarity—let it be systematically
unclear whether people are speaking sincerely or with an eye to their own
safety—and in at least certain contexts people's observation of one another will
leave them unsure of what their true attitudes are on any topic.

For a very dramatic example of how this can happen, consider Mao's China,
as that is depicted in a book like Jung Chang's *Wild Swans* (Chang 1991). She
describes a society in which it is common knowledge that no one, at any level
of the society or even the party, is in a position to criticise Mao with impunity: a
society in which, on the contrary, every word and deed of Mao's is held up as
the very essence of wisdom and virtue. In this society, what people say or fail to
say lacks any communicative message: it could be the product of fear or it could
be the product of approval or indeed disapproval; no one is in a position to
know. Whether they speak or remain silent, people will have become unreadable and inscrutable to one another. And in becoming unreadable and inscrutable, they will have lost their power to police one another by their estimative
attitudes; they will have left the field open to the unhindered influence of state
propaganda (see Kuran 1995: chs. 7, 13).

There is no need to go so far afield from the everyday in order to see how the
lack of forthright speech can undermine the economy of esteem. Consider
the workplace in which employees do not have the effective freedom to criticise
the doings or sayings, even perhaps the jokes, of the boss. Consider the political
party in which members do not have the freedom to raise questions about
anything dictated by received policy or ideology. Or consider the religious

congregation where no one dares to make a challenge to the dictates of the minister or priest or guru. In such communities, the scrutiny of others may have little or no power to police a person, independently of the policing effected by fear of the authorities. The economy of esteem, and in particular the intangible hand, will be incapable of achieving anything of significance.

There have been many attacks in recent times, mainly from the right wing of politics, on the cult of political correctness. This line of attack often suggests that if people are not pressured by those with well-worked-out views on politics, then they will inevitably achieve independence of mind; it tends to ignore the possibility that they may be subject instead to the pressures of tradition and, as it often is, prejudice. But still, there is something in the complaint. For it is clearly the case that when a movement of opinion has a political aspect and a political presence, there is bound to be a pressure on members not to break ranks: a pressure to keep and testify to the faith, whether that faith be leftist or libertarian, feminist or traditionalist, religious or atheistic. And when that pressure mounts to the point of seriously inhibiting members of the movement, the economy of esteem will tend to support conformism. In many circumstances, saying what's expected or saying nothing will be the only safe option—the only option that does not carry an unacceptable risk of demotion or ostracism. (On political correctness, see Loury 1994.)

Finally, a somewhat chilling line of thought. By some analyses, it does not require any particular repression or oppression for people's true attitudes to become inscrutable to one another (Noelle-Neumann 1984). Timur Kuran (1995: 88) puts the possibility forcefully: 'no one exhibits an absolute commitment to free speech. In practice, even people who consider themselves tolerant are prepared to regulate public expression, and thus public opinion, when it suits their own political goals.' The suggestion is that as people court one another's favour by falsifying the expression of their own views and preferences, they may make it unclear what they really think and feel. They leave others in ignorance of their true attitudes or, worse, they mislead others about those attitudes.

The forces of conformism are powerful, we agree, but we do not think that they are nearly as powerful as those of oppression and repression. While people may often find it attractive to conform to expectations, even at the cost of misrepresenting themselves, they will hardly do this universally in a society like ours. They may tell the host that they had a wonderful evening, for example (Kuran 1995: 3–4), but that's not necessarily what they will say to their closer friends. This is sufficiently a matter of common knowledge, indeed, for all of us to know that the parting comments made by guests are not necessarily reliable, and certainly not as reliable as the remarks they make later to their friends. The situation that prevails is quite different from the intimidating position of living under a dictatorship, or even under a code of political correctness.

One reason for this difference may itself stem from how the economy of esteem operates. The sort of society that is typical of contemporary democracies is fairly pluralistic, with different fashions and ideas and mores being relevant in different contexts. That being so, it will not generally further one's status in the economy of esteem to be seen as a conformist: as someone who routinely speaks and acts to the expectations of the immediate scene. Such conformism might force one to give palpably inconsistent expressions of attitude, thereby incurring the disesteem of those who notice. And, short of that extreme, it would tend to suggest an eagerness to please that is generally found disestimable. The desire for esteem is probably going to be better served by at least a show of forthrightness about one's thoughts and feelings. And the safest way of ensuring a show of fortrightness is almost certainly going to be by becoming forthright in fact.

Other failures of presentation?

There are many other presentational ways in which the economy of esteem may well be failing to deliver the goods of which it is capable. We consider two.

A first important question that arises with presentation is whether in holding up what someone does for praise or blame, we focus on the person or the deed. Do we approve of someone who does well, or disapprove of someone who does badly, as a person, depicting them as a virtuous and admirable agent or as a person with various flaws? Or do we approve or disapprove of them only in the act they perform, holding off from any more general assessment of their person?

There is a plausible line of thought in the literature which suggests that the most effective form of sanctioning is one that approves in their person of agents who do well and disapproves of the deeds—the deeds not the persons—of those agents who do badly (Braithwaite 1989). The idea is that people are going to be reinforced in their identity as someone admirable and virtuous by being approved of in their person, while the possibility of aspiring to the identity of such a person—with the motive to reform that is thereby kept in place—will be preserved when disapproval focuses only on their act. We ourselves find this idea plausible and, if it is sound, then of course it alerts us to a variety of ways in which familiar institutions, not least the institutions of criminal justice, may be failing to use the economy of esteem to best effect. But the truth is that more research is needed (though see Ahmed, Harris, et al. 2001). As things stand, we can only speculate about the motivational impact of act-centred versus agent-centred attitudes of esteem and disesteem.

A second example relates to the question of how far institutions should be tailored to promoting a certain level of performance on the part of everyone, on the part of the average—whether this be the mean, the mode, or the median—or on the part of high-flyers; we discussed this in Chapter 8. We naturally think that if it is important to have a universally satisfactory level of performance—if it is important to guard against a failure in the weakest link—then that argues for a very different style of presentation from what might be suitable for encouraging high average performance or high top performance, without any concern for performance in the lower ranges. But the truth is, as in the earlier case, that we do not currently have enough information to be able to do much more than speculate (Ahmed, Harris, et al. 2001: 15–16). For all that has been established with any degree of assurance, for example, focusing on high-flying performance may be best for encouraging average levels of achievement, or focusing on universal performance—in effect, on the performance of those who fly lower—may do better still.

5　FAILURES TO SHAPE PUBLICITY APPROPRIATELY

There are many ways in which our institutions may fail to provide the sort of publicity that will support the beneficial working of the intangible hand. But as with failures on the other two fronts, we can only hope to provide some salient illustrations; we are not in a position to develop anything more systematic. We describe five sorts of failure that involve respectively wasteful, motivated, unbalanced, prohibited, and frozen publicity.

Wasteful publicity

The most glaring way in which the system of publicity may fail is through leaving the pursuit of publicity—publicity for their respective levels of performance—to agents themselves; the topic was addressed in Chapter 10. In most contexts where this happens, agents will have a motive to publicise their own achievements, at least so far as this can be done without engaging the teleological paradox: that is, without earning the reputation for being an esteem-seeker, with a consequent loss—and possibly a net loss—in the esteem stakes. And if they each act on that motive, making efforts to publicise their own successes, then there are a number of more or less obvious losses in prospect.

One loss is that as they pursue publicity they will presumably devote less time or energy to the sort of performance for which they seek exposure, with a resultant decline in the level of performance overall. A second is that if they compete in the search for publicity, then they are each liable to end up no better than they would have been had there been no competition in the first place; so far as publicity relative to competitors is what matters, their individual efforts may only keep them on a par with one another: they may secure no advantage for anyone. And a third loss that is likely to follow on a competition for publicity and esteem is that as it becomes clear to everyone what is happening in the domain, a cynicism is likely to develop about whether there is any virtue whatsoever present in performers; and this, as we know, can erode the economy of esteem altogether, since no one can expect a cynical audience to be impressed by supposed evidence of virtue.

It may be thought that we are exaggerating the danger here. It may be said that in any case the teleological paradox is likely to inhibit the individual pursuit of publicity. But there are ways, as we saw, in which people can get around the paradox. They may covertly pursue publicity; they may appoint agents, in a more or less formal way, to represent their interests; or they may seek publicity for the performance of groups to which they belong, thereby indirectly achieving publicity for themselves.

The obvious way to get over the sort of failure envisaged is to have independent provision of publicity for the performers in a given domain. The performance of individual researchers or of the institutions to which they belong might be usefully broadcast under a centralised arrangement or by a watchdog body of some kind. And the same goes for the performances of politicians and journalists, lawyers and doctors, teachers and social workers, and so on. Such an independent source of publicity would not only avoid the waste associated with a competition for publicity. It would also serve well as a protection against underperformance or malperformance. In a situation where individuals contol much of the publicity given to what they do, those who perform badly may hope to be able to cover their tracks. But in a situation where publicity is provided independently, this hope should become less easy to sustain.

Motivated publicity

There is an independent failure associated with the decentralised pursuit of publicity that is worth distinguishing from the problem of waste. This is that as parties seek publicity for themselves, they are under a constant temptation to exaggerate their own achievements and, since relative performance is ultimately what matters, to denigrate the achievements of others and indeed to charge them with performing badly. Because the provision of publicity is motivated by the rival interests of the agents involved, it is in constant danger of being biased and unreliable. And even if the pressures of bias are heroically resisted by the parties involved, this may not always be apparent, so that the public addressed may be incredulous even in face of reliable evidence or testimony.

The problem of motivated publicity is most dramatically present in the world of politics where participants spend so much time lauding themselves and their party, and so much time running down the opposition, that it becomes almost impossible for the public to know what to believe. True, the media may serve as a more reliable source of information but here too it is hard for people to be sure of whether to believe what they hear or read. The media are often associated with particular sides in politics and even if they are not, they will certainly be accused of bias by those they criticise or those they fail particularly to praise.

But the problem of motivated publicity is not confined, of course, to the adversarial world of politics. It is also present wherever agents advertise their virtues, without fear of independent, credible adjudication: say, in spheres of professional or commercial service. One might have expected the market to provide such adjudication, as people show themselves willing to pay for reliable information and as it becomes profitable for information-providing bodies to form and to compete for a reputation as reliable guides. And indeed there are some cases where the market does very well in these respects: look, for example, at how reliable the best good food guides are. But there are problems that often beset this sort of development. The interest which members of the public individually have in gaining such information may be too slight to support a large, information-providing enterprise. And the interest of performers in not seeing such an enterprise get established may be sufficient to stop it from flying or even from getting off the ground. It may be possible for performers to inhibit entrepreneurs who would otherwise support such an enterprise, say by threatening to withdraw advertising from existing outlets that the enterpreneurs control. And it will often be possible for them to swamp the efforts of the enterprise envisaged, as they outspend it dramatically in the publicity they seek.

A good example of the sort of problem that arises here is provided by the lack of success that environmental monitoring agencies have had in establishing in public opinion an accurate sense of those companies that are environmentally responsible, and those that are not. Such agencies will depend on voluntary contributions, or governmental subvention, for their existence. And, short of having some dramatic scandals to reveal, they just cannot hope to be able to combat the massive advertising that a large oil company, for example, is capable of mounting in promotion of a responsible image.

The failure of motivated publicity, like the associated failure of wasteful publicity, argues for the merits of an independent, information-providing arrangement. Devising the institutional means of setting up such an arrangement is bound to be a difficult task, however, and we do not mean to suggest that the problem is as easily resolved as it is identified. We see no reason for despair on this front but we do see a powerful challenge for research into methods of institutional regulation and design.

Unbalanced publicity

The best example of unbalanced publicity probably arises in the area of criminal justice. Under existing procedures for the trial and conviction of offenders, and under the associated patterns of reporting, people are exposed to lots of negative publicity for any offence of which they are convicted; they are subjected to imprisonment in a ceremony of denunciation, for example, and this is often associated with a relative blaze of publicity. But that negative publicity is not balanced in any way by publicity for the remorse they may demonstrate; for the way in which they pay their debt to society, as it is described; or for any steps they may take to compensate the victims of their wrongdoing. Offenders are banished from the community of law-abiding citizens in theatrical light; they slip back into that community in darkness and obscurity.

This sort of imbalance is bound to have a damaging impact on the prospects for mobilising an intangible hand. The fear of ignominy may serve as a motivator that deters people from crime; it may even prompt many people to take criminal activity off the list of thinkable options (Tyler 1990). But the fact that there is little or no publicity available for those offenders who genuinely seek to reform or rehabilitate themselves is bound, equally, to remove a motive that might have worked effectively for the overall good. Under the existing regime of publicity, offenders may easily feel that there is no way back from the bad name associated with conviction: that with conviction the possibility of ever attaining a position of esteem in the wider community gets to be dead and buried.

The problem of unbalanced publicity may arise, not just when negative publicity dominates positive, but also when one sort of negative publicity dominates another. The best example of this is when the publicity given to false positives—that is, to acts that work for ill—dominates publicity given to false negatives: that is to failures to act for the good. Consider an institution which has come into being in many sectors of society in recent years: the ethics committee. While ethics committees can do great good in clarifying standards that people in a given domain are expected to satisfy—say, in the conduct of research involving human or animal subjects—they often operate under pressures of publicity that are unbalanced in this manner, with consequent dangers for how the institution will evolve (Pettit 1992).

The members of an ethics committee that examines and monitors research projects will clearly be exposed to the threat of bad publicity for approving a project that goes wrong in some way. For when a research project goes wrong, causing harm to subjects, or just giving them offence, that fact will often attract widespread publicity, perhaps in the courts of appeal that are available to complainants, perhaps even in the press. Thus the members of a committee must be on their guard against approving of that which may go wrong: that is, of committing false positives. But the members of the committee may have no reason in esteem to be equally on their guard about false negatives: that is, about refusing to approve of that which deserves to be approved. For those who will complain in this case—the researchers involved—will easily be cast as having a vested interest and will in any case be subject to censure for challenging the decisions of a designedly impartial umpire. The upshot is that, consequent on an imbalance in the publicity available, members of such a committee will find themselves with motives in esteem that argue for playing it safe rather than playing it honest.

The possibility of one sort of negative publicity dominating another may be illustrated, more generally, in any case where an individual or organisation has a choice between investing resources in the prevention of unspecified harms and investing resources in putting an actual harm right. Failing to prevent unspecified harms is not nearly so likely to attract attention and disesteem as failing to try to put an actual harm right. Failing to regulate for safety at sea will not generally cause a government much disesteem, for example, but failing to try to rescue someone in trouble at sea certainly will. And so here, as in the ethics committee case, there is a lack of balance that may occasion serious failures in the way the intangible hand operates.

There are other possible ways in which publicity may also be unbalanced: say through publicity being given to agents when it would be better given to acts, or through publicity attaching to the worst performers in an institution when it would be better given to those who perform well. The failure of unbalanced publicity, like the failures associated with regimes of publicity that are wasteful or motivated, may not be easy to put right. But there is still good point in drawing attention to them, for however difficult it may prove to rectify them, there is certainly no reason for despairing of a remedy.

Prohibited publicity

A different sort of failure in the economy of esteem occurs when, for reasons good or bad, the laws or conventions of a society prohibit a sort of publicity that might arguably be expected to work for overall good. We mention two examples of this. One is the prohibition in many societies on the provision of information on the income tax that is paid in a given year by individual citizens. And the other is the prohibition on access to information about how people vote.

It is notorious in many societies, as appears in the occasional scandal, that very rich individuals may succeed in organising their affairs so that they pay considerably less tax than ordinary, middle-income earners. This sort of tax avoidance, and in particular the widespread belief that avoidance occurs, may have a very bad impact on tax compliance overall and may have a demoralising, alienating effect on people generally. An obvious way in which to inhibit it would be to enable anyone to gain information via a website on the income tax paid by different individuals. Journalists would naturally have a motive for publicising high levels of tax avoidance on the part of prominent members of society. And if the rich and prominent generally expected such tax avoidance to become a matter of public knowledge, they would have a powerful incentive for not resorting to it. As it is, however, such individuals are protected from exposure in most societies, because of the privacy laws in force there. Those laws may work for good in other ways but it is surely worth considering whether they might not be relaxed with benefit in regard to something like the taxes that people pay.

The voting example of prohibited publicity is perhaps more tendentious. In large-scale electorates, voting is instrumentally insignificant, given the negligible chance that a single vote will make any difference to the outcome. But when voting occurs in conditions of secrecy—indeed, as it often is, when voting is subject to something like the seal of the confessional—then it will be socially insignificant too: it will not involve the voter taking a stand before others on how things should be collectively done. The secrecy of the vote will tend to make it inappropriate to ask others about their voting intentions; doing so may be like inquiring into something that is privy to a person and their god. And as this happens, there will be no motive in esteem why voters should take time and trouble over the decision as to how to vote; it is not as if they are likely to be regularly quizzed on the matter and prompted thereby to ensure that they can make a good show in discussion.

Can this problem be resolved, without reactivating the intimidation and abuse that is often cited, rightly or wrongly, as the reason why the ballot was made secret in the first place? We think in principle that it might (Brennan and Pettit 1990). Imagine an arrangement whereby people who go to vote are in a position to tell how others who happen to be in the booth at the same time are voting: this would be obvious, for example, were people required to go to one or another table in the booth, depending on their voting intentions. And imagine that there were safeguards in place against the possibility of intimidation: there might be a maximum on the number of people allowed in the booth at the same time, there might be a ban on people from the same address being in the booth together, a tribunal might be established with the power to determine that for reasons of widespread intimidation voting in a particular election should be secret, and so on.

We surmise that under this not very dramatic shift in current procedures, the culture of voting might shift so that people cease to think of it as a wholly private act; thus it could become acceptable for someone to ask another how they are disposed to vote. Were this to become acceptable, of course, then there would be room for the economy of esteem to operate, prompting people to inform themselves about candidates and policies and to make sure that they can keep their end up in discussions of voting intentions. And by most accounts that would be a socially desirable result.

The only test available for our conjecture as to what the change in procedures would mean would be to implement the reforms suggested, perhaps initially in restricted contexts, and to see whether the predicted result ensues. Studies of voter knowledge, and indeed voter involvement, would quickly reveal whether the changes had been successful. We think that the reforms might be worth investigating, for it is a melancholy fact about large-scale democracy that it often leaves people bored and alienated. Any reforms that improved the situation would surely be worth contemplating.

In maintaining this line, incidentally, we go along with the mature opinion of John Stuart Mill. Having defended the secret ballot thirty years earlier, on the grounds that it was needed to guard against intimidation, he argued in 1861 that things had changed for the better—he had experience of what had become a vibrant system of open voting (Fraser 1976)—and that voting should be exposed to the public eye so as to prevent it from becoming a socially insignificant, privatised act. 'People will give dishonest or mean votes from lucre, from malice, from pique, from personal rivalry, even from the interests or prejudices of class or sect, more readily in secret than in public' (Mill 1964: 306).

We should conclude this discussion of the bad effects of certain forms of prohibited publicity, however, by putting on the record that we are not outright opponents of privacy, or of privacy legislation, as our earlier discussion of the jury and of confidential references should make clear. We have been looking at how failures in publicity on the relevant performance of individuals, including failures ensured by existing law, can work to block the beneficial effects of the intangible hand. But the fact that there are such failures does not entail that from the point of view adopted here all publicity is good publicity. Certain forms of publicity will have effects unrelated to esteem—say, effects in the material economy (Posner 1981)—that argue for enforcing privacy: say, for reducing disruptive eavesdropping or the theft of ideas or personal defamation. But there are also effects of publicity in the economy of esteem that would argue for privacy legislation.

Certain kinds of publicity would block individuals from being able to affect the impressions that others form of them, for example, and to carve out a social identity of their own. Widespread publicity on a person's relatively dark past might do this, no matter how far they had reformed. And so would much publicity of the fame or infamy kind—to be discussed shortly—since this is hard for the individual to control. No doubt the capacity to present oneself to others, editing the impression one makes on them, carries with it the danger that those others will be duped. But that capacity is of the first importance in social and personal life, given that people each need to find a group among whom they can live in relative esteem. Considerations in the economy of esteem would argue for the protection of privacy in relevant areas, not make a case for opposing it on all fronts.[5]

Frozen publicity

The last failure in publicity that we mention will arise, so our analysis suggests, whenever the normal information available on a person's performance, be it good or bad, is blocked from having much effect on the esteem or disesteem in which they are held. Or if it is not blocked absolutely from having an effect, it is blocked in ordinary, run-of-the-mill circumstances.

---

[5] One further point worth recalling here is, of course, that there are some acts that are not disestimable if performed in private (acts related to hygiene and toiletry, for example), but that would be disestimable if performed in public.

The sort of blocking we have in mind can come about in two different ways. It may occur because there is too little known about the individual involved, so that others rely entirely on statistical cues for whether to presume the best or the worst. Or it may occur because in a sense there is too much known about the individual: it is a matter of common belief that the person is esteemed or disesteemed.

The first sort of problem is analogous to the problem at the core of the statistical theory of racism and sexism (Phelps 1972). According to that theory, racism or sexism may result from the fact that, say, employers believe that whites are better employees than blacks, or men than women: this, not necessarily on the basis of experience or research, but out of established prejudice. Not knowing the individual candidates they consider, and finding it too costly to seek out information, they let those presumptions dictate their responses. 'Skin color or sex is taken as a proxy for relevant data not sampled' (Phelps 1972: 659).

A parallel effect can materialise, obviously, in the economy of esteem, as we saw in Chapter 12. It may be that people take short cuts in forming opinions about others, letting prejudgements about groups dictate what they are in-clined to think about any member. Individual members of certain groups may find themselves rated by certain others in a manner that pre-empts their individual performance, and may find that there is little they can do to establish their personal credentials. They may confront the first version of what we describe as frozen publicity.

We argued in Chapter 12, that in this sort of scenario people may find it rational to act in the economy of esteem on behalf of a group to which they saliently belong. There is nothing much they can do to establish a personal standing for themselves and the most rational investment for them to make, at least in some circumstances, may be in an effort to lift the profile of that group: that 'vulnerability group', as it will be (Pettit 1997: chapter 5). But even if this relatively benign result ensues, it should be clear that the existence of the sort of frozen publicity envisaged may well work against the emergence of poten-tially beneficial norms. There won't be any point in a member of a minority working hard, for example, if prejudice is such that no performance is likely to make an impact. And this being so, there will be a serious block to the emergence or reinforcement of a norm in the area.

Is there much that can be done to counter this statistically based problem? If the statistical prejudices are ill formed, as surely in many cases they are, then the obvious solution is to make sure that more reliable statistics are gathered and promulgated. These statistics might show, at the least, that the best performers in the group who suffer discrimination do much better than the worst in other groups. But suppose that the underperformance imputed is a fact, perhaps being encouraged by the very failure associated with frozen publicity. What to do then? Subsidisation of individualised information or requirements that such information be sought would help. And if things are very bad, of course, then the motivation for individual members of the group to organise on behalf of the group as a whole will be correspondingly high, as argued in Chapter 12. There ought to be at least a possibility, then, that the group can act collectively to create opportunities for individual members to be given a chance to prove themselves.

The other variety of frozen publicity is associated with common belief—we discussed this at length in Chapter 8—rather than with statistically based esteem. Consider the case of a person who has done something evil—say, committed a crime—and whose evil action has received such widespread publicity that not only are they disesteemed by many people, as we may assume they are indeed disteemed; what also happens, crucially, is that everyone comes to believe that everyone disesteems them, everyone comes to believe that everyone does this, and so on in the usual hierarchy. Such common belief will mean that everyone has a powerful reason in testimony—the testimony, in effect, of everyone else—for holding the person in disesteem. And that reason may be so powerful that there is little or no chance of its being disturbed for many people by evidence of an improved performance on the part of the person. The only way of undoing the effect of the common belief would probably be for the agent in question to be given the opportunity of doing so spectacularly well in some context, that this achievement becomes itself a matter of common belief.

When someone is subject to a common belief that they are disesteemed, then we describe them as notorious or infamous. The corresponding effect on the positive side occurs when the fact that someone is highly esteemed, in whatever domain, also becomes a matter of common belief. Such a person, as we say, enjoys fame as distinct from infamy, celebrity as distinct from notoriety. And as it is going to be very difficult for someone notorious to reduce the disesteem in which they are held, so it is going to be difficult for someone famous to lose the esteem that they enjoy among people generally. It may take a spectacular fall from grace—one that itself surfaces in common belief—to remove them from the pedestal on which they are placed. We discussed this point in Chapter 8.

The frozen publicity that comes with notoriety and fame, like the statistical variety of the phenomenon, can make for a failure in the capacity of the economy of esteem to work for good. The prospect of notoriety is surely more repulsive and alienating than that of mere disesteem. And equally the prospect of fame is probably more attractive and engaging than that of ordinary esteem. But this motivational bonus, as we saw in Chapter 8, is partly out-weighed by an obvious disadvantage. For if the infamous are stuck with their notoriety, and the famous with their celebrity, then they are not going to be subject in the ordinary way to the discipline of an intangible hand. There will be little prospect for the infamous of redeeming their reputation, and little prospect for the famous—at least if they play it safe—of losing their reputation. And so neither will be susceptible in the manner of ordinary folk to the desire for esteem or the aversion to disesteem.

This observation probably has a sharper policy relevance in the negative case. John Braithwaite (1989) has argued that while exposure to a certain sort of shame can be a powerful force in steering offenders away from crime, the evidence suggests that anything in the nature of stigma—roughly, inalienable shame—fails to have the same effect, and actually increases the propensity of people to reoffend. This claim has been borne out in empirical work (Ahmed, Harris, et al. 2001). It fits exactly with our analysis, for offenders will certainly be stigmatised if it becomes a matter of common belief that they are held in disesteem.

There may not be much chance of doing anything to prevent fame and infamy materialising but there are surely measures that can be taken to prevent stigmatisation of this kind or, if stigmatisation occurs, to undo its worse effects. As with so many of the other failures reviewed in this chapter, there is a substantive challenge here for those who work in the area of regulation and institutional design. The challenge arises particularly with criminal justice systems and much recent research in that domain—and even some reform—bears directly on the issue (Ahmed, Harris, et al. 2001; Braithwaite 2002).

Other failures in publicity?

As in the case of failures in presentation, we should mention finally that there are many cases where, for all that we yet know with any certainty, there may be a serious failure of publicity. We illustrate the point by reference to a case mentioned in Chapter 9.

We have been assuming throughout this book, surely plausibly, that two factors are important from the point of view of orienting agents in any domain: first, the ideals that are held up in the relevant culture; and second, the beliefs in the culture as to how far those ideals are generally realised among those with whom agents will be compared. For this reason we opted to use the word 'standards', embracing the fact that it has both a normative and statistical significance, for the guidelines whereby people rate themselves—and expect to be rated by those who observe their performance. The standards in any domain will reflect two components that are relevant to presentation: the ideals generally espoused there and the information that is generally accepted about levels of relevant performance in relation to those ideals.

If this point is accepted then, as we saw earlier, in many areas there will be a calculation that has to be made by those who are in a position to reveal underperformance. If they reveal underperformance, thereby exposing the agent in question to disesteem (and perhaps a formal penalty), then they may hope to encourage others to try and avoid the same fate. But if they reveal underperformance, particularly underperformance of a significant sort, then equally they run the risk of activating a force that may have the opposite effect. They are in danger of affecting received beliefs as to how far others are underperforming—say, how far others are doing their bit in complying with certain regulations—and of having a negative impact on performance generally. If exposing a salient offender to disesteem leads people to believe that non-compliance is more common that they thought, then it may lead people to think that their own level of performance is actually better than they had imagined and that they may be less scrupulous without risking a particularly grievous level of disesteem.

The trouble in cases like this, of course, is that it is very difficult to obtain the kind of information that would enable one to tell whether a given sort of exposure will be productive or counterproductive from the point of view of the system as a whole. Thus consider the problem facing tax authorities who have to decide whether to prosecute a prominent person in the courts. While they cannot always be sure that they will succeed in such a prosecution, they can be reasonably certain that they will penalise the person in the economy of esteem. But they cannot be certain, just for that reason, that it is for the overall good of the community that they should take the person to the courts. For the exposure given may have the counterproductive effect of leading people to believe that non-compliance is more common than they thought and of thereby reducing the level of compliance overall. While recent research is beginning to provide us with a better idea of what to expect (Wenzel 2001*a*, *b*), there is still no convincing picture available of what the net effect of exposure is likely to be.

CONCLUSION

The ideal way of bringing this study to a close would have been to outline a programme of reform for activating the economy of esteem in the service of socially desirable results. But that is not something we are in a position to provide, given the need for empirical research on patterns in the economy of esteem and for empirically informed modelling of alternative arrangements. We settled, therefore, for something less. Having argued that whatever reforms are put in place they will have to be targeted on the fostering of certain norms, we went on to look at some more or less salient ways in which the economy of esteem, as it operates in familiar contexts, fails to support norms that would make, by most lights, for the overall benefit of society. Although the discussion focused on how we might rectify these failures in the hope of supporting beneficial social norms, we noted that it should also teach lessons on how we might hope to introduce such failures in the attempt to undermine various anti-social norms.

We distinguished between three broad sorts of failure. First, failures to ensure that people are predisposed, thanks to the absence of contrary pressures, to be moved appropriately by considerations of esteem. Second, failures to ensure that actions are presented in a light that can activate esteem motivation in a socially desirable way. And third, failures to ensure that publicity on people's performance is provided in a manner that triggers the desire for esteem, the aversion to disesteem, and that prompts kinds of behaviour that we are generally inclined to applaud.

We began the discussion of failures to guarantee that people are predisposed to be moved by considerations of esteem by looking at three measures which are used to foster a suitable predisposition among the members of a jury or indeed of many sorts of committee. The vetting of the jury is designed to make sure, so far as possible, that no one has a special interest in the outcome, the closeting of the jury that no one is subject to intimidation from outside, and the mixed membership that no one is likely to be pressured by in-group loyalties. We saw that these three dangers are often allowed to remain in other areas where the economy of esteem might work for good and that there is a presumptive case for reform in those areas.

Failures in the presentation of action may occur through failures to adjust any of a number of variables: the dimensions and ideals that are taken as relevant in the performance; the comparators in relation to whom agents are judged; and the public that does the judging. We distinguished between a number of ways in which such maladjustments can occur. One is the deactivation of virtue, which occurs when relevant ideals are left in obscurity; another the eclipsing of virtue, as when no one can expect to be taken as virtuous for performing well; another the destabilising of virtue, which occurs when the standards by which people may expect to be judged oscillate under the influence of exogenous factors; and yet another the suppression of the ordinary forces of esteem which will attend any regime that makes forthright speech difficult.

The last batch of failures we considered involve different ways in which the provision of publicity can undermine the operation of an intangible hand. Publicity may be wasteful, if it is left to each performer to publicise his or her own deeds, and the efforts that people make leave them no better off than if no one had sought publicity. Publicity may be motivated and unreliable, so far as performers are in competition and are naturally inclined to exaggerate their own achievements and to denigrate those of others or to charge others with misdeeds. And publicity may be unbalanced, prohibited, or frozen. It may draw attention only to one side of people's performance. It may be unavailable because its provision is prohibited in law. Or it may be frozen in a certain form, due to either of two factors: too little is known about an individual, and statistical cues reign unchallenged; or too much is known—the person is famous or infamous—and common opinion occupies an unchallenged place.

We are conscious that this list of presumptive failures in the design of familiar institutions is bound to be controversial. The kind of detailed empirical research needed to test and develop our conjectures more fully, as well as to explore the various other claims in this book, has yet to be done. We hope it will be done. There must be a serious cost to the understanding we achieve of our psychologies, our societies, and our institutional prospects, so long as the economy of esteem continues to languish in obscurity.

References

Abramson, J. (1994). *We, the Jury: The Jury System and the Ideal of Democracy.* New York, Basic Books.

Adair, D. (1974). *Fame and the Founding Fathers.* Indianapolis, Liberty Fund.

Adams, J. (1973). *Discourses on Davila (1790).* New York, Da Capo.

Ahmed, E., Harris, N., et al. (2001). *Shame Management Through Reintegration.* Cambridge, Cambridge University Press.

Akerlof, G. (1984). *An Economic Theorist's Book of Tales.* Cambridge, Cambridge University Press.

——and Kranton, N. (2000). 'Economics and Identity.' *Quarterly Journal of Economics* 115: 715–53.

Anderson, E. (2000). 'Beyond Home Economics: New Developments in Theories of Social Norms.' *Philosophy and Public Affairs* 29: 170–200.

Aquinas, T. (1958). *Summa Theologica.* Madrid, Biblioteca de Autores Cristianos.

Aristotle (1976). *The Nicomachean Ethics.* Harmondsworth, Penguin.

Axelrod, R. (1984). *The Evolution of Cooperation.* New York, Basic Books.

Ayres, I. and J. Braithwaite (1992). *Responsive Regulation.* New York, Oxford University Press.

Bardach, E., and Kagan, R. A. (1982). *Going by the Book: The Problem of Regulatory Unreasonableness.* Philadelphia, Temple University Press.

Barry, B. (1965). *Political Argument.* London, Routledge.

Baumeister, R. F., and Leary, M. R. (1995). 'The Need to Belong: Desire for Interpersonal Attachments as a Fundamental Human Motivation.' *Psychological Bulletin* 117: 497–529.

Baurmann, Michael (1996). *The Market of Virtue: Morality and Commitment in a Liberal Society.* The Hague, Kluwer.

Ben-Ner, A., and Putterman, L. (eds.) (1998). *Economics, Values, and Organization.* Cambridge, Cambridge University Press.

Bernheim, B. D. (1994). 'A Theory of Conformity.' *Journal of Political Economy* 102: 841–77.

Bikhchandani, S., D. Hirshleifer, et al. (1992). 'A Theory of Fads, Fashions, Custom, and Cultural Change as Informational Cascades.' *Journal of Political Economy* 100: 992–1026.

Bilgrami, A. (1998). 'Self-knowledge and Resentment', in B. S. C. Wright and C. Macdonald (eds.), *Knowing Our Own Minds.* Oxford, Oxford University Press: 207–41.

Black, D. (1958). *The Theory of Committees and Elections.* Cambridge, Cambridge University Press.

Black, J. (1998). 'Talking about Regulation.' *Public Law*: 77–105.

Blau, P. (1964). *Exchange and Power in Social Life.* New York, Wiley.

Bosco, L. and L. Mittone (1997). 'Tax Evasion and Moral Constraints: Some Experimental Evidence.' *Kyklos* 50: 297–324.

Boyd, R., and Richerson, P. J. (1996). 'Why Culture is Common but Cultural Evolution is Rare.' *Proceedings of the British Academy* 88: 73–93.

————(2002). 'Group Beneficial Norms Spread Rapidly in a Structured Population.' *Journal of Theoretical Biology* 215: 287–96.

————(forthcoming). 'Solving the Puzzle of Human Cooperation' , in S. Levison (ed.), *Evolution and Culture.* Cambridge, Mass., MIT Press.

Braithwaite, J. (1989). *Crime, Shame and Reintegration.* Cambridge, Cambridge University Press.

—— (1993). 'Shame and Modernity.' *British Journal of Criminology* 33: 1–18.

—— (2002). *Restorative Justice and Responsive Regulation.* New York, Oxford University Press.

Brehm, S. S., and Brehm, J. W. (1981). *Psychological Reactance: A Theory of Freedom and Control.* New York, Academic Press.

Brennan, G. (1996). 'Selection and the Currency of Reward', in R. E. Goodin (ed.), *The Theory of Institutional Design.* Cambridge, Cambridge University Press.

—— and Buchanan, J. (1981). 'The Normative Purpose of Economic "Science": Rediscovery of and Eighteenth Century Method.' *International Review of Law and Economics* 1: 155–66.

—— —— (1988). 'Is Public Choice Immoral? The Case for the Nobel Lie.' *Virginia Law Review* 74: 179–89.

—— and Hamlin, A. (1995). 'Economizing on Virtue.' *Constitutional Political Economy* 6: 35–6.

—— —— (2000). *Democratic Devices and Desires.* Cambridge, Cambridge University Press.

—— and Pettit, P. (1990). 'Unveiling the Vote.' *British Journal of Political Science* 20: 311–33.

—— —— (1993). 'Hands Invisible and Intangible.' *Synthese* 94: 191–225.

—— —— (2000). 'The Hidden Economy of Esteem.' *Economics and Philosophy* 16: 77–98.

Brown, L. (ed.) (1993). *The New Shorter Oxford English Dictionary.* Oxford, Oxford University Press.

Buchanan, J. (1965). 'An Economic Theory of Clubs' *Economica* 32: 1–14.

—— (1975). *The Limits of Liberty.* Chicago, University of Chicago Press.

Burke, E. (1987). *A Philosophical Inquiry into the Origin of our Ideas of the Sublime and the Beautiful (1757).* Oxford, Blackwell.

Chang, J. (1991). *Wild Swans.* London, HarperCollins.

Coase, R. (1937). 'The Nature of the Firm.' *Economica* 4: 386–405.

Coleman, J. (1990*a*). 'The Emergence of Norms', in M. Hechter, K.-D. Opp, and R. Wippler (eds.), *Social Institutions: Their Emergence, Maintenance, and Effects.* de Gruyter, Berlin: 35–59.

—— (1990*b*). *Foundations of Social Theory.* Cambridge, Mass., Harvard University Press.

Condorcet, M. de (1976). *Condorcet: Selected Writings.* Indianopolis, Bobbs-Merrill.

Congleton, R.(1989). 'Efficient Status Seeking: Externalities and the Evolution of Status Games.' *Journal of Economic Behavior and Organization* 11:175–190.

Cooter, R. D. (1994). 'Structural Adjudication and the New Law Merchant: A Model of Decentralized Law.' *International Journal of Law and Economics* 14: 215–31.

—— (1996). 'Decentralized Law for a Complex Economy: The Structural Approach to Adjudicating the New Law Merchant.' *University of Pennsylvania Law Review* 144: 1643–96.

Cowen, T. (2000). *What Price Fame?* Cambridge, Mass, Harvard University Press.

—— (2002). 'The Esteem Theory of Norms.' *Public Choice* 113: 211–24.

Darwall, S. (1977). 'Two Kinds of Respect.' *Ethics* 88: 36–49.

De Juan, A., Lasheras, M. A., et al. (1994). 'Voluntary Tax Compliant Behaviour of Spanish Income Tax Payers.' *Public Finance/Finances Publiques* 49: 90–105.

De Maria, W. (1995). *Whistle-Blower Bibliography.* www.uow.edu.au/arts/sts/bmartin/dissent/documents/DeMaria_bib.html.

Dharmapala, D. and McAdams, R. H. (2001). 'Words that Kill: An Economic Perspective on Hate Speech and Hate Crimes, *University of Illinois Law and Economics Research Papers.*', Champaign, Urbana.

—— —— (2003). 'The Condorcet Jury Theorem and the Expressive Function of Law.' *American Law and Economics Review* 5, 1–31.

Ellickson, R. C. (2001). 'The Market for Social Norms.' *American Law and Economics Review* 3: 1–49.

Elster, J. (1979). *Ulysses and The Sirens*. Cambridge, Cambridge University Press.

—— (1983). *Sour Grapes*. Cambridge, Cambridge University Press.

—— (1989). *The Cement of Society: A Study of Social Order*. Cambridge, Cambridge University Press.

—— (1990). 'Norms of Revenge.' *Ethics* 100: 862–85.

—— (1999). *Alchemies of the Mind: Rationality and the Emotions*. Cambridge, Cambridge University Press.

Feddersen, T., and Pesendorfer, W. (1998). 'Convicting the Innocent: The Inferiority of Unanimous Jury Verdicts under Strategic Voting.' *American Political Science Review* 92: 23–35.

—— —— (1999). 'Elections, Information Aggregation, and Strategic Voting.' *Proceedings of the National Academy of Science, U.S.A.* 96: 10572–4.

Fehr, E., and Gaechter, S. (2000). 'Fairness and Retaliation: The Economics of Reciprocity.' *Journal of Economic Perspectives* 14: 159–81.

Fletcher, G. J. O., and Clark, M. S. (eds.) (2001). *Blackwell Handbook of Social Psychology: Interpersonal Processes*. Oxford, Blackwell.

Fodor, J. (1983). *The Modularity of Mind*. Cambridge, Mass., MIT Press.

Frank, R. (1985). *Choosing the Right Pond*. New York, Oxford University Press.

Fraser, D. (1976). *Urban Politics in Victorian England*. Leicester, Leicester University Press.

Frey, B. (1997). *Not Just for the Money: An Economic Theory of Personal Motivation*. Cheltenham, Edward Elgar.

—— and Jegen, R. (2001). 'Motivation Crowding Theory: A Survey.' *Journal of Economic Surveys* 15: 589–611.

Fukuyama, F. (1992). *The End of History and the Last Man*. London, Hamish Hamilton.

Gaechter, S., and Fehr, E. (1999). 'Collective Action in Social Exchange.' *Journal of Economic Behavior and Organization* 39: 341–69.

Grabosky, P. N. (1995). 'Counterproductive Regulation.' *International Journal of the Sociology of Law* 23: 347–69.

Guerra, G. (2002). 'Crowding out Trust: The Adverse Effects of Verification. An Experiment.' *Oxford University Department of Economics Ms*. Oxford.

Gunn, J. A. W. (1993). 'Opinion in Eighteenth-Century Thought: What did the Concept Purport to Explain.' *Utilitas* 5: 17–33.

Hardin, R. (1982). *Collective Action*. Baltimore, Johns Hopkins University Press.

—— (1995). *One for All: The Logic of Group Conflict*. Princeton, Princeton University Press.

Hart, H. L. A. (1961). *The Concept of Law*. Oxford, Oxford University Press.

Heath, A. (1976). *Rational Choice and Social Exchange*. Cambridge, Cambridge University Press.

Heckathorn, D. (1989). 'Collective Action and the Second-order Free Rider Problem.' *Rationality and Society* 1: 78 –100.

Henrich, J., and Boyd, R. (2001). 'Why People Punish Defectors.' *Journal of Theoretical Biology* 208: 79–89.

Hirschman, A. O. (1970). *Exit, Voice and Loyalty*. Cambridge, Mass., Harvard University Press.

—— (1977). *The Passions and the Interests: Political Arguments for Capitalism before its Triumph*. Princeton, Princeton University Press.

Hirshleifer, J. (1983). 'From Weakest Link to Best Shot: The Voluntary Provision of Public Goods.' *Public Choice* 41: 371–86.

Hobbes, T. (1998). *On the Citizen*. Cambridge, Cambridge University Press.

Hollander, H. (1990). 'A Social Exchange Approach to Voluntary Co-operation.' *American Economic Review* 80: 1157–67.

Holmes, S. (1990). 'The Secret History of Self-Interest', in J. J. Mansbridge (ed.), *Beyond Self-Interest*. Chicago, University of Chicago Press.

Honneth, A. (1996). *The Struggle for Recognition*. Cambridge, Mass., MIT Press.

Hume, D. (1875). 'Of the Independence of Parliament', in T. H. Green and T. H. Grose (eds.), *Hume's Philosophical Works*, vol. 3. London.

—— (1967). *A Treatise of Human Nature*. Oxford, Oxford University Press.

—— (1983). *An Inquiry Concerning the Principles of Morals*. Indianapolis, Hackett.

—— (1994). *Political Essays*. Cambridge, Cambridge University Press.

Hurley, S. and Chater, N. (eds.) (2004). *Perspectives on Imitation: From Cognitive Neuroscience to Social Science* Vols 1 and 2. Cambridge, Mass., MIT Press.

James, S. (1997). *Passion and Action: The Emotions in Seventeenth Century Philosophy.* Oxford, Oxford University Press.

Jones, E. E. (1990). *Interpersonal Perception*. New York, Freeman.

Kamtekar, R. (1998). 'Imperfect Virtue.' *Ancient Philosophy* 18: 315–39.

Kaplan, S. E., and Reckers, P. M. J. (1985). 'A Study of Tax Evasion Judgments.' *National Tax Journal* 38: 97–102.

Kelman, S. (1987). 'Public Choice and Public Spirit.' *Public Interest* 80: 83–94.

Klein, D. B. (ed.) (1997). *Reputation: Studies in the Voluntary Elicitation of Good Conduct*. Ann Arbor, Michigan University Press.

Kreps, D., and.Wilson, R. (1982). 'Reputation and Imperfect Information.' *Journal of Economic Theory* 27: 253–79.

Krygier, M. (1997). 'Virtuous Circles: Antipodean Reflections on Power, Institutions, and Civil Society.' *East European Politics and Societies* 11: 36–88.

Kuran, T. (1995). *Private Truths, Public Lies: The Social Consequences of Preference Falsification*. Cambridge, Mass., Harvard University Press.

—— (1998). 'Ethnic Norms and Their Transformation Through Reputational Cascades.' *Journal of Legal Studies* 27: 623–59.

—— and Sunstein, C. (1999). 'Availability Cascades and Risk Evaluation.' *Stanford Law Review* 51: 683–768.

Latane, B., and Darley, J. (1970). *The Unresponsive Bystander: Why doesn't he Help?* New York, Appleton Century Crofts.

Leary, M. R. (2001). 'The Self we Know and the Self we Show', in G. J. O. Fletcher and M. S. Clark (eds.), *Blackwell Handbook of Social Psychology: Interpersonal Processes*. Oxford, Blackwell: 457–77.

Leeman, A. D. (1949). *Gloria*. Rotterdam, Wyt.

Le Grand, J. (2000). 'From Knight to Knave? Public Policy and Market Incentives', in P. Taylor-Gooby, *Risk, Trust and Welfare*. Basingstoke, Macmillan.

Levy, D. M. (1988). 'The Market for Fame and Fortune.' *History of Political Economy* 20: 615–25.

Lewis, D. (1969). *Convention*. Cambridge, Mass., Harvard University Press.

List, C., and Pettit, P. (forthcoming). 'An Epistemic Free Rider Problem?', in G. Macdonald (ed.), *Popper: A Critical Reappraisal*. London, Routledge.

Lively, J., and Rees, J. (eds.) (1978). *Utilitarian Logic and Politics: James Mill's 'Essay on Government', Macaulay's Critique, and the Ensuing Debate*. Oxford, Oxford University Press.

Locke, J. (1975). *An Essay Concerning Human Understanding*. Oxford, Oxford University Press.

—— (1993). *Political Writings*, ed. David Wooton. Harmondsworth, Penguin.

Loury, G. C. (1994). 'Self-Censorship in Public Discourse: A Theory of "Political Correctness" and Related Phenomena.' *Rationality and Society* 6: 428–61.

Lovejoy, A. O. (1961). *Reflections on Human Nature*. Baltimore, Johns Hopkins University Press.

McAdams, R. H. (1992). 'Relative Preferences.' *Yale Law Journal* 102(1): 1–104.

—— (1995). 'Cooperation and Conflict: The Economics of Group Status Production and Race Discrimination.' *Harvard Law Review* 108(5): 1003–84.

—— (1997). 'The Origin, Development and Regulation of Norms.' *Michigan Law Review* 96(2): 338–433.

—— (2000). 'An Attitudinal Theory of Expressive Law.' *Oregon Law Review* 79: 339–90.

Macdonald, G., and Pettit, P. (1981). *Semantics and Social Science*. London, Routledge & Kegan Paul.

McGeer, V. (2002). 'Psychopractice, Psychotheory and the Contrastive Case of Autism: How Practices of Mind Become Second Nature.' *Journal of Consciousness Studies* 8: 109–32.

—— and P. Pettit (2002). 'The Self-regulating Mind.' *Language and Communication* 11: 281–99.

Mackie, G. (1998). 'All Men are Liars: Is Democracy Meaningless?', in J. Elster (ed.), *Deliberative Democracy*. Cambridge, Cambridge University Press.

Madison, J., Hamilton, A., et al. (1987). *The Federalist Papers*. Harmondsworth, Penguin.

Mahoney, P. G., and Sanchirico, C. W. (2002). 'Norms, Repeated Games, and the Role of Law.' *University of Virginia Law School Working Papers*. Boston.

Mandeville, B. (1731). *Free Thoughts on Religion, the Church and National Happiness*. London.

—— (1924). *The Fable of the Bees, or Private Vices, Public Benefits*. Oxford, Oxford University Press.

—— (1971). *An Enquiry into the Origin of Honour and the Usefulness of Christianity (1732)*. London, Frank Cass.

Marks, G., and Miller, N. (1987). 'Ten Years of Evidence on the False Consensus Effect: An Empirical and Theoretical Review.' *Psychological Bulletin* 102: 72–90.

Milgrom, P., and Roberts, J. (1982). 'Predation, Reputation and Entry Deterrence.' *Journal of Economic Theory* 27: 280–312.

Mill, J. S. (1964 [1861]). *Considerations on Representative Government*. London, Everyman.

—— (1978). *On Liberty*. Indianapolis, Hackett.

Miller, D. T., and Prentice, D. A. (1994). 'Collective Errors and Errors about the Collective.' *Personality and Social Psychology Bulletin* 20: 541–50.

—— —— (1996). 'The Construction of Social Norms and Standards', in E. T. Higgins and A. W. Kruglanski (eds.), *Social Psychology: Handbook of Basic Principles*. New York, Guilford Press: 799–829.

Miller, W. I. (1993). *Humiliation*. Ithaca, Cornell University Press.

—— (1997). *The Anatomy of Disgust*. Cambridge, Mass., Harvard University Press.

Montaigne, M. de (1991). *The Complete Essays*. Harmondsworth, Penguin.

Montesquieu, Baron de (1977). *The Spirit of Laws*. Berkeley, University of California Press.

Munger, K., and Harris, S. J. (1989). 'Effects of an Observer on Handwashing in a Public Restroom.' *Perceptual and Motor Skills* 69: 733–4.

Nicole, P. (1999). 'De la charité de l'amour-propre', in L. Thirouin (ed.), *Essais de morale*. Paris, PUF: 3. 381–415.

Nisbett, R. E., and Cohen, D. (1996). *Culture of Honor: The Psychology of Violence in the South*. Boulder, Westview Press.

Noelle-Neumann, E. (1984). *The Spiral of Silence: Our Social Skin*. Chicago, University of Chicago Press.

Ogien, Ruwen (2002) *La Honte: est-elle immorale?* Paris, Bayard.

O'Neill, B. (2001). *Honor, Symbols, and War*. Ann Arbor, University of Michigan Press.

Ostrom, E. (1990). *Governing the Commons: The Evolution of Institutions for Collective Action*. New York, Cambridge University Press.

Oxford English Dictionary (1971). Compact edn., London, Book Club Associates.

Paley, W. (1825). *The Principles of Moral and Political Philosophy*, vol. 4, *Collected Works*. London, C. and J. Rivington.

Pettit, P. (1978). 'Rational Man Theory', in C. Hookway and P. Pettit (eds.), *Action and Interpretation: Studies in the Philosophy of the Social Sciences*. Cambridge, Cambridge University Press: 43–63.

——(1986). 'Free Riding and Foul Dealing.' *Journal of Philosophy* 83: 361–79.

——(1989). 'Decision Theory, Political Theory and the Hats Hypothesis' in F. D'Agostino (ed.), *Freedom & Rationality: Festschrift for John Watkins*, Kluwer.

——(1990). '*Virtus Normativa*: A Rational Choice Perspective.' *Ethics* 100: 725–55; reprinted in P. Pettit (2002), *Rules, Reasons, and Norms: Selected Papers*, Oxford, Oxford University Press.

——(1992). 'Instituting a Research Ethic: Chilling and Cautionary Tales.' *Bioethics* 6: 89–112; repr. in Pettit (2002).

——(1993). *The Common Mind: An Essay on Psychology, Society, and Politics* (pbk. edn. 1996). New York, Oxford University Press.

——(1994). 'Enfranchising Silence: An Argument for Freedom of Speech' in T. Campbell and W. Sadurksi (eds.), *Freedom of Communication*. Aldershot, Dartmouth: 45–56; repr. in Pettit (2002).

——(1995a). 'The Cunning of Trust.' *Philosophy and Public Affairs* 24: 202–25; repr. in Pettit (2002).

——(1995b). 'The Virtual Reality of Homo Economicus.' *Monist* 78: 308–29; repr. in Pettit (2002).

——(1996a). 'Functional Explanation and Virtual Selection.' *British Journal for the Philosophy of Science* 47: 291–302; repr. in Pettit (2002).

——(1996b). 'Institutional Design and Rational Choice' in R. E. Goodin (ed.), *The Theory of Institutional Design*. Cambridge, Cambridge University Press.

——(1997). *Republicanism: A Theory of Freedom and Government*. Oxford, Oxford University Press.

——(2000). 'Rational Choice, Functional Selection and Empty Black Boxes.' *Journal of Economic Methodology* 7: 33–57.

——(2001a). *A Theory of Freedom: From the Psychology to the Politics of Agency*. Cambridge and New York, Polity and Oxford University Press.

——(2001b). 'Two Sources of Morality.' *Social Philosophy and Policy* 18, 2: 102–28.

——(2002) *Rules, Reasons, and Norms: Selected Papers*. Oxford, Oxford University Press.

——and Smith, M. (1996). 'Freedom in Belief and Desire.' *Journal of Philosophy* 93: 429–49; repr. in F. Jackson, P. Pettit, and M. Smith (2004), *Mind, Morality, and Explanation: Selected Collaborations*, Oxford, Oxford University Press.

Phelps, E. S. (1972). 'The Statistical Theory of Racism and Sexism.' *American Economic Review* 62: 659–61.

Phillips, A. (1995). *The Politics of Presence*. Oxford, Oxford University Press.

Pope, A. (1971). *The Rape of the Lock*, ed. G. Tillotson. London, Routledge.

Posner, E. A. (2000). *Law and Social Norms*. Cambridge, Mass., Harvard University Press.

Posner, R. A. (1981). *The Economics of Justice*. Cambridge, Mass., Harvard University Press.

——and E. B. Rasmussen (2000). 'Creating and Enforcing Norms, With Special Reference to Sanctions.' *University of Chicago Law School: John M. Olin Program in Law & Economics Working Papers*.

Prentice, D. A., and Miller, D. T. (1993). 'Pluralistic Ignorance and Alcohol Use on Campus.' *Journal of Personality and Social Psychology* 64: 243–56.

Priestley, J. (1993). *Political Writings*. Cambridge, Cambridge University Press.

Putnam, R. D. (1993). *Making Democracy Work: Civic Traditions in Modern Italy*. Princeton, Princeton University Press.

Rawls, J. (1971). *A Theory of Justice*. Oxford, Oxford University Press.

Richerson, P. J., and Boyd, R. (1998). 'The Evolution of Human Ultra-Sociality', in I. Eibl-Eibisfeldt and F. Salter (eds.), *Ideology, Warfare, and Indoctrinability*. Oxford, Berghan Books.

———(2001). 'Built for Speed, Not for Comfort: Darwinian Theory and Human Culture.' *History and Philosophy of the Life Sciences* 23: 423–63.

Ricoeur, P. (1965). *Fallible Man*. Chicago, Henry Regnery.

Sabini, J., and Silver, M. (1982). *Moralities of Everyday Life*. Oxford, Oxford University Press.

Sally, D. (1995). 'Conversation and Co-operation in Social Dilemmas.' *Rationality and Society* 7: 58–92.

Samuelson, P. A. (1995). 'The Pure Theory of Public Expenditure.' *Review of Economics and Statistics* 36: 387–9.

Sandler, T., and Tschirhart, J. (1980). 'The Economic Theory of Clubs: An Evaluative Survey.' *Journal of Economic Literature* 18: 1481–521.

Scanlon, T. M. (1998). *What We Owe To Each Other*. Cambridge, Mass., Harvard University Press.

Schelling, T. (1978). *Micromotives and Macrobehavior*. New York, Norton.

Schroeder, C. M., and Prentice, D. A. (1998). 'Exposing Pluralistic Ignorance to Reduce Alcohol Use Among College Students.' *Journal of Applied Social Psychology* 28: 2150–80.

Selten, R. (1978). 'The Chain Store Paradox.' *Theory and Decision* 9: 127–59.

Selznick, P. (1992). *The Moral Commonwealth: Social Theory and the Promise of Community*. Berkeley, University of California Press.

Sen, A. (1998). 'Foreword', in A. Ben-Ner and L. Putterman (eds.), *Economics, Values, and Organization*. Cambridge, Cambridge University Press.

Sidgwick, H. (1907). *The Methods of Ethics*. Chicago, Chicago University Press.

Skyrms, B. (1996). *Evolution of the Social Contract*. Cambridge, Cambridge University Press.

Slote, M. (1989). *Beyond Optimizing: A Study of Rational Choice*. Cambridge, Mass., Harvard University Press.

Smart, J. J. C. (1987). *Essays Metaphysical and Moral*. Oxford, Blackwell.

Smith, A. (1976). *An Inquiry into the Nature and Causes of the Wealth of Nations*. Oxford, Oxford University Press.

———(1982). *The Theory of the Moral Sentiments*. Indianapolis, Liberty Classics.

Sober, E. (1983). 'Equilibrium Explanation.' *Philosophical Studies* 43: 201–10.

———(1984). *The Nature of Selection*. Cambridge, Mass., MIT Press.

———and D. S. Wilson (1998). *Unto Others: The Evolution and Psychology of Unselfish Behavior*. Cambridge, Mass., Harvard University Press.

Soltis, J., Boyd, R., et al. (1995). 'Can Group-functional Behaviors Evolve By Cultural Group Selection?' *Current Anthropology* 36: 473–83.

Song, Y. D., and Yarbrough, T. E. (1978). 'Tax Ethics and Taxpayer Attitudes: A Survey.' *Public Administration Review* 38: 442–52.

Stewart, F. H. (1994). *Honor*. Chicago, University of Chicago Press.

Sugden, R. (1986). *The Economics of Rights, Cooperation and Welfare*. Oxford, Blackwell.

Sunstein, C. R. (1990a). *After the Rights Revolution: Reconceiving the Regulatory State*. Cambridge, Mass., Harvard University Press.

———(1990b). 'Paradoxes of the Regulatory State.' *University of Chicago Law Review* 57: 407–41.

———(1996). 'On the Expressive Function of Law.' *University of Pennsylvania Law Review* 144: 2021–53.

—— (2002). 'The Law of Group Polarization.' *Journal of Political Philosophy* 10: 175–95.

Taylor, C. (1992). *Multiculturalism and 'The Politics of Recognition'*. Princeton, Princeton University Press.

—— (1995). *Philosophical Arguments*. Cambridge, Mass., Harvard University Press.

Taylor, M. (1987). *The Possibility of Cooperation*. Cambridge, Cambridge University Press.

Toennies, F. (1887). *Community and Society*. New York, Harper and Row.

Tucker, A. (1834). *The Light of Nature Pursued*. London, T. Tegg and Son.

Tyler, T. R. (1990). *Why People Obey the Law*. New Haven, Yale University Press.

—— Boeckmann, R. J., Smith, H. J., and Huo, Y. Y. (1997). *Social Justice in a Diverse Society*. Boulder, Westview Press.

Veblen, T. (1905). *The Theory of the Leisure Class*. New York, Augustus Kelly.

Vickers, J. (1986). 'Signalling in a Model of Monetary Policy with Incomplete Information.' *Oxford Economic Papers*. 38: 443–55.

Wenzel, N. (2001a). 'Misperception of Social Norms about Tax Compliance (1): A Prestudy.' *Canberra, Centre for Tax System Integrity, Australian National University.*

—— (2001b). 'Misperception of Social Norms about Tax Compliance (2): A Field-experiment.' *Canberra, Centre for Tax System Integrity, Australian National University.*

White, M. (1987). *Philosophy, The Federalist, and the Constitution*. New York, Oxford University Press.

Williams, B. (1993). *Shame and Necessity*. Berkeley, University of California Press.

Williamson, O. E. (1989). 'Transaction Cost Economics', in R. Schmalensee and R. Willig (eds.), *Handbook of Industrial Organisation*, vol. 1. Amsterdam, North Holland: 135–82.

Winch, P. (1963). *The Idea of a Social Science and Its Relation to Philosophy*. London, Routledge.

Young, E. (1968). *The Complete Works*, vol. 1. Hildesheim, Georg Olms.

Index

Abramson, J., 294
academia, 6, 151, 152–4, 235
   and esteem, 70, 72–3, 120–1, 181–2, 204, 209–10, 227
access to performance, 69, 70, 143, see also publicity
Adair, D., 6
Adams, John, 7, 25, 185–7, 187n
admiration, 21, 22, 23, 70
   mutual admiration, 197, 203–8, 213, 217, 233, 275
aggregate esteem, 99–101, 109, 116–7, 146
Ahmed, E., N., 57, 307, 308, 318
Akerlof, George, 2n
altruism, 51, 274–5
   primary and secondary, 274–5
Anderson, E., 274
anonymity, 31–3, 141, 146, 263
approval and disapproval: see also esteem
   attitudinal, 15–6, 275–6
   behavioural, 15–6, 275
   costliness of, 271–2
   moralised, 284–5
Aquinas, Thomas, 24
aristocracy, 8, 10
Aristotle, 8, 32, 42, 44, 262, 278
assimilation strategies, 235
association, 57–8, see also voluntary associations, involuntary associations
attachment, see love
attention, 20, 56–7, 59, 60, 61, 62, 122, 142, 153–4, 185–7, see also publicity
   avoidance, 183–4
   and exchange, 72
   and quality of performance, 154, 157

scarcity of, 153
   and voluntary associations, 196
attitude-dependent goods, 16, 66
attitudinal character of esteem, see esteem
attribution biases, 74–5, 75n
audience, 69, see also publicity
   quality, 84, 204–8, 210
   size, 26, 135, 142–5, 178, 180–3, 199, 200–3, 237; manipulation of, 180–3; and performance incentives, 142–5
autonomy, 261, 264
   of esteem relations, 30–1, 67, 217
average performance, see performance
Axelrod, R., 271n, 273
Ayres, I., 261n, 292n

backhand:
   intangible, see intangible hand
   invisible, see invisible hand
Bardach, E. R., 261n
Baumeister, R. F., 31
Baurmann, Michael, 9, 31
behavioural approval, see approval and disapproval
behavioural effects, see performance
behavioural trade-offs, 163
belief, see common belief
benevolence, 17–8, 83, 101, 104, 109–10, 162–3
Ben-Ner, A., 274
Bernheim, B. D., 2n
best-shot case, 121–2, 155, 158
Bikhchandani, S., 57, 147
Black, D., 147n
Black, J., 292n

Blau, P., 3
bootstrap effect, 126, 132–9, 284
Bosco, L., 166
bourgeoisie, 8
Boyd, R., 274, 279n
Braithwaite, J., 32, 57, 250, 261n, 274, 292n, 307, 318
Brehm, J. W., 261
Brehm, S. S., 261
Brennan, Geoffrey, 5, 74, 153n, 167n, 246, 285, 291, 295n, 314
British Academy, 198, 218
Buchanan, James, 167n, 196, 271–2, 271n, 276, 277, 285
Burke, Edmund, 25

capital effect, 151–2
Chang, J., 305
choice condition, 279–80
Christian values, 9
church, 172–3, 185, 219, 249, 298–9
Cicero, 9, 24, 46
civil society, 5, 248, 256, 257, 268, 287, see also voluntary associations
Clark, M. S., 26
cluster effect, 115–6, 118
Cohen, D., 8n, 9, 31, 268, 269
Coleman, J., 3, 270, 274
collective action problems, see free-riding
collective promotion, 40, 214–7
coming out, 193n, 236–7, 238–9
common belief, 110, 146–152, 162–8, 290, 317
    and average performance, 93, 164–7
    and esteem, 53, 56–7, 92–3, 146–52, 290, 317
    rationalisation of, 149
    reliability of, 162–4
    and standards, 110, 168
    and testimony, 146–8
common good, 4, 5, 162, 247, 250, 272, 289–91, 296, 297, 299

and the intangible hand, 247–51, 257–63, 267, 285–7, 289–91
common sense, 8
comparative character of esteem, see esteem
competition, 1, 2, 32, 34, 65, 212–13
    for esteem, 21, 34, 35, 50, 65, 68, 70–2, 98, 252; in performance, 70; in presentation, 71–2; in publicity, 70–2; wastefulness of, 182, 308–9
compliance, 69, 125–40
    actual versus perceived, 135–6
    attitudes to, 166–8, 273
    average, 93, 268
    and esteem-incentives, 125–39
    information about, 167–71
    norms of, 293
    tax-compliance, 94, 166–7, 169, 313
concealment strategies, 34, 39–40, 60
conditioning, 292n
Condorcet jury theorem, 147n
conformism, 30–7, 263–4
Congleton, R., 104
consumption goods, 4, 13, 30–1, 246
conventions, see norms
cooperation, 271–6, 280, 288
Cooter, R. D., 274, 278
corruption, 10, 17, 155, 163, 174, 234
countercultural groups, see culture
Cowen, T., 2n, 103n, 147
credibility, 169, 177, 274
criminal justice, 311
crowding out, 138, 261, 303
culture, 43, 318
    aristocratic, 10
    democratic, 264
    of generosity, 171
    and recognition, 188
    of silence, 172
    sub-cultures, 68, 245, 268; countercultures, 225–7, 229, 230; parallel cultures, 229, 230, 233, 234
cunning of reason, 45

Darley, J., 262
Darwall, S., 20
De Juan, A., 166
De Maria, W., 172
deception, 9, 26, 28, 39–40, 45, see also dissimulation
decisions:
  collective, 212, 231, 234
  political, 180, 296; and transparency, 152
  and uncertainty, 118–22
default exclusion, see exclusion
demand for esteem, see economy of esteem
democracy, 10, 188n, 264, 301, 302, 307, 313–5
detection problem, 259–60
Dharmapala, D., 246, 268, 301
dimensions of esteem, 17–21, 69, 70, 71, 299
direction of fit, 52
disapproval, see approval and disapproval:
discontinuities, 113
discretionary performance, see performance
discriminatory exclusion, see exclusion
disesteem, see esteem
dissimulation, 9–10, 38–9, 170
distribution of performances, 99, 113–16, 156–7, 189
  and aggregate esteem, 116–17
  and publicity, 142–5
dunce-cap policies, 142, 154–8

economics, 1, 2, 6–7, 24, 139, 195, 208, 254, 256
  and conception of the good, 251–2
economies of scale:
  in publicity, 196, 197–200
economy of esteem: see also intangible hand
  conditions of, 65–6

demand for esteem, 34–49; concealed demand, 39–40; and the teleological paradox, 35–46, virtual demand, 40–8, 278
  normative character of, 23,
supply of esteem, 50–64; coherence of, 51–62; concealed supply, 60; indirect supply, 56–8; virtual supply, 60–2; and voluntary associations, 214–19
egoism, see self-interest
Ellickson, R. C., 2n, 30, 246, 300
Elster, J., 27, 32, 35, 36, 37, 38, 39, 57, 225, 247, 268, 270, 272
enfant terrible phenomenon, 189–93
enforcement, 138
  costs, 276
  enforcement dilemma, 270–79, 285; resolution of, 274–9
environmental pollution, 102
equilibrium:
  multiple equilibria, 125–40
  simple model, 94–101; normative status of, 101–4
  three-range model, 113–18
equilibrium explanation, 47
esteem:
  anonymous and onymous, 29, 31–3, 141, 146, 263
  attraction of, 23–33; as instrumental good, 26–28; as intrinsic good, 29–31; marginal utility of, 115, 156; as primary good, 29; in today's world, 31–3
  character of, 15–23; as evaluative attitude, 16–18, 52, 93, 102–3; as comparative attitude, 18–21; as directive attitude, 21–3
  defective, 27–8
  external, 197–203
  internal, 203–8
  self-esteem, 13, 15, 16, 26, 28, 33, 262
esteem incentives, see incentives

esteem-seeking strategies, 68–74, see
    performance, presentation, publicity
esteem services, 55–62; see association,
    attention, testimony
  exchange of, 58–62; 72–3; 217–19;
    virtual character of, 60–2
ethics committees, 312
etiquette, 43
evaluation condition, 280
evaluative character of esteem, see
    esteem
exchange: see esteem services
exclusion, 223–30
  default, 224–7; discriminatory, 227–30
experts, 27
externalities, 54, 102, 103

fact-defective esteem, 27–8
fame, 57, 71, 146–52, 159, 205, 230, 315,
    317, 318
fashion, 149n,
Feddersen, T., 175
Federalist Papers, 296
feedback effects:
  compliance and esteem-incentives, 125
  performance and aggregative
    outcomes, 140
  performance and standards, 50, 65, 66, 99
Fehr, E., 274n, 280n
Fletcher, G. J. O., 26
Fodor, J., 30
folk psychology, 74, 75, 75n
formal law, see law
Frank, Robert, 2n, 197, 208–9, 219
Fraser, D., 314
free market, 3, 7, 77, 267, 310
free-riding:
  and involuntary associations, 231–4
  and norms, 270–1
  and voluntary associations, 211–17
  and whistle-blower dilemma, 175–6
freedom, 2, 10
  of entry and exit, 211, 222–9

of information, 152, 180, 297
of speech, 180, 305
Frey, B., 257, 262, 302
friendship, 61
Fukuyama, F., 20n

Gaechter, S., 274n, 280n
game theory, 169n
gift-giving, 52–3
glory, see fame
goal-specification, 155, 158
good (the): see also common good
  thick theory of, 253–5
  thin theory of, 251–2
government funding, 303–4
Grabosky, P. N., 261
group-selection, 278–9
Guerra, G., 257
Gunn, J. A. W., 8

Hamilton, Alexander, 10, 148
Hamlin, A., 285
Hardin, R., 246, 247, 268
Harris, S. J., 32, 57, 142, 307, 308, 318
Hart, H. L. A., 270
Heath, A., 3, 271n
Heckathorn, D., 103
Henrich, J., 274
hierarchies, 199–200
Hirschman, A. O., 7
Hirshleifer, D., 57, 122, 147
Hobbes, Thomas, 24
hole effect, 116
Hollander, H., 2n
Holmes, S., 8
homosexuals, 236, 264
honesty, 17, 18, 19, 37, 52, 67, 83, 87, 93,
    101, 170, 206, 268, 273, 293, 297,
    312
Honneth, A., 20
honour: see esteem
  aristocratic culture of, 8
honour-roll policies, 142, 154–8

human nature, 23, 25, 185, 206, 285

Hume, David, 8, 9, 19, 25, 27, 28, 46, 262, 285, 299

Hurley, S., 42

hypocrisy, see dissimulation

ideal-defective esteem, 27–8

ideal performance, see performance

ideals, 23, 69, 93, 103, 106–9, 110, 168, 301, 318
  and public life, 302

identity, 307

incentives:
  esteem incentives, 99, 117–18, 121, 155–6; and compliance, 126–35; and fame, 148–52; mobilising, 122, 152, 155–6
  of information providers, 167–71

income, 94, 173, 208–9, 313

individuality, 263–4

infamy, see fame

information:
  freedom of, see freedom
  and performance, 153–4, 164–7, 250
  and prevailing practice, 108, 138, 162–4
  and standards, 167–71, 301
  and whistle-blowing, 171–6

informational cascades, 57, 147

in-group loyalty, problem of, 295, 298–9

inhibiting alternatives, 42

inhibition effect, 181, 184, 214–17

innovation, 42

institutional design, 23, 152, 179, 243, 255–63, 285–7, 296, 318

intangible hand:
  criteria for guiding, 251–5
  dangers of, 263–4, 268–9, failures of; failures to shape predisposition, 294–9; failures to shape presentation, 299–308; failures to shape publicity, 308–19
  mobilising, 249–51, 289–321
  notion of, 245–8, 255–7

social benefits of, 247–51, 257–63, 267; inexpensiveness of, 258; effectiveness of, 259–60; virtue-compatibility of, 260–3

internal esteem, see esteem

intervention:
  and compliance performance, 133
  effects of, 135
  and incentives, 167–71
  and policy, 152–8

invisibility: see recognition

invisible hand, 4–5, 7, 10, 138, 243, 245, 246, 247, 255, 258, 265, 267, 269, 287
  and regulation, 255–6
  versus intangible hand, 246, 255–7

involuntary associations, 222–39
  advocacy of, 230–1
  basis for, 225–6
  and coming out, 236–7
  differences with voluntary associations, 223–9
  and exclusion; default exclusion, 224–7; discriminatory exclusion, 227–9
  and free-riding, 230–3
  and loyalty, 230–4
  and secrecy, 234–7

iron hand, 4–5, 243, 246, 255, 256, 260, 261, 265, 267, 287
  and regulation, 255–6
  versus intangible hand, 246, 255–7

isothymia, 20n

James, Susan, 24

Jegen, R., 257, 261n

Johnston, Samuel, 248

juries, 294–9
  and outside inhibition, 297–8
  and in-group-loyalty, 298–9
  and special interests, 296–7

Kagan, A., 261n

Kamtekar, R., 38, 247

Kant, Immanuel, 25

Kaplan, S. E., 166
Kelman, S., 167
Keynesian economics, 98n
Klein, D. B., 2n
knave, see sensible knave
Kreps, D., 169n
Krygier, M., 269
Kuran, T., 57, 305, 306

Lasheras, M. A., 166
Latane, B., 262
laurels effect, 151
law (formal), 138, 248, 300, 313
    and order, 231
    and regulation, 5, 138, 246, 250, 267–9,
        287, 300–1
    rule of, 291
law of opinion, 23, 263–4
Leary, M. R., 26, 31
Leeman, A. D., 9, 24, 46
Levy, D. M., 2n
Lewis, David, 53, 57, 147, 273, 282
Lively, J., 10, 30
location, see social context
Locke, John, 24, 248
Loury, G. C., 306
love, 16, 33, 61
Lovejoy, A. O., 6, 7, 24, 25, 26, 37, 38, 75,
    248, 262
loyalty:
    and involuntary associations, 230–4
    and voluntary associations, 211–17

McAdams, R. H., 53, 126, 127, 133, 138,
    246, 268, 275, 283, 300, 301
Macdonald, G., 76n
McGeer, V., 22, 74n
Mackie, G., 284
macro-behaviour, 104
Madison, James, 10, 148
Mahoney, P. G., 273
Mandeville, Bernard, 7, 248, 285
manipulation, 133

Mao's China, 305
marginal esteem, 85–7, 111, 144–5, 200–3,
    209
marginal utility of esteem, 88, 115, 151, 156
margins of adjustment, see esteem-
        seeking strategies, performance,
        presentation, publicity
market reputation, see reputation
material economy, 2, 66–8, 93, 197, 219,
    251, 253, 255, 315
    difference with economy of esteem, 93
media, 250, 264, 299, 310
megalothymia, 20n
micro-motives, 104
Mill, J. S., 263–4, 314–15
Miller, D. T., 26, 74, 166, 269, 277, 285
Mittone, L., 167
Montaigne, Michel de, 10
Montesquieu, Baron de, 10, 248
moral monsters, 45
multiplier effect, 96–99, 108
Munger, K., 32, 142
mutual admiration, 203–8
    trade-offs, 208–11

Nash equilibrium, 147
natural selection, 47
Nicole, Pierre, 25, 37, 45, 248
Nisbett, R. E., 8n, 9, 31, 268, 269
Nobel Prize, 58, 198, 199, 218
Noelle-Neumann, E., 306
norms:
    and common good, 269
    dangers, 268–9
    definition of, 267–8, 269–70
    emergence of, 286
    and enforcement dilemma, see
        enforcement
    explanation and prediction of, 279–85
    internalisation of, 278
    moral norms, 284–5
    and public policy, 285–7
    simple, 282–4

observer role 206–7
observer values, 103
Ogien, Ruwen, 9, 31
O'Neill, B., 2n
oppression, 305–7
Ostrom, E., 271
outside inhibition, danger of, 295, 297–8

pair-wise interactions, 273–4
Paley, W., 8, 9, 10
paradox of hedonism, see teleological
    paradox
Pareto optimality, 101–3
perception condition, 279–80
perceptions, see common belief
performance, 70–1
    absolute, 98
    and aggregate esteem, 99–100, 116–17
    average, 69, 92–99, 164–7, 200
    and compliance, 125–39
    dimensions of, 67, 69, 71, 109, 204, 299
    discretionary and non-discretionary,
        100–1, 108, 116, 117, 118, 150, 227
    failures to shape, 294–9; danger of
        special interest, 296–7; danger of
        outside inhibition, 297–8; danger of
        in-group loyalty, 298–9
    ideal, 93, 106–9
    individual, 85–91; relation with
        standards, 87–91
    standard, 93; as a range, 109–18
    three-range model, 111–18
personal autonomy, see autonomy
Pesendorfer, W., 195
Pettit, Philip, 5, 7, 16, 18, 22, 41, 47, 75,
    75n, 76n, 153n, 246, 257, 261, 262,
    270, 270n, 273, 275, 279, 281, 283,
    285, 289, 295n, 303, 305, 312, 314,
    316
Phelps, E. S., 228n, 268, 316
Phillips, A., 188n
Plato, 247
pluralism, 307

pluralistic ignorance, 166, 167, 247, 270n, 292
political correctness, 306–7
Pope, Alexander, 38, 295n
Posner, E. A., 26, 30, 273
Posner, R. A., 29, 315
power, 1–2, 67
    to expel, 211–12
    imbalances of, 260
    of norms, 280–5
    political, 246, 260, 302
predisposition, see performance
preferences, 251, 254
prejudice, see racism, sexism
Prentice, D. A., 26, 74, 166, 269, 277, 285
presentation, 70–3, 249–51, 286–7
    failures to shape, 299–308; deactivation
        of virtue, 300–2; destabilising of
        virtue, 303–4; eclipsing of virtue,
        302–3; masking of attitudes, 305–7
prestige, see esteem
Priestley, Joseph, 10
primary altruism, see altruism
prisoners' dilemma, 102, 162,
privacy legislation, 315
private vice, 7
professional probity, 110
prudence, 26, 174–5
public goods, 103n
public institutions, see social institutions
publicity:
    and effects on performance, 148–52
    as end in itself, 183–5
    failures to shape, 309–19; wasteful
        publicity, 308–9; motivated publicity,
        309–11; unbalanced publicity,
        311–13; prohibited publicity, 313–15;
        frozen publicity, 315–18
    policy, 152–8
    and reidentifiability, 146
    seeking and shunning, 178–94
    and size of audience, 142–5
public opinion, 45, 263–4, 306, 310, see
    also common belief, law of opinion

public policy, 138, 152–8, 249–51, 285–7,
    289–321, see also institutional design
public-spiritedness, 285
public virtue, 7
punishment, 122, 138, 272, 274, 274n, 277,
    278, see also sanctions
Putnam, R. D., 256, 269
Putterman, L., 274

quasi-exchange, 217–19

racism, 228–9, 316
random shocks, 135, 137
Rasmussen, E. B., 29
rational choice theory, 18, 269, 271
rationality, 66, see also self-interest
Rawls, John, 29
Ray, John, 248
reciprocity, 13, 50, 60, 61, 62,
    72–3
Reckers, P. M. J., 166
recognition, 20, 23, 33, 154, 179, 185–89,
    190, 192, 194, 237
    failures of, 185–89
recycling, 126, 133, 138, 280, 284
Rees, J., 10, 30
regulation: see also sanctions
    and detection problem, see detection
        problem
    dichotomous view of, 255–7
    intangible-hand regulation, see
        intangible hand
    and norms, see norms
    regulating the regulators, 259–60
reputation:
    market, 3–4, 30
    pooling, 197–203
resilience, 46–7, 62, 281, 283
Richerson, P. J., 279n
Ricoeur, P., 1
risk, 44, 113, 118–122, 151, 175, 235, 304,
    306, 319
risk effect, 151

Sabini, J., 274
Sally, D., 284
Sanchirico, C. W., 273
sanctions, 5, 192, 246, 255, 258, 265, 269,
    271, 284, 287, 307
    cost of, 272, 274, 276–77
    and enforcement dilemma, see
        enforcement dilemma
    intentional versus non-intentional, 246
    legal, 287, 300
Sandler, T., 196
satisficing, 44
Scanlon, T. M., 36
scarcity:
    of esteem, 20, 34, 65–6, 76
Schroeder, C. M., 148n, 166
secondary altruism, see altruism
secrecy, 234–7
secret ballot, 314
self-esteem, see esteem
self-interest, 8, 18, 24, 73, 174, 175, 211,
    260, 261, 268, 270, 272, 278
Selten, R., 169n
Selznick, P., 256
Sen, A., 278
sensible knave, 285
sexism, 316
shame, 57, 92, 154, 156, 250, 318
Sidgwick, H., 35
signalling model, 273
Silver, M., 274
simulation, see dissimulation
Skyrms, B., 273
Slote, M., 44
Smart, J. J. C., 35
Smith, Adam, 6–7, 10, 24, 156, 187, 245–6,
    277
Smith, M., 22
Sober, E., 270, 274, 279, 283
social context, 69, 106
social institutions, 71, 121, 174–5, 178,
    180, 210, 249, 255, 269, 285, 294, 307
social psychology, 74

Soltis, J., 179n
Song, Y. D., 166
sour grapes, 225
special interests, danger of, 295, 296–7
specialisation, 69
spontaneity, 36
standards, 318–19
    exogenous, 85–91
    perceptions of, 164–7; see also
        common belief
    as social constructs, 92–3
    standard performance, see
        performance
Stewart, F. H., 8
Stoic values, 9
subcultures, see culture
substitution effect, 181–2, 184
Sugden, R., 273
Sunstein, C., 57, 295, 301
susceptibility condition, 280

tax-compliance, 94, 163–4
Taylor, C., 20
Taylor, M., 271, 271n, 273
teleological paradox, 35, 36–46, 55, 72,
    217, 308, 309
    resolution of, 45–6
testimony, 56–61, 66, 68, 146, 147, 310,
    317
    and voluntary associations, 196, 197,
        205, 215, 217, 219
three-range model, 111–18
tidal effect of esteem, 105
tit-for-tat, 273
Toennies, F., 31
totalitarianism, 305
trade of esteem, 53–4
transmission of esteem, 54–5
trust, 269
Tschirhart, J., 196
Tucker, Abraham, 8–9, 25, 26
Tyler, T. R., 269, 278, 311
tyranny of majority, 268–9

unanimity rule, 175
uncertainty, 110, 113, 118, 162–4, 175,
    176, 205
upward bias, 163
utility, 157–8

values, see ideals
vanity, 37
Veblen, Thorstein, 7
Vickers, J., 169n
virtual demand, see economy of esteem
virtual supply, see economy of esteem
virtue:
    deactivation of, 300–2
    destabilising of, 303–4
    eclipsing of, 202–3
    economising on, 285
    and regulation, 260–3
    of rulers, 297
    scepticism about, 7–10
    spontaneous, 44
voluntary associations, 195–221
    choice between, 208–11
    and economies of scale, 198
    exclusiveness of, 203, 211–13
    and external esteem, 197–203
    and free-riding, 211–17
    hierarchical character of, 199–200,
        212
    and internal esteem, 203–8
voting, 313–14

weakest link case, 121–2
Wenzel, N., 166, 319
Whigs, 10
whistle-blower's dilemma, 171–6
White, M., 297
Williams, B., 27
Wilson, D. S., 270, 274, 279, 283
Wilson, R., 169n
Winch, P., 270
within-group effect, 209
Wolff, Christian, 25